Whalley cousin of Cromwell p 7?
vice-admiral Wm Penn 119

Cavalier and Roundhead Spies

Cavalier and Roundhead Spies

Intelligence in the Civil War and Commonwealth

Julian Whitehead

Pen & Sword
MILITARY

To DM

First published in Great Britain in 2009 by
Pen & Sword Military
An imprint of
Pen & Sword Books Ltd
47 Church Street
Barnsley
South Yorkshire
S70 2AS

Copyright © Julian Whitehead 2009

ISBN 978 1 84415 957 4

A CIP catalogue record for this book is
available from the British Library

Typeset in 10pt Palatino by Mac Style, Beverley, East Yorkshire
Printed and bound in the UK
By MPG Books Group

Pen & Sword Books Ltd incorporates the Imprints of
Pen & Sword Aviation,
Pen & Sword Maritime, Pen & Sword Military,
Wharncliffe Local History,
Pen & Sword Select, Pen & Sword Military Classics, Leo Cooper, Remember
When, Seaforth Publishing and Frontline Publishing

For a complete list of Pen & Sword titles please contact
PEN & SWORD BOOKS LIMITED
47 Church Street, Barnsley, South Yorkshire, S70 2AS, England
E-mail: enquiries@pen-and-sword.co.uk
Website: www.pen-and-sword.co.uk

Contents

Preface

This book provides an account of intelligence activity from 1642 to 1660. It does so against the background of the great events that took the kingdoms of England, Scotland and Ireland through civil wars to the formation of a powerful single republic, then back again to three monarchies. Before beginning this story it may be helpful to consider the nature of intelligence and how different it was in its seventeenth-century infancy from the technological giant it has become today.

The purpose of intelligence in any age is to provide assessments of the capabilities and intentions of those it is directed against in order to assist decision-making for future actions. In the case of military intelligence it seeks to provide information on enemy strengths, dispositions and intentions in order to assist the commander in planning his own strategy and tactics. In the case of foreign intelligence it seeks to learn the capabilities and intentions of foreign governments in order to help formulate foreign policy. In the case of security intelligence it seeks to identify the hostile activity of foreign intelligence services, and internal subversive organizations so that they can be neutralized.

Intelligence should consist of the cycle of collection, collation, evaluation and dissemination. Collection is the gathering of raw information from such overt and covert sources as are available. Collation is the sorting of that information in terms of subject matter, relevance, probability and reliability of source. Evaluation is the analysis of the patterns that develop to make judgements on the enemy's situation, capabilities and likely intentions in the form of assessed intelligence. Finally there is the timely dissemination of the intelligence assessment to those who require it, in a form that will best meet their needs.

An intelligence assessment only provides a snap shot of the situation at a particular time. Changing circumstances detected by the collection of further information and possible refinement in the evaluation of sources mean that it must be a continuing cycle of activity. Intelligence by its nature is most unlikely to provide a complete picture of the enemy or potential enemy against whom it is directed but strives to add sufficient pieces of a jigsaw of knowledge to enable enemy actions, capabilities and intentions to be assessed to a sufficient degree of likelihood that they can be the basis for planning an appropriate response.

Today intelligence collection is divided into human intelligence (HUMINT), signals intelligence (SIGINT) and imagery intelligence (IMINT). HUMINT consists of all information that can be collected by human beings. This may be from observation by military attachés, the use of agents and informants, visual reconnaissance of operations or the systematic extraction of information from prisoners through interrogation. SIGINT consists of communications intelligence (COMINT) and electronic intelligence (ELINT). COMINT is the interception of all types of communications, their decryption and translation as necessary and subsequent analysis. ELINT is the collection and analysis of electronic omissions such as those from communication facilities or radar sites in order to establish their location and draw conclusions from their levels and types of activity.

At a strategic level, collection sources cover the whole electronic–magnetic spectrum and can operate from platforms beneath the sea, on the surface of sea or land, in the sky and in space. The vast quantities of data collected from these great information vacuum cleaners is downloaded to their respective agencies and much is subsequently shared between inter-government intelligence alliances such as Canada, UK and US (CAN/UK/US) where it is assessed on a single-nation basis.

Even at the tactical level, huge volumes of information are collected from surveillance assets covering most of the electro-magnetic spectrum on systems such as JSTARS, ASTOR and a variety of unmanned aerial vehicles such as Phoenix and Desert Hawk, before being downloaded to their ground-stations and fusion centres. The military intelligence process no longer stands alone but is now an element of ISTAR (Intelligence, Surveillance, Target Acquisition, Reconnaissance) working in harmony together. The current watch word for this is 'network centric' by which is meant having the command, control and communications to ensure an integrated system whereby collection assets can be rapidly tasked so that their product is used for intelligence and/or target acquisition purposes. For intelligence the product goes to the all sources intelligence assessment cells and for target acquisition direct to the fire control systems for the artillery, missiles, bombs, etc. on platforms based on land, sea or air.

At the tactical level, the intelligence staffs of each of the three services carry out assessment and subsequent dissemination. At theatre level this is done on a tri-service basis. At strategic level assessment is carried out on a national basis. In the case of UK, the different lead agencies such as Government Communication Headquarters (GCHQ) for SIGINT and the Secret Intelligence Service (SIS) for overseas HUMINT bring their assessed information to various Cabinet Office committees where it is discussed and refined until put before the Joint Intelligence Committee (JIC) for approval. At JIC it receives any final amendment before being formally disseminated as a national assessment.

Intelligence does not just consist of the various elements of the intelligence cycle but also the management and support to make the system work effectively. Management and support covers such essential matters as determining intelligence requirements and the priorities for tasking the collection assets, as well as the overall management of the whole complex operation. This includes the development and procurement of new collection and processing systems and the management and training of the large number of professionals in the wide variety of expertise.

From this brief sketch of present-day intelligence it will be seen that it is a highly complex multi-billion pound international effort run with considerable professionalism and is usually capable of producing assessments of the greatest accuracy. However, intelligence today is still limited by its very nature of rarely being able to assemble all the pieces of the jigsaw puzzle and having to rely on judgements based on the balance of probabilities. The US/Allied invasion of Iraq which has resulted in a bloody and protracted peacekeeping operation occurred because of the intelligence assessment that Saddam Hussein possessed weapons of mass destruction. The fact that this assessment was subsequently found to be wrong serves to demonstrate that, for all the modern technology, intelligence remains a fallible art rather than an exact science. It also demonstrates the power of intelligence in decision-making and how its quality can be responsible for success or failure on a major scale.

Intelligence in the seventeenth century was severely limited compared with today but its nature was fundamentally the same. In terms of collection all elements of HUMINT were theoretically available in the early 1640s but little use was made of interrogation, as it would be considered dishonourable to use such techniques against a fellow gentleman who had surrendered. England had no standing army to provide professionalism in reconnaissance, still less any notion of camouflage and concealment. Agent handling was dangerously amateur and virtually bereft of tradecraft. Surveillance even in its static form was seldom used. There was no IMINT. Even the telescope had barely been invented and the few in existence were confined to astrological use. Virtually no thought was even given to the making of military drawings which in the next two centuries would be refined by the Royal Engineers into providing accurate representations of enemy defences before the invention of the camera. COMINT did exist but only in the form of the intercept of written communications. Although this source was available, a system for conducting intercept did not exist. Cipher was occasionally used to protect the security of sensitive documents but there was no formal cryptanalysis capability.

Not only were collection means severely limited but collation was virtually non-existent and evaluation usually little more than the confirmation of personal prejudices. The whole communication process necessary for transmitting the collection product and the dissemination of processed intelligence was only as fast as a ship or horseman, at a time when it took five days for a letter from London to reach Edinburgh. The traveller had to contend with roads that were at best muddy tracks with few signposts and any maps were usually incomplete or inaccurate. What is more the country had little apparatus for intelligence for the good reason that there was virtually no intelligence requirement.

Charles I's father, King James, had been paranoid about plots and assassination attempts, not without cause considering the Main and Bye Plots not to mention the Gunpowder Plot. This was not the case with Charles I. The Stuart dynasty was by then well established in the three kingdoms of England, Scotland and Ireland and there were no rivals for the throne or threats to his life. True there had been mounting dissatisfaction among the peers and gentry over Charles ruling without Parliament and so leaving them excluded from their traditional roles in government. Charles's dissolution of his 1629 Parliament had been particularly acrimonious and ended with several members of the opposition being imprisoned.

The period of the King's personal rule that followed 1629 saw what many regarded as flagrant infringements of ancient liberties. These included judicial and fiscal illegalities such as the misuse of the Star Chamber and the raising of taxes without parliamentary consent. Occasionally opposition to the King expressed itself, such as when John Hampden refused to pay Charles's tax of Ship Money, however this was settled in the courts and not with plots or insurrection. The strong Puritanism element of the country was becoming increasingly agitated that the Anglican Church was introducing Roman Catholic practices and that the Queen, herself a Catholic, was fostering Popery in the heart of the court. Again this did not manifest itself in any overt opposition, largely perhaps because there was no Parliament to give it voice.

As far as foreign affairs were concerned England had been at peace since 1630. While Continental Europe was obsessed with tearing itself apart in the Thirty Years' War, England was enjoying a period of commercial prosperity and had no immediate or potential enemies on whom it needed to collect intelligence. In 1637 this precarious but happy position of having no serious threat from home or abroad was put at risk when Charles tried to impose first bishops and then an Anglican-style prayer book on the Presbyterian Scots. Their response was to take the Oath of the Covenant to defend their faith and after protracted military manoeuvring and failed negotiations they advanced into England and captured Newcastle in 1640. From there they threatened to pillage the North unless their demands were met, including payment of £850 per day.

Charles had no option but to give into the Covenanter Scots' demands and to call a parliament to vote the money so urgently needed. In doing so he now faced members of both Houses who had added to their grievances of 1629 the additional causes for discontent from the period of personal rule. The years of pent-up resentment were now released in a determination by Parliament to give no help to the King until it had exacted major concessions. These he was not prepared to concede. This impasse between sovereign and Parliament was to cause the outbreak of Civil War in 1642, which is the starting point for this narrative.

With the advent of war came the need for military intelligence and with the subsequent establishment of the Commonwealth came additional intelligence requirements. These were to find out about sectarian opposition at home, Royalist plots and the support they might get from foreign powers, as well as military intelligence about the Dutch and Spanish, against whom the Commonwealth was to find itself at various times at war. Intelligence capability grew from virtually nothing in 1642 to 1658 when the claim could later be made in Parliament that 'Cromwell carried the secrets of all the princes of Europe in his girdle.'

List of Illustrations

Acknowledgements

As well as being indebted to all the authors listed in the notes and those who kindly agreed to the inclusion of their pictures as illustrations in this book, I would like to thank the staff of the Bodleian Library and my wife and family for their help and support.

Chapter 1

The Making of Two Armies, 1642

It was the worst time of the year for travelling but there seemed no option. In the streets of London angry mobs were violently demonstrating against the King and Queen. The royal family's safety was now at risk. On 10 January 1642 King Charles hurriedly set out from Westminster with his wife and three eldest children. The next time he was to return to his capital would be as a prisoner.

The dispute between King and Parliament had reached a new level of crisis. Two months previously Parliament had drafted the document know as the *Grand Remonstrance*. This catalogued grievances during the King's rule and demanded unprecedented parliamentary control of the running of the country. To Charles these demands were a direct challenge to his God-given authority as sovereign. Just at this time news reached London that Catholic rebels had massacred thousands of Protestant settlers in Ireland.

An army was clearly needed to put down this insurrection by Irish Papists. The Committee of Estates which was running Scotland in the absence of an Edinburgh Parliament sent a Scots force under Robert Munro to counter the rebellion in Ulster. Naturally England had to respond as well. His Majesty offered to lead an army but Parliament was reluctant to vote the taxation necessary to raise forces for the King. They felt that putting an army at the disposal of the King might give him the means to reverse the concessions they had recently gained from him. They may well have been right. The fundamental issue of who was to control the army was now in contest. In November Parliament reluctantly agreed to raise 8,000 men to be commanded by the Protestant Earl of Ormonde and included some small English contingents such as one led by Colonel George Monck. Whether Ormonde was under the overall command of the King or Parliament remained in question.

Most members of both Houses of Parliament distrusted the King and many even doubted his loyalty to the Protestant faith. They deeply resented that Charles had previously ruled for eleven years without Parliament and thus deprived both Lords and Commons of their historic role in the running of the country. Ever since His Majesty had been forced to call a parliament, these intrinsically conservative gentlemen had been growing in their opposition to the crown, following the lead of a small group of determined Puritans. This group was dominated by the astute John Pym. It was Pym who now began drafting a bill to put the trained bands and militia under the direct control of Parliament rather than the King.

Pym had become the hero of Londoners for championing resistance to royal courts and taxes and the introduction of High Anglican practices in the church. He had also become adept at inflaming the London mob to achieve his ends. On top of the graphic stories of Papist atrocities in Ireland, rumours were now being widely spread about Queen Henrietta Maria, Charles's Catholic wife. It was said that she was about to go to the Continent to raise troops to impose the King's will and still worse that she was somehow responsible for the Catholic Irish uprising in the first place. It seemed possible that Parliament might be preparing to impeach the Queen. After all, Parliament had already impeached the King's principal minister, the Earl of Strafford, and that had resulted in his execution.

Urged on by his queen, Charles decided to take decisive action. On 4 January His Majesty went to Parliament with some armed troops to arrest Pym and his fellow leaders for treason. The scheme backfired. Careless talk by one of the Queen's ladies-in-waiting had leaked the plan and when the King arrived at the Commons, Pym and the others had escaped by boat to the City of London. There they received the whole-hearted support and protection of the Corporation. The London mob was soon aroused and became incensed by what seemed a tyrannous act against parliamentary privilege. Just five days before the attempted arrest, rioters had attacked the gates of the Palace of Whitehall. Now, with armed apprentices and Thames watermen taking to the streets, far worse could be expected. Shops closed in the City, barricades were erected, Catholics houses were attacked and hundreds of citizens were milling angrily about the streets. It was with London in this uproar that the King removed himself and his family from his disaffected capital, travelling first to Hampton Court, then on to Windsor.

The day after the King left, Pym came out of his hiding in Coleman Street and proceeded in triumph by boat up the Thames to Westminster where he was met by cheering citizens. Parliament was in control of the capital and the machinery of government and Pym was in control of Parliament, but for all that the King was still King. Both Charles and Parliament felt there was still a slim chance of reconciliation. Charles made a gesture by assenting to Parliament's bill excluding all bishops from the House of Lords. Pym was not to be deflected and pressed on with the Militia Bill. It was unthinkable that the King could give up his royal prerogative of command of the army. His Majesty refused royal assent to the bill. The crunch had come. It was now clear to Charles that he must appeal to the loyalty of the country to uphold his sovereign rights over Parliament. To do this he required a clear sign of sufficient loyalty to the crown to overawe Parliament and remind the citizens of London of their duty. He needed an army.

The royal court on the move was usually an impressive sight. In normal circumstances it would have provided a glittering and colourful contrast to a grey winter day. This time when the King and Queen had left London they had no more than fifty guards and attendants and some hastily packed baggage. The subdued cortege which lurched off from Whitehall through the mud and potholes to Hampton Court was certainly no army or even the nucleus for one. Not only had the King little money and such a small number of followers but the kingdom's weapons, ammunition and artillery were concentrated in the Tower of London, soon to be under Parliamentary control.

Charles knew that he would have to proceed with caution in attempting to raise armed support. While at Windsor he played for time until it was safe for his beloved queen to escape the country. In February he was able to escort her to Dover, from where she sailed for the safety of the United Provinces with their daughter Mary, who had recently married the son of the Prince of Orange as a way of demonstrating the King's Protestant credentials. Henrietta Maria took with her some of the crown jewels to pawn or sell, in order to raise funds for the procurement of weapons and equipment. She also took the key to a cipher, which would enable her to communicate secretly with Charles, for Parliament had already started openly intercepting royal letters. This secure means of correspondence was not to be without its problems. The Queen was later to write to Charles:

> Be careful how you write in cipher, for I have been driven well nigh mad in deciphering your letter. You have added some blanks which I had not and you have not written it truly. Take good care of it, I beg you, and put nothing in it which is not in my cipher. Once again, I remind you to take care of your pocket and let not our cipher be stolen.

It is a comment on the style of Charles' government that the encryption and decryption of sensitive state communications between the King and Queen should be carried out by them personally, rather than by experienced secretaries. In many countries encryption and cryptanalysis were normal activities of government. This was most advanced in the Vatican Secretariat of State where Popes had long had an important department called the 'Cifra'. This was not only responsible for the creation of papal codes and ciphers and using them for papal correspondence but also the intercept of foreign mail and any cryptanalysis required. England had nothing of this sort. Indeed Charles regarded his wife as his principal emissary abroad who would seek help from all their connections in Europe. That was the Prince of Orange in the United Provinces, Charles's uncle the King of Denmark and Henrietta Maria's brother, the King of France. With the Queen personally engaged in these great matters of state, the official diplomats and crown servants became rather redundant.

Although Charles was taking measures for the protection of his family and security of his sensitive communications, he appears to have had no mechanism for obtaining intelligence on the threats posed to the monarchy. Of course he received information from his courtiers about what Pym and Parliament were planning but this tended to be just so much common knowledge, gossip and rumours, rather than accurate, assessed intelligence gathered from tasked sources. All rulers require intelligence about the capabilities and intentions of those who threaten the interests of their country and their own hold on power. This usually means collecting foreign intelligence on those states whose interests clash with their own and obtaining security intelligence on those groups plotting to overthrow the government. At the very minimum it was necessary to obtain intelligence on any threats to the life of the sovereign and their heirs. Most monarchs lived under a potential threat to their life. Charles's grandfather had been assassinated, as had his father-in-law Henry IV of France, and his own father James I had been the target of assassination plots. To counter such threats Queen Elizabeth had been served by Lord Burleigh as her astute principal minister, later followed by his equally gifted son Robert Cecil. She also had one of the great intelligencers of all time, Sir Francis Walsingham, her Secretary of State, whose successes included uncovering the Ridolfi and the Babbington Plots. James I inherited Robert Cecil, who thwarted the Gunpowder Plot.

After Cecil there was no principal minister of consequence to carry out the effective coordination of government and oversight of intelligence. There had been the powerful Duke of Buckingham but apart from conducting an inept foreign policy, he concentrated his energies on lining the pockets of himself and his cronies. After Buckingham's assassination in 1628, Charles made increasing use of his Privy Council. Thomas Wentworth, Earl of Strafford, and Archbishop Laud were the most prominent members of this otherwise lacklustre body. Wentworth could have been an effective chief minister but had been away in the North or Ireland most of the time and was now dead. Laud was no Richelieu and his influence had been mainly confined to religious matters where his efforts were to produce disastrous results. With the King's support he had attempted the introduction of High Anglicanism ritual across the church. These practices, such as removing altars from the centre of churches and placing them at the east end, seemed little short of popery to the Puritans. Parliament took their revenge and put an end to Laud's influence by committing him to the Tower.

In the absence of any major figure, the obvious post to carry out the function of chief minister was the senior Secretary of State. There were two Secretaries of State for executing the sovereign's foreign policy. One was responsible for the north of Europe (Scandinavia, Germany and the United Provinces of the Netherlands) and the other for the south (France, Spain, Portugal and Italy). It was to the Secretaries of State that England's ambassadors sent their dispatches from abroad, including any intelligence they had gained through their contacts and agents. They therefore became the foreign intelligence focus for their respective overseas areas. As England had been at peace for most of Charles's reign, there had been little requirement for overseas intelligence and so this aspect of their work had all but shrivelled away.

The Secretary of State for the South was the senior of the two and was usually also made responsible for countering subversion and treason at home. As there had been no rebellions or plots since Charles had become King there had been little requirement for any effort to have been put into gathering domestic intelligence. On top of this, Charles's Secretaries of State had not been in the mould of Walsingham. From 1625 to 39 the Senior Secretary of State had been Sir John Coke, described by

Clarendon as 'unadorned with vigour and quickness'. He had been forced to resign at the age of 75 following accusations of bribery. The other Secretary of State had been Sir Francis Windlebank, who had worked diligently to advance the financial position of himself and his family, then fled to France in December 1640 to escape the wrath of Parliament. It was a sign of the times that Parliament was not angry with Windlebank for any financial irregularities but because he was a Catholic and so might have a popish influence on the King. Sir Henry Vane had been appointed to replace Coke but had shown himself to be so much in league with Pym that he was dismissed. The replacements for Windebank and Vane were Edward Nicholas and the 23-year-old Viscount Falkland, both excellent choices. Nicholas had already proved himself to be a loyal and diligent servant as Secretary for the Council of War and Falkland was a man of talent and conviction.

From January 1642 Charles at last had two able Secretaries of State. The problem was that both were new to the job and trying to carry out their work on the move, following the King about the country far from the seat of government, with no infrastructure to support them and no intelligence network to inherit. To make matters worse, the one bit of governmental organization that they still had at their disposal, the ambassadors overseas, was being short-circuited by the Queen's diplomatic initiatives working directly for the King. Then there was the difficulty that His Majesty was usually more likely to take advice from some of his courtiers than the better informed Secretaries of State. Most prominent of his advisers was the 34-year-old, handsome Lord George Digby. It was no surprise that this eloquent, witty, amusing courtier, so elegant in dress and manners, should have become a favourite of first the Queen and then the King. As well as being charming, Digby had an infectious optimism and cheerful disposition which encouraged the King in these difficult times. The only problem was that his optimism was invariably misplaced and the quality of his advice may be judged from the fact that it had been he, along with the Queen, who had urged Charles to take the disastrous step of attempting to arrest Pym and the others.

As well as having to work in an incoherent and peripatetic seat of government, the two new Secretaries of State had assumed their appointments at a time of a major crisis whose complexity was without precedent and merely keeping on top of events would leave them little time to consider intelligence. In summary, the whole mechanism and infrastructure for intelligence so painstakingly and successfully created in the past two reigns had withered away with neglect. Moreover the government apparatus of which it was an element was falling apart. If the King was to have a successful outcome to his contest with Parliament his machinery of government would need a major overhaul, with an effective intelligence system created from scratch.

Charles may have had little or no intelligence system but he knew from his recent journeys to campaigns against the Scots that he enjoyed reasonable support in the Midlands and strong support in Yorkshire. As soon as the Queen had safely gone, he left for York. He had another reason for heading north. Hull was the second largest armoury and magazine outside the Tower, having been established as an arsenal for the wars against the Scots. Things did not go as the King hoped. As he moved to York there was little significant increase to his band of followers. In his absence Parliament had passed the Militia Bill into law as an ordinance without royal consent and started appointing lords lieutenant in each county to raise troops. Charles responded by appointing his own county commissioners to raise troops. The die was now cast and both sides began to openly recruit. In fact Parliament were well ahead of the game. Parliament already had the London trained bands which were the best militia in the kingdom and commanded by the able Philip Skippon. Parliament authorized the formation of an army of 10,000 and appointed the sombre, Puritan, pipe-smoking Earl of Essex as its commander. The majority of the navy supported Parliament and was put under command of Essex's cousin, the capable Earl of Warwick. Parliament was also confidently taking on the running of the machinery of government, for example sending its own diplomatic representative to the United Provinces.

In the mean time Charles had been to Hull only to find that the parliamentary-appointed governor refused to open the gates to him. Despite this setback Charles remained confident, secure in the certainty of his divine right of kingship. Of course, being the younger son of James I, he had not been born to be king. Charles had been a backward and sickly child raised away from court. He could not speak until he was 5 or walk till he was 7. The small pale stammering child with leg irons could hardly have been more different from his tall, handsome and outgoing elder brother Henry. But Henry died in 1612 and suddenly Charles found himself the unlikely heir to three kingdoms. With great determination he overcame his physical defects and concentrated on his studies, becoming both an excellent horseman and something of an intellectual with a particularly strong knowledge of theology. Charles fully accepted his father's concept of kingship, in which the monarch was appointed by God and was responsible to God alone for all aspects of his rule. Whereas James I had been prepared to temper this theory with expediency, Charles regarded it as an article of faith and would not compromise what he saw as his divine duty.

Charles was then a mature man of 42 with seventeen years of experience of kingship. He had presided over a period of national prosperity and in his own terms had worked hard for the best interests of his subjects. For a man of his convictions he had no option but to take decisive action to preserve the traditional powers and dignity of the monarchy. On 22 August he raised his standard at the strategic town of Nottingham, formally signalling a call to arms. The event was something of an embarrassment. More effort appears to have been put into the production of the royal standard than planning the creation of a trained force. The standard was absurdly long and required twenty men to put it up, only to have it blown down the next day. 3,000 local militia were paraded for the occasion but despite being harangued by the King and others at some length, only about 300 volunteered to serve. With time his force increased until it was of sufficient size for him to leave and march through the Midlands. On the march he heard some of his first encouraging intelligence when 'he received clear information from the well affected party in Shrewsbury that town was at his devotion'. At Shrewsbury his army consisted of 500 horse, five regiments of infantry (about 5,000 men) and twelve pieces of artillery, and was under the command of the elderly Earl of Lindsay.

By the end of summer both sides were drilling and issuing commissions to raise regiments. Apart from the largely ineffective provincial trained bands, recruitment was conducted on a semi-feudal basis. Landowners, such as the MP John Hampden, recruited troops from their tenants. In his case he raised a whole regiment at his own expense and provided them with smart dark-green uniforms. His cousin Oliver Cromwell had returned to his constituency of Cambridge, collecting supporters on the way, then secured the city castle and arrested the Commissioners of Array who were trying to recruit for the King. He then raised a troop of sixty horse with his own money and went off to put himself under the command of the Earl of Essex. Such groups of followers of individual gentry and nobility gradually assembled on each side and began dominating their surrounding areas.

By the autumn isolated skirmishes began breaking out between opposing groups. One such minor skirmish which occurred in September at Powick Bridge was to make the reputation of the victor, Prince Rupert. This tall, handsome, headstrong young prince was the younger son of Charles's sister Elizabeth, Queen of Bohemia, who had married the Elector Palatine. It had been her husband's acceptance of the throne of Bohemia for Protestantism which had sparked the Thirty Years' War. Rupert had been a child of the war. He was born in 1619, a month after his father had been crowned and a year before the Catholic League began hostilities by invading Bohemia. Rupert had attended his first siege at the age of 13 and at 18 commanded a cavalry regiment for a year before being captured at the Battle of Vlotho – not perhaps a great deal of military experience but more than most.

Charles decided to put his 23-year-old nephew in command of his Horse. This would turn out to be a brilliant decision as Rupert was a commander of genius. The royal cavalry had little armour so Rupert decided to employ this light horse in the heavy role and rely on the shock of close formation charge rather than the normal practice of advancing, then firing weapons and retiring. At Powick Bridge this tactic was a spectacular success and the Parliamentary force fled. Rupert's reputation was created as hero or demon, depending on whether the viewpoint was Royalist or Parliamentary. This reputation was to be fuelled by his extreme bravery in action and utter ruthlessness in victory.

By October both King and Parliament had assembled armies. Parliament had the advantage of numbers, arms, equipment and ordnance, together with the massive financial resources of the City of London. They also had the London trained bands, which had expanded to 6,000 strong. Most of the forces on both sides were groups of men following their local leader, with little training and accoutred with an assortment of uniforms, weapons and equipment. There were few leaders on either side with military experience. Noble rank and loyalty to the cause served as the main criteria for selection for senior command. Parliament's Lord General, the Earl of Essex, did indeed have a military background consisting of four years' service in the Netherlands and Germany followed by the disastrous 1625 Cadiz expedition, then nothing until the 1639 campaign against the Scots, where he saw no action. The important appointment of command of the Parliamentary Horse was given to the Earl of Bedford, who had no military experience whatsoever. There were exceptions such as Philip Skippon and Sir William Waller who had served in the Dutch Army. The Royalist side did rather better, having some experienced soldiers such as Prince Rupert, Sir Jacob Astley, Sir Ralph Hopton, Henry Wilmot and George Goring. Even so, military professionalism was thin on the ground. It was not assisted by the convention that many senior posts were given to grandees solely on the grounds that they raised large numbers of troops with their own money and semi-feudal local influence.

The royal army in October had expanded to about 14,000. This change in fortune had occurred because of strong recruitment in Lancashire, Cheshire and North Wales, largely through the influence of the local magnate the Earl of Derby. Although the King now had a reasonable-sized army, it was almost entirely manned by recent recruits, who required training. Two months was considered the minimum time to train an infantryman. There were eighteen postures for the pikeman and thirty-four movements for the musketeer, to be learnt and carried out in unison and appropriate formation. The whole military effort had understandably been focused on the recruitment, training and equipping of the cavalry, musketeers and pikemen. The individual regiments had just about managed to get their own quartermasters, waggoners, chaplains and surgeons. Some mercenaries had appeared on either side to man the artillery but both the Royalist and Parliamentary armies consisted of raw individual units with little or no cohesion between them. Command and control arrangements were at best vague and there were little or no staff officers to coordinate activities for the commanders, such as the management of intelligence.

Now that the armies were assembled, it was the aim of both sides to achieve a decisive victory before winter brought the campaign season to a close. The King planned to defeat Essex and then march on London to regain his capital and restore his supreme powers as monarch. Parliament wanted Essex to defeat the royal forces sufficiently convincingly that Charles would be obliged to make terms and accept the primacy of Parliament. With both armies about to be committed to fight it was now essential for each to have effective military intelligence. The type of military intelligence particularly required was operational intelligence on the strengths, dispositions and intentions of the enemy forces. The few professional soldiers on each side would have been well aware of this need. Rupert, for example, had read much military doctrine during his captivity and would have been familiar with the works of John Cruso, who wrote *Military Instructions for the Cavalry* and *Treatise of Modern Warefare* published in 1632 and 1640 respectively. Cruso placed great emphasis on operational intelligence as indicated in the following extract:

Every good commander must have these two grounds for his actions: 1. The knowledge of his own forces, and wants (knowing that the enemye may have notice of thereof and therefore must be always be studyinge for remedies, if the enemye should come suddainly upon him). 2. The assurance of the condition and estate of the enemie, his commodities and necessities, his councils and designs, thereby begetting divers occasions, which afterwards may bring forth victories.

Like all professional cavalrymen Rupert would have been clear about the importance of reconnaissance. Cavalry and dragoons were the usual sources of reconnaissance because of their ability to cover a wide area and report back quickly. Usually a troop of light horse of about twenty men commanded by a captain or corporal would be sent forward to locate the enemy and gather information regarding their strength and intentions. The musket-carrying dragoons were also used in this role, as these mounted infantry were particularly experienced in working as detached companies for a wide variety of tasks such as the escort of convoys or securing river crossings. Cavalry were not only known as a source of reconnaissance but also of intelligence, through the use of their trumpeters. It was accepted practice for trumpeters to be sent as emissaries from one side to the other. While conveying their message to the opponents, they would come up to or even into the enemy lines. They therefore had the opportunity to assess the strength, defences and combat effectiveness of the enemy at close quarters and report back accordingly.

Rupert was very familiar with these uses of cavalry from his own experience and as General of Horse would have wished to fully exploit their reconnaissance and intelligence roles. The problem he faced was that the King's army had only just been formed and it was more than a challenge to get this odd assortment of individual aristocrats, gentry and yeoman proficient at basic cavalry drill. Many would have had difficulty controlling unfamiliar horses massed together while keeping a hand free to use a sword or pistol effectively. Rupert set about the necessary combat training with considerable energy and professionalism but the teaching of the additional skills required for reconnaissance and intelligence gathering would have had to come later.

The Parliamentary army had been assembling at Northampton and on 10 September the Earl of Essex arrived to take command. Although at 14,000 they numbered roughly the same as the King's Army, they were better equipped but had less experienced commanders and fewer cavalry. His Majesty had left Shrewsbury on 12 October with thirteen regiments of foot, ten of horse and three of dragoons. Essex departed in pursuit of the King on 19 October with command of twenty regiments of foot, sixty-one troops of horse (most not organized into regiments at that time) and two regiments of dragoons. His force had been garrisoned over a wide area, including Hereford, Worcester, Coventry as well as Northampton, and would take time to concentrate. The Parliamentary army did not have anyone with the energy and experience of Rupert to begin training its cavalry and in any case having been dispersed they had been unable to conduct any centralized training. The Royalist horse may have had little experience in reconnaissance and intelligence gathering but the Parliamentary cavalry had virtually none. This was to show in the next few days as the armies manoeuvred about, unable to locate each other. In his advance towards London, the King had decided to take Banbury and the Royalist army was placed in quarters in the surrounding area. Essex's forces had advanced from Worcester to Kineton and had dispersed in the same area. A Parliamentary detachment looking for billets came to the village of Wormleighton, only to run into a Royalist party already there arranging quarters for Rupert. The detachment was captured and Rupert informed of the proximity of Essex's army. This must have come as a surprise as reconnaissance sent out by Rupert from Lord Digby's cavalry regiment earlier in the day had failed to locate any enemy. Rupert advised the King to occupy the high ridge overlooking Kineton three miles below. The ridge was called Edgehill, and thus the scene was set for the first major battle of the Civil War. If the reconnaissance and intelligence of the Royalist army had been poor it had at least been functioning, which was more than could be said for the Parliamentary force. The first that Essex heard of the presence of the King's army was at eight o'clock the next morning as he was going to church in Kineton. Essex immediately gave orders to deploy his army between Kineton and Edgehill.

By the afternoon of that day of 23 October both armies were deployed, although not all Essex's force had time to reach the battlefield. The Royalists army advanced down the hill to about half a mile short of the parliamentary line in order to provoke Essex to attack and the battle began. Rupert commanding the horse on the right wing and Henry Wilmot commanding it on the left both attacked the cavalry on the opposing wings with devastating effect. Rupert's tactic of the full sword charge sent the parliamentary horse into headlong retreat and the whole Royalist horse pursued until they arrived at Essex's baggage train where they stopped for looting. It was accepted military practice for the first line of horse to pursue their opponents off the field and looting was not only good sport but also an accepted perk at a time when army pay was at best irregular. What went wrong at Edgehill was that the second line of Royalist horse should have remained on the field to attack the flanks of the Parliamentary infantry, which were now exposed without the protection of their cavalry. The battle continued with the stronger parliamentary infantry beginning to gain the upper hand supported by two reserve regiments of horse which were then the only cavalry left in the battle. Two hundred Royalist horse eventually rallied and returned to restore the situation. As darkness began to fall the exhausted armies began pulling back, merely exchanging desultory musket fire until there was insufficient light to see their opponents.

The next morning both armies faced each other but neither felt they had sufficient advantage to resume fighting. In the afternoon Essex began to withdraw to Warwick and the King later moved back to Banbury which surrendered to him without a fight and then to Oxford which did the same two days later. The Parliamentary army had lost about 1,000 men and the Royalist about 500. The reputation of Rupert and his cavalry had been reinforced but their failure to remain on the field had lost the battle. The Parliamentary foot had proved effective and had even managed to capture the royal standard for a short time. The battle had resulted in a draw and both armies had missed the opportunity to destroy the other and secure the quick knock-out victory they needed. It is a matter of speculation whether with better reconnaissance and intelligence the Royalist army could have located Essex before his army had time to concentrate and force an engagement with superior numbers, thus changing history by creating a Royalist victory in the Civil War.

Essex's withdrawal had at least provided the Royalists with an opportunity because the road to London was now open. Rupert recommended taking a light column of 3,000 horse and foot the seventy miles to London to enter Westminster and overawe Parliament and the City. It is possible that this might have succeeded because the defences of London were not complete and the confidence of its citizens had been shaken by the initial reports of a parliamentary rout. Rupert was overruled and the Royalist army set about securing the area round Oxford, taking Abingdon, and then expanding to take Reading and finally Brentford. In the mean time Essex had joined up with General Skippon and his London trained bands at Turnham Green, with a total of 24,000 men. On 13 November the royal army arrived at Turnham Green and realized that they were completely outnumbered, withdrawing back towards Oxford. The opportunity to take London had gone as the Parliamentary forces were to grow greater and the city's defences become increasingly stronger. What was more, with London's population accounting for about one tenth of the population of the whole kingdom, it would always be relatively easy for Parliament to ensure that it had larger forces than the King. Charles was to retain his strategy of having London as his objective but if it had been briefly realistic in October 1642, it was no longer so from then on. There would be no hope of achieving victory unless he received substantial outside help or the parliamentary cause disintegrated of its own accord.

When the Royalists took over Kineton after Edgehill it was discovered that some of Essex's papers had been left behind. Among them were letters to Essex from Rupert's secretary, Blake, providing information on the Royalist army and asking for more money. This first case of espionage in the war came to a swift end with Blake being hanged in Oxford but intelligence gathering by both sides was just beginning.

The two armies now prepared for winter quarters in garrisons around Oxford and London respectively. The royal court set itself up in somewhat reduced circumstances in Oxford and life returned to some normality. A Master of Revels was appointed and courtiers could again concentrate on what they were best at: fashion, flirting, gossip and intrigue.

Chapter 2

For God and King, 1643

While Charles wintered in his new capital of Oxford, Pym and the other Parliamentary leaders were in London planning how to proceed with their stubborn monarch. Their principal demands to the King were that he should abolish the episcopacy and transfer command of the army to Parliament. It was clear from the intermittent negotiations that had been going on in the previous months that His Majesty would not budge on these points. The only hope of making him climb down was to completely defeat him in battle and Edgehill had shown that this would take time and effort.

Parliament was split into three general factions. Denzil Holles led a group who wanted a negotiated peace with the King. He was the second son of the Earl of Clare and had been a childhood friend of Charles. Unhappily, Holles's Presbyterianism and Charles's rule without parliament had destroyed the friendship and turned Holles into so strong an opponent that he was one of the MPs the King had tried to arrest. Although he championed liberty, Holles remained an aristocrat at heart who had no wish to see the King humbled but rather rule as advised by Protestant gentlemen such as himself. Then there was the group led by the former courtier Sir Harry Vane who wanted to dictate a peace to the King. In the middle were the majority, under the skilful leadership of Pym. These were not parties as such but general groupings whose members might move from one to another with changing circumstances. Predictably, Parliament was running the country by a system of committees. The Committee of Safety had been formed in July 1642 and was the principal committee for conduct of the war. The Committee was largely Presbyterian in membership, with Denzil Holles as a prominent member. One role of the Committee was to provide advice to Essex the Lord General. Unhelpfully, it was never clarified whether Essex was obliged to take this advice or merely give it his consideration. Parliament therefore suffered from no clear focus for military leadership and final decision-making. This meant that there could be uncertainty and ambiguity in strategy and the conduct of operations, right down to matters such as intelligence management.

By the spring of 1642 the Committee of Safety had set up groups of counties as military associations which could be deployed as directed. Of these, only three were to have any impact on the war. The Northern Association based in Yorkshire under Ferdinando Lord Fairfax; the Western Association incorporating the Midlands under Lord Grey of Groby and finally the Eastern Association under the Earl of Manchester. He was married to the daughter of the Earl of Warwick and had been the only member of the Lords who Charles had tried to arrest, along with Pym and Holles, the previous year. A neighbour of Manchester and one of his junior officers was Oliver Cromwell. Parliament therefore began the year with a more flexible organization, albeit one with a confused command structure.

The Royalist command structure was to all appearances very simple. The King, as head of state, was commander-in-chief. He alone was the final decision-maker on all matters. The army was run through his Council of War, which usually met in the King's quarters in Christchurch. The Council of War consisted of the two Secretaries of State and the principal military figures such as the Earl of Forth (Lord General), Rupert (General of Horse) and Sir Jacob Astley (General of Foot), together with Sir Edward Walker (Secretary for War). The Council of War also contained several of the King's closest companions such as the Earl of Bristol and his son Lord Digby. The whole unwieldy Council was up to twenty-five strong and split by factions, as much based on personal rivalry as genuine differences of opinion. Both Digby and Rupert were handsome men, the former blond the latter dark, but their differences went deeper than hair colour. The debonair and amusing Digby had been put out to find the gruff and impetuous Rupert a major rival for the King's favour. It did not take long before the clash of their personalities began to affect the war. Digby and his father had opposed Rupert's plan to advance on London immediately after Edgehill. The fact that Digby had next to no military experience, and that both Forth and Ashley had supported Rupert, had made no difference to the King's decision.

The proceedings of the Council of War were further hindered by Rupert's arrogance and unerring ability to insult anyone who disagreed with him. It had been Rupert's attitude at the Council of War before Edgehill that had so angered the Earl of Lindsay that he had resigned as General-in-Chief just as the troops were deploying for the battle. An argument had arisen over whether the infantry should be formed up in line abreast in the Dutch fashion as required by Lindsay or in the Swedish diamond formation, as proposed by Forth. When the cocky young Rupert waded in by taking Forth's side against Lindsay, it was just too much. Rupert had already angered Lindsay by stating that as a prince he would take orders only from the King. Lindsay resigned on the spot and stormed off to command his own regiment. He later died in the battle.

To complicate matters further, there was Charles himself. This pale, sad-looking middle-aged man with a stammer was only 5ft 4ins tall and lacked charisma but did carry himself with a cold regal gravity. He took pains to learn the art of war, was courageous in battle, merciful in victory and resilient in defeat. He was also vacillating, indecisive and unreliable. He was as likely to decide policy after a personal conversation with a courtier, as after carefully considering the advice of his Council of War. He was also quite likely to subsequently change his decision, leaving confusion in the wake. It must have been difficult for such a man to be receiving conflicting advice from the Rupert and Digby factions of his Council.

These difficulties were compounded by the personality of his Queen. Henrietta Maria returned to England in 1643 but, whether present in person or through correspondence, she was forever pressing her robust views on Charles or giving him a sound scolding if her advice was not taken. Charles deeply loved his wife and was strongly influenced by her uncompromising advice, which must have seemed a corollary to his own concept of divinely appointed kingship. As Digby was a favourite of Henrietta Maria, their joint approach to the King would often outweigh the more practical advice of his military experts.

By early 1643 this unpromising command structure was controlling three armies. There was the King's main army at Oxford, a small army in the South-West and a larger army in the North. The Army in the South-West was under the field command of Sir Ralph Hopton. The Northern Army was under the Earl of Newcastle who had command north of the Trent and, because of the distance, was given the powers of viceroy, even being authorized to bestow his own knighthoods. The Earl of Derby commanded Lancashire and was nominally under command of the Earl of Newcastle but, again because of the distance, his was effectively an independent command.

King and Parliament therefore both began the 1643 campaign season with a main headquarters, a principal field army and a number of smaller armies. They had both tried to dominate as much countryside as they could in order to gain access to recruits, finance and provisions. They achieved this dominance by garrisoning towns, castles and any country houses which were suitable for defence. It was possible for the cavalry from a particular garrison to control an area of twenty miles radius. Both sides attempted to interlock these arcs of influence to cover a wide area. For example, garrisons were placed in the towns round Oxford such as Banbury, Woodstock, Faringdon, Islip and Enstone and spread out to embrace Abingdon, Wallingford and Reading. Communications were only as good as a fast horse on atrocious roads and depended upon the ability to get changes of horses and avoid capture by the enemy. In such circumstances command and control was extremely difficult and local commanders were left to get on with their tasks on the basis of intermittent general directives.

The year 1643 had started well for the King. Hopton in the South-West head that the Parliamentary army was advancing towards him so decided to conceal his troops and six cannon in the broken ground on the brow of the Braddock Down. The Parliamentary forces had not bothered to find out the strength of Hopton's army, which had recently been reinforced and captured a large cargo of arms at Falmouth. On the sighting of what appeared to be Hopton's small army, the Roundhead cavalry charged. Too late the cavalry discovered themselves under heavy fire from the gorse. They turned and fled to Saltash where some then escaped to Plymouth by boat. Hopton's men pursued, capturing all their cannon, and the net result of the engagement was that Cornwall was cleared of Parliamentarians. This was a costly mistake for Parliament and the first battle of the Civil War to be lost as a direct result of intelligence failure.

Other engagements took place at this time that served to emphasize that many of the commanders on both sides had little or no concept of the need for intelligence. They were mainly landowners with no military background, whose only concept of tactics was drawn from the hunting field. Lord Herbert, son of the wealthy Marquis of Worcester, was a case in point. On 24 March he lost the newly recruited Royalist Army of South Wales after it was taken by surprise at Highnam, a village on the western side of Gloucester. Sir William Waller a professional soldier, MP and landowner, had been given command of the Parliamentary forces in the West. Waller had set out from the Parliamentary stronghold of Bristol, crossed the Severn Estuary with a bridge of boats just south of Gloucester and then marched through the Forest of Deane to take Herbert's army from the rear. It would seem that the Royalist scouting had been either so bad or non existent that Herbert had absolutely no idea of Waller's whereabouts. He had not even heard about the major event of building the pontoon bridge, which must have been the talk of the local countryside. In fact when Waller attacked in the early hours of the morning not only was Herbert away from his troops but he had left no officer of experience behind. Such was the chaos among Herbert's surprised army that his cavalry fled and virtually the whole infantry surrendered. As a result of this complete intelligence failure Herbert lost 14,000 men, together with a large supply of powder, arms and artillery.

Sometimes the value of reconnaissance was recognized but carried out so badly that again the result was intelligence failure. At about this time, at the other end of the country, another Royalist magnate was about to have a setback, this time in the advance to contact. The Earl of Derby with his band of ill-disciplined Lancashire retainers had been wreaking havoc across the county. Then Ralph Assheton, the local MP, raised a force for Parliament in the Rochdale area. On hearing of this, Derby led his men headlong after Assheton. Derby crossed the Calder at Whalley Abbey where he remained with his infantry and cannon and sent out cavalry forward, up out of the valley, to look for the enemy. Instead of sending a few scouts or a troop of dragoons for the reconnaissance he sent a large body of cavalry which, without a care in the world, went straight into the village of Padiham. Having seen Derby's advance, Assheton had concealed musketeers behind dry stone walls in the village who opened fire when the Cavaliers rode passed. Such was the effect of the surprise fire on the cavalry that they fled back to the main body. Assheton then took his men in pursuit and was joined by the villagers who had grabbed what improvised weapons they could lay their hand on. Derby's rabble of an army were so dismayed to see such an apparently large army charging down the hill towards them that they dropped their arms and ran. Derby only just managed to escape with a few of his troops. The King's army in Lancashire had been lost through ill discipline and intelligence failure.

It was at about this time that a chance meeting at a supper in London was to result in a marked improvement in one area of intelligence capability. The hostess for the supper was Lady Verris, a staunch Puritan, and among those attending was Sir William Waller's chaplain and her own chaplain called John Wallis. Wallis was a 28-year-old Ashford man who had been ordained two years previously while attending Emmanuel College Cambridge. Although a devout Puritan and deeply interested in theology, the young man had also spent time studying philosophy and mathematics. Waller's chaplain must have been engaged in army intelligence for he happened to mention that they had intercepted some Royalist correspondence but been unable to read it as it was in cipher. Wallis then offered to try to decipher it and the next morning presented Waller's man with plain text of the letter. In Wallis's own words 'by the number of different characters therein (not above 22 or 23) I judged that it could be no more than the Alphabet, and in about 2 hours time I had deciphered it ... and this was my first attempt at deciphering'. What might have seemed a party piece was not to be forgotten because soon after Wallis was to receive another intercepted enciphered letter to decipher. The letter was from Sir Francis Windlebank, the former Secretary of State, from his French exile to one of his sons in England. This was considerably more difficult than the first as it was written in numerical figures, extending to more than 700 characters It took him many attempts, over a period of several months, but he eventually cracked it. It was the experience he had gained from analysing the Windlebank cipher which he was able to use and build upon again and again when encountering future ciphers.

After this success more and more ciphers were sent to him for decryption. Later in life Wallis would become an internationally respected mathematician but from 1642 onwards cryptanalysis would always play an important part in his life and he was to become, in the words of Leibniz, 'the most famous decipherer now in Europe'. The Parliamentary cause was indeed fortunate to have stumbled upon someone of Wallis's mathematical brilliance and analytical skill to provide them with a GCHQ, albeit of only one person.

Although Wallis was centrally located in London, it could still take considerable time for ciphered material to be sent to him from the further corners of the country and for his plain text to return to the person requesting it. In this respect Wallis's capability provided little help to the Parliamentary tactical intelligence effort because the situation would have almost definitely changed with the passage of time. The huge intelligence advantage Wallis brought was in the area of strategic and political intelligence. These were areas that were far slower to change and, even if they did, could often still be used to advantage through propaganda.

While an obscure domestic chaplain was making his cryptanalysis debut there was one of the periodic semi-ceasefires which like all the others was to end in failure. A Parliamentary delegation went to Oxford to negotiate a settlement with the King. His Majesty was in no mood to consider Parliament's proposals and was more concerned with deciding the strategy for capturing London. Lord Falkland saw an opportunity to enhance the Royalist chances of taking the capital. He decided to attempt to subvert the MP and poet Edmund Waller, one of the moderate Parliamentary Peace Commissioners. Falkland somehow persuaded Waller to form a group of conspirators to carry out a Royalist coup. This would be activated when the King was ready to advance on London. The plan was to seize the Tower then take the principal Parliamentary leaders hostage. At the same time Royalists in London would declare the City for the King.

This plan was ambitious to the point of being farfetched. To succeed, the next step would be to give Waller, who had returned to London, the legal authority for the enterprise in the form of the King's Commission of Array. The question was how to get the Commission to Waller in London. Falkland decided to use for this task a war widow, Lady Katherine, whose husband had been killed at Edgehill. She was a lady of some note. Lord Aubigny had fallen in love with the Earl of Suffolk's beautiful daughter Katherine and they had run away to marry in secret fearing that they might not get official approval because he was the brother to the Duke of Lenox and so kinsman of the King. As it happened, both Charles and Henrietta Maria regarded the elopement as charmingly romantic, and the young couple returned to court and royal favour. Katherine had moved to Oxford after her husband's death but had received a Parliamentary pass to visit London. This was a perfect opportunity for Falkland, who asked Katherine to smuggle the Commission of Array to Waller when she returned to London. On 17 May she travelled to London with a box containing the Commission tied 'about the thighs'.

Among those recruited to the conspiracy was Waller's brother-in-law Tomkins. This Tomkins was overheard speaking about the plot by his servant who then reported it to Pym. The facts that Tomkin's servant had overheard the conversation while standing behind a hanging and had access to Pym strongly suggest that he was a Roundhead source. Pym as the de facto Parliamentary leader would have used agents but whether he ran them himself or others ran them for him, we do not know. It could even be that Pym exploited the Waller Plot in order to discredit Royalists in London. Whatever the truth of the matter, the conspirators were all arrested on 31 May and some hanged.

Waller decided it prudent to try to buy his life by giving details of all those implicated in the plot and so was reprieved and sent to the Tower. Katherine, for her part, fled for refuge to the French Embassy when she heard the news of the arrests. The embassy accepted her on the grounds of citizenship because of her husband's French title. Pym was not impressed by the French notion of asylum and had her removed to the Tower. Falkland was never to forgive himself for bringing such misfortune on the lady.

This ill-starred plot had not only completely failed but also given Parliament excellent material for propaganda. Falkland was right to be distressed over Lady Aubigny but the fact remains that he had managed to recruit a senior member of the opposing side, and through him others, to attempt to overthrow the rebel leadership. He had also arranged the successful use of a covert courier to communicate with his agent. Although the plan failed, knowledge that a senior member of their leadership could be subverted must have been a blow to Parliamentary confidence. Seeing this danger to morale, Pym turned the situation round by using the plot to tighten security. A special oath of loyalty to Parliament was written which all senior officials and members of Parliament were obliged to sign.

Meanwhile back in the West Country, Hopton found himself and his army at Lansdown facing the Roundhead army of Waller. The battle was a draw but there were heavy casualties on both sides. An exploding ammunition cart had temporarily blinded Hopton and his depleted army was exhausted. Hopton withdrew towards Devizes and Waller's larger force caught up with him. Hopton set about defending Devizes as best he could and sent to Oxford for reinforcements, which arrived two days later in the form of 1,800 horse under Henry Wilmot. Meanwhile the dapper overconfident Waller had been taking his time attacking Devizes and had ordered up beer, sack and brandy for his men. Waller had assumed that Essex's army would prevent any Royalist reinforcement getting through but on 13 July was informed by a scout that the Royalists were approaching. He quickly deployed to Roundway Down. Wilmot's horse attacked immediately and having driven off Waller's cavalry in confusion returned to the field to be joined by Hopton's Cornishmen who attacked Waller's infantry from the rear. Together they destroyed the Parliament's Western Army. Waller escaped the field with a small force, leaving behind 1,400 men dead or captured and all his cannon, ammunition and baggage.

There had been other good news for the Royalists regarding armaments because the Queen had managed to land at Bridlington in February with the arms and ammunition that she had purchased in the United Provinces. By this time the Earl of Newcastle had secured the North-East and was able to link up with Henrietta Maria in York. The armaments were put in two convoys, the second of which was accompanied by the Queen. Newcastle provided her with 3,000 foot and 1,000 horse for her journey south to meet a force under Rupert who would escort her to Oxford. The tiny bird-like figure of Henrietta Maria, accompanied by her favourite dwarf, pet dogs and monkeys, decided to play the general and lead her army. The Queen enjoyed calling herself the 'She-Majesty Generalissima', picnicking with her ladies beside troops in the field, riding with her officers at the front of the column and generally showing the world that she was a commander like her great father Henry IV of France.

Parliamentary ineptitude prevented her generalship ever being put to the test and her convoy eventually meandered to the rendezvous with Rupert at Stratford-upon-Avon on 11 July. Two days later she was reunited with the King and the court at Oxford could feel life was returning to normality. Henrietta Maria may have been a foolish and vain woman but she was also her father's daughter and succeeded in procuring and safely delivering 10,000 small arms, 32 guns and 78 barrels of black powder that were essential to the Royalist war effort. It must also be said that the fact that she had been able to take her slow-moving convoy halfway across the kingdom was an indictment of both Parliamentarian intelligence to locate her and the will of Parliamentary commanders to intercept her.

Once Rupert had returned from escorting the Queen he set off to Bristol where Hopton joined him. Rupert decided to take the city by storm and Hopton's already much reduced army died in great numbers attacking the southern forts but their brave exertions helped Rupert capture Bristol on 26 July. The second city in the kingdom was now in Royalist hands and with it the industrial base needed for arms manufacture. It must have been particularly satisfying for Rupert to take Bristol because he had tried to do so four months earlier in a failed covert operation. All towns had certain citizens who did not support whichever side was governing their town. Both the Royalists and the Parliamentarians made attempts to identify their supporters in the towns held by their opponents and establish contact with them in the hope of achieving an insurrection. Sir Edward Walker, the Secretary for War, also carried out the function of head of military intelligence. In this capacity he drew up lists of such potential sympathizers for the King. As far as Bristol was concerned, it became known that there were a number of seamen and merchants who were so worried about the loss of trade with Royalist Wales that they now supported the King. Their leader Robert Yeoman appears to have made contact with Oxford and communications were sent back to him from Royalist headquarters through a Doctor Marks.

Rupert arrived outside Bristol on 7 March, by which time a plot had been made for Royalists citizens to capture the city gates. The plan was that at midnight a Captain Hilsdon and some trusted soldiers would inspect the sentries guarding the gates then overpower them with the aid of a group of citizens. Having secured the gates they would then ring the church bells as a signal for Rupert's forces to enter the city. The Parliamentary Governor Nathaniel Fiennes heard of the plot and just before midnight sent in troops to seize all concerned.

It is not known to this day whether Hilsdon had been acting as a double agent for Fiennes or the conspirators had given themselves away by careless talk in the taverns where they made their plans. Whether or not this was an example of a good counter-intelligence operation by Fiennes, the investigations which followed certainly resulted in the exposure of virtually all Royalist sympathizers in the city. The leaders were hanged and the others suffered major confiscation of their property. There would be no hope of inside assistance for the Royalists in the future. Rupert had little option but to pull back as there was no purpose in besieging Bristol because it could always be relieved by the Parliamentary navy. Covert operations having failed, the only option left for capturing Bristol would be by difficult and bloody assault.

The summer of 1643 was the high point for Royalist fortunes. They had obtained urgently needed arms and ammunition, secured the vital city of Bristol and through a series of victories had won the South-West and North-East for the King. Charles was reunited with his Queen and there was confidence at court that His Majesty's rebellious subjects would soon be brought to obedience. Parliament had failed to fully exploit its overwhelming advantages such as its control of the main armouries, the navy and the great wealth and population of London. Essex had the main Parliamentary army tied down in the siege of Reading before it capitulated in April and then sickness in the ranks and discontent over lack of pay meant that he failed to press on to threaten Oxford. Harry Vane and the Parliamentary hawks began accusing Essex of deliberately avoiding battle with the King. The Parliamentary leadership was beginning to show cracks under stress.

Although Parliamentary failure was partly responsible for the Royalist successes, credit must also be given to the energy and leadership of Prince Rupert. As well as putting considerable effort into the supervision and training of the cavalry, he had captured Cirencester in February, Birmingham and Lichfield in April and then led several damaging raids on Essex's Army in June. One such raid turned into the Battle of Chalgrove Field, which resulted in the death of John Hampden, perhaps the most influential Parliamentary leader after Pym. Rupert appeared invincible and the fact that he was usually in the thick of the fighting and always managed to survive unscathed was explained in Parliamentary publications by him being made immune from gunfire by the Devil himself. He had even fostered his image of being a military demon by being 'clad in scarlet very richly embroidered with silver and mounted on a gallant Barbary horse'.

The Parliamentary military setbacks had brought morale to low ebb in London. It was to be lower still when Waller returned to London having lost his army and accused Essex of failing to prevent the Oxford reinforcements reaching Hopton at Devizes and so being responsible for the Roundway Down disaster and its corollary, the fall of Bristol. Parliament's two principal commanders were now at each other's throats. People took sides and both commanders had factions which tried to destroy the credibility of the other. Indeed Essex was so much criticized by Parliament that he offered his resignation and began proposing that there should be new negotiations with the King.

The Parliamentary cause looked as though it was about to collapse but Pym kept his head and managed to turn the situation around. He gave full backing to Essex who at least still had an army and persuaded Parliament to do likewise. This reversal of fortune was partly due to Pym's customary political acumen but had been made possible by two major mistakes made by the King. The first was when the Earl of Loudoun and a deputation from the Scots Council had visited the King in Oxford and offered to mediate between Charles and Parliament. The King, confident that victory would be his by the year end, regarded it as excessively impudent of the Scots to presume to interfere. The Scots were not even granted the courtesy of a private audience. Loudoun returned to Edinburgh to report the snub to his cousin. This was the canny, squint-eyed Marquis of Argyll, who was the Treasurer and Covenanter leader. He was a man with a religious mission to strengthen the Kirk and in doing so himself and Clan Campbell. As chief of the clan that dominated western Scotland, he had 5,000 claymores at his command and was not one to take offence lightly. He now decided that as there was to be no accommodation with the King: Scotland should now cooperate with the Puritans in the English Parliament to impose a settlement on the monarch.

The other major mistake concerned Ireland. The Irish rebellion of 1641 had gone from strength to strength because it became an alliance of the Celtic chieftains with the Catholic Anglo-Irish descendants of the Norman landowners. They had decided to bury their differences in the belief that the Puritanical Parliament of England would try to seize the land of Catholics and create new Protestant plantations. This was indeed a likely scenario. Irish leaders such as Sir Phelim O'Neill in the North and Lord Muskerry in the South formed a confederacy which controlled most of Ireland and had its capital in Kilkenny. So strong had the confederacy become while King and Parliament had been in conflict that it had established its own mint and was exchanging emissaries with Catholic countries. The 'Confederacy of Kilkenny' as it was called, had men under arms in each Province but its main forces were those of Owen Roe O'Neill in Ulster and Thomas Preston in Leinster. It also had a navy, which had joined forces with the privateers based at Dunkirk operating under Spanish protection to make a total of ninety sail.

Ormonde was Anglo-Irish just like his brother-in-law Muskerry but unlike him had been brought up in England as a Protestant. Ormonde controlled little more than Dublin and the Pale. There were also three other Protestant forces. The Scots contingent under Major General Robert Monro in Ulster, the Lagan Valley Protestants in West Ulster and the Earl of Inchiquin, the Protestant Chief of the O'Briens, in Munster. All these were often pinned down by Confederacy raiding parties. At their disposal to fight the Confederacy were nominally about 40,000 soldiers, mostly Scots but about 8,000 from Cheshire and North Wales. With the war in England the principal priority for both King and Parliament, these men had received neither the pay nor equipment to make them a motivated, effective force to deal with the Confederacy.

Back in Oxford, the King decided that the army in Ireland had the potential to make a significant contribution to the Royalist forces. On 23 April Charles took the fateful step of writing two letters to Ormonde in Dublin. The first was to make a truce with the Confederation and the second was to raise an army to join the Royalist cause in England. Neither were easy tasks, because the Council of Ireland was dominated by the Lord Justice, Sir William Parsons, and his Parliamentary supporters. Nevertheless, Ormonde dutifully began seeing how this could be engineered. In the mean time, the Queen had been told of Charles's Irish scheme while she was in York and decided to help matters along. When the Catholic Earl of Antrim, chief of the Irish MacDonnells, came to pay his respects to the Queen in York she accepted his offer to raise his clansmen for the King and ship them to the West Coast of Scotland. Such a move was attractive to Antrim because as well as serving the King he would be able join his Scottish clan relations the MacDonalds of the Isles and the Western Highlands, who were also Catholic. The combined clans would then be able to seize contested lands held by the Campbells, particularly in Kintyre.

Using Irish Catholic forces to invade Scotland or England on behalf of the King was a major misjudgement on behalf of the King but this intrigue would not have mattered so much if it had remained secret, at least for the time being. This was not to be. Antrim's boat was captured in the Irish Sea by a Covenanter patrol vessel as he returned home. Documents were found on him describing the plot. This could have easily been avoided if in the first place the documents had been encrypted and, more importantly, Antrim had had the wit to destroy them as soon as he realized he was about to be captured. This major security failure translated into a major intelligence success.

The documents were sent to Edinburgh where Argyll learnt that not only was the King to use the hated Irish Papists to invade Scotland but that they would very likely attack his own clan areas. The Scottish Council was dominated by Covenanters and they were furious. Loudoun summoned the Estates without the King's consent in order to vote money and in so doing broke with any pretence of answering to the monarch. The King had relied upon the Marquis of Hamilton and his brother the Earl of Lanark to look after his affairs in Scotland. From now on events were completely beyond their control and they could do no more than stand by as spectators. The vital piece of intelligence contained in the letters was sent with speed to England and gleefully received by Pym. By making the information public, Pym was able to transform a situation of despondency and defeatism to one of united rage against a ruler who planned to invade his own country with Irish Papists.

By the end of July, Argyll proposed a formal alliance with the English Parliament. Pym sent Sir Harry Vane to Edinburgh to negotiate terms. Things were now going well for Parliament but they would be improved further by another miscalculation made by the King a couple of weeks earlier. After the great success of the capture of Bristol, Charles had to decide the next step. He knew he must take London and this might be the time to advance on his capital while the Parliamentary commanders were quarrelling and some seemed to have little stomach for continuing the war. A royal promise of pardon and the approach of the Royalist army with the invincible Rupert in the vanguard might have been the correct balance of carrot and stick to encourage Parliament to sue for peace. Instead Charles decided to besiege the Puritan city of Gloucester which was being held for Parliament under the command the very capable Colonel Edward Massey.

When the Royalist Army reached Gloucester they found that the citizens had repaired their defences and were grimly determined to resist the King. The heroic defence of Gloucester struck a chord with the people of London who now clamoured for Essex to lead an army for its relief. Suddenly apprentices were flocking to enlist. News then reached London that Ormonde had carried out a coup in Dublin and removed Sir William Parsons and the Parliamentary sympathizers from the Council. This reinforced the truth of the information in the captured letters. Parliament authorized the raising of five new foot regiments and a thousand horse, together with £30,000 to pay them. In a matter of a few weeks Parliament had a large army under the undisputed leadership of Essex. On 22 August, the Lord General was able to review his 15,000 troops on Hounslow Heath. He could be confident that his men were highly motivated first to relieve Gloucester and then defeat the King.

Meanwhile Charles continued with the fruitless siege of Gloucester, rejecting Rupert's advice to take it by storm and deciding instead to breach the wall by mining.

While miners were being assembled for this work, the Earl of Montrose suddenly appeared at the Royalist camp outside Gloucester. He had decided that Argyll had now gone too far in his opposition to the King and brought vital intelligence that the Covenanters were planning to enter the war on behalf of Parliament and offered to raise a Royalist army in Scotland to oppose them. The King knew Montrose as a man of contradictions: on the one hand, a loyal Lowland aristocrat who was cheerful, charming and urbane; on the other, a staunch Presbyterian and successful Covenanter General who had waded through the Tweed in front of his troops to be the first to invade England back in 1640. Charles did not believe Montrose and forbade him to raise a Royalist army. The King had been assured by his Commissioner for Scotland, the Marquis of Hamilton, that the country would remain neutral until the winter and refused to believe otherwise.

Hamilton was almost extended family to the King. They were related and, as Hamilton was a descendant of James II of Scotland, he would be heir to the throne of Scotland if King Charles had no surviving children. Also, he had married the daughter of the murdered Duke of Buckingham who had been brought up like one of the royal children after her father's assassination. Hamilton was an ambitious man at pains to advance himself in the King's favour and exuded a confidence that he could easily control Scottish affairs. Despite the actions of the Scottish Council, Charles still had so much confidence in Hamilton's ability to keep the Covenanters on side that he elevated him to a dukedom. This confidence was entirely misplaced, as Argyll was able to run rings round this pleasant but mediocre magnate. The King thus had to choose between two contradictory intelligence assessments and it took him not a moment to decide in favour of the source he trusted, Hamilton. Montrose had burnt his boats with the Covenanter leaders and had been rejected by his sovereign, so he was left kicking his heels as an observer of impending calamity.

By 24 August the mines under Gloucester's walls were at last ready and Massey had refused a final summons to surrender. That night there was torrential rain and the powder was too wet to be ignited for the assault the next day. Meanwhile Essex was approaching slowly and cautiously. Essex had no wish to run into Rupert on the way and knowing the prince's aptitude for intelligence decided to try to counteract it by good operational security, including not lighting fires at night so that their position would not be seen. Despite this, Rupert located Essex's army at Stow-on-the-Wold. After a brief attack to test the Roundhead force, Rupert withdrew towards Cheltenham and sent word to the King of Essex's strength and position. When Essex arrived at Gloucester on 6 September he found the siege had been lifted and the Royalist army had disappeared.

Essex had achieved his mission and saved Gloucester but he realized that an equally difficult task now lay before him. He would have to leave some of his force to bolster the Gloucester garrison and then return to London without being ambushed by the King's army. News was also arriving that Exeter had just fallen to Rupert's brother Prince Maurice and so Essex could expect no help from the remaining Parliamentary supporters in the West Country. It was therefore an apprehensive

Essex who departed Gloucester with 4,000 horse and 10,000 foot. Rupert obtained intelligence of his movements and on 20 September the King's army blocked the way at Newbury with 6,000 horse and 8,000 foot. Essex could not avoid battle if he wished to return to London. Luckily for Essex he had with him Skippon and his brigade of well drilled London trained bands. Despite Rupert's repeated charges, the trained bands held their ground. When darkness fell and with the Royalist ammunition exhausted, the King withdrew towards Oxford. The way was left open for Essex to return to London and he took it.

Although the battle was in fact another stalemate, it was a great boost for Parliament. It had shown that Rupert's cavalry was not invincible and Essex was able to return to London as the hero of Gloucester. The tide was turning against the Royalists. Not only had they failed to defeat Essex but Lord Falkland, the Secretary of State, had been killed in the action. Falkland had been a sound and pragmatic adviser to the King and a promising intelligencer. His post as Secretary of State was given to Lord Digby.

In September the Royalists had been involved in another unsuccessful siege, this time of Hull where Ferdinando Lord Fairfax and his son Sir Thomas had been forced to withdraw. As Hull had strong defences and was being resupplied by the Parliamentary fleet, the Royalists had no chance of taking it. This posed a problem for Newcastle who felt that he could not advance south leaving the rump of the Northern Association Army at his rear in Hull. Cromwell, by now promoted Lieutenant General, was sent by Manchester to give support to Hull and arrived in the town on 22 September, meeting Sir Thomas Fairfax for the first time. The 30-year-old Fairfax, nicknamed 'Black Tom' because of his long dark hair, had fought alongside the Prince of Orange in 1629 and proved himself a daring and successful cavalry commander for the Northern Association. As there was little use for horse in a besieged town, it was agreed that Fairfax would ship his cavalry across the Humber and join Manchester's Eastern Association. Fairfax and Cromwell's force then combined with Manchester's and went on to besiege Bolingbroke Castle.

Sir John Henderson, the Royalist governor of Newark, set out to relieve Bolingbroke but was detected by Cromwell's forward reconnaissance. This intelligence enabled Manchester's force to prepare an ambush at Wincheby Ridge on 11 October. Cromwell successfully charged Henderson's force before it was deployed but his horse was shot under him. Fairfax then carried out a complicated manoeuvre, ending in a charge of the Royalist right, which won the day. Manchester had gained a victory thanks to his two cavalry generals. The Royalists were routed and retreated to Newark, leaving behind their supplies. The Battle of Wincheby Ridge resulted in 1,000 Royalist prisoners and secured Lincolnshire for Parliament. The origin of the success had been the effective deployment and efficient reporting of the reconnaissance forces. It was also the first joint battle of two Parliamentary leaders whose military genius was to clinch the outcome of the war.

In the same month the Royalists might have found consolation for their losses to the Eastern Association in the taking of Newport Pagnell by Sir Lewis Dyve.

Although no more than a small market town, Newport Pagnell was significant because it was the place Essex had selected as winter quarters for his army. Even more significant was its strategic position commanding the principal road and river connection between London and the eastern counties. If the Royalists could retain control of the town they would go a long way towards preventing produce reaching London. Also, control of Newport Pagnell would mean that the now resurgent Eastern Association would be cut off from London. Dyve's good work provided an excellent opportunity but he was desperately short of ammunition and so sent urgent messages to Oxford for replenishment.

Days passed and then weeks and for some reason no ammunition was sent, despite repeated letters from Rupert to Oxford emphasizing the importance of speed. On 28 October, Dyve saw no option but to withdraw from Newport Pagnell in response to an advancing Parliamentary force. As it happened the ammunition wagons were at last on their way to him but Dvye had not been told. This sad story of lethargy and incompetence shows how Royalist command, control and communications could break down. If it could fail in a matter of utmost operational importance, we can assume that similar failures were occurring in the management of intelligence. After all, both were largely the responsibility of the Secretary for War, Sir Edward Walker, described by Clarendon as 'A very importunate ambitious and foolish man that studied nothing but his own ends.'

While the Royalists had been concentrating on Gloucester, the situation in Scotland had got out of hand. Vane had arrived in Edinburgh and soon got down to business with Argyll. On 25 September an agreement called the Solemn League and Covenant was reached whereby the Scots would provide an army of 18,000 foot, 3,000 horse and artillery for Parliament in exchange for Parliament paying £30,000 per month and supporting Presbyterianism. All this time Hamilton had done nothing to prevent the summoning of the Estates or the treaty with the English Parliament. His inaction reeked of treason but was more a matter of being a bewildered bystander of events beyond his control.

This vital agreement with the Scots was one of Pym's last major acts before he died in December, probably of cancer of the lower bowel – though the Royalist press said of syphilis. Scots began raising an army through their well established method of local conscription. In this system all areas had to provide one in four men from a list of all men between the ages of 16 and 60. The writs for raising this force were amazingly authorized by Lanark and so officially went out on the King's authority! This major recruiting drive and the training that followed were organized by an experienced professional soldier, the tough, wizened little 63-year-old Alexander Leslie, Earl of Leven. Assisting him was his namesake, but no relation, David Leslie, the General of Horse.

Having made a complete hash of the King's affairs in Scotland, Hamilton and his brother Lanark rode to Oxford to explain to His Majesty. Charles refused to see them and realizing they had lost royal favour, Lanark bolted off in disguise to London to join Parliament. There was no proof that Hamilton had been disloyal but the circumstances were so negative that he was placed in custody. Charles was well aware that Hamilton was a potential heir to the throne of Scotland and it could well have been that he was manoeuvring himself into a position with the Covenanters to make a claim. Whether Lanark's behaviour was a result of a successful subversion operation by someone on the Parliamentary side is not known but belief in his disloyalty must have had a similar effect on Royalist morale to that of the Edmund Waller incident had had on Parliament in the summer.

Charles at last turned to Montrose to act as his leader in Scotland and finally gave him authority to raise a Royalist army. The Earl of Antrim had arrived in Oxford, having escaped his Covenanter captors and greatly impressed the King by announcing that he had made a deal with the Confederates and was now Captain General of Ireland. This was not strictly true, in fact not true at all but rather wishful thinking. The King had no reason to doubt the good news and decided on a strategy that Antrim should take his MacDonnells and other Irish to the West Coat of Scotland to link up with his Scottish clansmen and whatever force Montrose could raise, and so begin a Royalist offensive in Scotland. Although the autumn had brought setbacks for the Royalists, the King retained his optimism and the hope that an increased flow of troops from Ireland to England and Scotland would tip the balance.

After protracted negotiations, Ormonde at last signed the 'Cessation' or one-year truce with the Confederates. This was indeed only a truce. Owen Roe O'Neill wanted an independent Catholic Ireland and so continued raiding the King's garrisons. Protestant nobles like Inchiquin were totally against peace with the Papist rebels, as was Monro and his Presbyterian Scots who declared for Parliament. The decision to send an army from Ireland to support the King in England had not been well received by many of Ormonde's own troops. Among these was George Monck, the Governor of Dublin, who declined to take the oath of loyalty required of officers posted to England. As Ormonde valued Monck's military expertise he placed him under honourable arrest and sent him to England in the hope that the King might persuade him to do his duty.

Ormonde overcame his many problems and eventually managed to land about a thousand troops at Mostyn in Flintshire. Despite being poorly equipped these men managed to capture North Wales for the Royalists and then tried to link up with other Irish troops who had landed at Chester. The King had given the wild Lord John Byron command of all troops coming from Ireland. Byron concentrated the Irish contingents with his own men to make a force of about 1,500 foot and 1,800 horse. He then advanced on Nantwich, a fortified town on the River Weaver, which was the parliamentary headquarters in Cheshire.

Byron was not one for winning the hearts and minds of the local population. Wherever his force passed it would be long remembered for its drunkenness, looting and cattle rustling. Charles had secured a few more soldiers but given his opponents a propaganda victory. The Parliamentary press was swift to portray the King using marauding Irish Papists to invade England to crush his Protestant subjects. How much intelligence, if any, Parliament had of the timing of the arrival of the ill-disciplined Irish reinforcements is not known but the outcome was so much to their advantage that it did not matter. Byron's trail of armed robbery and organized vandalism eventually came to rest at Nantwich. As he did not have enough men to take the town by storm, Byron started the lengthy process of a siege just as the first snows of winter began to fall. The stakes were high, for if Nantwich surrendered Byron would dominate Cheshire for the King and Charles's great gamble on the use of forces from Ireland would begin to pay off. Only time would tell.

In December Parliament was focused on Scotland and the succession to Pym. Two people came to the fore. Oliver St John, the Solicitor General, had been Pym's closest associate and was regarded as his natural successor in the Commons. He was much respected for his intellect, legal knowledge and as a long-standing leader of resistance to the King. On the other hand he was not much liked – described as 'of dark and clouded countenance, very proud, and conversant with few but those of his own humour and inclination'. The other was the former courtier Sir Harry Vane who was equally religiously resolute but also had a charm and persuasiveness that had made him so successful as a negotiator with the Scots. Closely associated with both but busy away from Westminster on his military duties was Oliver Cromwell.

Part of the agreement with the Scots was that the Committee of Both Kingdoms would jointly manage the war. The Committee was established in Derby House, near Westminster Hall, early the next year. Lord Maynard led the Scots representatives; St John and Vane were the principal English members of the Committee. Both men were hawks in that they wanted a dictated peace with the King, but moderate in religion, believing in religious toleration within the Puritan wing of Protestantism. Those with this religious stance were termed 'Independents' which meant that they believed in congregations and their ministers being independent from outside authority be it bishops or the structure of the Kirk. Such men would be in no rush to introduce Presbyterianism to England. This stance of the Independents would become a cause of friction with Parliament's Scottish allies in the future.

In December the King saw an opportunity to drive a wedge between the Independents and the Scots and decided on another covert operation in London. The idea had come from Digby's father, the Earl of Bristol, who had been approached by a certain Thomas Ogle. It was Ogle's belief that a number of influential Independents in London would prefer allegiance to the King and the return of the bishops, if religious toleration was granted for Protestants sects, to becoming Presbyterian to please the Scots. A number of potential supporters for this scheme had been identified, including Sir John Wollaston the Lord Mayor, Colonel Mosley the Governor of Aylesbury and Riley the Parliamentary Scoutmaster General. Violet, a prominent goldsmith, was to be used to carry correspondence between the King and his hoped-for sympathizers. The general thrust of the plan was that the King would put forward new proposals for peace promising religious toleration which would be accepted by many influential Londoners and at the same time Mosley would hand over Aylesbury to Rupert who would advance through the town to London.

Unfortunately for the Royalists, their talent-spotting for conspirators had been literally cavalier as Digby's intelligence on them was plain bad. To add insult to injury, Mosley was acting as a double agent and passing all information about the plot to Vane and St John. The details of this plot, which was called the Brook Plot after one of the conspirators, Sir Basil Brook, were announced to Parliament by St John. This was followed by the usual flurry of arrests but of no prominent persons because no one of consequence had been involved. The Lord Mayor gave a generous banquet for Parliament and the Scots Commissioners and to all appearance the Scottish/English alliance stood firm. For Parliamentarians, 1643 ended with optimism that the coordinated efforts of the armies Essex and Leven would force the King to sue for peace.

Military professionalism was slowly developing on both sides, born through harsh experience in bloody encounters. Gradually there was a realization that operational intelligence on the enemy's locations, strengths and intentions was an important factor in deciding tactics. To obtain this operational intelligence scouts and intelligencers would be needed for all forces. Of course Rupert had been only too well aware of this and had been using scouts and intelligencers from the outset. Many Parliamentarians saw his ability to obtain good intelligence not as a result of establishing an effective structure for the purpose but as another facet of his miraculous invincibility.

Rupert was credited with being a master of disguise. It was reported that once, when disguised as a county gentleman near Worcester, he met an old woman and asked for something to eat. She invited him in and gave him some food and while chatting with him said that she hoped the plague would choke Prince Rupert. After the meal Rupert thanked her when he left and gave her money and a letter to the Mayor of Worcester, a Roundhead. The woman took the letter to the mayor which, when opened, reported her for giving food and shelter to Prince Rupert! Another of the many stories was that Rupert bought a load of apples from a farmer, changed clothes with him and then passed through the Parliamentary army selling apples. Having obtained all the intelligence he needed, he returned the apple cart to the farmer and told him to go to the Parliamentary army and ask them if they had enjoyed Prince Rupert's apples.

Although these stories are almost certainly apocryphal, they may have had a grain of truth in so far as Rupert did like to conduct reconnaissance himself and he tried to model himself on Gustavus Adolphus, who was well known for visiting enemy positions in disguise. The fear engendered by Rupert was such that even his dog was said to have special powers. His dog was a large white poodle called Boy. Boy, who followed him everywhere including into battle, was a dog of considerable character and wit. His accomplishments included being able to jump in air at the word 'Charles' and cock his leg at the word 'Pym' but many Parliamentarians believed Boy had more supernatural powers. It was widely thought that Boy was able to pass invisibly through the Parliamentary lines and then report intelligence back to his master. The fact that such a story could be believed may be a comment not only on the level of superstition of the time but also on the better intelligence system being developed by the Royalists.

By the beginning of 1643 both sides had established Scoutmaster Generals for their main armies. There was a general realization that intelligence should be run by a senior officer. Recognition of the importance of a Scoutmaster General was shown by them receiving pay of £1 a day at a time when a parish priest might get £20 a year. Henry Hexham, who had served as a quartermaster with English volunteers in the Dutch army besieging Breda in 1639, had written the most up-to-date English military manual. This was *The Principles of the Art of Militarie, Practised in the Warres of the United Netherlands.* In it he went so far as to say the Marshal of the Field (what we would now call chief of staff) should be head of intelligence and 'he should understand of what strength in horse and foot the enemy is and have an exact map of the country'.

Neither side was going to have such senior heads of intelligence, any more than they would be able to find decent maps, but they did at least tend to give sound officers the post of Scoutmaster General. Sadly few had any previous experience but they did at least provide a focus for operational intelligence and a potential conduit for intelligence reporting back to their respective headquarters in Oxford and London. The detachments and outposts of the armies and regional forces often had their own scoutmasters and thus there was the potential for an intelligence collection network. Sadly, this was seldom exploited. Just as operational control functioned on the basis of a main headquarters deciding strategy and then field armies and garrisons conducting tactical operations semi-autonomously, so it was with intelligence.

The intelligence collection sources used were cavalry reconnaissance, scouts and spies. This was wholly in keeping with the doctrine of the day – what John Cruso in his manuals described as 'spies, scouts and discoverers', who should be 'choice men valiant and discreet'. Both sides, therefore, had a rudimentary intelligence structure but it was still very immature. There was some flow of information upward but no dissemination of assessed intelligence and no intelligence management or collection planning from the centres. As is often the case, the intelligence system was only as good as the interest taken in it by the commander. Rupert strongly valued intelligence and used a reliable person, Sir William Neal, as his Scoutmaster. In addition Rupert always retained a hands-on involvement with intelligence. For example, in the Brook Plot, an informant had told him that the Parliamentary Governor of Aylesbury was prepared to secretly let some Royalist troops into the town so that it could be captured. Rupert left Oxford and was met outside Aylesbury by a contact of the informant. After talking to the contact for some time Rupert decided that it was a trap and sent the contact to Oxford to be hanged.

When discussing spies in his manuals, Cruso had made two valuable points: that you cannot have too many spies and that you must always be suspicious of spies;

these were lessons that Rupert had obviously learnt. Spies are not to be confused with scouts who were civilian-dressed members of their respective armies and collected information as directed by their scoutmasters. Their method of collection was usually by personal observation and by mingling in enemy-held areas then reporting what they heard. The word 'spies' can mean a number of things and it is convenient to divide them into modern categories. There are 'casual contacts' who provide information, either intentionally or not, to an intelligence gatherer by way of general conversation. The landlord of an inn is the sort of person who would hear lots of news and probably be happy to talk about it. There are 'informants' or 'numbered contacts' who intentionally provide information about the opposition in a covert fashion, usually in hope of payment. Then there are 'agents' or 'accredited sources' who are informants under the control of their intelligence handler. They probably make contact with their intelligence handler on a prearranged covert basis, are given direction on what information to try to obtain and how to get it and receive regular payments.

The intelligencers of the Civil War would not have known this terminology but would have recognized the general roles of the three types, although there would be blurring between the categories. The scouts of the civil war were a cross between low-grade undercover agents and reconnaissance. They would sometimes report back enemy activity from a safe distance and would also try to infiltrate enemy positions or territory to obtain information at close quarters. The great majority did little more than report hearsay and rumour and there are only a few records of scouts having casual contacts and even less of them recruiting informants. The few informants and agents tended to be recruited directly by scoutmasters or senior officials.

Casual contacts, informants and agents are all of value and take a long time to recruit, with the agent obviously taking the longest. Having decided the specific intelligence requirements, it is necessary for the intelligencer to identify those who would be likely to have access to such information. It is then necessary to identify among those with access who it would be possible to approach and whether any are likely be prepared to engage in espionage on grounds of conscience, character defect or because they are susceptible to bribery or blackmail. It is usually difficult to get alongside those with direct access and so the usual course is to talent-spot someone on the fringes of the access group who might eventually engineer indirect access or become promoted into a position of direct access themselves. All this takes time, patience and a high standard of intelligence tradecraft. In 1643 there had been little time to develop this process, as both sides were beginning from a standing start and the intelligence tradecraft, so effective in Walsingham's day, would have to be reinvented.

There were occasions when the recruitment process was dramatically shortened by what we would now call a 'walk-in': in other words, someone from the opposition volunteering to pass information. Walk-ins are always suspect because the volunteer may be mentally unstable or merely pretending to have information in order to receive payment. More dangerously, they may also be a double agent, as appears to be the case in Rupert's Aylesbury incident. For all that, some of the best agents in the Cold War began as walk-ins, motivated largely for ideological or personal reasons. During the Civil War there was a variety of strong ideological and personal reasons why someone might change sides and in doing so bring valuable information with them. These reasons included religion, family loyalties and rivalries and, most important of all, self-interest. For many it was only sensible to keep in with the winning side in order that their land and property would be relatively safe.

There was also the matter of conscience in fighting against one's sovereign. The Royalist battle cry was 'For God and King' and that of the Parliamentarians was 'For King and Parliament'. The Parliamentary side convinced themselves that they were not fighting against the King but against his evil advisers and were in fact fighting on behalf of the King to restore his good relations with his Parliament and subjects. Even the Covenanters swore 'To preserve and defend the King's Majesties's person and Authority'. After blood had been shed in such quantity at Edgehill, some of those who supported Parliament started worrying that the situation was getting out of hand and began doubting the logic of bearing arms against the King for his own good. Moreover the Royalist victories in the first part of 1643 made some wonder whether they had backed the wrong horse and what might happen to themselves and their estates in the event of a royal victory. In June, Rupert was particularly fortunate with the arrival of a well-placed defector. Essex had been attempting to move against Oxford and a force of 2,700 had been beaten back while trying to cross the River Cherwell at Islip. Colonel John Hurry, a Scots soldier of fortune, decided to change sides and in doing so brought Rupert detailed information on the dispositions of the Parliamentary army. This information was to be of assistance to Rupert in planning the various successful raids on the Parliamentary army that had stopped it in its tracks and brought calls for Essex's resignation.

The Royalist intelligence system also seems to have been developing quite well in the North. The Earl of Newcastle had appointed the Reverend Michael Hudson as his Scoutmaster. Hudson was a 38-year-old cleric who was a fellow of Queens College Oxford and had become a chaplain to the King. Charles called him 'his plain speaking chaplain' because of his bluntness. Whatever Hudson may have lacked in suavity he made up for in the soundness of his advice and zeal for the royal cause. It was these qualities that led the King to recommend him to Newcastle as Scoutmaster of the Northern Army. The actual degree of his success in that appointment can only be measured second-hand through the letters and journals of Sir Thomas Fairfax, who on several occasions mentions that the Royalists had intelligence of their movements and dispositions, leading to Newcastle dominating the North-East. Fairfax also writes about the poor intelligence available to the Northern Association at this time.

Rupert collected and exploited intelligence in a professional manner but it must be remembered that he was only the commander of the Royalist cavalry, not the whole army. During much of 1643 he had been rushing about the country as an independent commander achieving military success and using reconnaissance and intelligence for his own force. He had no responsibility for the strategic intelligence of the army as a whole. This lay with Sir Edward Walker who appears to have had little interest and less aptitude for the subject. Nor was he responsible for foreign or security intelligence which was the official domain of Digby and Nicholas, the two Secretaries of State. Foreign intelligence was of little concern because the overwhelming matter at hand was fighting the civil war against opponents who were not receiving any support from overseas. The abject failure of the Brook Plot had demonstrated that when Digby ventured into covert operations his intelligence expertise left much to be desired. In short, the intelligence successes of Rupert and to a lesser extent Hudson were successes in tactical military intelligence. Important though these were, they cannot disguise the lack of central direction and control of intelligence.

Although Royalist military intelligence appears to have been generally better than the Parliamentarian at this stage, a good intelligence structure was being created in Essex's army. In January 1643, Essex had appointed the MP for Bedford Borough, Sir Samuel Luke, as his Scoutmaster General with the additional responsibility of being governor of the Parliamentary depot at Newport Pagnell. Luke was a gentleman of character and energy. The son of Sir Oliver Luke of Woodend, Bedfordshire, Luke was a very short but dapper figure who, despite being a strong Presbyterian, was known for his excellent company, fine clothes and liking of good claret. He had been fighting for the Parliamentary cause from the beginning: first at Edgehill, followed by the siege of Reading, the relief of Gloucester and then the Battle of Newbury. He even had the distinction of having been twice captured at the Battle of Chalgrove Field and twice escaped. While he was at Chalgrove, a regiment of horse he had raised was surprised by Rupert at Chinnor, resulting in 50 of his men dead and 120 taken prisoner. Although he had not been present at the engagement he may well have taken to heart the need for good intelligence as the enemy of surprise. Whatever his motivation, he put considerable effort into recruiting a large number of scouts and establishing an extensive collection network. After a few months Luke was regularly receiving a substantial number of reasonable-quality intelligence reports.

With the King seeking support from Ireland and Parliament from Scotland, both had a new intelligence requirement to find out about the other's outside alliances. Until September the King had unwisely relied on Hamilton for intelligence on Scotland but could have made use of Montrose. Parliament had the more challenging task of finding out what negotiations were going on in Ireland in the confusion of the Catholic rising and with the west coast of England largely in Royalist hands. Moreover, Parliament had no way of knowing what support Charles might receive from his and his wife's continental relatives and so needed to obtain sources in France, Holland and Denmark. In other words it became important for Parliament to develop a foreign intelligence capability.

Foreign intelligence gathering is, by its nature, far more difficult than internal intelligence. Apart from the obvious problems of language and lack of local knowledge, agents have to operate in a hostile environment, quite possibly under the surveillance of the security intelligence organization of the host nation. Although these new intelligence requirements should have come into prominence by the middle of the year, there is little indication that either side made much progress in the matter. Parliament, for its part, would more than rectify this omission in the years ahead. However, in the winter of 1643 both contestants were concerned with the more pressing matter of how to achieve military victory with the Scots and Irish forces that had joined their respective causes.

Chapter 3

For King and Parliament, 1644

Parliament did not have long to wait in 1644 for a return on its Scottish investment. Leven invaded England on 19 January and began advancing south. The same month brought another blow to the Royalists, this time in Cheshire, where Byron and his troops from Ireland were besieging Nantwich. When news reached Parliament of Nantwich's predicament, Thomas Fairfax was ordered to take his force from Lincolnshire to relieve it. When Byron received intelligence that Fairfax was approaching he abandoned the siege and took up a defensive position north of the town. By the time Fairfax arrived on the outskirts of Nantwich he had a combined strength of 2,500 foot and 1,200 horse, therefore outnumbering Byron in the first, but being outnumbered in the latter.

On 24 January, the day before the battle, Colonel George Monck joined Byron's army. Monck had received an audience with the King in Oxford and been persuaded to return to his former troops who were now at Nantwich under Byron. On the same day as Monck's arrival, melting snow caused the River Weaver to burst its banks, washing away the only bridge and making the ferry unusable. This effectively cut Byron's force in two and made the ground of little use to cavalry which was his main advantage. When the battle began it was fought with ferocity and lasted for two exhausting hours. It ended when the regiments in the Royalist centre broke after Fairfax led a final charge which was followed up by the Nantwich garrison rushing out of the town to rout Byron's reserve regiment. With the battle obviously lost, Byron decided to save his cavalry and rode off to the safety of Chester, leaving his infantry to fight on. This they did until completely surrounded and forced to surrender. 1,500 of Byron's men became prisoners of war. This became a double blow to the Royalist cause when the majority elected to change sides and enlist in the Parliamentary army.

It could be said that the defeat at Nantwich was at least partly brought about by Byron having bad luck with the weather. Luck is an important factor in military operations but good commanders attempt to reduce the elements of chance to a minimum. Byron should have been able to acquire local knowledge of the likelihood of the Weaver flooding and its probable effect. Had he done so, he would have moved his whole force to a position where he would have been able to make best use of his advantage in cavalry. The fact that he did not could be regarded as an intelligence failure. Military intelligence today is not confined to the acquisition of information about enemies and potential enemies but about the whole environment as far as it can affect the operation. This is termed basic intelligence or engineer intelligence and covers such matters as ports and harbours, tides, capacity of roads and bridges and the availability of water – in other words, the information required for the logistic support of a force. Byron did indeed have bad luck with the weather but he might have been able to make his own luck by attempting to gain basic intelligence on his area of operations.

With Byron's defeat the King's long-awaited infantry from Ireland had been lost and Parliament had gained a victory. This victory was not confined to military significance, important though it was as a boost to Parliamentary morale and in marking out Thomas Fairfax as a major commander. The greatest victory was in propaganda which was able to portray Parliament defeating the Catholic Irish force that the King had used to invade his Protestant nation. The fact that nearly all the troops in the 'Irish' contingent were either English or Scottish Protestants, who had been recalled by the King from the campaign fighting the Irish Catholics rebels, was lost in the spin.

Among the officers taken prisoner at Nantwich was George Monck. Despite his sympathies for Parliament he was not prepared to abandon his allegiance to the King and join the Parliamentary army. He was therefore sent as a prisoner first to Hull and then to the Tower. There he was to remain till the end of the war, kept in reasonable conditions subsidized by a little money sent by his family. He passed his four years in captivity in the same way as Raleigh and several others had done with time on their hands in the Tower, by writing a book on military affairs, which was not to be finally published until after his death. Clearly authorship was not enough to absorb all his time for he fell in love with Anne, the daughter of a London farrier who was the Tower seamstress, and began an affair which would eventually lead to their marriage. This highly unsuitable match must have greatly distressed his family and friends. Monck was the second son of an impoverished Devon squire so his fortune depended upon him advancing his military career and with luck marrying an heiress. Now both hopes seemed gone. At that time any sensible person would have written him off as a having no prospects. But predicting the future is not always as simple as it seems.

Meanwhile Byron's mauled and a depleted force of cavalry limped its way to Shrewsbury. By the end of February, Shrewsbury had fallen and so lost the main Royalist recruiting centre for Wales. In the next couple of months a few more reinforcements from Ireland managed to dodge the Parliamentary fleet and cross the Irish Sea. They could pay a big price if they were intercepted. On one occasion the navy captured seventy men and two women making the crossing and threw them overboard to drown. It was felt to be sufficient justification that they were thought to be Papists. They may or may not have been. By April the Parliamentary fleet controlled the whole crossing area and reinforcements dried up. Over the next months Charles made desperate attempts to negotiate support from the Catholic Confederates but this came to nothing. A total of about 8,000 foot from Ireland came to support the King during the period October 1642 to April 1644. Had they come as a disciplined and well-equipped group they would have made an impact.

Instead, they arrived in dribs and drabs, neglected, mutinous and in rags. Many went absent on arrival in England and after the defeat at Nantwich only 4,000 of them remained in the King's service. Charles's hopes of reinforcement from Ireland had come to nothing.

In contrast, Parliament's Scottish reinforcements were proving successful and continuing their advance south. Parliament began besieging the Royalist fortified town of Newark-on-Trent. The governor called for reinforcements and Rupert was sent with a force to relieve the town, which he did on 22 March. A week later a bigger engagement took place at the village of Cherton to the east of Winchester. Sir William Waller had captured Alton and was threatening the road to Winchester with an army of 10,000. The Winchester road was being guarded by an army of the same size under the Earl of Forth and Sir Ralph Hopton. Sir Arthur Haselrig commanding the left wing of the Waller's cavalry outmanoeuvred the Royalist horse and began to rout Forth's infantry. Hopton just managed to slow the impetus of Haselrig's attack sufficiently for Forth and his army to retreat to Oxford.

This was the Royalists' first significant defeat and resulted in Waller being able to take possession of Winchester, Andover and Salisbury. It is tempting to speculate that, had Rupert been present, the outcome would have been different and, having defeated Waller, the King would have then been free to advance to the South-East. Instead, the King was now on the defensive, so much so that, having heard that the armies of both Waller and Essex were advancing towards Oxford, he feared he might be trapped in the city. Being concerned for the safety of his heavily pregnant Queen, Charles decided that she should go to the safer location of Exeter to have her ninth baby. On 17 April he accompanied her as far as Abingdon and then said his farewells, never realizing that this would be the last time he would see his beloved wife. Then it was back to Oxford to counter to the looming Parliamentary threat.

On 3 June Charles made a feint attack on Abingdon to put Waller on the defensive, then at night left Oxford with 7,000 men for Evesham. With Essex and Waller still advancing, Charles made for Worcester. Essex and Waller disliked each other both professionally and personally. Essex was a 53-year-old stolid aristocrat with little sense of urgency, whereas the slightly younger Waller was a shrewd professional soldier with the energy of a successful cavalry commander. Waller had gone so far as to complain to Parliament that it had been the negligence of Essex in not providing him with support the previous year that had caused the defeat at Roundway Down. Essex blamed Waller for remaining with his army at Windsor instead of coming to his assistance immediately after the first Battle of Newbury, when their combined forces would have easily outnumbered the King's. The enmity between the two men was further fanned by the rivalry that was developing between their different groups of supporters in Parliament.

Essex had the golden opportunity to unite with Waller's army, thus making a combined force of 16,000 which should have been able to easily defeat the King's 7,000 army, particularly as it was without Rupert and his cavalry. Instead, Essex, disregarding his orders from the Committee of Both Kingdoms, decided to take his 10,000-strong army to the South-East. His objective was twofold: to capture the Queen and to relieve Lyme, which was under siege by Prince Maurice. The King received the important intelligence about Essex's position from Maurice's scouts and so returned to Oxford to collect a further 10,000 troops in preparation for an attack on Waller.

Both armies came together in the Banbury area and advanced for a day side by side, separated by the River Cherwell. On 29 June, Forth sent a small force to seize Cropredy Bridge to the north of Banbury. Waller then succeeded in taking the area of the bridge with his full force of about 6,000 before the Royalist main body arrived. Following successful cavalry charges on Waller's front and rear, the Roundhead horse was defeated and the artillery captured. Charles could have gone on to destroy Waller's whole army but, hating unnecessary bloodshed, decided to offer terms. When Waller refused all terms, the King still pulled back. The Royalist victory saved Oxford but the royal clemency lost the opportunity of destroying the Western Association.

While trying to save his Oxford base, the King was well aware that the situation was getting dangerous for him in the North. Leven's Scottish Army had linked up with Sir Thomas Fairfax's horse, together with that of his father Ferdinando and the remains of the Northern Association. Newcastle and his Northern Army had been pushed back to York and on 22 April the combined Parliamentary force began besieging the city. On 16 May, Rupert left Shrewsbury with orders to relieve York. Picking up Byron and his few troops on the way in Chester and later those of the Earl of Derby, he advanced through Lancashire, taking Stockport, Bolton and Liverpool. On 13 June, Rupert received a letter from the His Majesty saying that he should relieve York as soon as possible and then return with all haste to join Charles at Worcester. The letter was overtaken by events because ten days later the victory at Cropredy Bridge meant that Oxford would be saved and there was no longer urgency for Rupert's return. Obeying orders, Rupert sped off to York where the situation had further deteriorated as Manchester with his Eastern Association Army had now joined the other besieging armies to make a joint force of some 27,000 men.

Parliamentary intelligence gained warning of Rupert's approach so the decision was made to block his advance by concentrating the armies at Long Marston. Rupert's scouts reported back this redeployment. Rupert therefore swung his 14,000-strong army north from Knaresborough and at Poppleton surprised a party of Manchester's dragoons guarding a bridge of boats across the Ouse. He took his army over the bridge and so achieved the relief of York having completely bypassed the main Parliamentary armies. This manoeuvre was typical of Rupert's brilliant generalship and also of his effective use of reconnaissance to provide vital intelligence. Conversely, for the Parliamentary armies this was a setback brought about by the failure to deploy reconnaissance to provide surveillance of all possible approaches. This failure can probably be attributed to a lack of coordination between the three armies.

Rupert, as always taking a lead in intelligence, had ordered that a captured Eastern Association trooper be brought to him for questioning. He asked just one key question, 'Is Cromwell there?' In fact the recently promoted Lieutenant General Cromwell was there with his cavalry. The 45-year-old Cromwell had not won any major battles but had a whole series of successes behind him. These were a variety of medium-sized engagements at Grantham, Burleigh House, Gainsborough and Winceby, which during the previous year had built him a reputation for success. On hearing that Cromwell was present, Rupert knew that he would be facing a formidable opponent, whom he was afterwards to give the nickname 'Old Ironsides'. More than that, he knew Cromwell's inclination for the offensive and realized that this would fit well into the strategy he was formulating of provoking Cromwell and his cavalry to attack at a disadvantage across a ditch covered by groups of musketeers. For success the whole strategy would depend, as always with Rupert, on speed – in this case, the speed of having all available Royalist Forces deployed for battle before the three opposing armies had got their act together.

Rupert had arrived outside York on 1 July and assuming he was in overall command sent a message to Newcastle to march out against the Parliamentary army at 4 am the next morning. Rupert wanted to attack without delay while he still had an element of surprise, then return to aid the King as soon as possible. Newcastle, well aware that his troops were exhausted from the siege, was infuriated to be given such apparently unreasonable and peremptory orders. Newcastle, a Cavalier grandee who had recently been created a Marquis, was the King's vice regent of the North. As a man of refinement and delicacy, he was deeply offended by this coarse treatment from so young a man, albeit a prince. Despite being deeply affronted, Newcastle joined Rupert at his headquarters on Marston Moor but left his second-in-command, Lord Eythin, to bring the main body of troops out from York. Eythin had served with Rupert in Germany and had been publicly blamed by Rupert for failing to provide him with support at Vlotho and thus causing his capture. Because of difficulties in getting the troops to obey orders and Eythin's dislike of Rupert, it was not till 4 pm that Eythin arrived and then with only 4,000 of the 5,000-strong force. Eythin then announced that he was not prepared to go immediately into battle as Rupert wanted. Rupert reluctantly agreed that they would postpone the battle till the next morning and the senior Royalist officers then went off to their coaches for supper.

With the Royalist army almost stood down, Leven and the Parliamentary Council of War saw an opportunity. At about 7 pm, amid torrential rain, the Parliamentary left wing began to advance with Cromwell's Eastern Association Cavalry at the head, followed by Leslie's Scottish dragoons and lancers. Then Cromwell broke into a tight, well-ordered charge down the hill towards Byron's cavalry on the Royalist right. Byron's cavalry rushed out to meet Comwell's charge and in doing so masked their supporting musketeers. Their front two lines were routed and began to flee. Rupert rushed into battle and attempted to rally Byron's men but was unhorsed in a melee and could only save his life by hiding in a bean field till he could find another mount. George Goring on the Royalist left rode through Sir Thomas Fairfax's opposing cavalry and then began plundering the baggage-train rather than returning to the main engagement. Meanwhile the infantry in the centre of both armies had begun ferocious fighting. Newcastle's foot, named the 'Whitecoats' because of their undyed woollen jackets, were more than holding their own against the advance of the Lords Manchester, Leven and Fairfax. Further to the Parliamentary right Goring's dragoons were causing heavy casualties, shooting from the position they had taken up in a long ditch in the valley between the armies. The situation became so utterly confused that Leven and Ferdinando Lord Fairfax, both thinking the battle lost, left the field. Cromwell hearing that the right wing was in serious danger, crossed to the opposite wing with his own cavalry and that of David Leslie. There they joined Sir Thomas Fairfax and attacked Goring from the rear. Having dealt with Goring, Cromwell and Fairfax's cavalry returned to attack Newcastle's infantry. The battle continued by moonlight until the cavalry of Cromwell and Sir Thomas Fairfax had demolished the Royalist army and the last few blood-spattered Whitecoats remaining standing were hacked down. The Parliamentary victory was overwhelming.

The largest battle of the Civil War was over. A few hours had transformed the Royalists' situation from the major success of the relief of York to a battle lost with 4,000 killed and 1,500 taken prisoner. The two great Royalist grandees of the North decided that the King's cause was hopeless. Derby departed for his estates in the Isle of Man and Newcastle left for Hamburg accompanied by Eythin. The northern Royalists were left leaderless, demoralized and deprived of the financial resources that had previously funded their campaign. Rupert left a garrison of 3,000 men behind to defend York but it surrendered on 16 July. By autumn virtually the whole of the North was lost to the King. Rupert managed to evade the Parliamentary forces and lead 6,000 troops south to rejoin the King but his reputation was severely dented. To the Parliamentarians he was no longer a figure of almost supernaturally invincibility and could now even be regarded as a figure of fun. The Parliamentary pamphleteers had immense pleasure describing how Rupert's banner had been captured, his dog Boy killed and provided illustrations of Rupert cowering in a bean field. There was endless other sport, for example, one of Rupert's other pet dogs had been captured and had its ears cut off 'to turn it into a roundhead'. Rupert's self-confidence had been severely hit and things would never be quite the same again.

There had been a variety of reasons for the Royalist defeat, not least that they were outnumbered by about 8,000, largely due to the presence of the Scottish army. The battle could have been avoided if Rupert had not felt that he should return to the King with such speed. Alternatively, there might have been a different outcome if the Royalist army had attacked immediately as Rupert wanted while they had an element of surprise. Rupert's poor handling of Newcastle and the feud with Eythin conspired to make this impossible. Had Goring brought his cavalry back to the main battle after his successful attack on the Parliamentary left wing he might have caused the rout that Leven and Lord Fairfax believed was occurring. Lastly, if Rupert had not been unhorsed, his leadership of the reserve might have been able to turn the battle. As well as being lost by the Royalists, Marston Moor was won by the emerging leaders of the Parliamentary army. It was Cromwell's decisive deployment of the Eastern Association horse to the opposite flank, and their disciplined fighting in conjunction with the horse of Sir Thomas Fairfax and David Leslie, which secured the victory for Parliament. The question arises over whether better intelligence could have altered the outcome of this important battle. The answer is no. If the Royalists had known that the Parliamentary army was going to attack in the early evening they would not have been caught by surprise and begun the battle at a disadvantage. However, the Parliamentary decision to attack was probably made at the last minute and it would have been virtually impossible for that information to be collected and communicated to the Royalists in time to be of use.

Unaware of the northern disaster, His Majesty was in good spirits in the South, greatly cheered by his defeat of Waller. True, Essex had relieved Lyme but he had not captured the Queen who reached the safety of Exeter where, despite illness, she had a successful birth. The baby, Henrietta Anne, was born on 16 June and soon after the Queen hastened to Falmouth and then for the safety of France and the protection of her sister-in-law, the Queen Regent Anne of Austria, after whom the baby was named. Essex had continued to disregard further orders from the Committee of Both Kingdoms to return to London and advanced deeper into Cornwall. Charles and his army went in pursuit.

Essex and his 10,000-strong army had arranged to go to Lostwithiel and be resupplied by the Earl of Warwick's fleet from its port of Fowey but a contrary wind prevented the ships landing. Sir Richard Grenville's Royalist army of 2,400 blocked Essex's further advance and the King's force of 14,000 blocked his return. Realizing he was cornered and outnumbered, Essex ordered his horse to break out from Lostwithiel. This they did on 2 September and eventually managed to reach the safety of Parliament-held Plymouth. Essex then left the infantry and artillery with Skippon while he escaped in a fishing boat to one of Warwick's ships and sailed off for the Hampshire coast. The troops were dismayed at the flight of their Lord General, cold, wet and short of supplies, and Skippon decided that, with morale low and no cavalry to support him, his only option was to surrender.

This was a significant victory for the King but could have been greater if it had included the destruction or surrender of Essex's horse. Virtually every military success achieved through surprise is achieved as a result of intelligence failure by the opposition. The Royalist intelligence could not have been expected to know the intention and timing of the breakout but there should have been sufficient reconnaissance deployed to ensure that there was enough warning for the Royalist cavalry to respond and, at the very least, pursue. For all that, Lostwithiel was a Royalist victory. Skippon handed over all his artillery and nearly 20,000 muskets but the King in his clemency agreed that the Parliamentary troops could march away if they agreed never to support Parliament again.

The soldiers who had surrendered were indeed fortunate not to have been taken prisoner. When the war began neither side was quite sure how to treat prisoners, other than badly. In November 1642, at Brentford, Lord Justice Heath tried and convicted for treason the captured Parliamentarians Colonel Viver and Captains Catesby and Lilburne. The latter was a firebrand who had long written libellous tracts against the King and in April 1638 had been whipped from Fleet Street to Westminster Hall for his pains. Now he not only protested strongly against the sentence but was equally incensed because he had been referred to in the incitement as a 'yeoman' and not 'gent' and offered to fight any two members of the court in trial by combat to prove his point. Meanwhile his wife Elizabeth informed Parliament of the sentence and as a result Parliament threatened to treat all captured Royalists as treasonous. Heath responded by quickly dropping the charges. Although after this it became normal practice to save the lives of prisoners, there were to be many future occasions in which those who had surrendered were either killed on capture or subsequently hanged or shot.

At best prisoners could expect harsh treatment. They would be invariably robbed of their possessions, often including their shoes and clothes, and subjected to jeers and rough handling. When Cirencester fell to the Royalists in February 1643 the 1,100 Parliamentary prisoners were first threatened with hanging then confined to Cirencester church for two days without food or water, after which they had to walk, bound and mostly shoeless through the snow to Oxford. On arrival at Oxford they were given the opportunity to join the King's army. All but sixteen agreed, knowing what to expect in captivity. The gaol in Oxford Castle was under the notorious Provost Marshall Smith and prisoners were kept crammed together, in deep excrement and on starvation rations. Royalist prisoners could expect no better and for those who found themselves on the prison hulks in the Thames the conditions were even worse than Oxford.

On the other hand, gentlemen could expect far better treatment, especially if they had sworn 'to be a true prisoner', in other words not to escape or fight again. England had a small population of only about five million and the landed classes would generally know each other in the same area and often be related or connected by marriage. It is interesting to note that Oliver Cromwell, a very ordinary squire from the Fens, could number eight fellow Members of Parliament as his relations. The common ties of land ownership were usually stronger than the bitterness of opposing sides and a person of quality had a reasonable chance of being exchanged with someone of similar status. An example of this was George Goring, the General of Horse of the Earl of Newcastle, who was captured by Sir Thomas Fairfax at Wakefield and sent without interrogation to the Tower. There he remained for nine months before being exchanged in April 1644 in time to join Rupert for Marston Moor. George Monck was not of sufficient rank or influence to be as fortunate and so remained stuck in the Tower until the end of hostilities.

Throughout the Civil War many hundreds of prisoners were taken on both sides but little attempt was made to obtain intelligence from them through interrogation. The traditional aid to interrogation was the rack but that was only used very occasionally at Oxford Castle and then only for amusement rather than to extract information. Unlike on the Continent, torture was not recognized by English Common Law. It was however a royal prerogative but had only been used once by Charles and that was long before the war and, as it happens, against an innocent man. The principal reason why interrogation was not used was that it would have been considered of no value. Intelligence is a perishable commodity and the tactical information known to an average prisoner after a battle would be completely out of date. It is true that captured officers might well have valuable strategic information but it would be unthinkable to put a gentleman through rigorous questioning. There were a few occasions when it was clear that a prisoner might have current information and then interrogation was used. Once such occasion was when Essex began besieging Reading soon after the King had withdrawn following Turnham Green. The Royalist garrison only had forty barrels of gunpowder left and decided to send Ensign Rupert Flower to the royal arms depot at Henley on Thames with a request for more. Flower managed to get through the Parliamentary besiegers, swim the Thames and pass through more Roundhead lines to reach Henley. Agreement was given to send more barrels by boat to Reading under cover of darkness. Flower then began his return journey with this news but was seen swimming back and captured. After torture, Flower revealed the plan and the barge was captured. Essex later received more reinforcements and as Reading remained so low on powder it eventually surrendered.

Although the North of England was virtually lost to the King there was at least some good news from his northern kingdom. In February Charles had made Montrose, Captain-General of Scotland. At the time this was a hollow appointment as there were no Royalist forces in Scotland and merely the promise that Antrim would raise Macdonnells to be sent across to the Western Highlands. Montrose travelled to the North of England and managed to recruit 1,300 followers. He then advanced into Scotland but as there was no sign of Antrim's troops, and with Argyll bearing down upon on his small force, Montrose withdrew back to Carlisle. It was no consolation to find that, despite the complete failure of the operation, the King had decided to make him a Marquis. Montrose realized that his troops would soon be located and crushed if they re-entered Scotland so dispatched them to support Rupert in the relief of York. He had retained just a handful of followers, foremost among which was his cousin and right-hand man, Patrick Graham of Inchbrackie, known as 'Black Pate' because his face was blackened from a powder explosion. After some time, word reached Carlisle that 1,600 Macdonnells were arriving from Ireland to support the King under the leadership of the physically huge and ferocious Scots warrior, Alasdair MacColla Macdonald. Montrose then decided to slip into Scotland with just Black Pate and one other, disguised as their groom. From positions of hiding this small team then fanned out to find news of Alasdair MacColla and eventually discovered that he and his Macdonalds were in Atholl.

Montrose also learnt that two clans of Atholl, the Robertsons and the Stuarts, had brought together 800 men to oppose the Macdonnells. On the morning of 28

August at Blair Atholl, the Robertsons and Stuarts began forming up for battle against Alasdair MacColla's men. The opposing armies then noticed two figures in the distance approaching them across the heather. The figures gradually came closer and then actually walked between the opposing ranks just before the battle was to commence. Suddenly it was realized that the leading figure was Montrose with a studded target on his arm, claymore at his side and in full Highland dress, followed by his kinsman Black Pate. As soon as Montrose was recognized, both sides gave great shouts of welcome. Their battle was forgotten and, after some conferring, Montrose was acclaimed their joint leader and all agreed to fight under the royal banner that he had brought concealed in the lining of his saddle. Highland history has some great moments of drama but the manner of Montrose's assumption of command at Blair Atholl takes the biscuit.

Montrose was gifted by any standards; an urbane aristocrat who was a scholar, poet, sportsman and both good-looking and good company. All this might have been forgotten if it had not been for that day at Blair Atholl which was to be the start of an adventure that would turn him into one of Scotland's greatest legends. The next year would prove Montrose to be an outstanding leader, tactician and exponent of guerrilla warfare. The 28 August 1644 demonstrated his ability, even when in hiding, to obtain the vital intelligence required and act on it with perfect timing. Sadly this was not always to be the case in his dramatic career but for now fortune was on his side.

Less than twenty-four hours after walking between the two forces with just one companion, Montrose was marching south to Perth at the head of 2,000 men. On 1 September his poorly armed force with just three horses defeated 6,000 Covenanter levies at Tippermure after delivering a ferocious Highland charge. Perth opened its gates to them and, having picked up arms, ammunition and supplies, Montrose moved on towards Aberdeen. As no Royalists could be spared to be left behind to garrison Perth it was soon occupied by Argyll who then took his army hard on Montrose's heels. Having picked up some sixty horsemen en route, the Royalists arrived outside Aberdeen to find the Covenanter forces drawn up for battle. After a long engagement, the Covenanters were routed, with the loss of 1,000 men killed to Montrose's loss of 20.

Leaving a sacked Aberdeen behind him, Montrose moved north with Argyll still in pursuit and burning as much Gordon land as possible to dissuade the powerful clan from supporting the Royalists. Argyll need not have bothered because the Marquis of Huntley, chief of the Gordons, was refusing all Montrose's requests for support and without his approval no Royalist Gordon laird would come out for the King. Montrose was not strong enough to fight Argyll so decided to lead him on a merry dance up the Spey, and through the Grampians and back to Atholl, with his lightly armed force and little baggage always managing to keep just ahead of Argyll's traditional and lumbering army.

A month later Argyll eventually caught up with the Royalists at Fyvie Castle and almost took them by surprise but Montrose beat off initial attacks then slipped away in the night. Argyll had to resume his pursuit. Then Montrose had a setback. Colonel Sibbald who had been with him from the beginning decided to defect to Argyll and took with him Montrose's latest plans for evading his enemy. Montrose immediately took counter-action by changing his plans and instead of moving as intended, stayed in position. Then leaving campfires burning, he silently withdrew at night with a light cavalry force screening his rear and once again evaded Argyll. At this point Argyll decided that enough was enough and that it was time to disperse his army to winter quarters and deal with Montrose when better weather returned. These early victories of Montrose were little more than successful raids but they were entirely unexpected and gave the King ground for hope that the Highlands might rise and force Leven to disengage his army from his siege of Newcastle in order to deal with the opposition at his rear.

October found the King in good spirits bolstered as ever by Digby's infectious optimism. On the other hand, there was general dejection among the Parliamentary leadership. There was a feeling that, despite Parliament's strong position, the way things were going it was never going to be possible to completely defeat the King. A growing number now believed that the only way forward was to come to terms with the King and avoid further bloodshed. Waller had been one of the first to express doubts about continuing the conflict by saying: 'Break the (Royalist) army never so often, his person will raise another.' Now Manchester found himself saying 'If we beat the King ninety and nine times, yet he is King, and so will his posterity be after him. But if the King beat us but once we shall all be hanged and our posterity made slaves.' Essex had already been accused of not wishing to confront the King in battle. This was partially as a result of Essex's naturally lethargy and also because he had no enthusiasm for bearing arms against his sovereign. In contrast, Cromwell was formulating a different solution to the military impasse with the King. Cromwell had seen how disciplined motivated troops under effective commanders could achieve a great victory like Marston Moor. He was beginning to form the view that, if Parliament could create a professional army under the right leadership, a final convincing victory over the Royalists could be won and the King forced to make terms.

In mid-October, the King had entered Salisbury and Waller's forces had withdrawn to Andover. Charles then moved to the north of Newbury while awaiting the return of Rupert. Meanwhile the Parliamentary army had regrouped. Colonel Sir John Hurry, the Scots officer who had defected to Rupert the previous year, now decided to defect back to Parliament. He rode to London and provided intelligence to the Earl of Manchester on the state of Charles's army. The vital information was that the King was separated from Rupert and had further weakened his force by having sent three regiments to relieve Banbury. Manchester responded by advancing with a combined force of 17,000 men to engage the King's army of less than half that number.

'Walk-in' intelligence had now made it possible to achieve a resounding, war-winning victory over the King. Personal differences were to prevent this occurring.

Manchester, like Essex, was now having second thoughts about the wisdom of trying to destroy the royal army and on top of that had fallen out with both Cromwell and Waller. With the Parliamentary military leadership in this disarray, their army took up position north of Newbury to block the King's return to Oxford and prevent any link up with Rupert. On 28 October Parliamentary attacks were beaten back and under cover of darkness Charles withdraw to Oxford and then to Bath where Rupert joined him. This Second Battle of Newbury had been another draw. The opportunity to destroy the King's much smaller force had been lost and there had not even been an attempt to pursue the Royalist army as it withdrew. Although the combined force of the King and Rupert was still considerably smaller than the Parliamentary army, Manchester dismissed Sir Arthur Haselrig's advice to attack them at Bath with the words: 'Thou art a bloody fellow. God send us peace, for God doth never prosper us in our victories to make them clear victories.' Given such an attitude there was little chance of a Parliamentary victory. With sickness rife, widespread desertion and the possibility of mutiny in Windsor, the decision was made for the Parliamentary armies to move to winter quarters. Any hope of a successful military outcome would now rest with the still relatively unknown Lieutenant General Cromwell.

Although the main English armies of both sides were setting up quarters for the winter, some military activity was still continuing. Leven and his Scots captured Newcastle on 22 November and thus secured the coal centre so important to London.

A couple of weeks later, back in Scotland, Montrose was setting out on what was to be his heroic march though the icy Grampians in the depth of winter to surprise the Campbells at their ancestral home of Inveraray. Out of the blue, a howling ragtag army of Royalist clansmen were pouring down Glen Shire to the banks of Loch Fyne and then on into Inveraray. The Campbells took to the hills and the town was soon put to the torch, then it was on again to burn and pillage the villages in the surrounding area. There could be no delay because the great Clan Campbell would soon take up arms. Montrose and his force therefore headed north to the safer Appin Stewart country, driving their captured cattle before them.

Meanwhile the Royalists, commanded by Sir William Vasasour, continued to besiege Gloucester, which remained defiant under Edward Massey. Vasasour decided to try subversion. On 19 November he wrote the following to one of the Parliamentary officers, a Captain Robert Backhouse: 'You may not only have your pardon, but raise youself a greater fortune, than the condition of those you serve are able to afford you. This you may gaine by the delivery, you may guesse my meaning of what place, which is not hard for you to do.' The person delivering the letter told Backhouse that he would receive £5,000 for carrying out the request of the letter. Although this was an inept approach, it is interesting to note that Vasasour had attempted to use veiled speech in his letter and tried to disguise the bribe by having it passed as a separate verbal communication. It transpired that Vasasour had chosen a poor target as Backhouse immediately informed Massey of the message. Massey instructed Backhouse to play along with the plot as a double agent. Covert correspondence continued between Backhouse and Vasascour for most of the winter, no doubt much to the mirth of Massey.

Winter also passed with Parliament again attempting negotiations with the King, which took place at Uxbridge in January 1645. As so many times before, nothing was to come of them. The real events of the winter were the proposals being made to Parliament. Cromwell, Sir Harry Vane and the war group in the Commons began formulating two objectives. The first was to create a single professional Parliamentary army under one commander that was properly equipped, trained and paid. As Cromwell said to the House: 'Until the whole army were remodelled and governed under stricter discipline they must not expect any notable success in anything they were about.' The second objective was to give this new army the leadership it required for victory. In Cromwell's terms this meant that it should be led by those of known godliness with proved military ability, regardless of their social background. Cromwell had already been openly sniping at Manchester for his lack of resolution. He took this further and formally complained to the House of Commons of Manchester's 'backwardness', 'aversion to engagements' and 'neglecting of opportunities'. Now he and others came up with a proposal to rid the army of those military leaders who had achieved their positions through birth rather than merit and who no longer appeared to have stomach for the war. On 9 November Cromwell introduced a proposal to the Commons called the Self-Denying Ordinance, in which no member of either House should hold command in the army. The motion was vigorously debated for ten days. It was generally supported by Vane's war party, and the Independents, and opposed by Holles's peace party, the Presbyterians and those with military appointments. On 19 December the Commons finally passed it and just before Christmas they sent it to the House of Lords, where it could expect a very rough ride when it was to be debated in the New Year.

The year closed with clear divisions in Parliament. Presbyterians were ranged against Independents, those for peace against those for war and reformists against those for maintaining the status quo – especially their own status. All this gave comfort to His Majesty who felt able to treat the Parliamentary peace negotiators with regal disdain. Whether the King's confidence was justified would depend upon the ability of Parliament to put its house in order.

The winter of 1644 is a good time to review the progress that was being made by the scoutmasters who had by then been in existence for about two years. The Scoutmaster General we know most about is Sir Samuel Luke, through the journal he has left us. He was given an official establishment of twenty scouts. These scouts were paid 5 shillings a day from which they had also to feed their horses but this compared very favourably to a cavalry trooper who received 2 shillings per day. In addition the scouts were also paid travelling expenses. In fact Luke appears to have had about ninety men working for him but many of these were messengers carrying communications between Essex, the Lord General, and his subordinate commanders. Aided by the rates of pay, Luke was successful in rapidly recruiting a large number of scouts and lost no time in putting them to work. It was not unusual for him to receive the reports of several scouts on any one day, with an average of about ten reports a week. He tasked them himself and the coverage stretched from Cambridge to Coventry to Bristol to Winchester. His principal area of intelligence interest was the Royalist headquarters of Oxford and second to that was the surrounding area it dominated, which extended as far as Reading.

Such was the level of Luke's activity that he soon got a name for himself. An extract from the main Parliamentary broadsheet *Mercurius Britanicus* describes him as follows: 'This nobel commander watches the enemy so continuously that they eat, sleep, drink not, wisper not, but he can give us an account of their darkest proceedings.' Then as now it was not wise to believe everything printed in newspapers. *Mercurius Britanicus* and the Royalist equivalent *Mercurius Aulicus* (edited by John Birkenhead, a notoriously devious fellow of All Souls) were as much instruments of propaganda as purveyors of factual information. Luke and his scouts worked hard but appear to have had very limited results. The scouts were good at bringing back information on what they saw and the following is a typical good-quality report:

> Wednesday 17 January (1644). Christopher Granger returned yesterday from Toster, and saith that there (are) about 700 foote and 3000 horse in the towne, and 8 peeces of ordnance, and hee heares there are about 1000 more horse quartered without the towne in and about Paules Perry under the command of Sir Lewis Dives. That they are all in great want of all manner of provision, and saith that 100 of them runne away the last weeke, but the commanders and officers fetcht them back againe.

This is a good report because it describes what we assume Granger has seen for himself and differentiates the information he had heard from others.

Despite the large number of intelligence reports of potential tactical value none of them appear to been acted upon. Clearly intelligence is only of value if it is going to be used for operations or countermeasures. The combat intelligence of Luke's scouts was not put to use. The prime reason for this is that Essex who received the intelligence was himself very inactive. He did of course manoeuvre his army on occasions, such as to besiege Reading and relieve Gloucester, but unlike Rupert he would not react to tactical opportunities.

As well as reporting troop dispositions, Luke's scouts were also effective at describing enemy defences, often in detail: 'Against Wadham college there is a mound cast up where there are two pieces of ordinance but the works were not finished', or 'On the south side of Abingdon there is a great drawbridge where there are 5 pieces of ordnance planted and 2 more in the market place.' The accumulation of this type of information could have been of considerable value. Although some towns such as Reading were besieged by Essex, no attempt was made to take them by storm so the information so carefully collected was never used. Through no fault of theirs, the successful efforts of Luke's men to produce intelligence ended as a pile of unused reports.

Although good at reporting what they saw, Luke's scouts were much less effective in obtaining accurate information on Royalist military intentions. It was not for want of trying and the scouts were constantly exposing themselves to arrest by sometimes spending several days in hostile territory. A typical report illustrating this is:

> 13 February 1643. Samuell Brayne returned from Oxford and informed that hee quartered for two nights past at the White Swann at Oxford and that hee saw Prince Rupert gathering his body of horses and dragoons together intending to march on Henley, and from Henley to Maydenhead with and intent to take those towns, and that my Lord of Dorsett intends to Manchester to take that.

The scouts' reports on intentions all seem to have been drawn from inn gossip, general rumour and hearsay. Some of the reports were complete rubbish, such as in one in February 1645 that '12,000 Highlanders and Irish are come to England very shortly, to help his Majesty against the Roundheads.' Time and again there are records of incorrect scout reports stating, for example, that Rupert was in Bristol when he was in Birmingham or Gloucester when he was in Lichfield. A typical example of a report on enemy intentions is from William Tuman on 3 March 1643 that 'Prince Robert's forces marcht out yesterday being Thursday towards Gloucester.' In fact Rupert had gone to Bristol in preparation for the Yeoman Plot to open the city gates. To make matters worse there was confirmation of this incorrect information on 7 March from Samuell Braine and then further confirmation by the scouts Robert Cox and Thomas Hitchman the day after. No doubt all these scouts were faithfully reporting the rumours that they heard but they were rumours rather than information from well-placed sources. Only the senior Royalist officers were aware of the military intentions and even they would have found it hard to keep up with the rapid changes caused by the King's indecision and Rupert's use of initiative and speed of movement. It is of course notoriously difficult to obtain accurate information on enemy intentions at any time. Luke's scouts did not have any sources with access to Royalist military planning and so they could not be expected to obtain such information.

Contrary to modern belief, in the Civil War it was very difficult to tell one side from the other. Most people dressed much the same and had the same hair length. Even in the extremes of appearance, dandies in lace and bows with large plumes in their hats could turn out to be Parliamentary supporters and a Royalist like Sir Marmaduke Langdale was far more austere in looks than the great majority of the Roundheads. Both sides took it for granted that they would be infiltrated by scouts and spies and were therefore reasonably security-conscious. This was particularly so in Oxford where the university supported the King but many of the townsfolk favoured Parliament. Some of Luke's scouts might have been thought to have Parliamentary connections but as so of many of citizens did, they were not immediately obvious as spies. That is not to say that their work was without danger. Spies if captured were condemned to death. Rupert had set the precedent when in December 1642 he hanged a spy 'upon the great elm near the Bell at Henley'. Later that month the Parliamentary governor of Reading hanged a Mr Boys of London as a spy and from then on hanging was the fate of anyone found collecting intelligence for the enemy.

Luke's scouts were fortunate because only one of their number, Francis Coles, was hanged. There were many occasions when Luke's men were arrested but they all appear to have used their ingenuity to regain their freedom. Richard Cross and Robert Sherwin managed to run away just after they had been arrested for questioning and William Richards succeeded in escaping from Banbury gaol. Others like Henry Hopkins, Henry Connington and Thomas Hitchman, although held and examined for several days, were able to talk their way out of their different situations. A typical example was William Harries who, in January 1644, was 'apprehended and examined overnight then released upon the entreaty of Mr Thomas Ambrose, son of his old master'. Many of the scouts probably came to attention as outsiders frequenting Royalist areas without clear reason but it was hard to prove guilt. This was especially so as their reports were all verbal and they do not appear to have made incriminating notes, indeed many were probably illiterate.

The scouts were largely just eyes and ears in enemy locations. Very occasionally they made use of what might be termed a casual contact. John Lane used Joell Steevens, a Reading grocer and Richard Clunne used Mr Spicer, a cornet in the King's army, but the information received was still gossip. There is an intriguing possibility that Luke was receiving some information from at least one well-placed source. The records for the Committee of Accounts show Luke receiving 20 shillings per day to pay 'a gentleman and servants residing at court' (i.e. the King's court at Oxford). As has been mentioned, Prince Rupert's secretary was in the pay of Parliament back in 1642 but there was a separate allegation that someone in the office of Sir Edward Walker, the Secretary for War, was also a Parliamentary agent. If this allegation is correct then Parliamentary intelligencers had done extremely well to obtain a source of such calibre. Assuming this was the case, we have no way of knowing whether the operation was directed by Luke or whether any of the scouts were involved as the handlers or used for covert communication. Whatever the case, Luke appears to have had some sources at court. It could be that these sources had access to provide some of the vital information on Royalist intentions that the scouts were not in a position to obtain.

Unfortunately, there are few records of the work of Royalist scouts. It may be assumed that they operated in basically the same way as Luke's but were more mobile. Luke was static at Newport Pagnell. Rupert was either at his lodgings at St John's College, the King's chambers at Christchurch or, most often of all, deployed in the field. His Scoutmaster General, Sir William Neal, would usually be with him. The Royalist scouts deployed with Rupert or other general's armies and operated very much in the reconnaissance role, penetrating deep into enemy territory. Ironically, the main information we have about Rupert's scouts comes from the reports of scouts of Luke and all refer to them with admiration. Typical reports are: 'That the King's scouts were as far as St Neats and Huntingdon, and all about Bedfordshire ... and upon recasins give intelligence to Oxford of the business and affairs of the county.' And 'He (Rupert) sends spies daily into our army which give him full intelligence of whatsoever happens here.' Allowance must be made for the awe with which Rupert and all associated with him were held. Nevertheless, the number of references to Rupert's scouts shows that at the very least they were extremely active. Given Rupert's professionalism and emphasis on intelligence it can be assumed that his scouts were indeed put to good use. One big difference between the scouts of Neal and those of Luke was that their intelligence was acted upon. This also seems to have been the case with other Royalist scouts. Henry Perryman, one of Luke's scouts, reported that 'on Wednesday last the Kings scouts came into Oxford and brought intelligence that Sir William Waller was advanced towards Worcester, and it was thereupon ordered that Prince Maurice should go and meet him'. Most of the Royalist successes of the first two years of the Civil War were down to Rupert's leadership, energy and tactical skill but the success of his operational decisions must have at least in part arisen from the good intelligence collected by Neal's scouts. Although there are few records of the activities of any scouts other than Luke's, it is fair to assume that by the end of 1644 both Royalist and Parliamentarian main forces had well-established contingents of scouts.

Royalist political intelligence was of course under the two Secretaries of State, Nicholas and Digby, with the former taking the lead. This activity had become of little consequence compared with the need for military intelligence to win the war. They received information from Royalist diplomats abroad and the King's supporters in Scotland and Ireland. This was almost entirely the management of official correspondence rather than covertly collected intelligence and very seldom included the running of any agents. One of the few exceptions was John Barwick, the son of a Westmorland husbandman, whose academic ability had enabled him to become a Cambridge don. Being a staunch Anglican he had shown his loyalty at the start of the Civil War by managing to smuggle some of the Cambridge college silver to the King in Nottingham. Charles was so impressed by his resourcefulness that he asked him to go to London to gather intelligence. Barwick established himself as chaplain to the family of the Bishop of Durham and so was able to operate from the bishop's large city mansion in the Strand. He gradually built up a network of agents, informants and sympathizers, the most prominent being an MP called Sir Roger Pope and a well-connected gentleman called Francis Cresset. Through them and others he was able to provide a reasonably good picture of public feeling in the capital and the activities of the Parliamentary leaders throughout the Civil War. Barwick reported this intelligence in cipher and had it covertly carried back to the Secretaries in Oxford using a network of 'adventurous women' employed by a bookseller called Richard Royston.

The man nominally responsible for Royalist strategic military intelligence was Sir Edward Walker, the Secretary for War. Sir Edward was also Garter King of Arms and his knowledge of heraldry and military ceremonial for state occasions was second to none. Unhappily, his expertise did not extend far into military matters and still less into the world of intelligence. He did a perfectly good job as Secretary to the Council of War and the handling of military correspondence to and from the King. Indeed this was his principal function and he appears to have had neither the time nor inclination to make any serious attempt to manage military intelligence. So it can be said that, apart from John Barwick, the only Royalist source of intelligence, other than official correspondence, was the largely tactical military intelligence provided by scoutmasters. It seems that they, like Luke, had expanded their remit from directing military reconnaissance to the running of casual contacts and the occasional agent. The professionalism in intelligence that was gradually developing on both sides came about because of the scoutmasters. The intelligence produced had so far made little impact on the outcome of the war but the expertise gained would eventually permeate beyond military intelligence and provide the basis on which a formidable government intelligence system would be built. However, in the winter of 1644 it was not any intelligence success but events taking place at Parliament in London which were to change the whole face of the war, including the scouting structure so carefully developed by Luke.

Chapter 4

New Model Army, 1645–1646

The Lords were completely opposed to the Self-Denying Ordinance. The generals such as Lords Essex, Fairfax and Manchester could see it for what it was: a ploy to remove them from command. Virtually all peers regarded it as monstrous to ban them from holding any military command, a role traditionally held by them since feudal times. The Lords threw out the ordinance but the Commons had no intention of being thwarted. On 11 January the Commons decided to go ahead with establishing a single army of 6,000 horse, 1,000 dragoons and 14,400 foot. They also agreed to bleed the existing armies of Essex, Manchester and Waller out of existence by diverting all funding from them to the new army.

A Lord General was appointed to command this reconstituted army. The choice had been difficult. Skippon was popular with the rank and file but being illiterate probably counted against him. Cromwell was an excellent general but distrusted. Sir Thomas Fairfax was also an excellent general and he had offended no one. His appointment would partially appease the Lords, as he was the son of Ferdinando Lord Fairfax. Things were moving fast. On 21 January the Commons voted by 101 votes to 69 to appoint Sir Thomas Fairfax Lord General and Skippon his Major General. Seven days later the Commons passed the ordinance creating the New Model Army. The Upper House had been outmanoeuvred. After some delaying tactics they passed the Self-Denying Ordinance on 3 April and Essex delivered up his commission. England's first professional army had been created. The 33-year-old Fairfax rode to Windsor to take up his command and begin the huge challenge of creating a single effective force out of the miscellaneous troops of three armies.

Just as Parliament was reorganizing its army in early 1645, so were the Royalists. Unfortunately for the Royalists, their changes were not to result in a better force. Lord Forth, the Royalist commander, had been wounded and Charles decided to appoint Rupert in his place. Such an appointment would have been deeply unpopular with Digby and those who shared his dislike of the King's nephew. For once Rupert showed diplomacy and recommended that Charles, Prince of Wales, should take command and that he would be his deputy. As Prince Charles was barely 15 and had little interest in military matters, Rupert became the commander in all but name. Partially to balance Rupert's elevation, the King made Lord Goring Lieutenant General of Horse. Goring was a gifted cavalry officer who walked with a slight limp as a result of a wound at the siege of Breda and was the archetypal Cavalier of the worst sort. Young, brave, amusing and good-looking he certainly was, but also a compulsive gambler, hard drinker and irrepressible womanizer. Not surprisingly his soldiers loved him.

Despite Rupert and Goring having served together at Breda back in 1636, they were rivals rather than comrades in arms and an antagonism had grown between them. The King was very conscious of this and split them up by sending Goring to a semi-independent command in the South-West. The early part of the year saw a number of unsuccessful Royalist engagements. Rupert failed to capture Abingdon, Goring failed at Christchurch and in Devon Sir Richard Grenville failed at Plymouth. With pay in serious arrears and supplies bad, the discipline of the Royalist army began to break up, particularly in the South-West. Grenville, Goring's Major General, was behaving like a medieval baron plundering surrounding areas, arresting people at will and then demanding a ransom. He even took the estates of his estranged wife and, when she sought legal advice, summarily hanged her solicitor. Goring had abandoned himself to debauchery and was encouraging his men to support themselves by pillage.

The King had further complicated the command arrangements by deciding that Prince Charles, the nominal commander, should be based at Bristol. Prince Charles was given his own set of advisers, the most prominent of which was Sir Edward Hyde, the third son of a Wiltshire squire. Hyde was a lawyer and MP who had joined the King's service at the start of the Civil War and risen rapidly to be made Chancellor of the Exchequer the previous year at the age of 35. Hyde had been a close friend of Falkland and was one of the few remaining good advisers left to the King. By sending the Prince of Wales and Hyde away to Bristol the King had confused the military command, put his heir in the company of dissolute commanders and deprived himself of one of the few servants who could offer sensible advice. Given this general environment it was hardly surprising that Royalists had no effective intelligence structure other than such scouts as were deployed with individual commanders, augmented by what rumour and correspondence made its way to the King's Secretaries. An added problem was that in February 1644 Sir William Neal, Rupert's Scoutmaster General, had been rewarded for his good work by being made Governor of Hawarden and the post was filled by Colonel Russe, who was not an officer of the same calibre.

The King's great hope remained with Ireland. He had expected that by February Ormonde would have come to an agreement with the Confederates and that they would be about to send a larger combined Confederate/Government army from Ireland to bring his English subjects to their senses. But try as Ormonde might, the best he could do was to obtain further extensions of the autumn 1643 ceasefire. There remained a number of intractable sticking points to achieving the King's objective. In the first place, the Catholic Confederates had been fighting against the Protestant Government forces for some years and had no wish to suddenly have them as brothers in arms. The feeling was mutual. Charles had written to Ormonde in February authorizing him to get a treaty with the Confederates 'whatever it cost'. This in effect meant agreeing to tolerate Catholicism. But the mere toleration of

Catholicism was now no longer enough for many Confederates. Urged on by Owen Roe O'Neill they now demanded the open exercise of their faith in all churches and cathedrals they had taken. Ormonde loyally pressed on with the difficult negotiations, with His Majesty refusing to see that he was expecting Ormonde to reconcile the irreconcilable.

The only good news for the King was coming from Scotland. Burning with determination to avenge the sack of Inveraray, Argyll had assembled an army of 3,000 to pursue and destroy Montrose. Argyll nearly managed to trap the Royalists between himself and the Mackenzies but Montrose's excellent scouts brought word of the approach of the Covenanter army. Realizing he would be outnumbered four to one, Montrose carried out one of the great flank marches in military history. He led his lightly armed force with no cannon and little baggage over mountains near Ben Nevis through the snow and ice. On 2 February Argyll's army at Inverlochy was taken completely by surprise in a dawn attack by an enemy they believed to be in winter quarters thirty miles to the north. Unable to withstand the shock of the downhill Highland charge, the Covenanters broke and were hacked down to the accompaniment of Royalist pipes gleefully playing the pibroch 'Sons of dogs come and I will give you flesh'. At the end, 1,500 Covenanters lay dead and Argyll had slipped away down Loch Linnhe in his black-sailed galley.

Back in England, while the Royalist forces were in some disarray, Fairfax was pressing ahead creating the New Model Army. This army was different in so many ways. The officers were all specifically selected for merit and support for the cause. Both officers and men were drawn from godly Protestants, whether Presbyterian or Independent. The ethos of the force was strongly religious, with services every day, numerous ad hoc prayer meetings and much psalm-singing. The former battle cry of 'For King and Parliament' had been replaced by 'God with us'. The levels of discipline and behaviour were made very high. The punishment for blasphemy was a red-hot iron bored through the tongue. Standard rates of pay were introduced, such as 1s 6d a day for an infantryman and 2s for a cavalryman and £1 10s for a colonel. The army was given the funding to pay for food, lodging and purchases from the civilian population, rather than stealing or at best requisitioning in exchange for worthless promissory notes.

A standard uniform was introduced of scarlet woollen cloth for the infantry and buff coats with breast and back plates for the cavalry. Prior to this, such uniforms as there were on either side depended upon the fashion sense and purse of their individual colonels. There were just a few regiments that stood out, such as Newcastle's White Coats or the green uniforms of John Hampden's regiment, but the rest looked much the same and there was little to tell even from their banners whether they were Royalist or Parliamentarian. It is true the Covenanters nearly all wore blue bonnets – but then again so did Langdale's Northern Horse. In battle each side had to use the expedient of extra markings, for example at Edgehill orange scarves were worn by Parliament and red by the Royalists. Sometimes the armies did not have any markers to hand, such as the Parliamentarians at the First Battle of Newbury when 'this day our whole army wore green boughs in their hats to distinguish us from our enemies'. From April 1645 the New Model Army began being completely fitted out with standard equipment and uniform. This had the obvious advantage of enhancing corporate identity and the self-esteem of the troops. Less obvious was the aid it gave to those engaged in reconnaissance and intelligence gathering who would have at last found it possible to differentiate between friend and foe.

The Parliamentary military intelligence organization was one of the many things to change with the introduction of the New Model Army. As Sir Samuel Luke was the MP for Bedford, the Self-Denying Ordinance debarred him from military command. It was generally recognized that he done an excellent job as Scoutmaster General and Governor of Newport Pagnell. He had not only run the vital depot effectively but ensured that its influence was felt in the surrounding area, as when he had surprised and overcome a regiment of Royalist horse at Islip the previous year. For Luke there was no question of temporary exemption to the ordinance, because he was out of favour. Luke was Presbyterian at a time when the Independents had gained the ascendancy in both Parliament and the army. Things came to a head when Luke arrested two captains for disobeying a Parliamentary order against unlicensed preaching. The officers appealed to their commanding officer Colonel Fleetwood and then to Fairfax, with the result that Luke was reprimanded. A short time later, on 26 June, Luke gave up his commission and so ends the record he has left us of his scouts.

As remnants of Essex's force, the scouts were part of an organization being disbanded to help create the New Model Army. Fairfax would create a new scouting organization to support his field army, based on mobile reconnaissance units rather than individual scouts reporting to a static base. It is likely that some of Luke's scouts joined the New Model Army but the organization he had created was now defunct. Despite this, the need for intelligence was well recognized in the New Model Army and was voted £1,000, compared with £500 for artillery. Lionel Warson was made Scoutmaster General. Procedures and security were tightened. For example, a standard secret code was introduced: 'G' for 'King', 'X' for 'Fairfax', 'OO' for 'Money', 'F' for 'Commons' and 'D' for 'Lords'.

While Fairfax was setting up the New Model Army, Cromwell had been in the West since February countering the Royalist threat to Weymouth. Sir William Waller had resigned under the Self-Denying Ordinance but Cromwell's commission was extended for forty days to allow him and his 7,000 men to harass the Oxford area and cut the King's communications between Oxford and the West. Fairfax, as Lord General, was answerable to the Committee of Both Kingdoms which was now dominated by the former generals Essex, Manchester and Ferdinando Lord Fairfax. The Committee ordered him to relieve Goring's siege of Taunton then to besiege Oxford. With some misgivings Fairfax obeyed the orders and the New Model Army deployed for the first time on 1 May.

The King had decided to leave Oxford and concentrated his army totalling 11,000 at Stow-on-the-Wold. There he held a council of war where, as so often, he received conflicting advice. Rupert wanted to go north to link up with Langdale and regain lost territory. Digby and others wanted him to block Fairfax's advance on Taunton. As a compromise Charles decided to split his army and went north with Rupert but sent Goring south with 3,000 horse. Rupert and the King's army decided to take Leicester which was stormed on 31 May with considerable bloodshed and pillage. So alarmed were the Parliament and the Committee of Both Kingdoms by the fate of Leicester that agreement was given to a request by Fairfax for Cromwell to be made Lieutenant General of Horse. They also agreed that Fairfax should direct field operations without reference to Derby House. Fairfax now had the freedom he needed to put his new army to best use and decided to advance against the King.

The King had moved to Daventry and Fairfax's reconnaissance made contact with the Royalist outposts on 13 June. Charles marched towards Market Harborough pursued by Cromwell and his cavalry who had now joined Fairfax. Goring had been recalled but was taking a long time to return. One reason was that poor discipline and no distinctive uniforms had resulted in Goring's left and right wings fighting each other for several hours on the march, believing each other to be the enemy. Intelligence now played an important part for Parliament because a letter was intercepted from Goring to Rupert saying that he would be delayed. The letter had not been encrypted and so Fairfax realized that he must attack as soon as possible. Rupert strongly advised the King to avoid battle until Goring had returned and some expected reinforcements from South Wales had arrived. Charles was persuaded by Digby to stand and fight where they were, near the village of Naseby and so crush what the Royalists derisorily referred to as 'the New Noddle Army'.

As the King's army was short of both powder and shot, Rupert then entreated that the King at least wait until his ammunition train had arrived. This again was overruled. By this time Fairfax's force was only six miles away but the Royalist army had no intelligence of its whereabouts. Rupert sent his new scoutmaster Russe to conduct a reconnaissance. As Clarendon describes, he 'went not far enough, but returned and averred, that he had been three or four miles forward, and could neither discover nor hear any thing of them, and presently a report was raised in the army that the enemy was retired'. Rupert had no faith in this report and sent out another party of horse and musketeers who had not gone a mile before it saw the vanguard of the Parliamentary army. This is a good example of a commander being sufficiently intelligence aware to recognize when their intelligence staff may have been in error and then take direct personal action to restore the situation.

On 14 June His Majesty's force of 3,500 horse and 4,000 foot took up position on a low hill, heavily outnumbered by Fairfax on the opposite hill with 6,000 horse and 7,000 foot. Cromwell who had arrived with 600 horse just before the battle, was placed in command of the cavalry. Fairfax then withdrew his troops out of sight just below the brow of the hill. At about 10 am, thinking that Fairfax was retreating, Rupert's cavalry attacked up hill and managed to break the Parliamentary right wing under Henry Ireton, pursuing them into Naseby village. As always in battle, the quiet intellectual Fairfax became a man transformed. He had lost his helmet, so with his long dark hair blowing in the wind he was galloping everywhere, now rallying Ireton's cavalry, now coming to the aid of Skippon's infantry who were being pushed back by Astley, and always closely directing the battle. On the other wing Cromwell routed Langdale's opposing cavalry but instead of pursuing it, attacked the unprotected Royalist infantry who were now very low in powder and shot. The King seeing the need to counter-attack was about to personally lead a charge of his Lifeguard and reserve, when the Earl of Carnwath grabbed his bridle to prevent him endangering his life. Charles's startled horse wheeled to the right and it was thought that the King was leaving the field. Charles then found himself swept along in a mass move to retreat towards Leicester. When Rupert returned to the field, the battle was all but over and the best he could do was to try to cover the King's retreat on the fourteen mile road to Leicester. The whole battle had lasted just two hours. The King had lost 1,000 killed to the Parliament's 150 and in the pursuit about 6,000 more Royalists were killed, 4,000–5,000 foot captured together with 5,000 horses and all the artillery and baggage. This was the decisive battle of the Civil War, fought by the King against the advice of his senior military commander and by Fairfax on the basis of good intelligence. It was lost by Royalist confusion and won by the superior control and discipline of the New Model Army's Ironside cavalry.

Despite the high standards of discipline in the New Model Army, it could not contain itself when it got to the royal baggage-train. There was of course the normal looting but a hundred women were put to the sword and many others had their noses slit. For the righteous Parliamentarians this was amply justified as they were thought to be Irish Papist whores. In fact they were mainly wives of the Protestant Welsh infantry. More positively, all the King's papers were captured. Virtually none of the correspondence was encrypted and it revealed all the Royalist objectives and plans. Any documents that were encrypted but had no plaintext with them were no doubt sent to John Wallis who had been rewarded for his cryptanalyst efforts on Parliament's behalf by being given the living of St Gabriel in Fenchurch Street and a Fellowship of Queens College Cambridge. This capture of the documents was both an intelligence and a propaganda coup. Admittedly some of those plans would now have to change because of the defeat and the known compromise of the documents but much was strategic and unchangeable. Most damaging to the Royalist cause were the letters going back to 1643 showing Charles had negotiated to obtain the support of the Irish Catholics and receive forces from Catholics on the Continent such as the King of France and Dukes of Lorraine and of Courland. That the King could ask foreign Papists to subdue his own country proved that the very worst fears about Charles were true. In a short time the printing presses of London had a field day publishing extracts from the documents in pamphlets such as *The King's Cabinet Opened*. This was another major propaganda victory coming on top of the well-known fact that the King had already brought over Irish troops to fight against Parliament. The King's image was forever changed and many concluded that he could never again be trusted.

Less important but still a damaging result of the publication of the letters was that they caused a deterioration in the King's already only lukewarm relations with his potential Continental supporters. No ruler would want to have their secret negotiations made public and any would be very wary of having future dealings with another ruler who cannot ensure secrecy. At the very least it completely undermined confidence in diplomacy and some of the revelations caused serious repercussions. For example, the Dutch found it most embarrassing that correspondence had been found suggesting a marriage between the Prince of Wales and a princess of Orange, in return for only providing arms and ammunition to the Royalists and not to Parliament. As the Dutch Estates had been carrying out a good arms trade with Parliament and were to all appearances close allies, the revelation was unhelpful to say the least. It was all the more galling because it had been no more than a Royalist proposal that was not being taken at all seriously by the Estates. The captured correspondence also revealed that the Prince of Wales was being offered in marriage to the Portuguese Infanta, Catherine of Braganza. The embarrassment to the Portuguese was even greater because the letters showed that the Portuguese Resident Antonio de Sousa had been abusing his diplomatic status by facilitating the secure passage of mail between the King in Oxford and the Queen in Paris. In short, the failure to secure the King's state papers greatly weakened his cause at home and his opportunity for support from abroad.

The King and his depleted army had moved to the Welsh borders. Despite the crushing defeat, His Majesty retained some optimism and wrote to the Earl of Glamorgan 'I am not disheartened by my late misfortune', as he was still hoping for reinforcements from Ireland. Charles, who loved intrigue, sent the Earl of Glamorgan to Dublin to secretly negotiate with the Confederacy behind Ormonde's back. Glamorgan was the son of the Marquis of Westminster, one of the most prominent Catholics in England. He was also married to an Irish wife, so seemed very suitable for the task of winning over the Confederates. Glamorgan was authorized to offer the Confederates all they wanted but on condition that the concessions to Catholicism were kept secret for the present and only made public at a more suitable time in the future. This proposal was not welcomed with any enthusiasm because most of the Confederate leaders had little faith in a secret treaty that could be repudiated by the King when he no longer needed their help. So both official and secret negotiations continued to drag on, with neither Ormonde nor Glamorgan making any headway.

The King and his army had begun moving northwards but Rupert had gone to the South-West to try to rally forces. Fairfax, after receiving the surrender of Leicester decided to advance into Somerset to relieve Taunton and defeat Goring. On 3 July just as he crossed into Dorset, Fairfax encountered a strange phenomenon called the 'Clubmen'. From the end of 1644 local groups in Worcestershire and Shropshire began defending themselves against marauding soldiers. These groups were neutral, led by local clergy or land owners and were prepared to defend their property by force. This movement spread particularly in the South-West in response to the excesses of Goring's troops. One of their slogans was 'If you offer to plunder our cattle, be assured we will bid you battle.' The armed Clubmen of Dorset now posed a potential threat to Fairfax and his response was to do all he could to obtain intelligence about them. He had several meetings with Clubmen leaders and eventually concluded that they were indeed neutral, rather than Royalist sympathizers. He also managed to gain their confidence by demonstrating that his army was disciplined and would pay for what it purchased.

Fairfax pressed on after Goring and was joined by Massey's Western Brigade of 2,200 horse and dragoons. Goring, with a force of 10,000, abandoned the siege of Taunton and prepared for Fairfax's arrival. Goring took up a temporary but strong position at Langport, while hoping for the arrival of reinforcements from Wales, and sent his artillery and baggage on to Bridgwater, where he intended to make his defence. Fairfax advanced to Langport and was not sure how to proceed, having seen the strength of Goring's position protected by the Rivers Yeo and Parrett. He then received information from his scouts that Goring had neither artillery nor baggage. Fairfax at once realized that this was a strong intelligence indicator that Goring was not in his final defensive position and wanted to retreat. Now was the time to attack. On 10 July the 10,000-strong force of Fairfax and Cromwell drew up on the other side of the valley and began bombarding Goring with their artillery. Fairfax sent 1,500 musketeers to cross the stream in front of Goring's lines and then secured a hedge-lined lane leading up the hill. At about noon, Fairfax ordered just 200 cavalry to go up the lane and charge Goring's cavalry at the top of the hill. The shock of the attack, which soon received the support of the musketeers, resulted in the disintegration of Goring's troops, who began to flee the two miles to Bridgwater. The second Royalist army had been defeated within one month: 3,000 Royalists had been killed and 1,400 prisoners captured together with 1,000 horses and 4,000 arms.

The job was not complete. Goring had withdrawn behind the 15-foot thick walls of Bridgwater and the support of his artillery. On 21 July Bridgwater was stormed in an action which showed that the infantry of the New Model Army were capable of being as brave and well-disciplined as the Ironsides. Seeing all was lost, Goring managed to escape the town with 2,000 cavalry. Fairfax sent Cromwell off to subdue some Clubman resistance in Shaftesbury and set about taking the remaining Royalist strongholds in the South-West. Bath fell to him on 31 July and Sherborne was captured on 15 August. Sherborne was also a Clubman centre and with its fall so ended the last important Clubman resistance to Parliament.

Despite the major Royalist setbacks in the South-West, the King could at least find some comfort in the news from Scotland. After winning the battle of Inverlochy, Montrose had moved on to Elgin and been joined by Lord George Gordon with 200 well-equipped cavalry. Not only could they provide him with additional shock in battle but also a much needed means of longer range surveillance and scouting.

Things were looking good but he still faced some significant problems. Although Huntley's son, Lord Gordon, had joined Montrose, the Marquis himself was still refusing to commit himself and so none of the Gordon lairds were prepared to declare for the Royalists. Moreover the clans who were with the Royalist army had a disconcerting habit of retuning home with their booty immediately after a victory. In the Lowlands there had been no sign of support for Montrose, indeed Argyll still had an army there that needed defeating. In addition William Baillie had been appointed Lieutenant General by the Convention of Estates and was concentrating an army at Perth. He was a professional soldier who had served under Gustavus Adolphus and acquitted himself well under Leven at Marston Moor. Montrose's success at Inverlochy had given the Estates such a shock that they ordered 1,500 men from Leven's army at Newcastle to join Bailey at Perth. This was good news for the Royalists in that their action in the Highlands had resulted in relieving the Scots pressure on the North of England but it also meant that Montrose was now facing hardened soldiers rather than levies. Baillie was also joined by Sir John Hurry to lead the cavalry who, despite defecting from Parliament and then back again, had been eagerly accepted by the Covenanters because of his known skills as a commander.

There was something else that was a problem for Montrose. He set great store by intelligence and many of his Highlanders had considerable experience of stalking and hunting game in the wildest terrain. Such men made ideal scouts. It was largely by Montrose's excellent collection and assessment of intelligence that he had been able to nearly always keep that vital one step ahead of his enemies and not be forced into an unequal battle. Perhaps it was too much to expect that day after day there could be no intelligence failure but they did occur. Though he was a brilliant tactician and exponent of surprise, he occasionally did not make best use of his intelligence collection to prevent himself from being surprised. The better deployment of reconnaissance, even on foot, would have given him sufficient warning of the approach of Argyll at Fyvie to enable him to have avoided battle. As it was, he eventually extricated himself enabling him to fight later at times and places of his own choosing and so turning a likely defeat into the resounding victories at Inveraray and Inverlochy. He had survived that time but Montrose could not afford to be lax over intelligence collection many more times in the future.

In early April Montrose's scouts brought him the vital information that Baillie and Hurry were temporally splitting their force. Baillie would go to Atholl to subdue Montrose's recruiting area and Hurry would go to Aberdeen to keep the Gordons in check. Montrose now urgently recalled the contingents of Black Pate, Lord Gordon and MacColla to make a force of 2,500 foot and 250 horse. First he went after Hurry and, although outnumbered two to one, defeated him at the village of Auldearn, outside Nairn. By the end of June the similar-sized armies of Baillie and Montrose met at Alford in Aberdeenshire. There, the Covenanters were routed and lost 1,600 dead but this great victory came at the price of the death of Lord Gordon whose cavalry had been of such value.

In a short time the Royalist army had increased to 4,000 foot and 500 horse. The Scottish Estates had gathered in Perth, having removed themselves from Edinburgh because of the plague, and were being protected by Hurry and 400 horse. Baillie had reassembled an army and had moved up to Perth. Montrose managed to bypass both Hurry and Baillie then cross the Forth into the Lowlands. Bailey pursued and on 14 August decided to attack Montrose who was just four miles away in the village of Kilsyth. The next day the Covenanter army of 7,000 came over high ground to face the Royalists' 5,000 below in the valley. After preliminary skirmishing, the Covenanters attempted to carry out a surprise right flanking attack from dead ground but the manoeuvre was seen. With the Covenanter force strung out and off balance, Montrose sent his infantry surging up the hill to strike at Baillie's centre. Soon the Covenanters were in chaos and beginning to flee, with the Highlanders cutting them down as they ran. Baillie fled the field and it was all over, bar the slaughter of those who could not escape fast enough. The last Covenanter army in Scotland had been decisively defeated and, with Leven still at Newcastle, Montrose commanded the only military force left in the kingdom. Glasgow opened its gates to him as did Edinburgh and most of the lords and lairds of the Lowlands were suddenly expressing their devotion to the King and his Lieutenant General. Montrose was now master of Scotland. Baillie and Argyll had gone to the safety of Berwick and Hurry had felt it opportune to turn coat for a third time and put his sword at His Majesty's disposal. Montrose's expedition had changed from a minor sideshow of the Civil War into a second front for the King and in doing so restored one of his kingdoms.

The surprising and exciting news from Scotland gave His Majesty new hope and he now decided to go north with a vague notion of linking up with Montrose. Instead of taking Rupert with him, Charles dispatched his nephew on the almost impossible task of defending Bristol, which was then in the grip of a plague. Rupert knew that the war was lost and was pressing Charles to negotiate while he could. In a letter to his friend the Duke of Richmond Rupert wrote: 'His Majesty hath no way left to preserve his posterity, kingdom and nobility, but by treaty. I believe it more prudent to retain something that to loose all.' As Rupert expected, Richmond had shown the King his letter and Charles replied:

> As for your opinion of my business and your counsel thereupon, if I had any other quarrel but the defence of my religion, crown and friends, you had full reason for your advice; for I confess that speaking either as a mere soldier or statesman, there is no probability but of my ruin. Yet as a Christian I must tell you, that God will not suffer rebels and traitors to prosper, nor this cause to be overthrown. And whatever personal punishment it shall please him to inflict upon me must not make me repine, much less give over this quarrel. And there is as little question that a composition with them at this time is nothing else but a submission which, by the grace of God, I am resolved against, whatever it cost me,

for I know my obligation to be, both in conscience and honour, neither to abandon God's Cause, injure my successors, nor forsake my friends.

Fairfax deployed his 9,000–10,000 force to besiege Rupert who had arrived in Bristol. After surrender negotiations had failed Fairfax decided to storm the city. Rupert had 3,500 soldiers, of whom a hundred a week were dying of the plague, and a three-mile perimeter to defend. Fairfax had 9,000–10,000 troops, about half from the New Model Army and half local Roundheads who had joined him from Somerset and Gloucestershire. On 4 September the assault began with considerable loss of life to the attackers but by sheer determination they managed to take Priors Fort. The Royalist garrison in the castle was now separated from the defenders on the walls. Rupert realizing his position had become hopeless, surrendered and was allowed to withdraw his forces from the city but forced to hand over all cannon and muskets. The second city in the kingdom was now back in Parliamentary hands. In the words of Walker, the Secretary of War, the loss of Bristol was 'the loss of all our magazines and warlike provisions, and so by consequence in very short time South Wales, the West and all other parts of the kingdom'.

Bristol was such a blow to the King that he felt completely let down by his nephew and regarded his surrender as treasonous. Rupert's elder brother, Charles Louis, the stateless Elector Palatine was in London courting Parliament and had just been voted a pension by them of £8,000. He was clearly cashing in on his royal blood and strong Protestant credentials to make himself available to the winning side as an alternative to Charles. Whatever the Elector's ambitions, none of the Parliamentary leaders considered him as a serious contender for the throne. Charles was not to know this but became deeply suspicious that all his nephews were plotting against him. Sir Edward Nicholas was dispatched to Rupert to inform him that he was removed from his command and banished him from the country. Rupert sent a message to the King appealing to see him but was refused. Rupert and his brother Maurice now rode to Newark where the Governor Sir Richard Willys, in defiance of the King's instructions, welcomed them. Although told that the King would still not receive him, he eventually forced his way into the King's presence. Rupert's angry outburst of accusations against Digby for ruining his reputation was heard by the King in silence.

The next day the King agreed to Rupert explaining his case to the Council of War, as a result of which he was exonerated. The King was so furious about the support Rupert had received from the Council of War and the Newark garrison that he removed Willys from his post of Governor and appointed Lord Belasyse in his place. Rupert and his supporters appealed to the King on Willys's behalf and that night it almost looked as though there would be a mutiny. Feelings were running very high on both sides and Willys challenged Belasyse to a duel. The next morning the King rode out to the marketplace to confront Rupert, Maurice, Willys and their supporters in the garrison. His Majesty made it quite clear that they should obey his commands or quit his service. Crestfallen, the protesters had no option but to sullenly disperse and Rupert then galloped off in royal disgrace. Some time later, Rupert brought himself to write two abject letters of apology to Charles who eventually conceded that he was no traitor, forgave him and allowed him to return to Oxford. Much as he loved his nephew, Charles could not bring himself to restore his command and so lost his finest general, most competent military adviser and best intelligencer. Willys was also pardoned and made a baronet as compensation for receiving his sovereign's unjust wrath but he would make his impact on intelligence nine years later.

The surrender of Bristol was devastating but there remained the hope that the invincible Montrose would restore the Royalist fortunes. This was not to be. Montrose had been received obsequiously by the majority of the Lowland leaders but all their promises of loyalty to the King fell short of practical help. The fact was that they hated and despised Montrose's barbarous Catholic Celtic army and had felt little affiliation to the remote sovereign whose interests they purported to represent. The Royalist army for its part was completely ill at ease away from the Highlands. As they were now the army of government and expected to be disciplined they were forbidden their great joy of plunder. Montrose's force melted away. MacColla took his Irish off to Kintyre to settle more scores with the Campbells. Other clansmen just wandered back to their homes with what loot they could carry. Before long the Royalist army was reduced to just 700 foot and 200 horse.

It was while at Dalkeith with these few troops that Montrose received intelligence that David Leslie had abandoned the siege of Hereford to return to Scotland and had already reached Berwick with 5,000 horse and 1,000 foot. It would have been Montrose's usual tactic to withdraw to the Highlands and so lure an opponent into favourable ground. This was no longer an option for he had received orders from the King to advance south to the border. Leslie had progressed to Gladsmuir in search of Montrose when he obtained intelligence of the exact location and disposition of the Royalist camp at Philiphaugh next to the village of Selkirk in the Ettrick Valley. This was almost definitely as a result of treachery by one of the Royalist officers thinking it prudent to get in with the stronger side – who it was will never be known for sure.

On the night of 12 September Montrose, who was quartered with his cavalry in Selkirk, went to bed saying that he was not to be disturbed. He was unaware that Leslie was just three miles to his north and advancing with all haste in order to attack the Royalist camp the next morning. Perhaps it was the pressure of events, but for whatever reason Montrose had been uncharacteristically careless about his scouts. The Scoutmaster, Captain Blackadder had removed the seasoned and highly effective Highland scouts and replaced them with Lowlanders. The logic behind it was that the Lowlanders knew the ground. Although these local scouts did indeed know their area, they had no military experience and so had little idea how to deploy effectively and provide the vital surveillance coverage of all possible routes of enemy advance. Montrose had at least deployed some pickets, the most important of which was a troop of horse under Charteris of Amisfield, which was at Sunderland Hall covering the northern approach to the Ettrick Valley.

In the middle of the night the troop were attacked and driven off with casualties but Charteris managed to gallop back to the Royalist camp and to report. Whoever received the report, presumably Blackadder, decided that the attack on Charteris was just some hostile local villagers and decided that the incident did not warrant waking Montrose. Blackadder did however send out scouts early the next morning when a thick autumn mist was lying on the ground. The scouts later returned to report that there was no enemy in a ten-mile radius. By now the Royalist infantry was beginning to cook breakfast and just as the first pots were ready on the campfires they looked up to see five squadrons of Covenanter horse bearing down on them with drawn swords.

Montrose was having his breakfast at Selkirk when a panting Blackadder rushed in to say that the infantry camp was under attack by Leslie. Montrose threw himself on his horse and galloped towards Leslie's cavalry, with the rest of his men following as best they could. The Royalist foot had managed to get their weapons and were just holding their own as Montrose and about 150 Royalist horse collided into the opposing cavalry. Furious fighting ensued but after a while it became clear that the Royalists were so heavily outnumbered and offbalance that there was no hope for them. Montrose was persuaded to leave the field with what horse he could rally and the Royalist foot fought on bravely until surrendering on Leslie's offer of quarter. The Royalist army in Scotland had been destroyed and along with it Montrose's reputation for invincibility. The Battle of Philiphaugh had taken place on the very day that Henrietta Maria had arranged a Te Deum in Paris to celebrate Montrose's victories and just two days after the surrender of Bristol. When the news of Philiphaugh reached the King it was clear even to him that the war was all but over.

After the battle, Montrose and his group headed for the Clyde and having forded the river then went on to cross the Forth and the Earn before at last coming to rest at Buchantry six days later. There he began to rally those who had escaped the battle. He now had the forlorn prospect of starting virtually from scratch the whole process of attempting to raise a Highland Royalist army. Significant as was the outcome of the Battle of Philiphaugh both militarily and politically, it also had a major human tragedy. Immediately after the battle Argyll took his revenge on the defeated Royalists. He persuaded the Council of War that the Royalists were all traitors and therefore exempt from quarter; 500 Royalist camp followers had already been butchered and 80 surviving women and children were marched to Linlithgow where they were thrown off the bridge to drown in the Avon. The infantry who had been granted mercy on the field were systematically slaughtered and the surviving senior officers were hanged without trial at the Market Cross in Glasgow.

The total rout of Montrose's force and the resulting Royalist calamity had been brought about by Leslie receiving the vital walk-in intelligence of Montrose's location and then acting upon it with speed and tactical efficiency. It had also been caused by Royalist intelligence failure, resulting from ineffective scouting aggravated by the poor weather conditions. Blackadder has much to answer for but it must be said that Montrose, as commander, bears final responsibility for allowing the slipshod intelligence management that would be responsible for destroying any Royalist hopes of prosecuting the war.

But the war went on. Digby was made commander of all Royalist forces north of the Trent but this was a hollow victory over Rupert. The main Royalist force of Langdale's Northern Horse had been defeated near Chester in September and Digby and the remnants were defeated at Sherborne in October, after which Digby and Langdale fled to the Isle of Man. The North was virtually lost for the King, except for Chester, which was stubbornly withstanding siege. Fairfax took his main force to relieve Plymouth then moved to Exeter having detached brigades to subdue Gloucestershire, Wiltshire and Hampshire. Cromwell took Devizes and then Winchester in November, followed by capturing Basing House, the stronghold of the Catholic Marquis of Winchester. Despite these successes, morale was now getting low as the war dragged on through a bitter winter with sickness rife and considerable shortage of supplies.

For the King, the particularly cold winter in Oxford was spent developing two contradictory political stratagems. He knew that the Scottish/Parliamentary alliance was close to breaking point because the Covenanters had not been receiving the payment promised to their army and it was plain that Parliament was taking no steps to establish Presbyterianism in England. Parliament for its part resented paying the Scots, who in their view had contributed nothing to the war except the occupation of Newcastle. Although Parliament was still against bishops, the pendulum was swinging away from Presbyterianism. The general breakdown of traditional authority that had occurred during the war had encouraged the flowering of a number of Protestant sects that were to be generally called 'Independents'. These had differing views but all agreed that congregations should come together as they wished, elect their own ministers and pay for their own churches. In short they wanted freedom to worship God as they pleased without any imposed authority such as was the case with Presbyterianism. Parliament was still dominated by those supporting Presbyterianism led by Holles but the Parliamentary cause was being dominated by Independents such as Vane and St John on Committee of the Two Kingdoms and Cromwell in the army itself.

The King put out feelers to both the Independents and the Scots in the hope that one or other would come to support him and so both fracture the Scottish/Parliamentary alliance and help cause a rupture between the Independents and the Presbyterians in the English Parliament. Associated with the Scottish part of these plans was an initiative by Cardinal Mazarin to rebuild the traditional French/Scottish alliance and through it to support the King against the Independents in Parliament. Mazarin had sent over a bright young envoy called Jean de Montreuil who began shuttling between the Scottish Commissioners in London, the King in Oxford and Argyll and the Covenanter leaders in Edinburgh. Meanwhile His Majesty was still continuing his negotiations with the Confederate Supreme Council in Kilkenny, openly through Ormonde and secretly through Glamorgan. This latter course had been complicated by the arrival in Ireland of Rinuccini, the Papal Nuncio, with the offer of financial support for Charles from the Pope. This support came at a price, for Rinuccini was determined to thwart any alliance between the Confederates and the King unless Ireland became a Catholic country. Naturally, Charles could not agree such a demand even in a secret treaty, so negotiations were further stalled.

At the beginning of the next year Fairfax decided to postpone attacking Exeter and began besieging Dartmouth. The outer defences of Dartmouth were stormed and the town surrendered. Fairfax was unable to return to Exeter because he received intelligence that Sir Ralph Hopton had gathered 5,000 Cornishmen to relieve Exeter. Goring had by this time left for France in an effort to raise support and that reliable and humane soldier Hopton had assumed command. Hopton had taken up a defensive position in Torrington and on 16 February 1646 Fairfax's advance guard of dragoons bumped into their outposts in the thick hedgerows around the town. This skirmish gradually turned into a full-scale engagement as more troops joined in. Fairfax gained control of the situation and the main assault began at 8 am the next morning. The Parliamentary infantry fought through hedgerow by hedgerow and eventually cleared the barricades for the cavalry who entered the town and completed the victory. At Langport the King had lost most of the cavalry available to him in the South-West, at Torrington he lost the last of his infantry.

At virtually the same time as the defeat at Langport news came of the fall of Chester after a long and heroic defence under Lord Byron. The only viable force left to the crown was the Prince of Wales's ill-disciplined 5,000 horse and 1,000 foot left in Cornwall, described by Clarendon as 'being only terrible in plunder and resolute in running away'. It was to them, rather than Exeter, that Fairfax now turned his attention. As a precursor to military engagement, Fairfax decided to employ a double agent in a psychological operations role. The agent was returned to Cornwall to spread information about 'the good condition of our (Parliamentarian) army and the desperate condition of theirs by the defeat given to them at Torrington'. How much effect this may have had we do not know but there can have been little doubt in the minds of Cornishmen that the King's cause was lost and, whatever the condition of Fairfax's army, it was still winning victories. Hopton decided to make a treaty with Fairfax to avoid further bloodshed and surrendered Exeter on 4 March. The same day, the Prince of Wales made for the safety of the Isles of Scilly. The only senior Royalist commander left was the 67-year-old Lord Astley, with just 700 horse and 2,300 foot, mainly raw recruits from Wales. Fairfax's scouts intercepted his correspondence and learnt his strength and position and at Stow-on-the-Wold the last Royalist army was swiftly defeated.

For the previous four months the King had been trying to further his attempts at alliance with the Irish Confederates and the Pope, the Scots, France and the English Presbyterians and the Independents who were the growing power in Parliament and the New Model Army. Each of the three initiatives was half-baked and had any one of them miraculously succeeded they would have been countered by the failure of the others. What were to put the nails in the coffin of these desperate designs were Royalist security failures and Parliamentary intelligence successes. It was already public knowledge from the documents captured at Naseby that the King was trying to get support from France and the Irish Confederates. Neither the Presbyterians nor the Independents were inclined to believe the word of a sovereign who was trying to get Catholic troops to invade his land. Then in the autumn of 1645 Digby won an engagement near Sherborne but in the confusion of pursuing the enemy lost all his correspondence on the King's affairs. Parliament was to learn of the King's current attempts to forge an alliance with the Confederates and other Catholics.

Had there been any doubt in Parliamentary minds about the King's intention to ally with the Papists, it would have been well and truly dispelled by more papers that reached Parliament in January. These papers had been found among the correspondence of the Archbishop of Tuam after he had been killed near Sligo and revealed the draft of Glamorgan's secret treaty with the Nuncio and the Confederates. The fact that this document was identified among many others as being so devastatingly incriminating, and that it was swiftly transmitted to Westminster, says a lot for Parliamentary intelligence collection. Despite his obvious lack of credibility, in March the King instructed Secretary Nicholas to write to Vane offering religious freedom to the Independents in exchange for their support. Vane never even bothered to reply. He had already received intelligence from the Parliamentary sources in Paris that the King was busy trying to form an alliance with the French and the Covenanters. Even His Majesty began to see that the chances of any of his ill-starred diplomatic initiatives prospering were unlikely in the least.

The King was now in Oxford with no army and Fairfax approaching. The options were to escape to France, which could prove difficult, or surrender. If it was to be surrender the question was would he get better terms from the Scots rather than Fairfax. Montreuil recommended surrendering to the Scots and said that he would go ahead to Newark to prepare the way. In the early hours of 27 April the King left Oxford accompanied only by Jack Ashburnham his Groom of the Bedchamber and Michael Hudson the former Scoutmaster for the Northern Army who had returned to Oxford as a royal chaplain after Marston Moor. Hudson had been chosen for his resourcefulness, knowledge of the enemy and of the local roads. In the interests of security, the King decided to accept the indignity of being disguised as their servant riding a packhorse, with his hair cut shorter and wearing a false beard.

It was no mean feat for Hudson to navigate the back roads avoiding Parliamentary forces and maintain the King's disguise on the journey, especially when staying at inns. The royal party reached Market Harborough where it was hoped that they might receive word from Montreuil, but none came. They moved on to Stamford from where Hudson went on to try to locate Montreuil and it was arranged that all should meet at the Swan Inn at Downham in Norfolk. Hudson arrived at the

Swan four days later having heard from Montreuil that he had contacted one of the Covenanter leaders, the Earl of Dunfermline, who had said that he could make no promises to the King other than to receive him in safety and with dignity if he should choose to come to them. Hudson's return was not a moment too soon because he discovered that the landlord was becoming suspicious of his unusual guests with their strangely cut hair and preoccupation with burning papers. The flight of the King from Oxford was already common knowledge and so Hudson wasted no time in getting His Majesty on the road again for Newark.

Travelling at night and resting only briefly at a tavern in Coppingford, at 6 am on 5 May the King arrived at the Saracen's Head at Southwell where Montreuil had arranged to meet him. Montreuil brought the senior Covenanter in Southwell to the King and His Majesty then announced that he wished to be taken to the nearby Covenanter headquarters at Newark to give himself up. From that moment the Civil War was over, bar the formalities. On 15 July the King ordered all strongholds to surrender but this took a little time to be transmitted across the kingdom. Rupert and James Duke of York were at Oxford, which after negotiation surrendered on 24 July. Under the terms, Rupert was banished and joined the Queen in Paris and James taken as a prisoner to join his youngest brother and sister at St James' Palace. On the same day that the Royalist headquarters surrendered, Charles Prince of Wales slipped away from the Isles of Scilly to Jersey, accompanied by Hyde.

By giving himself up to the Scots the King had been obliged to repudiate Montrose, who was ordered to surrender. On 22 July Montrose surrendered his thousand or so strong force to Middleton who agreed that the Royalists could return to their homes unharmed and that Montrose should leave Scotland. Less forgiving Covenanter leaders later tried to capture Montrose but he managed to escape in disguise to Norway. Royalist resistance in Scotland was now ended. In Ireland Ormonde had just reached an agreement with the Confederacy to send an army to England only to have it denounced by Rinuccini who threatened all concerned with excommunication. Owen Roe O'Neill supported the legate and joined forces with the Leinster army to surround Dublin. It was not until June the next year that Colonel Michael Jones landed in Ireland with 2,000 Parliamentary troops and Ormonde surrendered Dublin and other Royalist fortifications to him rather then let them fall into Catholic hands. Although this brought a formal end to the Civil War in all three kingdoms it was really all over by the summer of 1646. The war had cost over 20,000 lives but the King was still the King and nothing had been settled. What had changed, at least until some settlement was found, was the government of the country. The King was now a prisoner, with no Privy Council, still less an army or apparatus government to answer to him. The Royalist intelligence organization ceased to exist and the kingdom's intelligence was now in the hands of Parliament and the New Model Army.

Chapter 5

Captive King, 1647–1648

Having recovered from the surprise of their sovereign surrendering to them out of the blue, the Scots took the King to Newcastle to negotiate a settlement. Argyll, Leslie and the Scottish leaders assumed that Charles had gone to them because he was prepared to make terms and adopt the Covenant, for why else would he have done so? They gradually discovered that His Majesty was in no haste to make any concessions, least of all on religion. For the next eight months the King was subjected to endless lectures, sermons and discussions with Presbyterian ministers in an attempt to convince him to take the Covenant. He was treated with respect during this boring ordeal and could pass his free time in chess and golf. For all that, there was no mistaking that he was in real terms a prisoner. What was more, he no longer had anyone he could trust about him. Three days after the King's arrival in Newcastle, Hudson and Ashburnham had been tipped off that they were going to be sent to England as prisoners and so escaped – Hudson into hiding and Ashburnham to the Queen in Paris. Once Montreuil had realized that the Scottish alliance with the King and France was just not going to happen, he too went off to Paris. Charles was alone. His power was gone and his cause had evaporated but he lived in hope that if he played for time his adversaries would fall out among themselves. And so they did.

With the Scots holding the King and no Privy Council, England remained without formal government and had to rely on the wartime arrangement of the Commons working with the much reduced House of Lords and the Parliamentary committees. Now hostilities were over, it was essential to restore the normal organs of government under a settlement that would ensure that the King and his ministers were responsive to Parliament. Like the Scots, the English Parliament assumed this would be fairly swiftly achieved. No one could have guessed that negotiations with the King would continue on and off for two and a half years.

This period of political limbo was one in which factional intrigue was the principal covert activity rather than intelligence activity. To understand why this should be, we must examine the players in this power game. Parliament had split into two factions. There were the Presbyterians, such as Holles in the Commons and Essex and Manchester in the Lords. They wanted to fulfil their agreement with the Scots and make a settlement with the King which imposed Presbyterianism on England. They also believed that, as the army was unpopular, expensive and no longer required, it should be disbanded except for sufficient troops to subdue the Catholic rebels in Ireland. The Presbyterians were opposed by Independents such as Haselrig in the Commons and Saye in the Lords. They supported liberty of conscience and were tolerant of different sects as long as they were Calvinist in essence and did not pose a threat to law and order.

As the Presbyterians were in the majority in Parliament, the opposition to them would not have been of great consequence if it had not been for a new political force in the country, the army. The soldiers knew that it was their exertions which had won the war and now they wanted their due. The army itself was not united. There was general respect for Fairfax and common pride in the army's military achievements but discipline was undermined by the different forms of religious fervour that had sprung from creating an army of the godly. Religion was central to most people's lives but in the New Model Army it completely dominated daily existence, with constant sermons, prayer meetings and psalm-singing; all of which fostered extreme religious enthusiasm unrestrained by formal organization or liturgy. To this was added the conviction of different groups that military victory was God's sign that they were his chosen saints and that God intended to use their brand of worship as his means to build the New Jerusalem.

Although some members of the army were Presbyterians the majority followed Independent religious groupings such as Congregationalists or some of the new sects which had sprung up. For example there were the Millenarians who believed in the imminent coming of the millennium when Christ and his saints would rule for a thousand years. The liberty of conscience and freedom of thought that had thrown up differing religious beliefs also gave rise to new political ideologies. One such ideology was that of the Levellers who believed that, if souls were equal before God, so men should be politically equal, irrespective of whether or not they owned property. Such revolutionary views even went so far as to advocate universal male suffrage to replace the time-honoured principle of limiting voters to those with sufficient property to have a proven stake in the country. However, for all the army's differences there were some matters on which there was complete agreement. They were united in wanting pensions for military widows and disabled soldiers and settlement of arrears of pay, which in many cases were overdue by more than a year. Unless these demands were met, it was unlikely that the army would accept the politicians' plans for their disbandment lying down.

A clash between Parliament and army was postponed because all attention was focused on a settlement with the King, for it was from that settlement that all else could flow. In July, after much discussion and soundings, Parliament agreed to present His Majesty with the Newcastle Propositions. These required the King to abolish the episcopacy, hand over control of the army and navy and accept that all who had supported him in the war would be temporarily debarred from public office, with fifty being debarred for life. Parliament felt that these were reasonable terms to offer to a King who had been so comprehensively defeated. The King did not. It was back to the drawing board for the negotiators.

The year dragged on, with mounting frustration over the protraction of the negotiations and the army's resentment continuing to rise about its unfulfilled demands. The Covenanters become heartily sick of the King's stone-walling. They decided to rid themselves of the immediate problem and achieve a settlement with their English allies over the Scots' occupation of the North of England. In January 1647 the King was handed over by the Scots to Parliament in exchange for funding to pay off their army and return it to Scotland. The last of the Scots army duly crossed back over the border on 12 February. The King was taken south and arrived four days later at Holdenby Hall in Northamptonshire where he was put in the custody of a Presbyterian colonel. Michael Hudson had recently wangled his way into rejoining the King in Newcastle as chaplain and had brought secret plans for a Royalist uprising, but this ingenious intelligencer was not allowed to accompany the King to Holdenby. Charles was again alone.

Now that the King was in Parliament's hands it might be easier for them to come to a settlement with him. Essex, the leader of the Lords, had died in a hunting accident the previous September, so the Presbyterians were now led by Holles and Manchester, with Holles as the dominant voice. Things seemed to be going the Presbyterians' way; they held the King and there was a Presbyterian Lord Mayor who could bring the City to their side. Recent food crises and rises in prices meant that it was now urgent to save money and reduce taxation by disbanding the large army that was no longer needed in England as a counterbalance to the Scots army in the north. The total amount of money owed to the New Model Army, garrisons and county militia was the vast sum of £2.8 million. This just could not be allowed to continue to grow.

In February the Commons decided to disband all but 5,400 horse and 1,000 dragoons in England but retain some foot to send to Ireland. They also decided that there would be no more exceptions to the Self-Denying Ordinance and so not only would Cromwell have to resign but also Fairfax, who had recently become an MP. As though this was not enough, they also wanted all officers to swear the Presbyterian Covenant. As Cromwell and the majority of the army were Independents, it meant that the Presbyterian-dominated Parliament was now also in direct conflict with the army on religious grounds. On 25 May both Houses decided to go ahead with disbandment without addressing the issue of arrears or other grievances. For some time dissatisfied soldiers in regiments had been organizing themselves to voice their demands and became called 'Agitators'. Fairfax and his generals had complete sympathy with the views expressed by the Agitators, as long as they did not undermine discipline.

On 4 June a staunch Agitator called Cornet Joyce took a troop of 500 horse from Oxford and seized the King at Holdenby, then took him to a house near Cambridge. The King was now in the hands of the army and the Parliament was furious. It is believed but not substantiated, that Joyce had met Cromwell at his house in Drury Lane on 31 May. Whether or not Joyce had acted under Cromwell's direction we do not know but the Commons was sure he had. They ordered that he be arrested the next time he came to the chamber but Cromwell was ahead of the game. He had already left for army headquarters at Newmarket to where Fairfax had ordered the King to be taken. Fairfax definitely had no prior knowledge of the plot to capture His Majesty and although initially horrified by the event, soon realized its advantage to the army. He agreed to a document called the Solemn Engagement whereby the army would not disband until the arrears had been paid and other previous demands met, together with a religious settlement allowing freedom of conscience. He also agreed to a General Council of the Army being formed. This was to consist of the generals but also two officers and two soldiers from each regiment to represent the Agitators.

Fairfax then moved his army to St Albans to be nearer the capital. On 15 June the General Council drew up the Declaration of the Army claiming the army's right to speak for the people of England. They then demanded that eleven MPs should be expelled from Parliament 'for fermenting hostility against the army in Parliament'. Needless to say one of the eleven was Holles. Such unconstitutional pressure worked and the eleven offending MPs voluntarily withdrew from Westminster and Parliament voted one month's pay for the army. This was only a tiny fraction of what was owed but was a step in the right direction. Holles and other Presbyterians incited apprentices and Thames watermen to riot and call for the King's restoration. In fact on 26 July rioters entered the Commons chamber and forced through a vote that the King should be invited to return to London. Three days later, at the suggestion of Haselrig, senior members of both Houses of Parliament travelled to Fairfax's headquarters to ask for his protection. In their absence the remaining Presbyterian MPs elected a new Speaker and continued sitting. Fairfax ordered 9,000 foot and 7,000 horse to march on London. On 6 August the army occupied Westminster without resistance and both Parliament and order were restored. There could be little doubt now in anyone's mind where the real power in the kingdom resided. Soldiers were positioned at strategic points and the remainder of the army camped menacingly close to London at Croydon. The Commons felt it prudent to take steps to pay army arrears and began selling church lands to raise the money.

In parallel with these events the army had been devising its own settlement with the King. Major General Henry Ireton, a lawyer and husband of Cromwell's daughter Bridget, was the main architect of the draft, which was called 'The Heads of Proposals'. This should have been a much more attractive offer to His Majesty. Under this Parliament would control the armed forces and government appointments for just ten years but all those who had served in the King's army could be back in public life after just five years. Also neither bishops nor the Book of Common Prayer would be abolished. The Proposals were agreed by the General Council on 17 July and then put to the King. Of course the King had heard about the chaos in the capital and he again prevaricated. By now Charles was living at Hampton Court and although a prisoner he was able to enjoy a reasonably normal royal life and a measure of freedom including being able to indulge in his great love of hunting.

Fairfax being ill, it fell to Cromwell and Ireton to negotiate with the King but on 31 July he finally rejected The Heads of Proposals, hoping that he might get better terms from the Scots who had been in secret discussions with him through the Earl of Lauderdale. This was a considerable blow to Cromwell and Ireton who had made a genuine effort to give the King an honourable settlement. Matters were made worse for them because a rumour began that they were in the King's pocket. It was known that Cromwell and Ireton accompanied by their wives had dined with the King at Hampton Court and gossip had it that the relationship was so cosy that Cromwell might be bought by an earldom. Cromwell was in danger of alienating himself from the army, which was now hearing the strident demands of the Levellers. These followers of John Lilburne had produced a document called 'The Agreement of the People' and in October presented it to the General Council of the Army. In essence the Levellers regarded the senior officers of the army as 'grandees' and believed that the rank and file should formulate a political settlement without reference to the King. The Levellers also felt that they and not the Agitators were the true voice of the army. Parliament had recognized that they could trust John Lilburne 'no further than you can throw an ox' and committed him to the Tower but so strong appeared Leveller support in the army that Fairfax agreed to discuss their proposals. On 28 October the discussions began in Putney with Cromwell in the chair, as Fairfax was ill, and Colonel Rainsborough the main advocate for the Levellers demanding a new parliament and universal male suffrage. John Wildman, another Leveller, went even further, calling for the punishment of the military grandees for treating with the King and for the King himself to be impeached. The Putney Debates dragged on for several weeks of strident and extravagant demands with no prospect of accommodation until Cromwell could take no more and dismissed the delegates back to their regiments. The Debates may have allowed Levellers to let off steam but they had also given the disparate leadership the opportunity to come together as a movement. These men returned to their regiments to foment opposition to the military leadership with renewed confidence. Printed addresses were distributed to soldiers in London telling them not to trust their officers. Three regiments were won over and the Levellers began to assemble supporters at Ware in Hertfordshire.

While the army was facing this serious challenge by the Levellers, across in Ireland there was still the unfinished business of the Catholic uprising that seemed no nearer ending than when it began five long years before. After Ormonde had left Ireland he had gone to join the Queen in Paris. Parliament filled the appointment of Lord Lieutenant with Viscount Lisle, son of the Earl of Leicester. Lisle decided to gather together competent officers he could trust. When Lisle had served in Ireland in 1642/3 he had known Monck well and so he asked the permission of Parliament for him to be released from the Tower and returned to duty in Ireland. This lucky stroke of fortune for Monck was agreed on condition that he took the Covenant and a rather long oath. The oath reflected the unresolved constitutional position of the time and included preserving the right and privileges of Parliament and also 'the honour and happiness of the King's Majesty and that of his posterity'. This he did and arrived in Cork in February 1647, only to leave a few months later when Lisle was dismissed by Parliament for falling out with the powerful Earl of Inchiquin who had defected to Parliament the previous year. In the absence of a Lord Lieutenant, Michael Jones as commander of Parliamentary forces assumed the role and recalled Monck to Ireland, where he arrived in September. As well as Jones's force in Dublin, Parliament had the English settlements round Londonderry and uncertain allies in Inchiquin in Munster and Robert Munro with the remnants of his Scots in Carrickfergus. The Confederacy army of Leinster had recently been defeated by Jones but they still had Owen Roe O'Neill's army of 8,000 men who dominated Ulster and were using it as a base to attack the Pale. In short Ireland was an unstable patchwork of armed groups and shifting alliances.

Scotland was at least at peace, but with its King a prisoner of the English Parliament and no one faction of the Committee of Estates in control. These were indeed complex and confusing times with no proper government in any of the three kingdoms, let alone of Great Britain. Over a year and a half had passed since the King's surrender but still no formula had been found for re-establishing a head of state. The English Parliament had been governing the Parliamentary-controlled areas of the country during the Civil War and now did so for the whole of England. This administration was exercised through committees supported by a form of civil service reporting to a Parliament deeply divided by factions and at loggerheads with the army, the real power in the land. The one potential force for stability, the army, was itself becoming dangerously split by the Levellers who were congregating in opposition as whole regiments.

What then of intelligence at this time? About the only activity that was continuing was that of Parliament's envoys abroad sending sporadic dispatches back to Whitehall. Many of these representatives had been given generous budgets to pay informants during the Civil War and had built up a reasonable network of sources. Even this potentially good stream of intelligence became haphazard, as the envoys were more likely to write to friends of their own faction than to committees whose leadership was unclear. It would be fair to say that all the factions were scheming to strengthen their positions and find new allies. In this situation the different leaders were in effect using their own informal network of personal connections to further their ends and gain intelligence on the intentions of the other players in the political game. The army still had its scoutmasters and intelligence organization but this was for military intelligence and, as there was no longer a Royalist army, it had no immediate role.

It is interesting to note that Lionel Warson the Scoutmaster General was quite deeply involved with negotiations with the Levellers and as early as 14 July was present when the subject was being discussed at the General Council. This could indicate that Warson was merely being used as a staff officer at a time when there was little requirement for his intelligence function. Alternatively, it might have been that the Army Council had tasked Warson and his intelligencers to find out as much as possible about the Levellers movement. The latter would be an interesting case of military intelligence moving into the role of counter-subversion.

The Royalists too were scheming and trying to gain information on potential friends and definite foes. The Queen and her principal adviser Lord Jermyn were in France attached to the court of Anne of Austria who had become regent on her husband's death. From there they were able to gain a limited intelligence picture from information passed by Cardinal Mazarin, when it suited him, as well as from Royalists in England. The Queen was still able to carry out correspondence secretly with the King and in cipher. Since her illness at the time of the birth of her baby she had given up working on the cipher herself and left it to her secretary Jermyn. This task was soon delegated by urbane and idle Jermyn to a junior secretary, the poet Abraham Cowley.

In October the Queen had been joined by Prince Rupert. Far from Rupert assisting in intelligence or indeed anything else constructive, he immediately challenged Digby to a duel. The Queen forbade the duel but antagonism lingered on. Charles, Prince of Wales, was still in Jersey and Hyde was in no rush to see him joining his mother and her squabbling supporters with their half-baked schemes at a Catholic French court. Hyde for his part was also busy trying to understand and influence events through correspondence to his Royalist contacts.

As for the King, he had given his parole and was allowed a surprising amount of freedom at Hampton Court. He was able to receive visitors such as the Scottish Commissioners and even have some of his advisers and household about him. Colonel Whalley, a cousin of Cromwell, was responsible for the King's custody at Hampton Court. Whalley tried to ensure that Charles could only send or receive authorized correspondence and not speak to visitors without a reliable person to monitor the conversation. Despite this the King managed to keep up to date with both public events and secret schemes, such as discussions with the Scots to restore him if he became a Presbyterian and Mazarin's promise to the Queen of 10,000 French troops. A number of those allowed access to the King managed to pass secret information. Among those was Lady Aubigny who had been released from the Tower, gone to the Continent and had recently married Viscount Newburgh. She had decided to resume her covert activities and managed to regularly smuggle enciphered letters between the King and Queen.

Charles was also receiving other covert correspondence at Hampton Court. As Clarendon wrote: 'the King every day received little billets or letters usually coveyed to him without a name, which advised him of designes upon his life'. This all related to the Levellers and a supposed or real plot by them to murder the King. Indeed Cromwell's own sources had told him as much and he wrote to Colonel Whalley: 'Dear Cousin Walley there are rumours of some intended attempt on his Majestie's person. Therefore I pray have a care of your guards.' Whether Charles really believed these reports or merely used them as an excuse is not known but on the evening of 11 November he escaped from Hampton Court via the back stairs and through the Privy Garden to the river path. There he was met by three members of his bedchamber, Berkley, Legg and Ashburnham, who had a boat to cross the river where they had horses waiting. So far so good, but the question was where to go. Should it be Scotland and the Engagers, France and the Queen, or somewhere safe in England? On the advice of John Ashburnham the King decided to make for the Isle of Wight, which was under the governorship of Colonel Henry Hammond, a Parliamentary officer believed to have sympathies for the King. Hammond's father had been a royal chaplain and Ashburnham was sure he was a secret Royalist. On arriving at the Isle of Wight this proved to be bad intelligence. A rather embarrassed Hammond received the King with courtesy but it soon became clear to Charles that he was to be held in open arrest at Carisbrooke Castle. A more thorough assessment of Hammond would have established that, despite his father, he was a firm Parliamentarian, not least because he was married to Cromwell's cousin, the daughter of John Hampden.

The King was still able to receive visitors and swiftly sent Berkley as his representative to the Army Council at Windsor Castle. Berkley explained that His Majesty had fled Hampton Court because he feared assassination by the Levellers and now wished to reopen negotiations. This cut no ice. As far as Fairfax and the army leadership were concerned, the King had broken his parole. In the couple of weeks between Charles's escape and Berkley's visit to Windsor the Leveller threat had receded. On 15 November, Fairfax carried out a review of troops near Ware in Hertfordshire. Two regiments arrived without officers, wearing '*England's Freedoms Soldiers Rights*' in their hatbands. Fairfax made a speech promising regular pay, pensions and indemnity then snatched the manifesto from some of the Levellers' hats and arrested all the ringleaders who were court-martialled and found guilty on the spot. Pardon was then granted to all but three who where made to draw lots and the unlucky one was shot by the other two at the head of his regiment. Army parades are seldom so eventful. The soldiers loved it and with confidence that Fairfax would deliver on his promises, began shouting 'The King and Sir Thomas!' Fairfax's leadership and decisive action had done much to restore army discipline but the Leveller movement had not been completely wiped out.

Cromwell and Ireton had spent about five months trying to reach a settlement with the King and had risked their credibility with the army in doing so. In response to their efforts, Charles had peremptorily rejected the generous terms of the Heads of Proposals and then broken his parole by escaping. They both felt completely let down by the King and considered there was no point in further negotiations. They gave vent to their views by denouncing the King at the Army Council meeting on 26 November, the day before Berkley arrived as a royal emissary. This complete change in their attitude to the King had also been brought about by some intelligence through the mysterious case of the 'Saddle Letter'.

There are different accounts of the circumstances surrounding the Saddle Letter incident but they all tend to agree on the same core story. This was that Cromwell obtained intelligence from a source close to the King that a messenger carrying covert royal correspondence would stop at the Blue Boar Inn at Holborn at 10 pm on a particular night on his way to Dover. The messenger was duly arrested and found to have a letter sewn into the skirt of his saddle. The letter was from the King to the Queen saying that both the Scots and the army were competing for his support but that 'he would close with the Scots sooner than the others'. Once Cromwell read this he is reported to have said: 'finding that we were not likely to have any tolerable terms from the King, we immediately from that time, resolved his ruin'. It would seem that it was this intelligence more than the King's rejection of the Proposals or his escape that finally convinced Cromwell that Charles should be removed. If so, it was a piece of intercept intelligence that was eventually to lead to the King's execution and the creation of a republic.

Although a prisoner, the King was in an open arrest and still allowed to negotiate with both the English Parliament and the Scots Commissioners. The Scots Commissioners, the Earls of Lanark and Lauderdale backed by the Duke of Hamilton, made a secret treaty with the King on 26 December called the 'Engagement'. By this Charles agreed to introduce Presbyterianism for a trial period of three years and the Scots would invade if the English Parliament refused to return him to the throne. A copy of this secret treaty was placed in a lead box and buried in the grounds of Carisbrooke Castle. This treaty was not merely secret from the English but also from the majority of Presbyterian Scots because the provisions would be totally unacceptable to the Marquis of Argyll and the Covenanters.

The English army leadership knew nothing of the Engagement but realized from the Saddle Letter that something of the sort was afoot and Cromwell used his Scottish contacts to gain more information. In the words of Clarendon '[Cromwell] had constant intelligence from thence of the advances they made'. This intelligence is most likely to have come from Argyll and his informants. Cromwell and the Army Council knew enough for two things to become clear to them. One was that the army would have to be ready to deploy against the Scots Engagers, the other was that the King could not be trusted and a constitutional settlement would now have to be imposed upon him.

It was just three days into the new year of 1648 that Cromwell and Ireton got Parliament to agree the Vote of No Address, in which they decided to resolve the question of the country's government without reference to the King. The vote was carried with the biblical quotation 'Thou shalt not suffer a hypercritic to reign' ringing in every ear. The Committee of Both Kingdoms was dissolved and replaced by a Committee of Safety based at Derby House, which began functioning on 20 January with preparations to get onto a war footing. At last the scoutmasters had an enemy and could revert to their proper role. Perversely for an army preparing for war, 20,000 men were disbanded by the spring. This reduction was part of a deal Fairfax had made with Parliament in exchange for the granting arrears of pay. This smaller army resulted in an increase in the quality because many of those who were dismissed were Levellers and malcontents.

Colonel Hammond was holding His Majesty in close confinement and Ashburnham, Berkley and Legg were all expelled from the Isle of Wight. They did however remain at hand with horses ready, in the hope rescuing the King. News that the King was now held a complete prisoner and that Parliament had refused to deal any more with him resulted in an upsurge of public sympathy for Charles. This coincided with a number of plots Henrietta Maria was hatching for risings throughout the three kingdoms. An important element of these plans was that Charles should escape. There had already been the escape of his son, the 14-year-old James Duke of York, from St James' Palace in London. A Colonel Joseph Bampfylde had been chosen for the task. This shadowy figure was a charming, handsome 26-year-old adventurer from Devon who had joined the King's army in 1639 to fight the Scots and been given command of a Royalist regiment during the Civil War. His natural abilities lay less with military affairs than with intrigue. Somehow he came to the notice of the King who in 1642 decided that he should go to London as an agent 'to penetrate the designs of the two parties in Parliament'. Bampfylde was one of the first of a small but new category of person that had been thrown up by the Civil War. He was a professional spy. Clearly he had proved himself sufficiently in this espionage role in London to be trusted with the delicate covert operation to free Prince James.

Bampfylde engineered the prince's escape with the assistance of his mistress Anne Murray, whose mother had been a royal governess. He visited the prince to explain the plan and obtain his measurements with the aid of a ribbon. Anne had then taken the measurements to a tailor who, despite being surprised by the vital statistics, made a dark mohair dress and scarlet petticoat. The duke cleverly managed to obtain the keys to the privy garden and, having already got his captors used to him playing hide and seek, made his escape during one of these games. Bampfylde was waiting for him outside with a cloak and periwig and took him away by coach and water to a safe house near Westminster Bridge. Anne was waiting and soon dressed the duke in his new female wardrobe. Then he was whisked off by barge to Gravesend and on to the safety of France. All in all, a most satisfactory covert operation, the success of which had ensured that the Duke of York could not be turned into Parliament's puppet king.

Although Charles was under strict confinement at Carisbrooke, one of his guards named Firebrace felt compassion for him and began smuggling correspondence to and from the King when he was on duty outside his door. A crevice in the doorframe was used to hide the documents and Charles was able to pick them up when he passed through. Firebrace then became bolder and tried to arrange the King's escape. He obtained a silken cord and tied it round the bars of the King's window and then climbed down to the ground to make sure that it was safe. His Majesty attempted to follow but got so firmly stuck in the bars it was only with great difficulty that the monarchical head could be pulled back into the room. Escape would have to be deferred.

Despite additional security, Charles still managed to carry out secret communication with his wife and supporters. This was largely due to the comely young redhead, Jane Whorwood. Her stepfather had been a Groom of the Bedchamber to Charles.

She had first visited the King when he was held in Holdenby on the pretext of delivering funds from her stepfather. Although searched before seeing the King, she had still been able to deliver a letter in cipher which she deposited behind the hangings in the royal chamber. When the King was moved to Hampton Court she again visited him to bring money. She had then begun planning the King's escape with William Lilly, an eminent astrologer, but was pre-empted by Charles own escape to the Isle of Wight. Jane followed the King to Carisbrooke and, despite the restrictions, managed to get herself accepted as a regular visitor, as it was generally mistakenly assumed that she was the King's mistress. Throughout the autumn of 1648 Jane carried secret correspondence to and from the King and was constantly trying to come up with ways for his escape. Her most prominent attempt was to bring in a phial of nitric acid she had obtained from Lilly in order to weaken the bars on the King's window. This did not work and His Majesty remained behind bars.

About this time there started rumblings of discontent across the country. This was as much because of dissatisfaction with life under Parliamentary rule as in support of the Royalist cause. There had been high taxes, poor harvests and most of the fun of life had been banned, such as Christmas festivities, Sunday games, plays and maypoles. On 27 March, the anniversary of Charles's accession, there were riots in several towns and 3,000–4,000 apprentices came down Fleet Street shouting 'Now for King Charles'. In May Colonel John Poyer, Governor of Pembroke Castle, declared for the King and was supported by his garrison who were angry about disbandment and delays in pay. Poyer was joined by other officers and before long there were assorted groups totalling 8,000 men under arms. Cromwell was dispatched with five regiments and rapidly recovered Carnarvan. By early July the Royalists had been completely routed near Cardiff and Poyer had surrendered Pembroke Castle to Cromwell. Wales was subdued but there were now other Royalists to deal with.

There was a brief time in April when apprentice riots looked so grave in London that the Lord Mayor took refuge in the Tower and 3,000 men of Surrey surrounded Parliament demanding the restoration of the King. Fairfax soon restored order, only to find Kent in revolt and Rochester becoming Royalist on 22 May. The elderly Earl of Norwich arrived on the scene at the end of the month: he was declared general of the insurgents and occupied Maidstone. Altogether there was a total Royalist force of 11,000 in Kent but it was dispersed in Maidstone and several other towns. Fairfax with just 4,000 troops advanced on Maidstone where after a night of heavy fighting he defeated the 2,000 Royalists in the town. The revolt in Kent crumbled and Norwich took his small force to join the 4,000 men Sir Charles Lucas had raised in Essex. With Fairfax hot on their heels, the Royalist sought the safety of Colchester. There they defended themselves from Fairfax's besieging troops and waited for relief from the Scots.

The Duke of Hamilton had returned to Scotland and the King's favour. As the leading Engager he had promised Charles a force of 40,000 Scots in exchange for tolerance of Presbyterianism. Now his promise was put to the test. The Kirk denounced the pact with the King as a complete religious sell out. They had always insisted that Presbyterianism should be fully established in England as well as Scotland and were in no mood to compromise their souls. With this resistance the most Hamilton was able to deliver was 10,000 and that had been a very slow process. At least that number would include 3,000 Scottish veterans from Ireland who Robert Monro was arranging to send over under command of his nephew George. Sir George Monro was an officer of considerable standing who had commanded the Swedish left wing at the great battle of Lutzen. Unfortunately for Hamilton, Scotland's two foremost generals Leven and David Leslie would not join him, which, given his almost complete lack of military experience, was a major blow. He therefore turned to the Earl of Callander to be his Lieutenant General. Callander was indeed an experienced soldier but had an arrogant, inflexible manner that made him almost impossible to work with.

Meanwhile, Sir Marmaduke Langdale had raised his Northern Horse and with just 100 men surprised Berwick. The next day, Carlisle was taken for the Royalists. Langdale was now waiting impatiently for his enlarged force to be joined by Hamilton. At last Hamilton's army arrived on 8 July but the Presbyterian Scots regarded Langdale's men as Papists whom they would much prefer to fight against than alongside. At Kendal, Hamilton's army was joined by Sir George Monro with his men from Ulster. Callander refused to treat Monro as an equal and the bad blood which resulted led to Monro and his men being left behind at Kirby Lonsdale to await the arrival of artillery from Scotland. The rest of Hamilton's unhappy band made a slow advance to the Preston area. Partially because of the need to forage, Hamilton had allowed his force to spread to such an extent that there were twenty miles between Langdale in the vanguard and Monro at the rear.

In the mean time, Cromwell's force had marched from Wales with amazing speed, then joining Major General Lambert had advanced towards Preston with a combined army of 8,600. Given that Hamilton had a total force of nearly 14,000 the Royalists still had a major opportunity of victory if only their force could be concentrated. Despite the odds against him, Cromwell had decided on the daring move of crossing to the north bank of the Ribble to attack Hamilton from the rear rather than following the south bank of the river to block the Scots advance. Cromwell's movement was picked up by Langdale's scouts who brought him reports that a large Parliamentarian force was just sixteen miles away to the east at Stonyhurst. Langdale reported this back to Hamilton and Callander at Preston who discounted the report believing that Cromwell could not have covered the distance from Wales in the time and assumed Langdale had merely bumped into a group of Lancashire Roundheads. To make matters worse, Callander got Hamilton's agreement to send the cavalry forward from Preston towards Wigan, thus even further distant from the threatened attack.

At first light on 16 August Langdale's scouts captured some prisoners who said that Cromwell was no more that six miles away. Having got this confirmation of the intelligence, Langdale himself rode at once back to Hamilton at Preston. Again Hamilton refused to take note of the intelligence or even begin recalling his horse and concentrating his force as a precaution. By the time Langdale had returned to his position, Cromwell's men were on his defences. Langdale's 3,000 foot and 600 horse were completely outnumbered by Cromwell who had achieved a local three to one superiority of numbers despite an overall numerical disadvantage of two to one. After six hours of heavy fighting Langdale began a retreat that turned into a rout, with most of the Royalist army still south of the River Ribble not having taken any part in the action. Langdale's force was almost totally destroyed except for some horse, which went north hoping to link up with Monro.

The news of the surprise defeat hit the spirit of the Royalist army, which was already demoralized by lack of food, supplies and ammunition. Hamilton at last realized he must concentrate his force and distance himself from Cromwell by heading south. Callander's plan for this was a complex night-time manoeuvre in the pouring rain which fell apart and soon deteriorated into a disorganized fighting retreat. The running battle took place over three days, with the tired and dispirited Royalist taking ever more casualties. Hamilton decided to save the remnants of the horse and left the infantry to surrender at Warrington. Of the three main Royalist leaders, Hamilton was obliged to surrender at Uttoxeter and later executed, Langdale was captured in Nottingham and Callander escaped to the Continent. About 3,000 Scots had been killed and 10,000 prisoners taken. The vital intervention of the Scots for the royal cause had been squandered because of a commander's refusal to believe confirmed intelligence. Once news of the defeat reached Scotland, Argyll and the Covenanters swung once again into the ascendancy. They invited Cromwell to Edinburgh where he stayed sufficient time to assure himself that Argyll was a true partner and that the Covenanters were in reasonable control of Scotland.

The great victory at Preston had been achieved by Cromwell's brilliant manoeuvring of a well-trained and motivated force against an ill-equipped and disunited Royalist army under incompetent leadership. As we have seen, intelligence failure was a significant factor in the Royalist defeat but some credit for victory must be given to the success of Parliamentary intelligence. After receiving the surrender of Pembroke Castle on 11 July, Cromwell began his remarkable march to intercept Hamilton's invading Scots. He had taken a circuitous route, going eastwards as far as Leicester then on to Doncaster where he joined up with artillery and supplies from Hull before uniting with John Lambert. All this time he was maintaining contact with Lambert who was harassing the Royalist advance and thus able to have a reasonable idea of Hamilton's location. From there on Cromwell sent scouts probing into the Ribble Valley until they located Langdale's force and established that it was separated from the main Royalist army. It was Cromwell's good intelligence on the disposition and strength of the Royalist army that led him to concentrate his troops at the decisive point and so win numerical superiority. All this could only have occurred as a result of good scouting and this is much to the credit to Cromwell's scoutmaster, Major Sanderson. History records tantalizingly little about this officer other than in some intelligence accounts which show that he paid spies such as Thomas Gooley 5 shillings a day for 'going into the enemies quarters near Berwick' after the town's capture and others as much as 12 shillings for observing enemy strengths. What we may conclude was that his professionalism assisted Cromwell in achieving his first major victory as a commanding general.

The defeat of Hamilton was a body blow to the Royalists at Colchester. Norwich and the other leaders surrendered to Fairfax after a siege from mid-June to the end of August in which the besieged had been reduced to eating cats and rats. The land battle was over but there was still some unfinished business. On 27 May the Downs Squadron at Deal had revolted and declared for the King. This was mainly because they did not wish to serve under the radical Colonel Thomas Rainsborough whom Parliament had appointed Admiral to replace the Earl of Warwick. Six men-of-war from Deal sailed under command of William Bratton to Holland with the intention of putting themselves under the command of James Duke of York.

When Henrietta Maria heard of this she called for Charles Prince of Wales to go to Holland and take command. This he did, accompanied by Prince Rupert and Lords Hopton and Colepeper, each of whom heartily detested the others. The constant wrangling and opposing advice of these three was to bedevil planning throughout the expedition. Having obtained the loan of some Dutch vessels, a fleet of nineteen ships was assembled. Prince Charles sailed to the south coast of England unopposed but did not decide to do the obvious and go to the Isle of Wight to rescue his father. This was because he was carrying out negotiations with the Engager's representative Lauderdale with a view to then linking up with Hamilton and his Scots army. Charles then sailed to the mouth of the Thames and began correspondence with the City about opening their gates but managed to alienate them by demanding exorbitant ransom for merchantmen he had captured. Parliament had realized its mistake and reappointed Warwick but his small squadron was blockaded in the Thames by the Royalist fleet.

Time passed in discussions with Lauderdale, who was demanding among other things that Charles rid himself of Rupert, who responded by threatening to throw Lauderdale over the side. Meanwhile, Warwick received reinforcements from Portsmouth to defend London and the Thames. The Royalist fleet could have attacked earlier but the moment had passed, Having then heard of the defeat at Preston, Charles decided to sail back to Holland. The whole naval operation was a missed opportunity for the Royalists who might have persuaded London to declare for the King or at the very least rescued Charles. Instead they seem to have been paralysed by indecision resulting from severe factional and religious disagreement. To cap it all, Warwick followed the royal fleet back to Holland and managed to persuade Bratton and several of his rebel ships to return under his command.

The Second Civil War had led to large numbers of armed bodies appearing in different parts of England, Scotland and Wales to support the King. Even an important element of the navy had changed allegiance. This was a very testing time for the army and the Independents, especially as Holles and the Presbyterian faction in Parliament could make mischief with the King while they were distracted by operations. This Royalist opportunity was wasted by an inept and squabbling leadership. When we compare the military professionalism of Fairfax and Cromwell with Hamilton and Norwich we see now that the enterprise was doomed, but it might otherwise have been a close-run thing.

A small contributory factor to the success was the effective intelligence of the New Model Army which was able to keep the General Council pretty well informed of the enemy situation across Great Britain. It is also likely that intelligencers had gained quite a reasonable knowledge of some of the Royalist plans. As Hyde wrote: 'The Parliament had too many spies and agents in Paris not to be informed of whatsoever was conspired there.' Also those Royalists sent to England by Henrietta Maria and Jermyn were well-known figures, far from discreet and were easily identifiable. Typical was the Earl of Holland who was distributing Royalist commissions in London before the uprising with little secrecy. He almost definitely came to the attention of Parliamentary intelligencers but being the brother of the Earl of Warwick was not arrested.

Although the Royalists had lost the Second Civil War in major engagements some mopping-up operations were required to completely restore peace. Isolated pockets of Royalist resistance held out for some time with bravery and determination. One such example is that of Sir William Compton, third son of the Earl of Northampton, who bravely withstood a thirteen-week siege at Banbury until the end of August. Another case was that of Woodcroft House in Hampshire. This was defended by the Reverend Michael Hudson and former Scoutmaster General to the Northern Army. After he had escorted the King to Newark to surrender to the Scots, he tried to escape to France but was arrested at the Channel ports. He then succeeded in escaping again but was finally captured and sent to the Tower. This resourceful intelligencer later managed to escape from the Tower disguised as a tradesman with a basket of apples on his head and then made his way to Lincolnshire to raise support for the King.

When the Royalist uprising occurred, Hudson was given command of Woodcroft House with the commission of a colonel. Woodcroft was besieged and when the door was eventually broken down, Hudson continued the defence from the battlements. In the fighting he was thrown off the roof but managed to save himself by catching hold of a gutter. The attackers then cut off his hands and he fell into the moat. Parliamentary soldiers dragged him from the moat and bludgeoned him to death with muskets and then cut out his tongue to take away as a trophy. He had lost his life and estate in the service of the crown and his wife and family were left to exist on charity. Hudson was one of several members of the clergy who became good intelligencers but he is their finest representative of the church militant.

There was also some Parliamentary mopping up to do in Ireland to punish Robert Munro for sending his nephew George and the majority of his troops to join the Duke of Hamilton. The war now won, Parliament sent orders for all Royalist sympathizers in the army of Ireland to be arrested. Monck found that some Scots officers had a grudge against their commander Robert Munro and so with their help gained information of his whereabouts. With this intelligence Monck was able to surprise Munro still in bed in Carrickfergus and send him under arrest to England and the Tower. Thanks to his effective use of intelligence, Monck had rehabilitated himself and his military career was back on track. A thankful Parliament made Monck governor of Belfast. The island of Ireland was still largely in rebel Catholic hands but at least all government Protestant forces were now loyal to Parliament.

While the uprising had been taking place Charles remained a prisoner in the Isle of Wight, still hoping to escape or be rescued. One incident helped to relieve his frustrating period of confinement. Colonel Hammond had appointed a reliable man called Osborne as gentleman usher to the King but as time went by he succumbed to Charles's charm. One of his tasks was to hold the King's gloves at meals and he decided to communicate with His Majesty secretly by placing notes in the finger of the gloves. For a time he was able to supply the King with information about the situation on the uprising and then he was able to warn him of an assassination plot. Osborne had heard a rumour that a Captain Rolf, an officer of the guard appointed by Cromwell, was planning to remove the King from Carisbrooke Castle and kill him. It was unlikely that there was any truth in the story but both Osborne and the King believed it. Another escape plan was made. Charles sawed through his window bars in readiness. Unfortunately for Charles, one of the soldiers betrayed Osborne to Rolf who informed Hammond. On the night planned for the escape he looked through his window and saw unusual activity so went straight to the bedroom where Charles was found together with the insecure window. The only positive result was that Osborne escaped and lived to tell the tale.

Just as it appeared that the Royalists had been dealt a final blow, they returned as a problem in Ireland. In February 1648 Ormonde had joined the Queen's court in Paris. In August he was commissioned by the Queen to return to Ireland and the next month arrived in Cork where he was welcomed by Lord Inchiquin who had become suspicious of the Independents in Parliament and switched back to being a Royalist. Ormonde then set about mobilizing both Protestants and Catholics to the King's cause. Had Ormonde been sent earlier, his operations would have coincided with the Royalist uprisings on the mainland and might have had a positive influence on their outcome. As it was, for the time being, this was just a military sideshow and there were more pressing matters to engage the attention of the army leadership.

With the leading Independents such as Ireton and Cromwell still far from London, the Presbyterian members of the Commons under Holles decided to again open negotiations with the King in September. This was anathema to the Independents but the army was still deployed completing the mopping up and they could do little to impose their will. These negotiations took place at Newport in the Isle of Wight and the King was again allowed more freedom and to have access to advisers such as the Duke of Richmond. Despite endless entreaties over a period of two months, the King would still not give any ground. As usual he was playing for time, trying to make secret deals with the French, Scots and Irish though his advisers, who were also busying themselves with schemes for his escape. He was also able to maintain secret correspondence with the Queen using a new cipher devised by Abraham Cowley. In late November, just as the negotiations with Parliament were about to break up, Charles suddenly conceded all the main demands such as the abolition of the episcopate and the loss of command of the army. He did this because he knew that time was at last running out as the army was moving back to London and the Independents were now openly calling him 'that man of blood' and demanding he be brought to trial. He had left it too late. Cromwell ordered the King to be put in close custody and transferred to the dank austerity of Hurst Castle at the end of a bleak shingle headland on the Solent.

For the Presbyterians too time was running out. On 1 December the House of Commons listened with favour to Holles's proposal that the Newport Agreement with the King should be accepted. The debate was long and a vote was postponed till 4 December. By that time Fairfax had arrived and quartered his men in and around Westminster and Cromwell and Vane put the case to the Commons against treating with the King. Nevertheless the Presbyterians won the vote with a majority of forty-six. Two days later on 6 December Colonel Pride's infantry replaced Skippon's trained bands guarding the two Houses of Parliament. Pride himself stood by the door of the Commons with Lord Grey of Groby, who had a list of Presbyterian members, and arrested fifty-two of them as they arrived to take their seats. The next day the same happened, by which time a total of forty-seven members had been imprisoned and ninety-five excluded or fled, among them Sir Samuel Luke. The Independents could now continue Parliamentary proceedings without the inconvenience of opposition. This purged House of Commons, soon to be called the 'Rump', immediately voted to declare the Newport Agreement monstrous and invalid. The depleted House of Lords passed the motion the same day.

The Independents now decided to bring the King to Windsor and a strong party of horse was dispatched to Hurst Castle under a richly dressed officer adorned in scarlet and gold lace. What appeared to be a Cavalier fop was none other than Colonel Thomas Harrison, a veteran of Edgehill and Marston Moor, who had been elected to Parliament in 1646. Despite his love of fine clothes Harrison was a Puritan of the most austere sort who would later become the leader of one of the most extreme sects, the Fifth Monarchist Movement. The choice of the grim, uncompromising Harrison to escort the King did not bode well. Things were looking desperate for the King and escape was now a vital necessity. Lady Newburgh (formerly Lady Aubigny) and her husband had managed to maintain secret correspondence with the King and arranged a plan for him to escape during his journey to Windsor. The plan was for Charles to say that his horse was lame and ask to stop at the Newport's home, Bagshott Lodge. Once there, Lord Newburgh had arranged to have very fast horses for the King and his immediate attendants to make their escape. Other fast horses were placed further along the route so that Harrison and his men would be unable to catch them. Charles agreed to the plan and as he approached Bagshott told Colonel Harrison that his horse was lame. Harrison merely provided another horse but allowed the King to stop for lunch at Bagshott Lodge. After lunch, Harrison made a pointed remark that the King's party now seemed to be mounted on exceptionally fine horses and Charles decided that it was too risky to try to escape. There had been little prospect of success for this plan but it was to be the last desperate hope for the King's freedom. Charles was duly delivered to Windsor then the next day taken to St James' Palace.

For a Puritan, Christmas Day was not of course a time of holiday or celebrations and so a routine Army Council met on 25 December. As it happened, the discussion was far from routine, for Ireton began stating what so many of the Council had felt for some time. He proposed that the King, whom he described as the 'capital enemy', should be brought to 'speedy justice'. The next day Cromwell rose in the Commons and called for the King to be tried. The House responded with general approval. Many of the MPs supporting the idea of a trial would have had no real notion of the consequences that would stem from the unstoppable chain of events that now took place. The logical conclusion was inescapable. There was no point in putting the King on trial unless he was to be found guilty. If he was found guilty, the only safe course was his execution. As no heir to the King would ever forgive those who had caused the execution, this would mean an end to monarchy. Without a monarchy England would become a Republic for the first time in history, with no precedent to show where that might lead.

Events now accelerated, forced on by Ireton and Cromwell who knew they must act quickly and decisively to achieve the necessary outcome. On 28 December the Commons read an ordinance establishing a special court to try the King consisting of 135 commissioners who would act as both judge and jury. This was passed on 1 January. On 6 January the Commons made themselves the supreme power in the country by Act of Parliament and the decision was made to charge the King with treason. On 10 January an obscure but compliant judge was dredged up and appointed President of the Court. It was John Bradshaw, the Chief Justice of Cheshire. The venue decided upon for the court was Westminster Hall, where both Edward II and Richard II had been brought to trial. With everything in place, all that remained was to keep pressure on the commissioners to ensure that as many as possible would turn up and do what Cromwell regarded as their duty

On 20 January Charles appeared before the court. The King conducted himself with dignity and presented a clear and cogent defence without any sign of his usual stammer. The obvious illegality of his trial weighed little against the outcome that was required and Bradshaw sentenced him to death and the warrant was signed. On 30 January the King, still in perfect composure, made a short address to the group about him on his scaffold outside the Banqueting House. A few moments later, the executioner raised his severed head and a great groan rippled across the awestruck onlookers.

In Charles's address he had said that he 'died a martyr to the people' and he was going 'from a corruptible crown to an incorruptible'. There is no way of telling whether he was correct on the last point but we may be certain that was what he fervently believed. Charles lost both his crown and his life and historians have tended to brand him as a failure who brought about his own downfall by refusing to compromise. However, it is hard to see how any monarch would have accepted the demands made by Parliament. Would Queen Elizabeth I have agreed to hand over control of the militia or have her ministers selected by Parliament? Charles had to take a stand and in doing so found himself in a civil war which he had little chance of winning without the manpower, money, resources and government structure provided by London. However good his generals and supporting elements such as intelligence, there was no real chance of winning unless the Parliamentary leadership fell out and so failed to bring their superior forces to bear. They nearly did, but then the creation of the New Model Army under Fairfax and Cromwell ended that possibility. As for his years of imprisonment, Charles again had little option but to play for time in the hope that his opponents would fall out. Again they nearly did, but Cromwell's determination and standing in the army brought the protracted negotiations with the King to an abrupt end. Had Charles's delaying tactics succeeded then he would have been regarded as an astute politician but they did not and he is often dismissed as a bigot.

The King should at least be given credit for upholding what he and many others believed in. As a direct result of Charles not compromising on his regal rights, it meant that his son eventually returned to the throne with all the traditional powers of the monarchy intact. Charles did indeed die a martyr. He was not a martyr to the people but to the traditional powers of kingship. Today we may see Charles as a major obstacle in the advance towards parliamentary democracy but he saw himself as the custodian of the powers of kingship held under divine authority. His bravery in refusing to compromise his beliefs should at least make him a deserving contender for a crown incorruptible.

It remains to consider the impact of intelligence in the outcome of the Civil War. It must first be stated that wars are won when one contestant ceases to offer any significant armed opposition to the other either because they have accepted surrender or their forces have been destroyed. This in turn is brought about as a result of the accumulated outcome of different engagements on battlefields and at defensive positions such as fortified towns, castles or great houses. The results of these engagements are determined by many important factors such as the numerical size of the forces, their levels of experience, training and morale, together with their quality and quantity of weapons, equipment and supplies. Among those important factors are the strategy and tactics used by the commanders. War-winning strategy and battle-winning tactics are the product of the flair and professionalism of military leaders but this successful decision-making usually depends on an accurate knowledge of the enemy's disposition, strengths and weaknesses – on intelligence.

Good intelligence cannot itself determine the outcome of a war but it may well bring about the decisions of the general that create battle-winning tactics, as was the case at Preston. Unfortunately there were many occasions when squabbling among leaders led to in bad military decisions, such as the King's decision to fight at

Naseby without waiting for reinforcements, which had more impact on events than any amount of good intelligence. It should also be noted that security is the other side of the coin to intelligence and that one antagonist's security failure can be the other's intelligence success. Also that security failure can also seriously undermine morale. This could not have been demonstrated better than by the capture of the King's correspondence after Naseby which proved that Charles was plotting to use Irish Catholics and foreign Catholic powers to invade England. The effect of this security failure was to dismay the King's supporters, encourage his enemies and lose him the waiverers.

As has been seen, intelligence played an important part in many of the major events in the Civil War but it was not so important that it affected the outcome. Its real significance was that throughout the war both sides had a growing awareness of the value of intelligence in both military and political planning and also the importance of security in preventing those plans falling into hostile hands. As a result scouts and agents were brought into use, letters were intercepted, ciphers broken and the intelligence process began to be given a structure. Perhaps most important of all was a general realization that information was a commodity which could be sold at a price to an intelligencer. All this provided the foundation on which a great intelligence structure would be built which would became the lynch pin of Commonwealth success.

Chapter 6

Dawn of a Republic, 1649–1651

It might have seemed that the army command had engineered the creation of a republic but that was not so. Fairfax, the Lord General, had not been involved in Pride's purge and had withdrawn as a commissioner for the King's trial. In fact his wife, Lady Fairfax, had even shouted from the public gallery during the trial 'Oliver Cromwell is a traitor!' She was not far from the mark. The bewildering pace of events leading to the trial and intense pressure for a guilty verdict had been the work of a small group led by Cromwell and Ireton. Now that they had achieved their end, they maintained the momentum, with Ireton busying himself drafting a constitution for a republic.

Fairfax had become rather marginalized and decided to return to his estate at Nun Appleton. He remained Lord General but had left the way open for Ireton and Cromwell to proceed as they pleased. On 6 February the Commons voted to disband the House of Lords of which Fairfax was a member, having inherited his father's title the previous year. The next day they abolished the monarchy. On 14 February a Council of State was elected by the Commons to run the country. This was presided over in the first instance by John Bradshaw, the man who had sentenced the King to death. It included those who had engineered the trial such as Cromwell, Ireton, Vane and the zealous Thomas Scot, MP for Aylesbury. New judges were appointed, a new great seal made for the 'Commonwealth of England and Free State' and new coinage minted with the motto 'God with us'. In no time at all the machinery of government for a republic was in place, together with its appropriate Commonwealth trappings.

The Scots were less than happy. No one had consulted them about bringing their King to trial, let alone executing him. In Edinburgh on 5 February Prince Charles was proclaimed King of Scotland. Lady Newburgh and her husband had escaped abroad after their abortive attempt at the King's escape and had now joined his heir in Holland. We know tantalizingly little about Lady Newburgh's covert operations but can assume they were many from Clarendon's description of her as 'A woman of very great wit, and most trusted in those intrigues which at that time could be best managed and carried out by ladies.' Sadly she was soon to die but one of her final known acts was to establish covert correspondence with Lanark who had succeeded his executed brother as Duke of Hamilton. As a result, four Scottish commissioners were sent to The Hague to negotiate with Charles about returning as King of Scotland on condition that he took the Covenant and imposed Presbyterianism on the three kingdoms. Montrose, who had also joined Charles, persuaded him not to agree to the Covenant being enforced anywhere other than in Scotland.

Fierce quarrels took place between the supporters of Montrose and the Covenanters on how to proceed in Scotland. Matters were not helped when a group of Montrose's supporters assassinated Dr Dorislaus, the English Parliament's representative to Holland, while he was quietly having supper. Dr Dorislaus was a Dutchman who had served as judge advocate in Essex's army and so was the natural choice as the Commonwealth's representative in Holland, charged with gathering intelligence on the Royalists and making an alliance with the United Provinces. As soon as his presence was known, the poor man became a sitting duck for Royalist reprisals and so only lasted a matter of days in the post. What had been for many Cavaliers an amusing and thoroughly justified escapade was seen in a different light by the Dutch authorities. They made it clear that such behaviour was unacceptable on their soil. So cold became their relations that Charles felt obliged to move his small court to join the Queen in Paris. Just before leaving, Charles informed the Covenanter Commissioners that he rejected their terms. They returned very irritated to Scotland.

In Ireland there had also been strong condemnation of the King's execution. This had swelled support for Ormonde, who had already strengthened his position by making peace with the Catholic Confederacy of Kilkenny in January. Ormonde proclaimed Charles II as King and expected to obtain the support of both Jones in Dublin and Monck in Belfast. Both declined, saying that they took their orders from Parliament, but neither was in a strong position. Inchiquin and Ormonde's Royalists dominated all Munster and Leinster outside Dublin. The other Parliamentary base of Londonderry was surrounded by forces under O'Neill who had an army of 7,000 in Ulster which was also a threat to Monck in Belfast. The latter was having other problems, with many of his Scots troops refusing to support the Parliament that had executed their king. On top of everything, the Parliamentary commanders were short of the pay and supplies needed to hold their forces together. If Ormonde could come to an agreement with O'Neill and launch a joint attack on Dublin, Ireland might well become Royalist. The Irish problem was getting steadily worse.

On the Continent the picture was more encouraging for Parliament. It might have been expected that every crowned head would be straining for revenge against the English Parliament for the execution of one of their number; but no. The rulers of Europe were all preoccupied. France was busy with its war with Spain and Spain was more interested in maintaining trade with England than rocking the boat. The various princes of Germany were focused entirely upon recovering from the devastation of the Thirty Years' War, which had only ended the previous year. The United Provinces, being a republic, was sympathetic and any Royalist influence that might have been exerted by William II of Orange as Stadtholder was lost because he had fallen out with the Regents in Amsterdam.

Before long even those rulers to whom republicanism was anathema were happy to support Parliamentary finances by buying up King Charles's belongings at bargain prices. Queen Christina of Sweden bought pictures and jewels as did Arch Duke Leopold of Flanders. Don Alfonso de Cardinas, the Spanish Ambassador in London, bought so many pictures that it took eighteen mules to transport them from Corunna to Madrid. Even Mazarin, the host of Henrietta Maria, bought carpets and bed-hangings for his own Paris palace. Foreign intervention was not therefore an immediate problem for the English Council of State but clearly action would have to be taken about Ireland. Before this, a more immediate problem would have to be resolved and it came not from Royalists at all.

The Levellers should have been delighted to have seen the removal of the monarchy, but extremists are seldom satisfied. The Levellers now regarded Cromwell as a usurper of kingship and therefore no better than a king himself. In April a small army mutiny occurred in London when troops refused to serve in Ireland until various demands were met. This was put down by both Cromwell and Fairfax, who had returned to command. The Levellers were able to capitalize on the general discontent within much of the army after a hard winter and with many soldiers still not in receipt of their back pay. Lilburne was writing inflammatory documents such as *England's New Chains Discovered* and his supporters began trying to widen their support by appealing to the rural poor.

The Levellers and their associates were soon to learn that Fairfax and Cromwell had few qualms about dealing with indiscipline. Lilburne and other leaders were put in the Tower and there were public punishments in the Palace Yard of Westminster. This backfired and the punished soldiers were treated as heroes by the populace. Leveller mutinies then began flaring up in Oxfordshire, Gloucestershire and Wiltshire. Cromwell and Fairfax marched rapidly towards Salisbury where 1,200 mutineers had gathered, then pursued them to Burford, where they took them prisoner. On 17 May three of the Levellers were executed in Burford churchyard and the remainder pardoned. Fairfax with his usual flair for leadership then issued a declaration saying that most of their military grievances were being met and won their agreement to serve in Ireland. The other mutineers soon surrendered but it took till about September before the Leveller movement appeared under control.

During this period military intelligence was of paramount importance to Fairfax and Cromwell, both in understanding the causes of mutiny and in locating the main bodies of mutineers. Scouts were again being used to obtain the necessary tactical intelligence to neutralize individual mutinous regiments. An example of this was Colonel Reynolds at Banbury who had two-thirds of his regiment go over to the Levellers led by Thompson, one of his captains. Reynolds attacked Thompson and not only put him to flight but managed to rally much of his regiment. The job was not complete because a Lieutenant Rowley had escaped into hiding with the remaining rebel horse. Reynolds went south to deal with Rowley and was able eventually to locate him through his scouts, with the result that these Levellers were all killed or captured.

The Leveller threat had made it clear to the Council of State that high-quality intelligence was essential to identify and counter the threats being posed to the fledgling Republic. They decided to appoint a head of intelligence and selected a senior member of the Council for this important position. On 1 July Thomas Scot was appointed, in the words of the *Commons Journals*, 'to manage the intelligence both at home and abroad for the state'. A few days later he was allocated £800 a year for the task. Scot was a lawyer from Buckingham who had been an ardent supporter of the Parliamentary cause. He had been one of the first MPs to demand the King's trial, had worked closely with the small group of Cromwell, Ireton, Harrison and Vane who engineered its outcome, and like them had signed the death warrant. It was Scot who had given orders for Archbishop Parker's body to be removed from its grave and thrown on a dunghill. With such credentials his loyalty to the Republic was unquestionable. He was already a prominent member of the Council of State, and sometimes even referred to as 'Secretary of State' for the Commonwealth. With his natural ardour, strong political power base and funds of £800 a year, Scot seemed in an excellent position to direct the Commonwealth intelligence effort. Balanced against this, he had no intelligence experience himself and would have to set up an effective intelligence apparatus virtually from scratch. The Council did give Scot one useful starting point and that was oversight of the Committee of Examination chaired by John Bradshaw. This was responsible for examining witnesses and suspects and therefore a most valuable source of intelligence. In the months ahead Scot would work with energy and dedication to find other key sources of relevant information to create an intelligence organization worthy of the Commonwealth.

Leaving Scot to get on with recruiting suitable staff and deciding how to go about intelligence collection, the Council of State's attention was firmly fixed on Ireland. Cromwell had been made Lord Lieutenant of Ireland and with the Levellers under control could at last leave in July to take up his appointment. By this time Ormonde had an army of 13,000, consisting of Catholics of the Kilkenny Confederation, Lord Inchiquin's Munster O'Briens and some of Monro's Presbyterian Scottish army. In addition Ormonde was attempting to negotiate a truce with O'Neill, leader of the Catholics in Ulster and Connaught, in exchange for religious toleration. Monck had been obliged to abandon Belfast and base himself at Dundalk. He knew that Cromwell would soon be coming with a large English force but thought he might arrive too late. He decided to make his own three-month truce with O'Neill in the hope of buying time. He then wrote to Cromwell in England as the newly appointed Lord Lieutenant explaining what he had done. Cromwell was privately pleased by the move but the Council of State was furious. Meanwhile Inchiquin had captured Drogheda and then laid siege to Dundalk. Monck could not hold the town without support and so surrendered and was granted safe passage to England. There he travelled first to Cromwell, preparing his army for embarkation at Milford Haven, then on to London and a very unhappy Council of State. The Council decided that Monck should be called to answer for his actions at the bar of the House of Commons and Thomas Scot was given the task of preparing the evidence against him.

While a disgraced Monck was getting ready to defend himself and Cromwell was embarking his army to sail for Ireland, Ormonde had begun to lay siege to Michael Jones in Dublin. Jones had 5,000 men, Ormonde had an army of 19,000. Ormonde was no great general but had used his diplomatic skills to bring together a formidable force. This was to be his zenith. On 2 August Jones made a sally from Dublin an hour before sunrise which caught Ormonde's army completely by surprise at Rathmines. The Royalists fled in confusion, leaving behind 4,000 dead, 2,000 prisoners and all the artillery and baggage. Dublin had been saved and Ormonde's depleted army had to retreat to regroup and lick its wounds. Once the news of the Rathmines victory reached London, Parliament was in a joyous and generous mood. Monck was merely reprimanded and went off to Devonshire to take over the family estate which he had inherited after his brother's death. To all appearance his military career seemed at an end and he would have to content himself with country pursuits. In the time it had taken Cromwell to complete his sea journey to Dublin, the Royalist field army had received a severe setback that had lost its momentum and initiative. Jones had proved himself an outstanding general and the morale of government troops in Ireland was now sky high. The astounding victory of Rathmines was proof positive that God was on their side.

Cromwell and Michael Jones were not the only able generals in Ireland in August 1649. There was also Prince Rupert but he had turned admiral and led his seven ships into Kinsale harbour some months before to use as a base to attack Parliamentary shipping. Parliament deployed a naval force to counter this threat, while at the same time keeping a fleet to guard the Channel. Colonel Blake, one of the three newly appointed generals-at-sea to replace Warwick, took a squadron to blockade Rupert's force in Kinsale. There Rupert would remain till the end of the year when he managed to give Blake the slip and sailed to Portugal as a new base to attack government shipping. However, for now, with other Parliamentary squadrons patrolling to the north and offshore from Dublin, the Royalist naval threat in Ireland had been neutralized. Cromwell could concentrate on the main purpose of his expedition: to completely subdue the Catholics and at last avenge the massacres of 1641.

Before departing for Ireland, Cromwell had been meticulous in his preparations. The operation was a major logistic exercise requiring 130 ships to be enlisted to transport 12,000 troops, 9,000 horses, 56 cannon, 6,000 bags of powder. The procurement and assembly of the rations and equipment for this force was in itself a major undertaking. Cromwell had also been diligent in building up his intelligence and covert capabilities. In June he had managed to intercept Lord Broghill, a younger son of the Catholic Earl of Cork as he came through London on his way to France to obtain a commission from Charles. He persuaded Broghill to change sides and become his Master of Ordnance in Ireland. He also exacted agreement that Broghill would get his tenants in Munster to desert to Parliament, but not until the right moment.

Cromwell obtained a large intelligence fund to take with him. He knew that, in a country with so many clan rivalries, money could well be an important way of swaying allegiances. He began almost at once to start offering bribes to the Munster ports. It was Cromwell's plan to secure the ports on the east coast from Drogheda in the north to Cork in the south. As it turned out the intelligence fund was hardly necessary because Cromwell was to gain his objectives not by stealth or covert activity but by sheer military terror.

As soon as Ireton and the main body of the army had arrived, Cromwell advanced on Drogheda. On 10 September he began bombardment but the governor Sir Arthur Aston refused to surrender. The following day a breach was made but was repulsed. Cromwell led the next attack in person and the town was stormed. The order 'no quarter' was given, although most of the garrison had surrendered: 3,500 soldiers and civilians were killed and Aston was clubbed to death with his wooden leg. The only clemency was that thirty soldiers were spared so that they could be sold as slaves in Barbados. For Cromwell this was divine retribution on the Papists. As he says in one of his own letters: 'A righteous judgement of God upon those barbarous wretches, who have imbued their hands in so much innocent blood.' Colonel Venables was sent to Ulster and Cromwell advanced on Wexford via Dublin burning villages on the way. On 2 October Wexford was called to surrender but the governor refused. Two of Inchiquin's regiments deserted and took the nearby garrison of Youghal for Cromwell. After further bombardment surrender was agreed but once again the 'no quarter' order was given. The whole garrison of 2,000 was killed, together with many hundreds of civilians. Cromwell's 'shock and awe' tactics at last began to take effect and when his army arrived at New Ross two weeks later, the garrison surrendered and was allowed to march away. Cromwell's force was by now tired, depleted with illness and short of rations. He decided not to advance further, being in no condition to tackle Waterford, but Cromwell was still able to continue his campaign through his secret arrangement with Lord Broghill.

Broghill sailed from Bristol to Wexford in October then on to Munster where he raised 1,500 troops from his family estates then linked up with some of Inchiquin's Royalist troops under a Colonel Townsend near Cork. Broghill persuaded Townsend to defect to Parliament and, with the help of two other like-minded colonels of Inchiquin in the Cork garrison, took possession of the town. Soon after other Munster towns followed, including Kinsale. Cromwell was then able to take his force to Cork for winter quartering and the opportunity to reflect on his progress. With the exception of Waterford, he had virtually achieved his first strategic objective. In addition, Coleraine and Carrickfergus had also been taken. Balanced against this, Ormonde's remnant force had now been joined by O'Neill in Kilkenny with 2,000 troops. Also there was all the rest of Catholic Ireland yet to subdue, before an attempt could even be made to govern a people who had previously always proved ungovernable. By 29 January Cromwell was in the field again, marching into Tipperary, and on 28 March had taken Kilkenny. In early April, Clonmel had fallen to him but this was as far as he would go. The Council of State now requested his urgent return to England because of a new crisis. Ireton was appointed Lord Deputy and left to complete the work and, as Michael Jones was one of those who had died of sickness during the winter, Edmund Ludlow was made acting commander-in-chief.

The crisis was Scotland. As Cromwell was crushing Royalist hopes in Ireland, Charles had been trying to improve his fortunes through Scotland. The Council of State had been well aware of this from the start because of the excellent intelligence they had been receiving from Walter Strickland, the Parliamentary envoy in Amsterdam. A typical and very accurate report, as early as October the previous year, was:

> Montrose hopes to raise a thousand horse and three thousand foot, and with them visit his countrymen. My Lord Kinnoul who is well known in England, I hear, is gone to take possession of some island in Scotland … there is in Amsterdam a ship in which arms and ammunition bound for Scotland for the use of Montrose as I am informed. If there be any in Scotland who desire such information, it is well they knew it. It is to be sent to some of the Isles, some say the Orkades … Montrose is expected in Hamburg.

Montrose had indeed raised and dispatched a fleet, much of which had been wrecked or scattered in gales. In December they finally landed in the Orkneys with just 400 men – mainly Danish infantry. In March the next year Montrose joined this bridgehead in the Orkneys, having been scouring Europe for recruits, arms and funding. The next month he crossed to the mainland after increasing his force by 1,000 Orkney levies. He then advanced to Carbisdale on Dornoch Firth where he camped in an entrenched hilltop position. David Leslie at Inverness had already begun moving his 4,000 force north against Montrose and sent a forward column of 250 experienced men under Colonel Strachen to harass the Royalists till his main body arrived. By the afternoon of 27 April, Strachen had reached a wooded area just four miles from Carbisdale and his scouts had begun reconnoitring Montrose's position.

Robert Monroe of Achness and his three sons were Montrose's scoutmasters and they reported back to the Marquis that there was only a single troop of Covenanter horse in the area. Montrose then sent Major Lisle, an English Royalist, to conduct further reconnaissance with his cavalry and he too reported back that there was only one troop of enemy horse. For reasons that will always remain unclear, Montrose now ordered his whole army to advance from the safety of their entrenched position down the hill to face what was thought to be small body of enemy. Lisle and his cavalry then attacked Strachan's forward troops who pulled back with Lisle's few men in pursuit. Strachan then charged with a hundred horse into the unsuspecting Lisle, whose men immediately fled back, riding into their own infantry. The shock of Stachan's charge so terrified the inexperienced Orkney levies that they fled. It was thought that these extra troops were the main body of Leslie's army which was in fact still at Brechin. Montrose ordered a withdrawal, which turned into a rout when he was wounded and his horse was killed under him. The outcome of the battle was decided in minutes but the slaughter continued for hours.

Montrose only managed to make his escape by swimming a river and eventually making his way alone to the mountains of Sutherland disguised as a peasant. There he reached the safety of the house of one of his former officers, Macleod of Assynt. While Montrose was resting his host decided to capitalize on the situation and betrayed him to the Covenanters for £10,000. Montrose was arrested and taken to Edinburgh where Argyll had much pleasure avenging the burning of Inveraray by ensuring he was sentenced to a traitor's execution. On 21 May Montrose was hanged on a gibbet thirty feet high and then quartered with his head stuck on the Tollbooth spike. His limbs were sent to the four major cities of Scotland to be displayed above the main gates. Montrose's intelligence failure at Carbisdale had cost him his life and the lives of most of his followers.

Even while Montrose and his army were actively serving their King, Charles had again been negotiating with the Covenanters. With Montrose defeated, Charles thought it expedient to completely throw in his lot with the Covenanters. Although Charles despised everything about the Covenanters, desperation had convinced him that they offered him the only way to recover the crown of Scotland and, through that, England. On 2 June he set sail for Scotland, accompanied by the new Duke of Hamilton. Just before landing Charles took the required oath to uphold the Covenant. As a result of Carbisdale, the Covenanters dominated Scotland and the Marquis of Argyll dominated the Covenanters.

Argyll welcomed Charles as King amid great public support and celebratory bonfires. So far so good, but things began to move in ways Charles had not anticipated. He was Defender of the Faith and Supreme Governor of the Church of England but he was now officially a Covenanter and expected to behave as such. His natural humour, cynical wit and philandering disposition had to be sharply repressed. To cap it all, negotiations even began for him to marry Argyll's daughter, Lady Ann Campbell. Charles might be able to prevaricate about the marriage but he had no manoeuvre when it came to matters of state. Like it or not he had to defer to the wishes of Argyll on whom rested his present position and future hopes. An unholy alliance had been created between the grim Covenanters and a flamboyant young man from the Continent, who happened to be legal heir to the English throne

It was no wonder that the English Council of State was in panic. Just as they thought that the defeat of Montrose had destroyed Royalist aspirations in Scotland, suddenly Parliament's former allies the Covenanters had rallied to their King and could soon be marching south. Intelligence of the impending Scots attack was coming in from many sources, not least those of William Rowe, the Scoutmaster General. As it happened much of the information that was being presented as intelligence was just rumour. The Scots at this stage had not created a force for the invasion of England, let alone moved it to the border as the intelligence reports made out. Nevertheless it was the intelligence reports that were believed and on that basis virtually the whole Council of State felt a pre-emptive attack on Scotland was essential. The notable exception was Fairfax who, as commander-in-chief, was not prepared to lead an English army against Scotland which was still officially an ally.

Fairfax and his inconvenient principles made for a difficult situation. Although Cromwell had been the architect of the Republic and principal leader of the Council, Fairfax was still the figurehead commanding widespread respect in the army and among the Commonwealth's civilian supporters. If the Council lost the support of someone of Fairfax's stature it might fatally wound the credibility of the new Commonwealth. Understandably, Cromwell and fellow members of the Council began trying hard to either persuade Fairfax to change his mind or to find some formula whereby a force could be sent against the Scots while he remained in London as commander-in-chief. The final crunch came on 20 June when the Council of State discussed the intelligence assessment of the Scots' military activity and what should be the English response. The Council was agreed that Scotland had taken up a military posture on the border. The debate centred on the question of the Scots' intentions. In military intelligence it is relatively easy to build up a reasonable picture of an enemy's deployment but usually far more difficult to assess intentions. Fairfax felt it would be morally wrong to take up arms against the Scots when there was no confirmed intelligence that they were about to invade. The following dialogue took place:

Fairfax: What warrant have we to fall upon them unless we can be assured of their purpose to fall upon us.

Cromwell: 'That there is to be war between us, I fear is inevitable. Your Excellency will soon determine whether it be better to have this war in the bowels of an other country or of our own, and that it be will be in one of them I think without scruple.

Fairfax: If we were assured of their coming with their army into England, I confess it were prudence for us to prevent them, and (if) we are ready to advance into Scotland before they march into England: but what warrant have we to fall upon them unless we can be assured of their purpose to fight us?

Harrison: I think, under your favour, there cannot be greater assurance or human probability of the intentions of any state than we have of theirs to invade our country, else what means their present levies of men and money, and their quartering soldiers on our borders? It is not long since they did the like to us, and we can hardly imagine what other design they can have to employ their forces.

Fairfax: Human probabilities are not sufficient grounds to make war upon a neighbouring nation.

The intelligence assessment of likely enemy attack had thrown up the moral and legal question of whether a pre-emptive attack was justified. Deciding the operational response to such intelligence has always been difficult and remains so today. Fairfax stuck to his principles and seeing that he was outvoted decided that it was more honourable to resign as commander-in-chief than to take part in the operation. On 26 June Fairfax formally laid down his commission and on that day Parliament declared war on Scotland. An Act was quickly passed appointing Cromwell Lord General and commander-in-chief of all Commonwealth forces. Fairfax retired to his home in Nun Appleton to the south of York to devote his time to the management of his estates and his hobbies of writing poetry and cultivating roses.

Although Fairfax had become marginalized at the period of the King's trial and execution he had remained the most prominent member of the Council of State, with considerable public support. As commander-in-chief he could have become the leader of the new Republic had he wished it, especially if he had seized the chance when Ireton and Cromwell were out of harm's way in Ireland. He was after all only 38 years old while Cromwell might be regarded as 'over the hill' as he was now 51. But it was not in Fairfax's character to seek power and the opportunity passed him by. So with Fairfax gone and Ireton in far off Ireland, Cromwell became the most powerful man in England and poised to become a major figure in his country's history. The catalyst to bring about this major event had quite simply been the intelligence assessment that Scotland would invade England.

The intelligence assessment was incorrect but it became a self-fulfilling prophecy. Hearing that the English army was marching against them, the Scottish Estates voted to raise an army of 60,000. The nominal commander of this force was the elderly Lord Leven but the actual command rested with David Leslie. Cromwell wasted no time. Leaving Major General Harrison as senior commander in England, he left London on 28 June with about 12,000 men and taking as his generals Fleetwood, Lambert and Whalley. Cromwell had already appointed a Scoutmaster General for Scotland, one George Downing. He was unusual in having been brought up in New England and been one of the first graduates of Harvard. He had come to England to support Parliament, serving first as a chaplain to Colonel Okey's dragoons and then to Haselrig's regiment. As so often happened clerics were used as intelligencers and we can only assume that he had shown sufficient aptitude with Haselrig that Cromwell decided to appoint him on the good salary of £365 a year.

Cromwell's plan was to collect troops from garrisons on his march northwards and to summon as many good officers as he could into his army as it advanced. One of those summoned was a surprised but delighted Colonel George Monck. Additional regiments were picked up in Durham and Newcastle, including a newly raised regiment of men from Berwick and Newcastle which Monck was given to command; it would later be called the Coldstream Guards. Cromwell's force numbered 16,000 by the time he crossed the border into Scotland on 22 July.

So far from massing an army for the invasion of England, Leslie's deployment was entirely defensive. Indeed he had withdrawn every man of military age from the counties of east Lothian and Berwick. Six days after crossing the border, Cromwell made his first contact with outposts of Leslie's force of 23,000 but the Scots pulled back to Edinburgh. Leslie had calculated that if he evaded battle, the English army would be gradually worn down by the difficulty in obtaining supplies and the traditional wet Scottish weather. For over a month Cromwell tried every means to bring the Scots to battle but Leslie remained elusive and always in occupation of the higher ground. The weather was atrocious and Cromwell's army was without tents, so this and difficulties in supplies brought on sickness. Then, following some skirmishing, Cromwell withdrew his army along the coast back towards the small port of Dunbar, with the Scots marching parallel on the high ground above them. On 2 September Leslie occupied an immensely strong position called Doon Hill that could look down on the dispirited English who had now reached Dunbar.

Because of illness only 11,000 of the English army were fit enough to fight. They had their backs to the sea and were outnumbered two to one by the Covenanter army, which could now block the route to Berwick and south to the safety of England. Leslie's cautious strategy was about to reap its reward. At this critical moment the Committee of Estates of the Covenanter army got it into their heads that Cromwell was about to retreat back to England and so ordered the Scots troops to prepare to cut him off. Taking the Bible as their military textbook they decided that their army should 'fall like Ehab on the Moabites'. Despite Leslie's protests, he was overruled by this committee of clerics and the Covenanter army began to spread out and descend from its strong position in preparation for attacking the English the next day. During this manoeuvre Cromwell realized that the Scots cavalry on Leslie's right wing had become exposed and out of contact with the main body. Cromwell immediately called his senior officers and made plans to attack this vulnerable right wing. At dawn on the wet and stormy day of 3 September, the attack was launched with six cavalry regiments under Fleetwood, Whalley and Lambert and Monck's three infantry regiments in the centre. The Scots were taken by surprise but put up a brave resistance till Cromwell threw his own regiment of horse into the attack. The shock of this onslaught was sufficient to put the Scots cavalry to flight. They then rode through the infantry of their main body and a rout began.

In Cromwell's words the Scots were 'made by the Lord of Hosts as stubble to their swords'. About 3,000 of Leslie's army were killed on the field and 1,000 more in the pursuit, with 10,000 taken prisoner. Hundreds of these prisoners were to die of starvation as they were marched to Durham where they were eventually locked up in the cathedral before being shipped out as forced labour to Virginia. Leslie had fled to Sterling and on 7 September Cromwell entered Edinburgh. Could this Royalist disaster have been averted by good intelligence? The answer is no. Cromwell's brilliant decision to attack was a tactical one made on the spur of the moment and he could not have even foretold it himself. What had made Cromwell decide to attack had been the intelligence from Lambert's scouts who had been shadowing the move of Leslie's right wing and reported them out of contact with their main body. The Royalist failure was a direct result of the Covenanter ministers' meddling initiative of urging an attack contrary to Leslie's carefully considered defensive strategy. The Committee of Estates had made their fateful decision based upon their civilian assessment that Cromwell was about to retreat to England, an assessment that had no basis in intelligence or fact.

As the Covenanters still controlled of Perth and Sterling, Cromwell and Lambert set about subduing the Lowlands, which they achieved by the end of the year. The first day of 1651 saw the 21-year-old Charles being crowned at Scone, with Argyll actually placing the crown on his head. Argyll must have felt that not only was he a king-maker and power behind the throne but likely to have his own grandchild as a future Scottish monarch if he pushed through Charles's marriage to his daughter. Although Charles seemed under Argyll's complete control, the coronation changed the whole dynamics of power. Charles was now officially King and astute enough to play the card for all it was worth. He took every opportunity to appear in public as King and before long even the hardened Covenanters were beginning to show him the respect due to their sovereign. Meanwhile the Covenanter army had again grown to 20,000, largely from being joined by Highland Royalists. Charles was officially commander-in-chief of a substantial force. This in itself reduced the influence of Argyll and correspondingly gave Charles more authority as King. Angry at his waning influence, Argyll returned to the Highlands in a huff. Charles was fortunate to have a military breathing space to consolidate his position as several months passed with no major activity while Cromwell was inactive through illness. On his sick bed Cromwell formulated a plan to establish a military foothold on the north bank of the River Forth which could then be used as a base to attack Leslie in Stirling.

Monck was chosen to take 1,500 men in boats from Leith and carry out an amphibious assault on a small port of Burntisland on the opposite side of the Firth of Forth. Leslie had made sure that the English forces were under close surveillance and Monck's little flotilla was spotted soon after it set out. Leslie's men lit beacons to signal that an attack was coming and the Covenanters of Fifeshire rushed to the defence of Burntisland, making it too strong for Monck to make an opposed landing. With a storm blowing up to make the Firth dangerous for small craft, Monck had no option but to return to Leith. This incident reflects well on the deployment and vigilance of Leslie's scouts and also on them being practical enough to overcome difficulties in communications by the use of beacon sites. Although there are no other records in this period of beacons being used to disseminate intelligence warnings, it is likely that this time-honoured method of communication would have been used elsewhere.

Monck did succeed in capturing two Covenanter strongholds and was promoted to major general for this good work but in truth the English army had not got any further towards defeating Leslie during the whole four months Cromwell had been ill. By the end of May Cromwell had fully recovered. In July another attempt was made to make a bridgehead across the Forth. This time Colonel Robert Overton led 1,600 men in boats across the river and established himself at North Queensferry. We don't know whether Leslie's scouts had been negligent or the crossing was so fast in the calm summer weather that there had not been time to mobilize opposition to the landing. However it came about, the result was that Overton had gained the vital bridgehead on the north bank which enabled Lambert to cross and defeat a 3,500 strong Covenanter force at Inverkeithing near Perth.

The battle at Inverkeithing opened the way for Cromwell to take the bulk of the army across the Firth of Forth and advance to Perth on 1 August. It surrendered the next day. Perth was a natural objective as it was the Royalist/Covenanter seat of government but more importantly by advancing to Perth Cromwell both threatened the Covenanter supply lines to Sterling and left the Lowlands unprotected and thus open to the Scots to advance to England uncontested. This was a deliberate ploy on Cromwell's behalf to flush the Covenanters out of the security of the Highlands. Charles and Leslie, his commander, saw the way south open, took the bait and decided to march south via Glasgow to North-West England then on to the ultimate prize of London.

Apart from seizing what appeared a tactical opportunity, Charles's decision to go south was based on the assumption that the Royalists in England would rise up and join him. This assumption was wrong. Lack of good intelligence meant that Charles and the Scottish army was completely out of touch with the situation in England. England was a country dominated by an army that had very conclusively won a bloody civil war. The situation called for revenge on Royalist 'malignants' and the imposition of draconian measures to secure the survival of the Commonwealth State. For example, immediately after the execution of the King all ports had been closed and borders sealed, thus cutting all communications to and from the country until it was safe for them to be resumed.

Republican England was defending itself by setting up the apparatus of a police state, including that vital ingredient, an intelligence service under Thomas Scot. The Council of State had appointed Captain George Bishop as Scot's assistant and Secretary of the Committee of Examinations. Bishop was a Bristol man and a Quaker of the extreme type that existed at that time. He had taken part in the Putney Debates where he was even at that early stage calling for the King's execution. On starting work for Scot, Bishop became responsible for source handling and soon threw himself into agent recruitment. Naturally his involvement in examinations gave him a good opportunity to pressure suspects into deals whereby they could be granted leniency in exchange for becoming informants. As he had a natural flair for covert intelligence gathering and the money to pay informants, it was not long before he was establishing an increasingly effective network. It had been one of Bishop's informants who had unearthed the first Royalist plot in England since the King's execution. This is when Charles had sent undercover Royalists from Scotland in the autumn of 1650 to start risings in Chester, Liverpool, Hull and Norwich. Only Norwich had got off the ground and that been swiftly dealt with. At about the same time Scot had received information that a Eusebius Andrews was planning to seize the Isle of Ely in the name of the King Charles II. Scot organized an operation in which one of his agents managed to win the confidence of Andrews to such an extent that he was eventually prepared to write down the plan. This was sufficient evidence to result in Andrews's arrest and subsequent execution and lead to nine other conspirators being later brought to justice. Although Andrews and his group had posed no serious threat, the operation was a neat piece of tradecraft and the penalties imposed must have deterred others from active resistance.

In April 1650 there had been the first meeting of the Western Association for the Restoration of the Monarchy. This took place at Salisbury under the guise of a race meeting. It was just a few local landowners led by Colonel Francis Wyndham and Sir John Paulet, neither men of significant wealth or influence. They established a small circle of Cavalier gentlemen who would like to bring about Charles's restoration but had no intention of taking up arms in the immediate future. Throughout the country the estates of Royalist leaders had been seized and many Royalists had fled abroad. Those who had stayed were keeping the lowest possible profile, just hoping that by complying with the new regime they could hold on to at least some of their land. Parliament had officially termed all Royalists 'delinquents' and ruled that two-thirds of their estates were to be sequestered. Some 700 Royalist estates were to be sold that year just to make ends meet. This was a time for Cavaliers to think first and foremost of ensuring the survival of at least some of their family inheritance. There were of course some ardent Royalists who would risk all for the cause. One such was Sir Marmaduke Langdale who, after the Battle of Preston, had made it to Widmerpool disguised as a woman but was then arrested and imprisoned in Nottingham Castle. Later he escaped to London, disguised this time as a clergyman. There he was taken in by the Royalist agent John Barwick and stayed with him pretending to be an Irish clergyman driven out of his parish by the Papists. With even men like Langdale lying low, there was little hope for Charles as he left Scotland on 5 August to gather support in England.

Although there were few, if any, Royalist grandees in England likely to come to Charles's support, there was the Earl of Derby, the Royalist magnate for Lancashire, who was sheltering in the Isle of Man. The intention was that Derby would bring over men from the island to join up with Charles's army. Although Charles's intelligence was poor but it must be said that he did have one man who stands out as a good intelligencer. This was Isaac Berkenhead. Unfortunately for Charles he was a double agent and passed the information about Derby's landing to his Commonwealth handler. As a result, the Isle of Man contingent was defeated at Wigan by Colonel Robert Lilburne and Derby only managed to escape the fighting. He eventually reported to Charles with just himself and a handful of followers.

As soon as Cromwell received intelligence that Charles was heading for England, he ordered Monck to assume command in Scotland, Lambert to follow the Scots/Royalist army with 3,000 horse and Harrison in Newcastle to harass Charles's flank, while he advanced south with Charles Fleetwood and the main force of 10,000. The advance of Charles's army was so rapid that Harrison was unable to intercept them and by 22 August they were at Worcester. Although well received in the city, Charles was unable to gain more recruits en route because his army was regarded as Scots invaders rather than Royalist. The few Royalist volunteers who had come forward were turned away by the Committee of the Kirk who refused to accept anyone unless they took the Covenant.

Thomas Scot's intelligence organization had been daily winning its spurs during the Scots/Royalist invasion of England. By this time Scot had built up a considerable database of known Royalists. Added to this, one of Bishop's agents, a certain Thomas Coke, was able to provide precise details about Charles's advance to Worcester. As a result Scot was able to identify and arrange the arrest of some 200 Royalist sympathizers on the path of the likely advance, including the Duke of Richmond and Lord Beauchamp. Deprived of English supporters Charles and Leslie decided to take up a defensive position round Worcester and stay there in the hope that they might receive reinforcements from Wales. No reinforcements appeared and the Royalist forces remained 16,000 strong and in a sorry state, with many of them shoeless and without weapons.

Cromwell had collected reinforcements on his march south including 2,000 under Colonel John Desborough and Lord Grey of Groby, and arrived outside Worcester on 28 August to join forces with Fleetwood and Lambert. Cromwell now had a well-equipped army totalling 31,000. The Scots/Royalists had taken up defensive positions in three areas on the outskirts of Worcester. These were south of the city, protected by the Rivers Teme and Severn; at Fort Royal to the south-west covering the London Road and finally Leslie and his cavalry to the north of the city. Cromwell deployed his forces roughly facing the two Royalist positions to the south and south-west and placed his artillery to the east on the high ground at Perry Wood. With Commonwealth militia advancing on Worcester from the north, the Scots/Royalist army was trapped. They decided to make a break-out on 29 August to capture Cromwell's gun positions at Perry Wood. If this succeeded they might have a chance of bursting through the Commonwealth encirclement and even making a dash for London. Cromwell received intelligence of this emanating from a Puritan tailor called Guise in the city. The treachery of Guise was discovered and he was hanged in Worcester the next day but this was too late to prevent the Royalist break-out being decisively thrown back by Cromwell's prepared force.

Cromwell now ordered the construction of pontoon bridges. On 3 September, the anniversary of the Battle of Dunbar, Cromwell launched a two-pronged attack. Fleetwood used a pontoon to cross the river at the Severn/Teme junction and aimed his attack at the Scots commanded by Hamilton. Hamilton and his infantry were pushed back into the city. Cromwell used the second pontoon to cross the Severn and made his attack from the east. Charles himself led a daring counter-attack on Perry Wood but was thrown back and soon all the Royalist infantry were pushed into the city with Commonwealth forces in hot pursuit. For some reason Leslie and his cavalry remained to the north of Worcester taking no real part in his countrymen's increasingly desperate attempts to halt their pursuers. The situation now turned to one of rout and carnage. Before long, 2,000 Scots lay dead or dying in the narrow streets and twisting alleys of Worcester. Charles just managed to escape on horseback with Henry Wilmot through St Martin's Gate with only seconds to spare. Others were less fortunate: 3,000 were killed and 6,000 taken prisoner, including Leslie, Hamilton and Derby. The Third Civil War was over and 190,000 lives had been lost since the wars had begun in 1642. Charles, King of England, Scotland and Ireland, found himself on the run with a £1,000 price on his head. He was to spend the next forty-two days in various disguises and hiding places until he got to Brighton and managed to board a collier bound for Normandy.

Chapter 7

Commonwealth of Three Nations, 1652–1653

In the year or so while Cromwell had been dealing with Scots Royalists, his son-in-law Ireton had been making sound progress in Ireland. There had been some initial setbacks in 1650, particularly in Ulster where the Bishop of Clougher had been elected the commander of a 6,000-strong Catholic Ulster army following the death of Owen Roe O'Neill. Ireton brought the bishop's military career to an abrupt end when he defeated him at Letterkenny, then had him hanged, drawn and quartered in Londonderry for good measure. This was yet another blow to the Irish Catholic Royalists whose loyalty had been stretched to breaking point by Charles taking the covenant in Scotland. Ormonde's position had become virtually untenable, but he had loyally continued on in post. Then the news came through of the Scots defeat at Dunbar. With all hope now gone, Ormonde decided he could do no more and sailed for the Continent in December. The final blow to the Royalist cause in Ireland came ten months later when the long siege of Limerick ended with it falling to Ireton on 27 October 1651. Formal Royalist resistance was at an end and all forts were in Parliamentary hands. Although there were still many small but significant pockets of Catholic resistance, Ireton had achieved his principal military objective. In less than a month from this success he was dead from the plague.

For Cromwell this was a serious personal loss. Not only had the husband of his daughter Bridget been snatched away but also a close friend, who had been his right-hand man, both militarily and politically. Cromwell had learnt the shocking news of Ireton's death while still elated by his Worcester victory when being received in London as a hero. Parliament had voted him an annual pension of £40,000 and decreed that 3 September should always be kept as a public holiday in his honour. But this was no time for either private grief or public esteem. Cromwell's immediate task was to appoint a replacement for his Lord Deputy in Ireland. Lambert, being Cromwell's best general, was the obvious choice but he eventually rejected it when Parliament decided to downgrade the post in a cost-cutting exercise. In the mean time Bridget Ireton had found consolation for the loss of her husband in the arms of General Charles Fleetwood and the two soon married. It was Fleetwood who was now appointed commander-in-chief and civil commissioner and so Cromwell again had a son-in-law holding the key position in Ireland. Fleetwood was a safe pair of hands who had fought well at Dunbar and Worcester but lacked the imagination and flair of Lambert. Although a pleasant enough Northamptonshire gentleman, he was an exceptionally pious Puritan even for those times. Fleetwood was to carry out his Irish duties with religious fervour and soon after his arrival in Dublin presided over the trial of 200 Irish Catholics who were thought to have taken part in the 1641 uprising. The lack of substantial evidence about events twelve years previously did not hinder the due process of law. They were all executed.

Cromwell had been away from government, busy with the Levellers, Ireland and Scotland, for the greater part of the time from the King's execution to the end of 1651. He is such a major historical figure that it is sometimes assumed that he was governing England during this time, but this was not the case. As the army commander he was a person of considerable potential power but had to exert that influence from a distance through friends and correspondence. The Council of State whose President was Sir Arthur Haselrig was carrying out the government of England to the tunes called by the Rump Parliament dominated by Sir Harry Vane. As the Rump was chiefly concerned with promoting the interests of its members and their cronies, this was not the quality of government hoped for from a republic. Despite this uninspiring leadership, the government in England was working reasonably well. This was because the Council of State was fortunate in being supported by committees and a bureaucracy, which had been steadily developing into an effective civil service. The fact that John Milton had been made Secretary of Foreign Tongues (later called 'Latin Secretary') in March 1649 is an indication of the intellectual quality and moral standing of some of these new government servants. By 1652 the government apparatus of England had acquired a new confidence drawn from experience in both administering a now united country and in dealing with foreign nations, most of whom seemed eager to encourage good relations.

The archetype of the sort of person who was now conducting the administration of government was John Thurloe. He was the son of a Puritan rector from Abbess Roding in Essex who had come to the attention of Oliver St John while training in London as a Chancery clerk at Furnival's Inn and been taken on as St John's clerk in 1637 at the age of 21. By good fortune the young Thurloe had hitched himself to a rising star. St John married Cromwell's first cousin Elizabeth in 1638, became MP for Totnes in Devon in 1640 and Solicitor General the next year, then a member of the Committee of Both Kingdoms in 1644 and Chief Justice of Common Pleas in 1648. Meanwhile Thurloe took on increasing responsibility in St John's private law practice and had his first official appointment in January 1643 when he was made one of the secretaries to the commissioners of Parliament at the negotiations with the King at Uxbridge. The next year Thurloe was admitted to Lincoln's Inn and in 1648 Parliament made him Receiver of Cursitors Fines under the Commissioners of the Great Seal at £350 a year. In February 1650 he was appointed one of the Treasury officials responsible for the drainage of the Isle of Ely.

In March the next year Thurloe had something of a career breakthrough when he was made secretary to Oliver St John and Walter Strickland on their mission to Holland. The job itself was scarcely more important than posts he had held previously but it put him in daily contact with his influential patron who could assess his qualities at close quarters and reward him accordingly. More importantly the post also made him known to the Council for it was he who wrote the reports to them on the progress of these important negotiations. On four occasions he sailed back to England to personally brief the Council, increasing his profile still further. As it happened he was already well known to the most important member of the Council as he had been acting for Cromwell in a legal capacity. As a result of St John marrying into the family, Cromwell had put his private legal work in the hands of St John's law practice. The person who actually looked after the affairs of the Lord General was John Thurloe. He carried out a variety of tasks, such as being a trustee for an estate belonging to the children of Henry Ireton and Bridget Cromwell and representing Cromwell at the Admiralty Court over interests in a vessel from Waterford.

Thurloe had been making a name for himself on several fronts when an opportunity that would change his life came out of the blue. In early 1652 Walter Frost the Secretary to the Council of State unexpectedly died. A replacement was needed and such was the way things were done in those days, the successor who immediately came to mind was Frost's son, who had been his father's assistant. Fortunately the Council at length concluded that sentiment should not cloud their judgement and that Thurloe was far more talented than the young Frost. On 29 March the job was given to Thurloe and with it an annual salary of £600 and a house in Whitehall. A meteoric rise indeed, stemming as always from the luck of being at the right place at the right time but also from his talent and energy. Thurloe was small in stature with long brown hair, a wispy moustache and dressed in the subdued puritan fashion – not someone to stand out in a seventeenth-century crowd. His qualities belied his rather unprepossessing appearance. He had shown himself to be a loyal, dedicated, energetic, intelligent and ambitious 32 year old who had built up considerable experience of government and the workings of the new order. It was men such as Thurloe who were beginning to provide the administration of the Republic with a high level of professionalism in all the essential activities of government, including intelligence.

Cromwell's return to the scene of government was bound to upset the way Parliament and the Council of State had been running the country. As always Cromwell had clear views on what was necessary. He wanted an Act of Oblivion to help unite the country by pardoning all Royalists who had opposed Parliament before Worcester. More importantly he demanded dissolution of the Rump Parliament and new elections. The Rump was largely made up of religious Independents like Cromwell and the majority of the army, but their religious stance was all they had in common. Cromwell regarded the Rump as a self-seeking oligarchy composed of ungodly men whose principal aim was to perpetuate their position of privilege. The Rump for their part eyed Cromwell with the greatest suspicion. He had returned a national hero after Worcester and was now residing in the King's former apartments at Whitehall and Hampton Court. Cromwell appeared an overmighty citizen who could always use the army to impose measures born of his unshakable convictions.

Despite all Cromwell's efforts in the Council of State and key committees, Parliament went its own way and decided not to dissolve until 3 November 1654 and watered down the Act of Oblivion so as to make it near useless. Cromwell and his army were not having the influence that they believed was their due. As the year progressed, fortune turned further against them. In November Parliament decided to sell Hampton Court where Cromwell had been living since returning from Worcester. At the elections for the Council of State Cromwell was re-elected but Fleetwood was not, thus reducing the military influence. Then Parliament made a big blunder. The army had been getting very restless because of arrears in pay when Parliament announced troop reductions of 21,000 in England and Scotland. On 26 December Cromwell got Colonel Pride to stand once more at the door of the House but the members did not take the hint.

While these power struggles were going on in the background during 1652, other major events were taking place for the Commonwealth. Relations with the Dutch had been deteriorating through rivalry for the seas. The Council of State were put out about the Dutch spurning Oliver St John's overtures of friendship the previous year and began remembering that their co-religionists were also England's commercial rivals. The Dutch had been taking an increasing amount of the three kingdoms' mercantile trade and fishing in home waters without handing over the customary tenth of their herring catch. In October Parliament passed the protectionist Navigation Act. This made it a requirement for all English exports to be transported in English ships and for all imports to be carried by either English ships or the country of origin. The Dutch were thus debarred from English trade at considerable economic loss. The States General sent over three ambassadors to try to negotiate a lifting of the ban but protracted negotiations only resulted in further deterioration of relations.

In March 1652 the English fleet of some sixty vessels was put on readiness and Robert Blake was appointed its commander. Blake was a stocky, plainly dressed Somerset man who had defended Lyme against Prince Maurice and then as a colonel led the long and heroic defence of Taunton where he had ordered the thatch to be taken off the roofs off houses to feed his cavalry horses and declared that he would eat three of his four pairs of boots before he surrendered. Since becoming a general-at-sea he had distinguished himself in harassing Rupert's fleet from Ireland to the Mediterranean and was now ready to take on the Dutch. A flare up between the two nations appeared inevitable; it just needed an occasion for ignition. That occurred two months later when Dutch ships refused to dip their flags as salute to English ships, which provoked Blake into exchanging shots with a squadron under Admiral Martyn Tromp. Although Cromwell himself wished to avoid clashing with another Protestant republic, the general view was that such Dutch impertinence in the English Channel could hardly go unanswered. The English Parliament declared war and the navy began seizing Dutch merchantmen whenever they could be found. This war was to go on for two years to the disadvantage of both parties, causing havoc to trade and fishing, both essential to each country's economy.

In Ireland Fleetwood was continuing the work of Cromwell and Ireton by savagely subduing the country. As areas were dominated they came under a new Commonwealth order. All Catholics were excluded from positions of trust; this meant not only government office but professions such as barristers and teachers. In May 1652 came the official end of hostilities when the Commonwealth and the Irish Parliament at Leinster signed the Kilkenny Articles. On 12 August the English Rump Parliament passed an Act of Settlement of Irish Land in which half the land of Ireland was transferred to either Fleetwood's soldiers or Commonwealth creditors. The Catholic Irish occupying the confiscated land were to be forcefully transferred to Connaught. This act of ethnic cleansing had to be borne on top of the death and destruction of the civil war and crop failures which had led to widespread starvation. So harsh had life become that by the end of the year the population of Ireland was 855,000, compared with one and half a million in 1641.

There might be a formal settlement but the Catholic resistance continued under the leadership of Lord Muskerry. Occasionally 2,000 rebels would be put in the field but for the most part it was a campaign of skirmishes and ambushes, followed by dispersion to the hills when superior Commonwealth forces appeared. It would take an army 33,000 strong to keep any semblance of order in Ireland during the Commonwealth. Naturally intelligence was important to the Commonwealth forces and the Scoutmaster General Henry Jones did his job with vigour but with ultimate frustration. He was to describe the Irish as 'cursed people' and came to realize that whatever the tactical advantages were gained though successful operations based on good intelligence, there could be no peace in Ireland unless it was wanted by all its inhabitants.

Scotland had reaped the whirlwind of the Worcester campaign. After capturing Stirling in August 1651 Monck had sent a force to Alyth, where the two Committees of the Kirk and Estates were surprised, together with Leslie and several noblemen. A total of 300 were arrested and packed off to prison in England. Many Scottish magnates had been captured at Worcester, or subsequently fled to France, so the loss of the 300 left Scotland virtually leaderless. Now, almost a year to the day after Worcester, Dundee was stormed, leaving 800 dead, many of whom were women and children. As in Ireland, Commonwealth terror worked and the remaining towns soon opened their gates. Having overcome all military opposition, Monck became ill and handed over to his able deputy Richard Deane to complete the English domination. In December came the final humiliation, when the English Rump Parliament passed political union with England and abolished the Edinburgh Parliament, the Executive Committee of Estates and the General Assembly of the Church. The government of Scotland was to be by eight commissioners appointed by the Rump. All crown land was forfeited to the Commonwealth, as was the land of anyone who had supported Hamilton. To cap it all, a levy of £130,000 was imposed on the Scots to maintain the army sent to subdue them.

By the end of 1652, both Scotland and Ireland were effectively united to England under direct rule. Henry VIII of England had become King of Ireland, and James

VI of Scotland had inherited the crowns of England and Ireland. It had been James's great wish to bring the three kingdoms closer together as a single unity but the Westminster Parliament had opposed this. Charles too had wanted unity but his attempts to impose even some religious uniformity had been one of the causes of the Civil War. Now by an interesting irony it was the English Parliament which had achieved this Stuart goal of a single state. The difference was that this state was a republic, not a united kingdom and was to be kept in obedience not by consent but by a powerful army.

To hold together this new state whose birth had caused such bloodshed and resentment would need an intelligence apparatus as powerful in its own way as the army itself. Thomas Scot and George Bishop had the challenge of expanding and enhancing the intelligence department to meet this requirement. As we have seen, Scot was receiving interrogation reports from the Committee of Examination and both he and Bishop had made great strides in establishing a network of agents and informants. There was another major source of intelligence collection and that was the interception of Royalist communications. As early as May 1649 the Council of State had issued a warrant to Captain Edward Sexby to 'go to the foreign post, seize the letters of persons holding correspondence with the enemy, and bring them to the Council'. Sexby was a cavalry officer who had served as a trooper in first Cromwell's and then Fairfax's own regiments of horse. He was also one of the leading young officers involved in setting up the Council of Agitators and a supporter of the Levellers. In short he was a man known for his loyalty and energetic support for the republican cause. No doubt Sexby succeeded in obtaining the correspondence required but it was hardly a covert operation. This highly unsubtle method of intercept was to be refined in time. In March 1650 the Council decided to assume the authority for appointing the Postmaster General. The job was given to their Attorney-General, Edward Prideaux. Working in cooperation with Prideaux, it was now relatively easy for George Bishop to arrange the intercept of ordinary mail. For example it is recorded that in June 1650 the Council's sergeant-at-arms was dispatched to a post stage twenty miles from London on the York road to intercept the outward mail and then ride to the next stage and take that as well. Again rather a clumsy way of going about things because it meant that legitimate mail was also disrupted, including that of the government service!

Although intercept collection was less than subtle, Scot was able to make use of an expert when it came to dealing with letters written in cipher. That expert was of course Dr John Wallis who had continued to provide his cryptographic services since he began working for Parliament in 1642. In June 1649 Wallis had been rewarded for his war effort by being given the post of Salvian Professor of Geometry in Oxford, replacing a Royalist. The fact that Wallis was without any formal mathematical education had not been seen as an impediment to this selection. As it happened, the previous year Wallis had done investigations into the nature of quadratic and cubic equations and made an intense study of Oughtred's *Clavis Mathematicae* then produced his own theory of angular sections. He had gone on to establish the recognition of negative solutions and their geometrical representation as line segments in the special case of the equations based on angular sections. It is unlikely that the Council knew or cared about any of this when they rewarded their cryptanalyst, who just happened by fortunate coincidence to be the greatest British mathematician prior to Newton. The value of Wallis's work for intelligence is best judged by it being described by Thomas Scot as 'a jewel for a prince's use'. Thanks to the energy and dedication of Scot and Bishop and the analytical skills of Wallis, a comprehensive system was in place for the intercept of the national mail service.

Fortunately for Scot and Bishop, following the subjection of Scotland and Ireland there were no immediate internal threats to the Commonwealth of any significance. They therefore had the time to prepare for a future which was likely to be less benign. The Royalist resistance in England had shrunk to next to nothing. Such Royalist resistance that remained centred on the handful of Cavaliers in Hampshire and Somerset known as the Western Association. They had been just that too far south to have provided support for Charles at Worcester and in any case were not prepared to organize themselves into a military force. They had however been of service in the young king's escape from Worcester. After the battle Charles had with him Charles Gifford, a Catholic, who suggested refuge in his Boscobel estate. In a journey that had included swimming a river and hiding in a tree and several priests' holes, Charles was passed on through a network of Gifford's Catholic connections via Mosely Old Hall to Colonel Lane of Bentley Hall. Lane's daughter Jane then took Charles on the next stage disguised as her servant riding behind her on the same horse. They travelled with various adventures to her sister at Abbots Leigh from where it was hoped to find a ship at Bristol.

Wilmot, who had escaped with Charles from Worcester and reunited with him at Mosely, found that all the ports in the area were being closely watched. Wilmot then wrote to Colonel Francis Wyndham for help. So it was that Jane Lane and her 'servant' went south to Wyndham's home near Sherborne in Somerset. This was to be Charles's base for several weeks from which he left only to return again as various opportunities of a sea passage fell through. On 6 October Charles set off again on a horse, this time behind Wyndham's cousin Juliana Coningsby, and travelled to Heal House near Amesbury to stay at the home of a relation of Edward Hyde. Then it was on via Hambledon to Brighton where a ship was eventually found that enabled Charles and Wilmot to leave England on 15 October, pretending to be illegal duellists escaping the law. Despite the search of the Boscobel estate and the rough questioning of Gifford and others, the network for the escape was not compromised and Wyndham and his Western Association could continue their low-key resistance.

Charles II returned to Paris after his Worcester escape and found his mother living almost penniless in the Louvre with the Fronde riots raging outside and Queen Anne of Austria and Mazarin having fled the city. He also found there was no hope for support through his sister Mary, because her husband, William II of Orange, had died from smallpox. Six days after his death Mary had given birth to a son and a major family quarrel broke out over who should be the guardian of this new Prince of Orange. Mary was already unpopular for her haughty manner and refusal to learn Dutch; now she was no longer the wife of the Stadtholder but merely a widow in a foreign country trying to gain control of the Orange estates, which were in any case in deep debt. Although Charles could now expect no help from Mary, he had hoped that the Dutch war with England might give an opportunity to find common cause with the United Provinces. He offered Rupert's fleet and even to serve as an admiral in the Dutch navy but all overtures were rejected. Then Turenne captured Paris in the autumn 1652 and Anne of Austria returned, together with the 13-year-old Louis XIV, enabling Charles's position to improve somewhat. Charles secured the promise of an annual pension from the French crown of £600 a year; the bad news was that it was rarely paid. Worse, Mazarin was beginning to distance himself from Charles. The true French relationship with the exiled English court became clearer at the end of the year when Antoine de Bordeaux was sent as France's envoy to London. Although not titled 'ambassador', this was de facto recognition of the Commonwealth and a strong indicator that France wanted to ally with the English republic.

Rivalries, squabbling and the odd duel still bedevilled Charles's unhappy and impoverished court and all was observed by Scot's spies, including the progress in forming a government in exile. Sir Edward Hyde had returned from Spain in 1651 where he had been ambassador. Now he was promoted to join Sir Edward Nicholas as Secretary of State. A Privy Council was formed with those two steady loyal servants, Lord Jermyn and Ormonde, as well as more mercurial figures such as Wilmot and Buckingham. Different individuals and groups would gain ascendancy in the Privy Council in different circumstances but Hyde slowly began moving into the position of the King's most trusted adviser. Unlike Charles's aristocratic inner circle, Hyde's background was that of a gentleman of modest means who had become a lawyer and then an MP before entering the service of Charles I. As such he had a far better understanding of the feelings of the majority of Englishmen. Added to this was his shrewd brain, and complete dedication to the House of Stuart and the Church of England. This consummate crown servant was a workaholic driven by the goal of regaining the throne for Charles. However, his high moral standards, fussy manner and undisguised disappointment that his master was not spending enough time at his paperwork caused tensions between the 43-year-old government servant and the 22-year-old monarch.

It was to Charles's credit that, despite most of those close to him being better company than Hyde and more daring in their plans, he usually took the advice of the older man. For the most part that advice was to do nothing. That meant not trying to get foreign armies to invade England or encourage half-cock rebellions but wait until the situation arose when the majority of his subjects were ready to welcome their King's return. Doing nothing kept Hyde immensely busy. He needed to have the clearest possible view of the situation at home and abroad to be able to recognize when the time was becoming ripe for action. In order to do this he needed the best intelligence he could gain. Sir Edward Nicholas was officially responsible for intelligence but Hyde decided that additional effort was required. The problem was that Hyde had little enough money to pay for his own board and lodgings and certainly none to spare for paying informers. He therefore had to rely on the information he could obtain from Royalist sympathizers either when they visited the King in Paris or through covert correspondence.

One of Hyde's most useful covert correspondents was John Barwick, Charles I's former secret agent in London. During the King's imprisonment he had been a principal route for communications between him and Royalists on the Continent and after Charles's execution he had continued as a live letterbox, posing as a Dutch merchant and using the cover name of James van Delf. This was eventually discovered by a Post Office employee and he was arrested. Bravely he prevented the compromise of his sources by refusing to give any information under examination. On being released from the Tower in August 1652 he and his brother Edward continued to communicate information when they could, right up to the Restoration. Hyde worked tirelessly building up a network of such contacts but his great achievement was being able to make accurate assessments of what he heard. He soon learnt to distinguish wishful thinking from reality. The many reports of the Commonwealth's forthcoming demise or widespread support for the King could be put down to the overenthusiasm of the authors. Less palatable news was more likely to be true.

While Hyde was trying to establish an intelligence network for the Royalist court in exile he was well aware that the actions of the Stuart Court were under the scrutiny of Commonwealth spies. Hyde was very security conscious and did his best to make others close to the King similarly circumspect. One of the more effective Commonwealth agents at the Stuart court in Paris was none other than Colonel Joseph Bampfylde, the long-standing Royalist agent who had successfully organized the escape of James, Duke of York. After the King's execution he had been captured and imprisoned in the Gatehouse from where he escaped to the United Provinces. While crossing the Channel he had a duel with the brother-in-law of his former mistress, Anne Murray, over having proposed to Anne while omitting to mention that he was already married. The outcome of the duel was mixed. On the one hand Bampfylde clearly won the encounter but having shot his opponent through the head he found that he was not welcomed when he arrived at Charles's court. Seeing that he was getting nowhere with the Royalists first in Paris and then in Scotland, he had returned to England in 1652. It was at this stage that he changed his allegiance and was taken on by Scot as a Commonwealth agent. He was arrested later in August of that year and brought before the Council of State who ordered him to leave the country. This was merely a ploy to ensure that he retained credibility as a Royalist. Before long he had got himself at least tolerated at the Stuart court in exile and was sending long and detailed dispatches back on Royalist plans and activities.

By the end of 1652 the intelligence apparatus of the Commonwealth was winning the intelligence war but a more important contest was about to break out as to who was to run the Commonwealth. The army was getting increasingly disenchanted with the Parliament on whose behalf they had fought the Civil War. A clash between them was becoming inevitable, with the potential to release forces which might tear the newly formed Republic apart. The dramatic result of this contest would make itself known as soon as the spring of the next year.

The new year of 1653 was not greeted with any optimism. There was a general air of dissatisfaction throughout the three countries of the Commonwealth. The blame for all ills, from the price of coal to high taxation, was laid squarely at the feet of the Rump. The army was becoming increasingly restless and in January began a series of long prayer meetings with officers from all areas congregating in London for a showdown with the Rump. One such officer was George Downing, the Scoutmaster General for the army of Scotland whose intelligence efforts had contributed to the victories of Dunbar and Worcester. He travelled down to London to extend his career into the political arena. There were also activists such Harrison and the Fifth Monarchists who wanted to establish the reign of Jesus Christ on Earth and were becoming particularly impatient with a Parliament that showed absolutely no sign of trying to bring that situation about.

The army leadership came to general agreement that the Rump should dissolve itself as soon as possible to make way for a new parliament. However, far from showing any inclination to dissolve, the Rump was planning its own extension. There were rumours that Sir Harry Vane, the leader of the largest faction in the Rump, was engineering the selection of Presbyterians as MPs to support his group. When Cromwell entered the Commons in mid-April he was not well received and someone even shouted that it was time to choose a new Lord General. Cromwell did not respond but kept his own counsel, unsure of how to proceed with a Parliament which was blatantly incapable of bringing about the godly nation that was the prime objective of the Commonwealth.

On 20 April Cromwell suddenly acted decisively. Harrison brought him the news that Vane was about to push through a bill to fill vacant parliamentary seats with Presbyterians. Cromwell's frustration with Parliament at last boiled over. He brought thirty musketeers with him to the House and, leaving them in the Lobby, took his seat. At first he listened quietly to the debate and then rose to speak himself. He began in measured tones by commending Parliament and then as he began pacing up and down the chamber started to criticize the members, finally proceeding to harangue them unmercifully for their failings. Warming to his theme he went on to say: 'For shame! Get you gone! Give place to honest men; to men who more faithfully discharge their trust. You are no longer a parliament. The Lord has done with you. He has chosen other instruments for carrying on His work.' At the crescendo of his invective a signal was given and his musketeers entered. Cromwell ordered the Speaker Lenthall down from his seat and dissolved Parliament. When the last MP had been removed, Cromwell locked the chamber door, put the key in his pocket and stalked off to the Cockpit to meet his Council of Officers, then on to Derby House to inform Bradshaw, the Chairman of the Council of State, that he and the whole Council were dismissed, including Thomas Scot.

In four years, first the monarchy had been disbanded, then the House of Lords and now the remaining Rump of the House of Commons. Sir Harry Vane and the like, who were Independents in terms of religion but at heart traditionalists whose principal concern was to look after the interests of the propertied classes, had gone with the dissolution. Whatever were the faults of the Rump, and for the army they were many, they had been all that was left of the country's legitimate Parliament. Now they had been dissolved by the bad temper of one man. This was a military coup. When Charles I had gone to the House of Commons to ask for them to hand over the five MPs back in 1642, London went into an uproar of indignation that was to spark the Civil War. Surely Cromwell's total trampling of the whole Parliament would see a reaction of even greater ferocity in defence of freedom. But times had changed. Dramatic and unexpected as was the dissolution of Parliament, in the words of Cromwell 'there was not so much as the barking of a dog'. The Rump was gone and unlamented and the populace tacitly accepted that the power in the country now rested with the Council of Officers and the Lord General. There was no doubt in anyone's mind that Cromwell was now running the country and it was interesting to note that from that time it became customary for people to raise their hats to Cromwell, a courtesy previously reserved for the King.

What Cromwell and the Army Council wanted was a system of government based on a Council of State and a single chamber parliament that was an 'assembly of saints' consisting of radical Independents who would build the 'Godly nation'. Their first step was to set up a smaller Council of State which sat with Cromwell to select 140 men 'fearing God and of approved fidelity and honesty' from persons put forward by independent Puritan congregations. Those nominated to attend this parliament were then summoned to Westminster by Cromwell as commander–in–chief. What had not been realized by Cromwell during the nomination process was that a significant number of the new godly MPs were Fifth Monarchists. These were religious radicals like General Harrison who believed that the monarchy of Christ was about to be established on earth and so not exactly the ideal people to address the practical issues confronting the Commonwealth.

On 4 July Cromwell opened the new Parliament, which was dubbed the 'Barebones Parliament' after one of its members Barbon, who had been nicknamed 'Praise God Barbones'. There were some gentlemen among the new MPs, such as Colonel Montagu and the West Country magnate, Sir Anthony Ashley Cooper, but it was people such as Barbon who characterized it. A sectarian preacher, who was a leather seller from Fleet Street, Barbon could hardly be more different from knights of the shires and country gentlemen who had preceded him throughout England's history. This parliament was revolutionary not only because its members were the nominated godly but also because the nominations had included six members for Wales, five for Scotland and six for Ireland. It was therefore the first parliament representing the whole of the united dominion of Great Britain and Ireland that the Commonwealth had become.

The new Parliament set to work with religious gusto. Having elected a Speaker they spent the rest of the first day from 8 am to 6 pm in prayer. The first few days continued with this emphasis on religious devotion over business of the day and it was not until 9 July that they got round to appointing a new Council of State which included Cromwell and his senior generals, but also had Anthony Ashley Cooper and Colonel Montagu as members. The Parliament then picked up momentum and began to go its own way, coming up with a variety of reforms including the introduction of civil marriage, revising the Excise, reorganizing the Treasury and the abolition of the Court of Chancery. They then turned to reform the law and anxious lawyers began to fear that these religious zealots were going to overthrow the whole system of British jurisprudence and replace it with the less lucrative Law of Moses.

Cromwell and the Council of Officers found that they had created a force that they could not control. In June John Lilburne the Leveller had written a pamphlet against his former friend Cromwell whom he accused of being a 'robber', 'murderer and 'usurper'. He had been put under surveillance by George Bishop and then arrested for treason and thrown into Newgate Prison. Lilburne petitioned the new Parliament but they declined to interfere and give their support for the imprisonment. Lilburne then went before the criminal courts and was acquitted, much to the annoyance of Cromwell. The fact that Lilburne was soon again causing unrest, and at last was imprisoned in the Tower by Parliament for seditious libel, did not make Cromwell forgive Parliament for failing to support his imprisonment in the first place.

With the Dutch war still in progress the Council of State began to turn its attention to intelligence and on 8 July gave Thurloe complete control over the management of foreign intelligence. To the Council this appointment must have made a lot of sense because Thurloe was already Secretary to the Committee of Foreign Affairs. It made less sense to George Bishop who had been previously handling this work and was merely confirmed in his post of Secretary to the Committee of Examinations. This was in effect demotion and Bishop was not happy. With immediate effect from Cromwell's dismissal of the Rump Parliament Thomas Scot had ceased to be a member of the Council of State or even an MP and so had lost his mandate to be head of intelligence. In the confusion following this coup no one had been appointed to replace Scot. For the two and a half months that had passed we must assume that, as Bishop was Scot's deputy, he had stood in as unofficial acting coordinator of intelligence. Bishop must have hoped that given his excellent record as intelligencer he would eventually be given the official post by the new regime. Instead he found that the top job remained unoccupied and his own post of head of foreign intelligence was given to Thurloe, a man Bishop must have regarded of as one of Cromwell's cronies.

A couple of weeks prior to Thurloe's appointment Bishop had found himself excluded from the receipt of postal intercept information, despite having been largely responsible for setting it up. This had occurred when Isaac Dorislaus told Bishop that in future he would report only to Thurloe. Dorislaus was the son of Parliament's highly regarded envoy to The Hague who had been assassinated back in 1649. Dorislaus the younger was an accomplished linguist and had been recruited to Scot's Intelligence Department in January 1653 to operate under cover of Solicitor to the Admiralty Court with a salary of £250 a year. He was allocated an office conveniently located next to the main sorting office and became responsible for processing all intercepted mail. Combining his linguistic skills with enthusiasm for the task, he had soon shown his worth and before long he had increased his expertise by becoming adept at recognizing both handwriting and seals. It was Dorislaus who carried out the analysis on the letters and it was he who sent those in cipher to Willis and received the plain text transcripts back again. Dorislaus also had considerable influence in the Post Office because when the Council decided to privatize the postal system they had rented it out to his brother-in-law, John Manley, for £6,300 a year. In short Dorislaus had become the intelligence coordinator and analyst for the government's intercept operation.

With Thurloe in the ascendancy and Bishop associated with the ousted Scot regime, Dorislaus decided to change horses. This is shown from in the following extract of a letter from Dorislaus to Thurloe:

> I will manage that business for you with that secrecy and dexterity to your owne heart's desire; and am resolved henceforward not to impart one sillable of any thinge I know to any living soule but yourselfe, who am now wholly engaged to you; and you will finde me reall, faithfull, and true in every particular trust or word you shall impose upon me.

As a result of this stab in the back, Bishop had found himself debarred from all intercept intelligence product just when he was trying to assert his assumed authority as acting head of intelligence. It is therefore no wonder that he wrote a letter of protest to the Council, saying that his intelligence work had brought him:

> little advantage except the loss of my calling, the prejudice of my estate, the wearying out of my body, breaking of my health, neglect of my family, and encountering temptations of all sorts, prejudices, censures, jealousies, envies, emulations, hatreds, malice, and abuses, which the faithful discharge of my duties has expressed me to, in no small measure, besides the mischiefs decimated on me by the enemy, and the keeping of £600 and sometimes £1,000 always ready by me of my own money, to carry on my correspondence when the Council had no money in their treasury.

Clearly life as an intelligence officer was not all fun.

The Council merely ignored Bishop's letter and confirmed Thurloe in his new appointment with its responsibilities for foreign intelligence. Bishop resigned and returned to his native Bristol, with the result that the Commonwealth lost its most experienced intelligencer. Thurloe had been in receipt of foreign intelligence as Secretary to the Council and aware of collection methods through being Secretary to the Committee of Foreign Affairs but he now needed to become an intelligencer himself. As always Thurloe threw himself into this further increase in responsibilities with energetic dedication.

Meanwhile relations between the Council of Officers and their specially selected Parliament had become stretched to breaking point. This was over Parliament's desire to cut expenditure but at the same time continue the Dutch war, which Cromwell wanted to end. By December things came to a head. Early in the morning of 12 December General John Lambert and some others went to the Commons before most members arrived. The moment the Speaker took his chair, Lambert's group proposed a motion to resign the Parliament to the Lord General. This was then carried in the absence of most of the members and Parliament was officially closed. Those MPs who did not leave immediately were then removed from the chamber by musketeers. It was the second military coup in the space of one year.

The experiment of rule by a godly parliament had failed. The Council of Officers led by Lambert now came up with a new concept of a 'Commonwealth in a single person', assisted by a Council of State elected by a Parliament. A new constitution to put this in place had been drawn up during that November by Lambert. This was named the *Instrument of Government* and was the first written constitution in British history. Lambert's draft went through various amendments. Should the 'single person' be called 'King', which would offend republicans in the army, or 'Lord Governor', which sounded more republican and less permanent? Eventually, 'Lord Protector' was chosen and the *Instrument* reached final agreement by the Council. Then in the name of the army, Lambert asked Cromwell to take up the office of Lord Protector of the Commonwealth of England, Scotland and Ireland. On 16 December Cromwell dressed in black with a broad gold band around his hat was driven by carriage through streets lined with soldiers to the Court of Chancery. There in front of the Lord Mayor, Aldermen and Councillors of State, Cromwell received the sword of state and cap of maintenance and was formally asked by Lambert to become Lord Protector. On Cromwell's agreement, a clerk read out all the forty-two articles of the *Instrument of Government*.

The new constitution still gave principal power to Parliament because only they could make legislation or raise taxes and any act passed by them would become law after twenty days even if opposed by the Lord Protector. Furthermore, Parliament could not be dissolved for five months and a new Parliament had to be called within three years of the dissolution. Parliament would consist of 340 MPs for England and Wales, 30 for Scotland and 30 for Ireland. MPs would be voted for by an electorate of persons with property worth more than £200, excluding of course Papists or anyone who had supported taking up arms against Parliament. Although the Lord Protector could make peace or war, he had to have the support of the Council of State, indeed the Protector was expected to be advised by the Council in all things. The Council of twenty-one was already nominated and included Lambert, Fleetwood, Skippon, Desborough, Ashley Cooper and Montagu. John Milton was confirmed as Latin Secretary and Thurloe was confirmed as Secretary to the Council.

Throughout the political manoeuvrings and coups d'etat, Thurloe had been helping to keep the administration of the Commonwealth working effectively as Secretary to the Council. As the Council met five days a week at 8 am and sometimes had additional sessions, it was a busy job to prepare for each meeting and then arrange for the implementation of any decisions. The job was made more complicated by the post of Lord President of the Council being rotational so Thurloe had to react to each new president's way of doing business. Added to this Thurloe was also carrying out work as a commissioner for the Isle of Ely and still doing the odd bit of legal work for Cromwell.

Thurloe was a married man with three children but just how much his wife Ann would have seen of him can be imagined. It had become less in December the previous year when the post of Secretary to the Committee of Foreign Affairs was added to his portfolio and with it a pay rise to £800 a year. He had taken on this additional work with his customary energy and as we have seen had been rewarded, if that is the right expression, by being put in charge of foreign intelligence. As no one was appointed to replace Scot, Thurloe would find himself drawn more and more into coordinating all aspects of intelligence. Thurloe was able to inherit the good work begun by Scot and Bishop on the interception of mail and the examination of suspects. He would also be able to take over many of the sources that Scot and Bishop had managed to build up at home and abroad. Scot had succeeded in getting the Intelligence Fund increased to £2,000 a year and been able to establish a large number of sources in France and also some in Denmark and the United Provinces. A few were high quality, for example, Scot later claimed that during the Dutch war he obtained 'the minutes or heads of every night's debate in the Closet Councils and whole resolutions (of the Dutch) as often as possible'.

The Dutch war had not gone away. There had been a lull in hostilities during the 1652 winter period because of delays in the provision of supplies. During this lull it was decided to give Blake more support by creating two additional generals-at-sea, the now recovered George Monck and Richard Deane who had taken command in Scotland when Monck became sick. It was testament to their amazing success in Scotland that the country was considered sufficiently stable to manage without them. Colonel Robert Lilburne (brother of John, the Leveller leader) was left to command Scotland. So it was that in early 1653 the English fleet under Blake, Monck and Deane, and with Vice-Admirals William Penn and John Lawson, concentrated in the hope of engaging Admiral Tromp. On 18 February Tromp was eventually located near the Isle of Wight. The Dutch fleet consisted of some seventy or eighty men-of-war protecting about 175 merchantmen. A running battle ensued over three days that took the two fleets to Cap Gris Nez where Tromp managed to disengage in the dark and reach the safety of his home ports. The Dutch lost eleven men-of-war and thirty merchantmen. Blake had been wounded and his fleet badly damaged but had only lost one man-of-war. Following this satisfactory outcome the English fleet returned to Portsmouth to replenish and prepare for the next round.

It was not until May that a fleet was again ready. As Blake was unwell, it set sail under Monck and Deane in quest of Tromp. It took them a month of sailing from the Texel to the Orkneys then back to the Dutch coast before they received accurate intelligence of Tromp's location. This delay in locating the enemy was typical of the whole problem of naval intelligence. The home port of an enemy force would be well known but unless that port was blockaded while the enemy were in port it would be difficult to know when they took to sea or in what direction. Even when there was a blockade, it was sometimes possible for the enemy to slip through unnoticed as Prince Rupert had done at Kinsale. Blockading in winter was unheard of because it was the custom of navies to stay in their own ports for refitting during the bad weather. In other words the navy had campaigning seasons just like the army and if a navy set sail before its opponents had arrived off their home port then they could be anywhere on the high seas.

Naval intelligence had to rely on information that might be picked up from ports or merchantmen that had been stopped and boarded for questioning at sea. Navies did have their own reconnaissance vessels, usually small fast ships such as barques which were dispatched to locate the enemy fleet, but unless there was reasonable information in the first place on roughly where the enemy were sailing, it was a matter of looking for a needle in a haystack. In the case of Monck and Deane they at last received information that Tromp had been seen off the English coast, so hastened back across the North Sea to Southwold Bay. On 2 June the information was confirmed when they sighted the Dutch fleet of ninety-eight warships and five fire ships. Monck and Deane then joined with the two other squadrons under Lawson and Penn to make an English fleet of one hundred and ten men-of-war and five fire ships.

At 11 am the battle began a couple of miles south of the Gabbard Sandbank on the Suffolk coast. At 3 pm at the height of the action Deane was killed by chain shot as he stood next to Monck on their flagship. Although drenched in blood Monck coolly covered Deane's body with his cloak so that the men would not be demoralized. With Blake still unwell, Monck assumed full command then counter-attacked. By the time darkness had fallen Monck's squadron had destroyed four Dutch warships. When the battle resumed the next day Monck's squadron led the pursuit of the Dutch to Ostend. There the English fleet was joined by a slightly recovered Blake with an additional eighteen men-of-war. The battered and outnumbered Dutch fleet then sought the safety of the shallow waters of the Walcheren at the mouth of the Scheldt. In total the Dutch had lost twenty ships while Blake's fleet had lost none, although twelve were damaged. The English fleet was now sufficiently strong to establish an effective blockade of the Dutch coast under Monck's command.

On 27 July Monck decided to concentrate the English fleet of 120 sail off Texel because of poor weather. Tromp and his vice-admiral de Ruyter brought their fleet of about 100 sail out of the Walcheren with the intention of breaking the blockade that was keeping Vice-Admiral de With's squadron of twenty-seven warships bottled up in Texel. On 29 July Monck's reconnaissance ships brought him the information that Tromp had left the Walcheren and so he went in pursuit. This allowed de With to take his squadron out of Texel and the next day join up with Tromp off Scheveningen. At about 5 pm that day the leading English frigates made contact with what had then become the combined fleet of Tromp and de With. The ensuing engagement was still inconclusive by the time night fell and was then disrupted by gales. These abated on the morning of 31 July when Tromp launched an attack on Monck's vanguard and a bloody battle raged for five hours during which Tromp was killed by a musket ball. De Ruyter took command then sped to the safety of Goeree and de With made for Texel. The victory went to Monck whose fleet had destroyed ten Dutch ships and badly damaged many more but the English fleet was also badly battered and returned to Southwold Bay having lost a thousand men dead or wounded.

While the majority of the English fleet was licking its wounds, Monck and Lawson took a force of sixty-two ships to the Texel to surprise de With. This would have had a great chance of success had it not been for an intelligence failure. Information was received that de With had already gone to the Baltic. Monck decided that his ships were not able to withstand the autumn gales and therefore returned leaving only some frigates to attack Dutch merchantmen. No sooner had Monck gone than de With left the Texel with his fleet to escort over 300 merchant ships to Norway. An opportunity for a decisive victory over a smaller force had been lost and the majority of the English fleet spent the remainder of the year back in port while the war went on with no engagements.

During this quiet period of hostilities Cromwell began some very strange negotiations that Thurloe must have been obliged to facilitate. The Dutch defeat off Gabbard Sands in June had encouraged them to consider peace negotiations. Cromwell got the notion that there should not just be peace between what he saw as the two main champions of Protestantism but that the countries should actually unite to become a Protestant super state. In July the Dutch sent emissaries over to London to put feelers out for peace and were more than taken aback by Cromwell's proposals. In the discussions over the days that followed Cromwell got increasingly carried away with enthusiasm for his scheme, while the Dutch listened in polite amazement.

Cromwell did not help his case by telling them that their naval set back arose because 'You have appealed to the judgement of heaven. The Lord declared against you.' Warming to his theme he went on to tell them how fortunate the Dutch would be to be united to such a superior nation as England, which was receiving God's favour. All this may well have been very true but was less than tactful. These bizarre discussions continued for a couple of months with little effect while the war continued to damage the economies of both countries.

The *Instrument of Government* in general and the post of Lord Protector in particular had not gone down at all well with some of Cromwell's former friends. This was particularly so of the Fifth Monarchists who considered, with some justification, that the 'Good Old Cause' of republicanism had been sold out. Major General Thomas Harrison, who had been so close to Cromwell and so much trusted by him, now denounced the Protector. He did not mince his words and openly described Cromwell as 'the dissemblingest perjured villain alive'. For this he was summoned to Whitehall, removed from command and arrested. A little later he was released and allowed to return to his home at Newcastle under Lyme on condition that he did not leave the area. He went surprisingly quietly. For the moment it looked as though resistance from the diehard Republicans had evaporated but beneath the calm there were still many supporters of the 'Good Old Cause' who kept their feelings to themselves but would never forgive Cromwell.

Fortunately for the Commonwealth, Royalists at home and abroad were in such disarray that they were unable to turn this period of instability to their advantage.

Charles was still in Paris with no money and frozen out of contact with the French royal family while Mazarin was actively considering an alliance with Commonwealth England. When the Dutch war had broken out, Charles decided to make another attempt at a Royalist rising in the Scottish Highlands in the hope that Commonwealth forces would be too stretched to respond effectively. In June he appointed General John Middleton, who had fought with distinction at Worcester, to be the Royalist commander but it would take him many months to cobble together enough ships, men and weapons to sail for Scotland. In the mean time the Earl of Glencairn led the Royalist call to arms and soon other leaders including Lorne, the son of Argyll, had all declared for the King. This was good Royalist timing with Monck away as a general-at-sea and just Colonel Robert Lilburne left behind to command the depleted garrisons of Scotland. Although this Royalist uprising never posed a serious threat to the Commonwealth control of Scotland, it was to prove a serious running sore that was to give Lilburne increasing anxiety as the year wore on.

With the Western Association effectively dormant, another Royalist organization came into being. This group centred on Sir William Compton, the third son of the Earl of Northampton, who at the age of 17 had bravely taken Banbury in 1642 then in the Second Civil War had joined the Earl of Norwich and suffered the appalling privations of the siege of Colchester. After the surrender of Colchester he had been imprisoned but was later released and like other prominent Royalists returned to a low-profile life on his estates. In fact Compton had become the leader of the main Royalist resistance movement. He brought together a small cell consisting of the Earl of Oxford, Lord John Belasyse, Sir John Grenville, Colonel John Russell, Colonel Edward Villiers and later Sir Richard Willys. The fact that Willys had challenged Belasyse to a duel during the emotion of Rupert's appeal to the King at Newark would not assist in the group's cohesion. This group was to be called the 'Sealed Knot' because of their emphasis on secrecy and restricted their communications to Hyde alone. The only person who knew of their existence other than Hyde and Charles was Ormonde.

The Sealed Knot were realists and, being based in the Puritan-dominated eastern counties, had no intention of starting an armed uprising which they knew would fail. In November 1653 Charles gave formal recognition to the Knot as the focus for Royalist resistance in England and instructed them to discourage any half-baked attempts at insurrection which would not stand a chance against a disciplined army. They were told to: 'Live quietly, without making any desperate or unreasonable agitation or giving advantage to those who watched them to put them imprisons or to ruin their estates and families.' The policy was to wait until a situation arose for an uprising that would to have a really good chance of success.

There seemed no prospect of such a situation occurring in the foreseeable future. December and the creation of the Protectorate had seen a major change. Earlier in the year Cromwell was by far the most potentially powerful man in the country as Lord General but it just might have been that he could be outmanoeuvred. Certainly shrewd politicians like Sir Harry Vane had thought that they had a chance of doing so before Cromwell used his military position to dissolve the Rump Parliament. In those uncertain times there might have been other outcomes such as Cromwell having tired of trying to influence the Barebones Parliament and deciding to retire to his estates like Fairfax his predecessor as Lord General. Cromwell was after all 54 years old, which was the average life span of anyone surviving to 14 in those days. However, Cromwell was of a different mould from Fairfax and, with his conviction that he had a God-given mission, there was little chance of him ending his days pottering about his home in Ely.

By the *Instrument of Government* Cromwell was Lord Protector for life. Of course he was just one of a triumvirate of Protector, Parliament and Council and in some ways the junior partner. But he was still commander-in-chief and so could always be expected to gain his objectives in extremis by force, as long as he held the support of the army. He was also head of state for life, with the title of Lord Protector which had been used in previous periods of English history such as at the time of the Duke of Somerset's protectorate during the early part of Edward VI's reign, and so was little different from an elected king. The Commonwealth now had an unambiguous ruler whose face would be depicted on its coinage and to whom foreign countries could send ambassadors. It also had a major figurehead who symbolized the Commonwealth and was thus going to be at very high risk of assassination. The personal security of the Lord Protector would now become a significant additional responsibility for the Commonwealth intelligence and security organizations.

Chapter 8

Protectorate Established, 1654–1655

Cleaners, carpenters and painters were busy at the Royal Apartments at the Palace of Whitehall in January 1654 getting them ready for the Lord Protector. Cromwell was now called 'Your Highness' and took on many of the attributes of a monarch including bestowing knighthoods. Internationally his position as ruler of the Commonwealth of the three former kingdoms had real stature. The previous year the various engagements in the Dutch war had culminated in a major British victory. Although Cromwell eventually had to accept that the Dutch had no appetite for unification with Britain, a peace treaty was eventually signed in April. Before too long France, Denmark, Portugal and Sweden would also make treaties with the new Protectorate. Cromwell now gave audience in a chair of state on a dais in the Whitehall Banqueting House. Ambassadors were obliged to bow to him on entrance, halfway towards him and finally in front of his chair and repeat the same ceremony on leaving.

How depressing must have been news of this sort for Henrietta Maria and Charles in Paris, desperately trying to raise credit to cover basic living costs. The outbreak of the Dutch war had given Charles the hope that it could be turned to his advantage. The war's conclusion had not only brought peace between the United Provinces and the Protectorate but Cromwell had inserted a clause in the treaty that the House of Orange would be banned from holding public office in Holland. Charles's sister and young nephew were now well and truly out in the cold with no chance of giving him any assistance.

Whatever way it was looked at, Cromwell appeared to be in a commanding position. He had a fully supportive Council of State composed of old comrades such as Fleetwood, Lambert, Desborough and Monck. As Parliament would not be assembled until September, the Protector and his Council were able to rule for nine months by the issuing of ordinances and push through the measures they wished. For all the importance of generals such as the flamboyant Lambert, the creation of the Protectorate had brought one unassuming man into a position of central importance. Under the *Instrument of Government* the Council had been given greater powers than before and so too had its Secretary. Cromwell had appointed Thurloe his Secretary of State, responsible to him for all aspects of government. The Stuart kings had two Secretaries of State, Cromwell gave all the power, and with it the work, to one man – a man who was also head of secretariat for the Council of State, as well as having particular responsibility for foreign affairs and foreign intelligence. A huge task for anyone but Thurloe was up to the enormous job and gathered round him a small but effective staff. Records for early 1654 are slightly contradictory but drawing the information together it seems that Thurloe's immediate department consisted of:

Philip Meadowe, Latin Secretary: £200
Colonel Dendy, Sergeant-at-Arms: £365
Gualter Frost, Treasurer for Contingencies: £400
John Milton: £150
10 underclerks (probably including Henry Sobell, William Jessop and James Nutley): 5s per day and 6d a mile riding
12 messengers: 5s per day
10 sergeants-deputy (reporting to Colonel Dendy): 3s 4d and 8d a mile riding
5 officers to attend the Council: 3s to 7s per day
Robert Stebbins, to make the fires in the clerks' rooms: 2s a day
2 women cleaners: 2s a day

This required a total departmental pay figure of about £5,000 per year.

The members of the department would have set their hands to most things but four of them concentrated on foreign affairs: Philip Meadowe, John Milton, Henry Sobell and William Jessop. Milton had gone totally blind in 1652 so had been given an assistant to read and write for him but he died in February 1653. A replacement was needed and Philip Meadowe, a 27-year-old linguist, was recruited for the job. Over time Meadowe took on more and more of Milton's work, leaving the great author time to concentrate on writing works of government propaganda such as *Defensio Secunda*. By 1654 assisted by the newly recruited Andrew Marvell, Meadowe was doing much of the translation and drafting most of the letters of accreditation and other diplomatic documents. In recognition of this, Meadowe was promoted to Latin Secretary and branch head. Milton remained with his status in no way diminished as the government's much respected mouthpiece abroad.

It is hard to judge how many of this small department spent their time on intelligence duties. Certainly the management of foreign affairs would have required some time spent on handling and assessing intelligence. As has already been noted the Sergeant-at-Arms could be employed on intelligence tasks such as the interception of mail and he would be assisted when necessary by sergeants-deputy. Presumably at least some of the underclerks must have spent part of their time engaged on intelligence for internal affairs. We know from records for March 1655 that Issac Ewer, the son of Thurloe's half-brother William, was the clerk responsible for handling all intelligence payments. This small team of clerks were covering virtually all aspects of the government's central administration, doing everything from acting as the secretariat for both the Council of State and the Lord Protector to carrying out the functions of a civil service. How such a small number of individuals managed to keep on top of all these activities in highly challenging and changing times is a minor miracle but they did.

Those likely to raise a voice of dissent against Cromwell had been defeated or were in the process of being neutralized. Lilburne the Leveller leader was safely incarcerated but there were others such as the Anabaptists who did not welcome the Protectorate. Powell and Feak, two Anabaptist preachers in Blackfriars, denounced Cromwell from their pulpits as 'the beast in the Apocalypse' and soon found themselves in the Tower. Other Anabaptists, like Colonel Alured of the army in Ireland, who could not accept the Protectorate with good grace were simply removed from their appointments. The Fifth Monarchists remained opposed to Cromwell. Having been expecting the reign of Christ they did not find the reign of a Protector an adequate substitute. To be on the safe side, their vociferous leader, Major General Harrison was given a spell in the Tower.

All these overt demonstrations of disloyalty to the new regime were easily identified and dealt with but there was always covert Royalist activity. Thurloe had received two intercepts in January referring to secret Royalist meetings which alerted him to the existence of the Sealed Knot. About the same time Thurloe received information about a plot through the examination of a Roger Coates. He had revealed that the leader of the plot was John Gerard, a 22-year-old former ensign in the Royalist Army. As it turned out Gerard was not a member of the Sealed Knot and appears to have been acting independently. The main details of Gerard's plot were revealed a week later by the examination of a different prisoner by Colonel John Barkstead, the Lieutenant of the Tower. Barkstead was an ardent Congregationalist from London who had joined the Parliamentary army in the Civil War and been one of the commissioners who had sentenced the King to death. By 1650 he had risen to being colonel of the regiment guarding the City of London. Two years later, his stern unswerving devotion had led to him being entrusted with the Tower. While never using torture, his treatment of prisoners undergoing examination was less than benign. Barkstead's examination revealed that the plan was to use thirty mounted men to attack the Protector and his escort when travelling to Hampton Court where it was his custom to spend his weekends. The date set for the attack was Saturday 13 May. As Thurloe knew the details of this assassination plan as early as 9 March, arrangements were made for the Protector to travel by water on the day concerned and for his men to collect information on those who turned up for the attack. When the conspirators discovered that their target had failed to materialize they decide to implement a fall-back plan, an attack on Whitehall Chapel on 21 May. On the day of this intended attack Gerard and about forty others were arrested. Thurloe had kept his nerve and allowed the conspirators almost to launch their operations and in so doing had been able to obtain the maximum amount of intelligence about the plots and all those implicated.

Thurloe examined Gerard personally on 5 June but failed to obtain anything other than complete denial of involvement. Peter Vowell an Islington schoolmaster was examined the next day and also denied all knowledge of the plots. Barkstead had more luck when he examined another of the prisoners, the Leveller John Wildman, who stated that Vowell was one of the leaders and had wanted the plot to go ahead even after Gerard had been arrested. Others also began speaking under examination and soon the whole plot was revealed, including Gerard's leadership and their intention after the successful assassination to attack the guards at St James and Whitehall in the hope of inspiring a general rising. Thurloe's investigations revealed that the whole plot had been a half-baked idea with zero chance of success and in his words had no backing from 'persons of honour or interest' but 'some desperate fellows come from France' who had managed to get the support of 'several people of desperate fortunes' who were 'the scum and faeces' of the Royalists.

The leaders of the highly unpromising scheme were tried, after which Vowell was hanged, Gerard beheaded and three others transported to Barbados. Wildman was rather surprisingly released, as was a Thomas Henshaw, which suggests that deals might have been done in exchange for information. Otherwise little mercy was shown to participants of this foolhardy escapade. The Protectorate was taking no chances and the consequences of treason were made clear for all to see. It also sent a message about the efficiency of the security organization that must have made Royalists think twice before committing themselves to the cause of Charles Stuart.

For Thurloe this was a minor milestone because it showed that his duties had widened from responsibility for foreign intelligence to the coordination of intelligence for internal security. In his operation against the Gerard Plot Thurloe had made best use of intercept, surveillance, interrogation and source handling. It was the latter that was to indicate that the contest between Protector and King had become personal. Colonel Bampfylde, the man Thomas Scot had recruited as an agent to penetrate the Stuart court, was now being run by Thurloe. Bampfylde had been so successful in winning Charles's trust that he was soon selected to go on a mission to Scotland. He had returned to the Royalist court in September the next year but two months later a letter was intercepted by Hyde showing Bampfylde to be in Thurloe's pay. Bampfylde got wind of this and, once again demonstrating his innate tradecraft, managed to secretly slip away from Cologne. Although no longer a member of the Royalist court, Bampfylde had been able to provide Thurloe with some useful information about the Gerard plot but perhaps the most significant was the following report: 'Upon this you may rely, that the King both knew of it, approved of it, and looked to it as the only and most necessary means to set all his other designs in motion.' From this information it was clear that Charles was prepared to support the assassination of Cromwell and could therefore expect no quarter himself from the Protector.

The personal security of the Lord Protector was of the highest importance and a number of measures had been put in hand for his close protection. The principal of these was the formation of a mounted Life Guard. Cromwell had been first authorized a Life Guard when he became Lord Lieutenant of Ireland. This guard consisted of '80 gallant men … in stately habit' who accompanied him from London to Bristol and then on to Ireland. He retained this guard when he returned to London as Lord General and on becoming Protector it became his Highness the Lord Protector's Life Guard of Horse. This well-equipped and mounted force in breast and back plates was commanded by Colonel Charles Howard, a former Royalist who had proved his loyalty to Cromwell beyond doubt at the battle of Worcester where he had been wounded while fighting courageously against Charles's forces. These specially selected members of the army received double the pay of normal troopers and would escort the Protector as he travelled, much in the same way as today the Sovereign's Escort accompanies the Queen as she rides by coach for the State Opening of Parliament. Their task was to keep a distance between the crowd and the Lord Protector and to defend him from attack.

The responsibility for the static protection of the monarch traditionally rested with the Yeomen of the Guard which in the Protectorate was renamed the Life Guard of Foot. The difference between them and their royal predecessors was that instead of being in scarlet they wore the velvet-collared grey coats of the Protector's livery welted with silver and black lace. The captain of this guard was the loyal Walter Strickland the former Parliamentary Ambassador in the United Provinces and member of the Protector's Council. It was the responsibility of the Life Guard of Foot to control access to the Protector in whatever location he was residing. At the Palace of Westminster or Hampton Court at the weekends, they would man the entrances, patrol the palace and grounds and occupy what had been previously called the King's Guard Chamber. The job of those on duty in the Guard Chamber was to ensure that only persons who were authorized were granted access beyond that point. The arrangements for access to the Protector were much the same as for a monarch: that is, a series of rooms leading to the inner sanctum where the ruler would conduct sensitive discussions. The typical palace layout for a monarch could have included as many as seven rooms beyond the King's Guard Chamber: the Presence Chamber, the King's Eating Room, the King's Privy Chamber, the King's Withdrawing Room, the King's Great Bedchamber and then the King's Little Bedchamber and finally the King's Closet. The Privy Chamber was the principal ceremonial room where for example ambassadors would be received and the Withdrawing Room would be reserved for people such as ministers and senior members of the Royal Household and the Closet was in effect the sovereign's private study and where only the closest advisers would be invited.

Although this same procedure was adopted in general terms for the Lord Protector, Cromwell tended to use only the first four of the chambers. After a visitor was authorized entry to the Guard Chamber by the Life Guard of Foot it then fell to another set of guards to authorize access to the Privy Chamber or beyond. These were traditionally the Gentlemen Pensioners but under the Protectorate they were renamed the Ordinary Pensioners, 'ordinary' in those days meaning staff officers in regular attendance. These guards were those closest to the Protector and were drawn from members of the Life Guard who were regarded as particularly loyal. Cromwell understandably placed great emphasis on ensuring that all his guards had a strong personal loyalty to him which, together with the fact that there were three different types of Protectoral guards under different trusted commanders, provided a good mechanism for reducing the chance that they might be suborned into an attack on his life. That said, the close protection afforded by the Protectoral guards was not in itself a guarantee of security.

Whether King or Lord Protector was occupying a palace there were always numerous members of the public trying to have access to him or his influential advisers, either in search of appointments and advancement, or to seek redress for supposed grievances. The problem of control of access must have been a nightmare. There was no pass system and people would be authorized access on the basis of recognition. The guard's orders were simply 'to suffer no strangers to pass through unless they be known'. As many of Cromwell's closest advisers were members of the army they would usually be easily recognized by the guard members, which made matters simpler. Balanced against this, these senior officers could also pull rank on the guards to gain access to restricted areas to which they were not authorized. An added problem was that an authorized person might well arrive at the Guard Chamber with a number of people whom they insisted should accompany them to have an audience with the Protector or a meeting with one of his Council.

Given that a significant number of extremists of one sort or another from Fifth Monarchists to Anabaptists were still serving in the army it would not have been difficult for some of them to get sufficiently close to Cromwell in one of his residences to carry out an assassination. Naturally the Lord Protector was even more vulnerable when he was outside the relative security of a building. He was in constant risk of being stabbed by a Royalist or religious crank in a crowd situation or more likely being shot from a distance as he rode by. There was no doubt about it, Cromwell was at high risk of assassination and the protective security measures available were strictly limited. Under these circumstances intelligence was vital so that those plotting assassination could be identified, located and neutralized before the flimsy protective measures were put to the test.

Although opposition to the Protectorate in England appeared to have been largely silenced, there was still the matter of Glencairn's Royalist force in the Highlands. Colonel Robert Lilburne had been pleading with the Council for more money and troops to no avail. With the Dutch war coming to a close, Cromwell decided George Monck was no longer required and so ordered him back to command Scotland, where he arrived in April. Unlike poor Lilburne, Monck was given funding and additional troops. He was also fortunate that while he was travelling to Scotland Colonel Morgan had advanced from Aberdeen and defeated a Royalist raiding party led by Glencairn at the head of the Cromarty Firth. Balanced against this good news was that Middleton had landed about six weeks before and so Monck would have a new Royalist force to contend with. This information was by no means a surprise. As early as November the previous year Thurloe had received intercept of a Dutch dispatch that Middleton had obtained a licence to export weapons and munitions, which clearly indicated he was preparing a force. Then in January he received a further intercept that Middleton had sailed from the Low Countries with 300 officers.

Glencairn had been obliged to hand over command to Middleton but to add insult to injury Middleton had made Sir George Monro his second-in-command instead of Glencairn. After nearly killing Monro in a duel, Glencairn went off in disgust with his own men, thus splitting the Royalist army. Monck's plan was to deal with Middleton first and destroy him before he could reach the Lowlands. To this end he divided his force into two mobile columns. One he commanded himself and the other was commanded by Morgan. In mid-June Monck received intelligence that Middleton was at Loch Dutch with 3,000–4,000 men. Monck attempted to trap Middleton between his own force and that of Morgan but the Royalist general escaped through the mountains to the north. Now followed a relentless pursuit of the elusive Middleton, which led through mountains and glens as far as Dunain. There, Monck received the information from the Governor of Blair Atholl that Middleton was marching south with 400 men to Dunkeld near Perth, rather than north as Monck had supposed. There was now a chance that Middleton might outmanoeuvre him and reach the Lowlands, so Monck sent orders to Morgan to march south to cut Middleton off in the Grampians. Morgan at last caught up with Middleton at Dalnaspidal near Loch Garry and won a decisive victory over tired and depleted Royalist forces. Three hundred prisoners were taken and the majority of Royalists who survived the battle fled back to their homes, leaving a wounded Middleton to lead just a handful of followers to Caithness.

Monck decided not to pursue either Middleton or Glencairn any further but to devastate large tracts of the Highlands and leave the two demoralized and diminishing Royalist forces to the ravages of winter with inadequate rations or quarters. During the autumn most of the Royalist chiefs surrendered to Monck and Glencairn was captured. By the winter Middleton began negotiating terms for surrender then escaped abroad early the next year. The Royalist rising was well and truly over. This was largely thanks to Monck's leadership, tactical and logistic skills. The success was also due to Monck's own excellent intelligence service that had been able to keep track of two small very mobile enemy forces operating in the near perfect guerrilla terrain of the Highlands. With peace restored his intelligencers were put to good use in providing security intelligence about potential opposition in the Highlands. In fact Monck encouraged his whole force to be intelligence gatherers and charged his officers 'to look for discontented spirits' of any type. be they Royalist, Fifth Monarchists, Quakers or Anabaptists. From this initiative his intelligencers were gradually able to build up a pretty comprehensive picture of potential opposition and then arrange to stamp it out whenever it developed into a potential threat.

Four months earlier there had been the Ordinance of Union between Scotland and England and Ireland. A new coat of arms had been designed for the British Republic with the cross of St George in the first and fourth quarters, the lion of Scotland in the second quarter and the harp of Ireland in the third quarter.

Scotland and Ireland were no longer independent countries but junior partners of a union in which they were merely allowed to elect some of their own members to the English Parliament. After Dalnaspidal this subjugation was no mere passing constitutional or heraldic nicety; it was reality. Fortresses were built at Leith, Perth, Ayer, Inverlochy and Inverness and the garrisons for these strongpoints were to eventually dominate the whole country. With Monck's officers active in gathering intelligence through informants from these strategic positions there became little or no chance of any organized resistance. The Scots nobles and clan chiefs were in absolutely no position to do anything other than acquiesce to Monck's rule and were even denied their traditional pastime of feuding with each other. Monck's tight grip was a blow to Scottish freedom but it brought with it peace and stability. Before long a contemporary could write: 'A man may ride all Scotland over with switch in his hand and a hundred pounds in his pocket which he could not have done these five hundred years.'

The failure of the Glencairn rising had been a major setback for Charles but he had more immediate problems. Mazarin had made no secret of negotiating a treaty with Cromwell and while doing so had frozen his relations with the threadbare Stuart court. As Mazarin intended, Charles's position in Paris became untenable and so he had little option but to leave France and begin wandering the Continent. Mazarin's final incentive for Charles to be on his way was a promise that his pension would actually be paid for once. The only other positive result of his departure for Charles was that Henrietta Maria had been left behind in the Louvre. The Queen was no longer the lover of dancing and masques whose gay personality had enlivened the formality of her husband's court, but an embittered widow much given to lecturing her son. Charles could now feel free of the constraints of his mother or indeed Mazarin. But what could he do with little or no money and less friends? He was not welcome in the United Provinces, the Channel Islands were now under the Commonwealth and so the principalities of the Holy Roman Empire close to the Spanish Netherlands were about as near as he could get to his kingdoms.

Charles's small impoverished group went first to Spa, where he was joined by his equally unwanted sister, Princess Mary of Orange, then to Aachen, followed by Cologne, Dusseldorf and back to Cologne. All the time he was under the surveillance of Thurloe's agents. One reported back at that time: 'For all his dancing, I believe he [the King] has a heavy heart.' And so he might have. Charles had hoped that Cologne would be a good centre from which to collect money granted to him by the Imperial Diet but with the princes of Germany still licking their financial wounds after the Thirty Years' War, virtually no money was forthcoming. This was such a low point for Charles and his mini-court that they began clutching at straws. The wildest schemes were being actively considered to help replenish the royal coffers. One was for James, Duke of York, to marry Duke of Lorraine's illegitimate daughter and be given the independent throne of Ireland. Reason prevailed and all parties soon realized this was a complete non-starter and it was discreetly dropped. Charles eventually began to realize that no amount of imaginative plans for furthering his cause had any chance of success while all the rulers of Europe were courting Cromwell. Even the Pope had begun putting out feelers to come to some accommodation with Cromwell in exchange for better treatment of Roman Catholics in Britain. Charles had little option but to wait and hope that a major ruler would fall out with the Protector and therefore decide to give him some support. In the mean time money was rapidly running out and credit getting daily more difficult.

Back in England, Cromwell was busying himself conducting reforms by the issue of ordinances. Chancery was now rearranged to his liking and the Church was purified of those not considered sufficiently pious. Two commissions were established, one for the examination of clergy applying for an incumbency and another commission for expelling 'scandalous, ignorant or insufficient ministers'. Cromwell did this with the highest motives and the commissioners he chose included Presbyterians and even the odd Anabaptist as well as Independents such as himself. The sect to which a minister belonged was of less importance than his piety and ability. For all that, the end result was to purge the Church of those who were likely to speak out against the Protectorate. Given that the Church was such an essential element of everyone's life and its ministers a major influence in opinion-making, the purge was a helpful instrument in winning hearts and minds for the support of the new regime.

On Cromwell's lucky day, 3 September, the first Protectorate Parliament assembled. After a succession of prayers, Cromwell rose from his chair of state and gave what he termed the 'Free Parliament' a speech lasting several hours. This 'Free' Parliament was based upon a £200 property franchise and had excluded Catholics, Episcopalians and Royalists. To be on the safe side the election process had been closely monitored to ensure the exclusion of those former friends of Cromwell who could be no longer relied upon, such as Lord Grey of Groby. Had there been a truly free parliament at that time it would have been largely Presbyterian with a good representation of Episcopalians and Royalists, with Republicans and Independents in a minority. In fairness, it must be said that the Parliament was probably as free as it could be under the circumstances. For all the limitations it was at least the result of the first parliamentary elections for fourteen years.

This Parliament had the urgent task to establish the Protectorate and begin resolving the many issues which continued to cause division in the Commonwealth. It was unlikely to have been able to achieve this if its members had included those known for strident opposition. Although Cromwell had attained the semi-regal office of Lord Protector he had never set out to gain power. As a deeply religious man he had found himself as Lord General in a unique position to influence events. He saw it as his destiny to create a united and godly republic out of all the bloodshed, dissent and bickering that had followed the King's execution. It was Cromwell's devout hope that this new Parliament would be the instrument for bringing about the unity, prosperity and godliness that he knew were so urgently needed across Great Britain and Ireland. He was to be disappointed.

Despite the selection process there were 125 former members of the Rump among the MPs, including Bradshaw, Haselrig, Thomas Scot, the Leveller John Wildman and the former Speaker William Lenthall. They were all still smarting from the dissolution of the Rump. The new Parliament elected Lenthall as its Speaker and then proceeded to debate its own legality for eight days, raising such questions as whether it had been legal to dissolve the Rump and questioning the authority of the Protector. John Thurloe had been elected MP for the Isle of Ely and being the principal secretary to the Lord Protector was in effect the government spokesman in the House. He was later to use these words to describe the atmosphere in this unhappy parliament: 'The truth is, there was so little consistency and agreement among themselves, and so violent and strong parties contradicting each other, that it was scarce possible for them to come to any resolution among themselves that might be for the public good.'

The level of bloody-mindedness was such that Thurloe was completely unable to get his fellow MPs to carry out any legislation at all. Cromwell decided to step in. He went to the Commons and told the members that God and the people had called him to be head of the nation and only God and the people could take the office from him. He then informed the MPs that the entrance to Parliament would be shut and no one would be readmitted unless they signed an engagement that they would be true and faithful to the Protector and would uphold the government of the country. Although somewhat dazed by this turn of events, 140 MPs signed the engagement document almost immediately and within a month 300 out of the 400 members had signed. Staunch Republicans such as Bradshaw, Haselrig and Wildman refused to sign and were excluded.

The reduced Parliament, while not challenging the principles laid down in the *Instrument of Government*, now started to debate its details and consider minor limits to the Protector's powers. Early the next year they went further and produced a militia bill stating that the militia 'could not be raised, formed or made use of' without Parliament's authority. This was the same challenge to the Protector as had been made to the King, and as in 1641 could not be countenanced. 22 January 1655 was exactly five lunar months after Parliament had been assembled and so the minimum time for which it could sit under the *Instrument of Government* before it could be dissolved by the Protector. Cromwell dissolved Parliament that very day.

In his speech dissolving Parliament, Cromwell accused them of quibbling over details while the country was in danger. In hindsight this appears a slight exaggeration but it was true that there had been threats to the Protectorate. The immediate threat of this time came not from Royalists or Fifth Monarchy men, but from Republicans and Levellers who had admired Cromwell but regarded the Protectorate as a betrayal of their cause. In October a petition had been drawn up by Colonels John Okey, Matthew Alured and Robert Saunders, drafted by Major John Wildman, who had become the leading Leveller now that John Lilburne was in prison. The petition challenged the legitimacy of the Protector and demanded a 'full and free Parliament' to establish the freedoms that the Levellers had listed in the *Agreement*. Informants reported this to Thurloe who had Alured's rooms searched where the petition was found. The three colonels were arrested. Alured was cashiered and imprisoned, Okey and Saunders were court-martialled and deprived of their commands.

At the same time, and probably related to this, was a conspiracy by Major General Robert Overton, an ardent Republican in Scotland. Overton was a well-educated Yorkshire man who had fought at Dunbar, been governor of Edinburgh and then promoted to major general and given command of Western Scotland. He had next been made Governor of Hull, which had become important during the Dutch war. With the war over he decided to travel down to London to see Cromwell about a better paid command. During his interview with Cromwell Overton said with greater honesty than diplomacy that if Cromwell 'did only design the setting up of himself, and not the good of these nations' he could not support him. Cromwell replied 'Thou were a nave if thou wouldst' and, deciding Overton was loyal, gave him command of North Scotland under Monck.

It seems that Overton was not convinced by Cromwell's assurance that he would put his country before himself and while he was in London went to see Wildman. On returning to Scotland he wrote to Wildman saying that he knew a number of people who 'would stand right for the Commonwealth'. Then in December Overton met a group of officers in Aberdeen and drafted a letter to be circulated to other dissidents to meet in Edinburgh on New Year's Day. It is great credit to Monck's intelligence organization that he soon heard of this plan. Monck ordered Overton to immediately report to him. When Overton failed to comply he was arrested. On being searched he was found unwisely to have the following verse in his pocket:

> Protector, what's that? 'Tis a stately thing
> That confesseth itself but the ape of a King;
> A tragic Caesar acted by a clown;
> Or a brass farthing stamped with a kind of crown.

He was sent under guard to London. Although there was no actual evidence that Overton had committed either treason or insurrection, there could be no risks taken over the loyalty of a senior officer. He was committed to the Tower where he stayed for the remainder of the Protectorate.

A similar situation arose in Ireland at about the same time. Fleetwood decided to sack his second-in-command in Ireland Lieutenant General Edmund Ludlow for disloyalty. Ever since the formation of the Protectorate, Ludlow had been openly refusing to recognize the post of Protector or Cromwell, whom he described as a 'usurper' and 'false hypocrite'. Fleetwood, who had some sympathy for these republican views, was typically weak over this slander of his father-in-law and for months and months just turned a blind eye. Only after it was proved that Ludlow had been responsible for printing pamphlets against the Protector, and only then because of pressure from Henry Cromwell, did Fleetwood have him removed.

Another senior officer opposing the Protectorate was therefore relieved of his command but in this case Ludlow was allowed to remain free.

What all these incidents demonstrate is that Cromwell's intelligencers now had to keep a keen eye out for those who had so heartily supported him and his republican stance in the past. Cromwell was fortunate in having a man he could rely upon to take on the huge responsibility of coordinating all aspects of intelligence. Since the summer of the previous year John Thurloe had taken on responsibility for all aspects of intelligence. This was much the same as combining the functions of today's Security Service (MI5) and Secret Intelligence Service (MI6) under one director. Thurloe had also retained his post as both Secretary of State, Secretary of the Council of State and remained an MP and government spokesman in the Commons.

Although as a Secretary of the Council of State Thurloe would have been able to have some say in the shaping of policy, it was both his role and inclination to be a public servant responsible for ensuring that the policy of the Protectorate was effectively implemented. The policy of the Protectorate was in effect the policy of the Protector for whom he had the greatest respect. Cromwell was 55, a man of passion, a military leader, outgoing and at times even a boisterous practical joker. Thurloe was 38, small, quiet, hardworking, earnest and a somewhat highly strung civilian; yet the two men seem to have hit it off and became friends. When the loyalty of former colleagues such as Scot became doubtful it must have been a relief to Cromwell to be able to give so much responsibility to a friend he already knew he could trust with his life.

It is a mark of how close the two men had become that in late September the previous year Thurloe had accompanied Cromwell and a small retinue on a picnic in Hyde Park when en route to Hampton Court. Horses were a particular passion of Cromwell and he had been recently presented with six fine Friesland coach horses by the Duke of Oldenburg, the ruler of a small Protestant state in Lower Saxony. After the meal, being the man he was, Cromwell decided that Thurloe should travel in the coach while the postilion mounted one of the horses and he tried his hand as coachman. Cromwell was an excellent equestrian and all went well at first, then something spooked the horses and they bolted. The postilion was thrown, the carriage nearly overturned and Cromwell was catapulted from his seat onto the pole, then with his legs entangled with the harness he fell under the carriage. As he fell a loaded pistol went off in his pocket without injuring him but no doubt frightening the horses even more. He was then dragged along by his foot until his shoe came off and, disentangled, he fell free. Thurloe and attendants rushed to Cromwell who had suffered no more than severe bruising and the loss of his shoe.

The facts of the matter are not clear but it would seem that Thurloe tried to come to Cromwell's rescue and in doing so had jumped from the moving coach, fracturing his ankle and receiving very bad bruising which was to keep him off work for a couple of months. The incident not only tells us something of the relationship between the two men but is a lesson on how unwise it is for a high- threat person to take unnecessary personal risks. The death of the Protector would have had an equally damaging effect on the Commonwealth whether he died by an assassin or an avoidable accident. The danger Cromwell found himself in on that day seems to have checked any desires he had to take the sort of risks that might have been acceptable for an adventurous private citizen. In future his Life Guard almost always accompanied him and he always had his personal weapon as a defence of last resort. Before very long his life was to be again at risk but this time it would be from an assassination plot.

Although Cromwell relied upon Thurloe for intelligence he had always done pretty well in keeping himself informed of events, particularly in the army. Well before Thurloe had taken up office, Cromwell had his own very effective network of friends in the army. A small taste of this may be seen from the diagram in Appendix 2 showing Cromwell's connections just through his own family. Since becoming Lord Protector Cromwell had been very careful not to distance himself from the army on which his power rested. It was, for example, his custom every week to dine with his senior officers at Whitehall Palace so that he was up to date on the feelings and issues of the moment. In many ways Cromwell was his own head of intelligence.

Intelligence was not needed just for providing internal security and stability of the Protectorate; it was also needed to look after its overseas interests. Foreign affairs for the Republic was far more complex and wide-ranging than it had been under Charles I. England had not been involved in any overseas wars since Charles's peace with France in 1630. After that came the period of personal rule during which Charles was focused on making ends meet at home. Then there were the problems in Ireland and Scotland and the breakdown of relations with Parliament. During all this time Charles had quite enough to concentrate his mind on at home to be concerned with foreign affairs.

Only with the Civil War did Charles take an interest in foreign affairs and that was restricted to the matter of seeking support for his war effort. This limited diplomatic activity was carried out amid the disruption of the war and in competition with the Parliament's overseas envoys. Charles never gained the overseas support he so desperately sought and for the years of captivity leading to his execution was a monarch in name only with no government service, who could do no more than send out clandestine pleas for help. The rulers of Europe had been too fully occupied by the Thirty Years' War to be much concerned with a lame-duck England. As a result the country had become marginalized.

With the formation of the Commonwealth England once again had a single government and within three years that government had control of all three former kingdoms. Once Europe began recovering from the horrors of the Thirty Years' War and returning to commercial enterprise, it remembered that Britain was a major trading nation that could no longer be ignored. Also Britain now had the New Model Army whose discipline and professionalism were receiving widespread respect and some of whose best officers, such as Blake and Monck, were now commanding a large navy. A country with such an army and navy would be a valued ally to France or Spain who were once again squaring up for conflict. Suddenly Britain mattered and the rulers of Europe had important economic or military incentives to foster good relations. The Commonwealth was also to have its own agenda for foreign affairs which was more ambitious than anything seen since Elizabeth I's time, fifty years before.

The foremost foreign affairs objective of the Commonwealth was to persuade countries whose rulers might have sympathy with Charles II to withdraw all support. The principal country of concern was France, where Charles and his mother had been living as poor relations to the French royal family. The next most important objective for the evangelical Commonwealth was to promote the Protestant cause. This was a matter of alliances with the leading Protestant nations such as Sweden (whose monarch also ruled Finland and Estonia), Denmark (which then included Norway) and the United Provinces. This was complicated by several factors. First, Sweden was in bitter conflict with Denmark, its traditional enemy, and the United Provinces were allies of Denmark. This situation was to deteriorate further when Queen Christina of Sweden later abdicated in favour of her cousin Charles X and he began to prepare to attack both Denmark and Catholic Poland-Lithuania, the largest state in Europe, which was in turn allied to Austria-Hungary and through them the Spanish Netherlands. Apart from these main players there were other important Protestant states in or close to the Baltic such as Protestant Brandenburg which could greatly influence events depending upon whether they came down on the side of Sweden or Denmark.

Another objective for the Commonwealth was to promote British commerce. This simple objective was fraught with difficulties when it came to dealing with potential Protestant partners. The Dutch were major trading competitors of Britain, so this commercial objective triumphed over the spiritual one when the two countries went to war in April 1652. Commercial matters further muddied the diplomatic waters because the English Eastland Company was also a major trading partner of Sweden, the enemy of Denmark, which was allied to the United Provinces. Britain relied very heavily on Sweden for its iron, wood and hemp to maintain both its merchant shipping and a large navy which was now expanding at a rate of about five major ships a year. Strong though Protestantism was as a unifying force, it could not always compete with traditional national enmity or commercial reality. All this made for highly delicate circumstances in which to advance the Protestant cause and required the best possible intelligence to have a chance of succeeding, or at any rate not completely backfiring.

Cromwell brought his own slant to these objectives when he became Lord Protector. First, as we have seen, he had always been uncomfortable with the war with the United Provinces and brought it to an end in April 1654. Secondly, he decided to oppose Spain and in doing so champion Protestantism against the most powerful Catholic country and instigator of the hated Inquisition. This stand also fitted well with promoting trade and economic prosperity, because it allowed attacks on Spanish vessels and possessions, all in the name of religion. Challenging Spain also appealed to Cromwell emotionally because he had a high opinion of Elizabeth I and looked back to a time when a sovereign and Parliament worked in harmony and England was a major power that could defeat the Spanish Armada.

Once Cromwell was decided upon something and convinced that he was God's vessel, there was no stopping him. To achieve the various foreign-policy objectives needed not only alliances with natural allies such as the Protestant states of Scandinavia and the Holy Roman Empire but also with the enemies of Spain, and so that meant Catholic France and Portugal and more exotic rulers such as the Grand Duke of Russia and the Sultan of the Ottoman Empire. Thurloe was left with the task of implementing this ambitious work, including obtaining the intelligence on which decision-making could be based. This work was not to be carried out by Thurloe as a matter of duty but with the same zeal as his master who regarded the Spanish as 'the greatest enemies Jesus Christ hath in this world'.

Although Cromwell failed to get anywhere with his scheme to make Britain and the United Provinces a single Protestant super-state, the peace treaty did at least bring cooperation with the Dutch. The other Protestant power the Commonwealth had been keen to work with was Sweden. The feeling was mutual as Queen Christina of Sweden had wanted England as an ally against her Protestant neighbour Denmark and had sent an envoy to London in December 1651. To cement this relationship Cromwell made Sweden the first country to be sent an envoy of the status of ambassador. The urbane Bulstrode Whitelocke was selected for this post and departed for Sweden in April bearing a sword, inlaid spurs and a painting of Cromwell as gifts for the Swedish Queen. Whitelocke's principal mission was to create a commercial alliance but it went without saying that Cromwell and Christina, the daughter of the great Protestant hero Gustavus Adolphus, would work together in the face of any threat from Catholic nations. With the Dutch war out of the way and an alliance with Sweden, Cromwell could now decide how to confront Spain.

During 1653 both Spain and France had been eager to court the Commonwealth. The Spanish Ambassador had offered to take Calais for Britain if the Commonwealth would support Prince Condé who was leading the Spanish troops against the French. Condé was the principal prince of the French blood royal, a man of considerable wealth and an outstanding general who had become a national hero when he had defeated the Spanish at the Battle of Rocroi back in 1643. He was also an arrogant and ambitious overmighty subject who had fallen out with Mazarin and Anne of Austria and decided to take his sword to the service of his former enemies. Naturally, Mazarin was just as eager to win British support for France against Condé and Spain. Condé was also making his own overtures to Cromwell, suggesting that Britain would be given the use of La Rochelle and Bordeaux in exchange for military assistance. Cromwell decided to use covert means to decide whether to help Condé and the French Protestants. In October he sent the German-born military engineer, Joachim Hane, to France make secret contact with the French Protestants and assess the potential of La Rochelle and Bordeaux as bases. Hane travelled under the cover of being a merchant called Israel Bernhard. This early example of engineer intelligence was nipped in the bud when Hane was recognized and subsequently arrested. As it happened, Cromwell had sent another secret agent to the French Protestants, Jean Baptiste Stouppe, who did manage to get through. Stouppe was able to return to Cromwell with the assessment that Condé was not to be trusted. It was this piece of intelligence that dissuaded Cromwell from pursuing any possibility of alliance with Spain and Condé against the young Louis XIV.

Once Cromwell was installed as Protector, France and Spain began another round of seeking British support for their continental war. In January 1654 Mazarin sent over Baron de Baas as a special envoy to try to win Cromwell round. The next month the Spanish Ambassador Alonso de Cardenas formally proposed an alliance against France. Not to be outdone, Antoine de Bordeaux, the French Ambassador, was instructed by Mazarin officially to recognize the Protectorate. A secret diplomatic bidding contest then broke out between France and Spain for England's military support. In March the Spanish were offering £120,000 a year for an alliance, in May France offered £200,000 which was then matched by Spain, who later in the month put it up to £300,000. Cromwell was briefly tempted by this offer but when it became clear that Spain could not raise the promised amount he reverted to his normal gut feeling of hating all things Spanish. It has to be said that he was not too happy with France either. Not only was France, like Spain, a Papist country but it had been conspiring against him. Thurloe had uncovered evidence that de Baas had been plotting with a French Anabaptist Theodore Naudin to incite Anabaptists in the English army to assassinate Cromwell. Although de Baas was immediately declared *persona non grata* and ordered to leave England within three days, Cromwell decided to maintain relations with France. Negotiations resumed with Bordeaux but Cromwell and the Council of State had decided against supporting any country in a continental war and merely to have a commercial treaty with France. Commercial treaties had already been signed with Sweden and were soon followed by ones with Denmark and Portugal. Commercial realism had come to the fore but Protestant power projection was to be not far behind.

Spain still appeared the world's richest country, based on its control of the resources of much of Central and South America, not least the silver mines of Polosi in Peru. Spain also dominated the West Indies and refused to allow other countries to carry out trade in the Caribbean. They had even attacked the British colony of Santa Cruz four years previously. By June 1654 Cromwell and the Council had almost gone firm on a plan called 'the Western Design' to attack the Spanish West Indies, both for profit and Protestantism.

It took another five months to prepare for this covert expedition and on Christmas Day the Western Design force left Portsmouth under Admiral Penn and General Venables. They took with them secret orders that were not to be opened until they were far out to sea, directing them to attack Spanish possessions in the West Indies. Penn and Venables had a fleet of sixty ships carrying 4,000 troops but those troops were far from normal New Model Army quality. They had been gathered by instructing various regimental colonels to provide a certain number of men.

Naturally they took the opportunity to get rid of their worst soldiers, described by a contemporary as 'common cheats, thieves, cut purses and suchlike persons'. Added to this, Desborough and the Committee who organized the West Indies expedition had provided little money for pay and had sent them off with insufficient arms, equipment and rations.

The Western Design was not helped by its command being equally divided between two people who had a hearty dislike for each other. As though this was not enough, the whole expedition was based on faulty intelligence that had totally underestimated the Spanish military strength in the West Indies. This arose because Cromwell bypassed Thurloe and took as his expert adviser on the Spanish Main a former Dominican priest now turned Protestant, called Thomas Gage. It was true that Gage had lived as a priest in the West Indies and Central America and had published a very popular book in 1648 called T*he English American: A New Survey of the West Indies.* The trouble was that Gage had not been back to the area since he left in 1640, so was hardly up to date.

Gage had all the Protestant ardour of a convert and his hatred of Catholicism and Spain chimed well with Cromwell's Protestant crusade. He told Cromwell that Spain had become so weak that it could be easily ousted from the West Indies. In particular he advised that Hispaniola (today the island of Haiti and the Dominican Republic) and Cuba could be taken without much difficulty, after which all Spanish possessions in Central America could be captured within two years. This was heady stuff to Cromwell who could see himself achieving a magnificent conclusion to the work begun by his beacon of Protestantism, Queen Elizabeth. In this instance Cromwell heard from Gage what he wanted to hear and the Western Design was launched with totally unrealistic expectations. On opening their orders at sea on Christmas Day 1654 Penn and Venables decided to sail first to Barbados and then to smaller English settlements like St Kitts in order to pick up supplies and reinforcements. It transpired that the 5,000 men levied were of even lower standard than those already in the expedition and shortage of provisions resulted in the whole force being put on half rations.

In mid-April 1655 this large but highly unpromising force launched its attack on Hispaniola, intending to capture St Domingo. So far from taking the Spanish by surprise, the English force was ambushed and given a thorough mauling in which 1,000 men were lost. There was nothing for it but to retreat with ignominy and sail away. Although the attack on Hispaniola had been a complete disaster, Penn and Venables still had about 7,000 troops and so decided to seek success against Spanish possessions elsewhere. They sailed for Jamaica. The total population of Jamaica was about 2,500, compared with Hispaniola's population of over 30,000, and being lightly garrisoned was a realistic target for the English force, even taking into account its poor morale, training and equipment. The force landed on 10 May and seven days later, after it took Villa la Vega, the principal town, the Governor surrendered. The island was now technically a British possession but the English troops were completely unprepared for tropical conditions and had not even been issued with water bottles. Within six months about half would die through disease, while a month or so after the Spanish capitulation both commanders sailed separately home to explain their actions.

The news of the capture of Jamaica eventually came back to London but did nothing to counter the massive blow to Protectorate confidence caused by the disaster of Hispaniola – the first military reversal since the formation of the New Model Army. To many, including Cromwell, it indicated that the Protectorate might no longer enjoy God's support. In fact he wrote 'It is not to be denied that the Lord hath greatly humbled us in that sad loss sustained at Hispaniola.' Cromwell was also furious and did not consider that poor planning and above all atrocious intelligence were the root cause of the failure. Penn and Venables were sent to the Tower on their return. In time Cromwell was to recognize that God had granted Britain Jamaica with its strategic position in the Spanish Main as a means to prosecute war against the Spanish. Twenty-eight men-of-war were sent to patrol Jamaica and orders were given for the island to be colonized from volunteers from New England and Scotland and a thousand pressed Irish girls. The plan to send the Irish girls did not materialize but the management of it gives an interesting glimpse of Thurloe's steely devotion, for he wrote on the subject: 'Concerning the young women, although we must use force in taking them up, yet it being so much for their own good, and likely to be of so great advantage to the public, this must be done.'

Cromwell's initial reaction to the taking of Jamaica may have been disappointment over securing an apparently unimportant island but King Philip IV of Spain was understandably furious at the loss of his possession. He instructed Cardenas his ambassador in London to make the strongest formal protest. When the protest was made Cromwell countered by saying that the attack on Jamaica was no more than self-defence by England after all the offensive activity by Spain over the years from the Armada onwards. Cardenas reported back to his King that Spain and Britain would soon be at war.

Two months before the departure of the Western Design expedition, Cromwell had dispatched another fleet to project Protestant Britain's power but in this case it was to the Mediterranean and commanded by a now recovered Robert Blake. Although Blake's fleet of thirty sail was just half that of Penn and Venables, when he passed the Straits of Gibraltar he was commanding the most powerful British fleet to have entered the Mediterranean since the Crusades. The objective of the expedition was to seize French merchantmen and if possible locate and destroy the French fleet under the Duke of Guise which was planning an assault on Naples. In this Blake failed because he was unable to locate Guise but he succeeded in his other objective, which was to overawe those Mediterranean countries that had caused offence to the Protectorate. First was Tuscany whose Grand Duke had allowed his ports to be used by Prince Rupert to sell English ships that he had captured. On his way Blake passed close to the shores of the Papal States to make the point to the Pontiff that Britain could with little difficulty visit him in his capital. When the fleet arrived off Leghorn, handsome compensation was offered by the Grand Duke for allowing the illegal sale of English vessels.

With no sign of the fleet of the Duke of Guise, Blake now turned his attention to the Mediterranean pirates who had caused such losses to British and other shipping. Blake went first to Tunis and requested the Dey to release English slaves who had been taken from captured English merchantmen. The Dey's reply was unhelpful. He told Blake that he should look at the strength of his fort at Porto Farina and the size of his fleet that was anchored there and engage them if he dared. Blake's response was meekly to sail away to Sicily. With the Dey assuming he was far away Blake then departed Sicily for Porto Farina where he destroyed the castle and shore batteries, then proceeded to sink the whole Tunisian fleet. Having made his point but lacking the ground forces to take the matter further, Blake then took his fleet to Algiers. On arriving at Algiers, Blake obtained the Dey's agreement to the release of English slaves on payment of their value and to sign a treaty promising to punish any of his subjects attacking British vessels in the future.

Now that all pretence of friendship with Spain had gone, Cromwell decided to attempt another attack on Spanish commerce and sent Blake secret orders to intercept the Spanish silver convoy on its way to Cadiz. Blake therefore left the Mediterranean to lie off Cadiz in the hope of intercepting the convoy. No sooner had Blake arrived on station than the Spanish fleet in Cadiz of thirty sail was dispatched to shadow him. This was a direct result of a British security failure.

Colonel Edward Sexby had been a leading Agitator who had became a prominent Leveller, then a strong supporter of the Commonwealth. He had been given command of a regiment in Scotland but had been court-martialled by Monck for financial irregularities in 1652. Although cashiered, this does not seem to have been a bar to government work, probably because back in 1647 he had been employed by the Council on intercepting foreign correspondence. Scot decided that he would be suitable to go on a secret mission to France to try to negotiate an alliance with the Fronde rebels in Bordeaux. This came to nothing and on finding that a warrant had been issued for his arrest he only just escaped the city of Bordeaux by climbing over the town wall at night. On returning to England he reverted to his Leveller views and became implacably opposed to Cromwell as Lord Protector. He began distributing pamphlets attacking Cromwell and trying to form alliances with anyone who shared his opposition to the Protectorate, particularly disgruntled Presbyterians and disappointed Republicans. He then seems to have decided that even a Stuart monarch was preferable to a Puritan Protector and defected to the Royalist cause. With some like-minded Anabaptists he made his way first to Brussels and then to Spain with a vague hope of raising an army to invade England and overthrow Cromwell. This handful of extremists would have been able to do little damage to the Protectorate had it not been that Sexby had been one of Scot's agents. Sexby had knowledge of the orders given to both Blake and Penn's fleets and passed the information to the Spanish authorities. It was as a result of this intelligence that that the Spanish fleet set sail to shadow Blake's ships. As Blake was not authorized to initiate action against the Spanish fleet who were merely keeping his ships under close observation, there was an impasse. After some time Blake received information that the silver convoy was delayed and so he returned to England in October to refit. Philip IV responded to Blake's obvious designs on the silver fleet by declaring a trade embargo on English goods and withdrawing Ambassador Cardenas. The Protectorate and Spain, although not formally at war, were now in a state of commercial hostilities which was not too much different.

Blake had succeeded in projecting British power into the Mediterranean, proving correct one of Cromwell's favourite sayings that 'a ship of the line is the most effective ambassador'. On the other hand Blake had failed in his mission to attack the French fleet because he could not locate it. This emphasizes the difficulties of obtaining naval intelligence, relying as it did for the most part on the luck of coming across other shipping who had current information about the enemy's whereabouts. As it happened, this lack of intelligence luck was probably just as well because Cromwell had since gone firm on making an alliance with France – an alliance which had become essential, given the state of hostilities with Spain.

While this extension of British influence was going on in the Mediterranean and West Indies, an event occurred which was to have a major impact on British foreign policy. There was a Protestant group in the Savoy Alps called the Vaudois whose religion had been tolerated by the Duke of Savoy as long as they remained in their homelands. With the passage of time the Vaudois had moved to other areas of Savoy and an ultimatum was given to them to either convert to Catholicism or sell up and return to the mountains. The Vaudois refused and six regiments were sent to drive them back to the mountains. Of the six regiments, three were Irish Catholic mercenaries who had left Ireland because of the Commonwealth's severe anti-Catholic policy. These Irish regiments relished the opportunity to strike back against Protestants and carried out their work with brutal religious enthusiasm. The result was a series of massacres of the Vaudois.

When news reached England of this tragic but far-off event, there was outrage. Not only was it a brutal attack against Protestantism, of which the Protectorate saw itself a champion, but it had been done by the hated Papist Irish. All Protestant Britain was up in arms and no one more than the Protector himself. Action was called for, but what? A military expedition against the Duke of Savoy was out of the question, so other ways had to be found to show solidarity with the Vaudois. The first was a national disaster appeal fund for the homeless Vaudois, which rapidly raised the amazing sum of £38,228. This was sent via envoys to Geneva for distribution. The second was diplomatic action. Thurloe managed to persuade the Swiss to declare war against Savoy to avenge the brutality. Cromwell decided that the time was now right to agree to France's long-standing requests for a treaty. Mazarin was delighted to hear that France would be able to count on British forces as allies against Spain. He was less pleased to find that the price for friendship was to put pressure on the Duke of Savoy, a fellow Catholic. It was a price that he was reluctantly prepared to pay and before long the exertion of French influence over the Duke had extracted agreement to religious liberty and security for his Vaudois subjects.

There was also a second price to pay for Mazarin and that was to ban Charles II and leading Royalists from French territory. This was easier to grant as Charles and his entourage had left France the previous year and Mazarin had been keeping the Royalists at arm's length during his protracted peace negotiations with the Protectorate. The treaty between Britain and France was at last signed on 24 October. For very different reasons, France and Britain had become timely allies against the superpower Spain. Sir William Lockhart was dispatched by Cromwell to be ambassador to France. This was a wise choice because not only could Cromwell trust Lockhart as the husband of his niece Robina Sewster, but Lockhart had the personality to quickly establish a personal friendship with Mazarin. By spring the next year the alliance had become closer still, with France agreeing to provide 20,000 men and England her fleet and 6,000 men to wage war against Spain in Spanish Flanders. Their initial objectives would be to capture Gravelines for France and Dunkirk and Mardyck for England. The increasing warmth of the Anglo-French entente had the corollary that Charles II was obliged to seek an alliance with Spain. This was signed soon after and the terms were that Charles II would return Jamaica and remove all British subjects from Spanish territories in the West Indies, if the Spanish army helped him regain his throne.

By the end of 1655 the principal dynamics for the foreign affairs of the Protectorate were set. It was clear that there was going to be no peace dividend from the end of the Dutch war. Although the large army and navy were costing the Protectorate a fortune, keeping up their strength and supplies was essential to promoting the ambitious foreign policy. It was the job of Thurloe and his small team to manage this highly active and challenging foreign policy which required the maintenance and development of allies in a war with one of the two superpowers of Europe. This was even more complex given the number of powers in a Europe consisting not just of states but of principalities, duchies, bishoprics and free cities, whose friendship or otherwise might help to tip the balance more or less in Great Britain's favour.

It should be remembered that Thurloe and his team were not just efficient government functionaries but men dedicated to Cromwell who shared his brand of religious zeal. Milton, in between drafting his Latin letters to different states requesting their condemnation of the Duke of Savoy, was privately dictating the sonnet, which begins:

> Avenge, O Lord, thy slaughtered saints, whose bones
> Lie scattered on Alpine mountains cold!

For Thurloe and the others it must have been exhilarating to know they were the principal administrators of the revolutionary Commonwealth of Britain which, being an instrument of God, was able to bring its influence to bear on the great nations of Europe. In the words of Andrew Marvell, Cromwell 'once more joined us the Continent'. They put their trust in God and the Protector's interpretation of God's will but they well knew that faith was not enough and it would be by their exertions that the Lord's will would become manifest. Part of that hard work was to ensure that intelligence was in place to assist the Protector in making decisions that would further the interests of the Commonwealth, and so the Protestant cause.

The sources of foreign intelligence were several and included the use of agents and interception. The traditional source for any government was that gathered by ambassadors, their staff and agents. Ambassadors and other envoys received diplomatic protection and then as now it was accepted by their host nations that it would be part of their role to collect information. This was tolerated as long as it was done discreetly and the host nation security would do its best to ensure that foreign diplomats were not able to penetrate the inner workings of government. The use of envoys/ambassadors by the Commonwealth had got off to a bad start. They might have diplomatic immunity but they were not immune from Royalist assassination. In June 1652 Anthony Ascham the Commonwealth representative in Spain had been assassinated, as had Doctor Dorislaus the Commonwealth envoy to the United Provinces three years before. Gradually Commonwealth representatives became established in foreign capitals and elevated to the position of ambassadors, until by 1654 there was a significant and growing number able to send intelligence reports back to London.

As well as using ambassadors abroad for the collection of intelligence it was also expedient to target foreign ambassadors based in London. The Commonwealth continued the royal office of Master of Ceremonies which was the post responsible for protocol and the management of foreign ambassadors. This covered everything from the reception of ambassadors at Greenwich to their first presentation to the Protector and all their future dealings with the court till their final departure. The man who held this post from 1649 to 1660 was a former Royal Master of Ceremonies, Sir Oliver Fleming. It must be assumed that, as his duties required him to have the closest possible relations with foreign diplomats, he would use the position to obtain information from them, their staff or their correspondence.

By September 1655 there were about thirty foreign representatives in London, which was in itself great testament to the importance of Protectorate Britain to European rulers. In fact interest in the Protectorate Britain was being taken by rulers at the extremities of Europe and beyond. The Sultan of Morocco sent Cromwell a lion and a leopard as gift and an envoy from the Prince of Transylvania arrived in London proposing an alliance against Poland and Austria, only to be followed a bit later by an envoy from King John Casimir of Poland arriving to request Britain invade Archangel to distract Russia from attacking Poland. As Cromwell had already dispatched his own envoy, Prideaux, to the Tsar to seek commercial concessions, the Polish proposal did not get far. Although there were a number of diplomatic feelers from these more exotic countries, the Protector was mainly concerned with fostering relations with ambassadors from nearby Protestant countries and of course France and Portugal, his Catholic allies against Spain. The best examples were Nieupoort the Dutch envoy and the Swedish ambassador, Peter Julius Coyet, both of whom Cromwell regarded as personal friends whom he would regularly invite to dine and play bowls. When Coyet departed England in May 1656 Cromwell knighted him and gave him a 'handsome sword with a rich scabbard', a gold chain and 'a fair jewel with his Highnesses picture', altogether worth £600, as well as four horses and a hundred pieces of white cloth said to be worth £4,000. Intentionally or not, by talking to a friend from an allied foreign power Cromwell must have obtained insight into Swedish affairs that was itself of valuable background intelligence.

This brief description of foreign affairs in 1654 and 1655 may give a feel for the confusion of the times and how active, extensive and ambitious was Protectorate diplomacy. Thurloe and his staff had the enormous challenge of providing intelligence to support this complex diplomatic decision-making. They were not to be found wanting.

Chapter 9

Security of the State, 1655

Active and eventful though the Protectorate's foreign affairs were in 1655, the security of the Commonwealth at home remained the highest priority. Bampfylde had provided Thurloe with information about plans for a Royalist uprising and gave various names of those who might be implicated, including Belasyse, Russell and Compton of the Sealed Knot. A little later Thurloe received intelligence of an arms purchase in London which sounded highly suspicious. On 1 January 1655 a number of arrests were made of gunsmiths, arms dealers and suspect Royalists. Thurloe began examining those arrested, who were sticking to a cover story that it was a consignment for colonist in Virginia. When crates of weapons were found in Staffordshire and Derbyshire the cover story was destroyed and prisoners were re-examined in earnest by Thurloe, assisted by William Jessop and George Firbank. Although more consignments of weapons were recovered it was very difficult to produce sufficient evidence that would be able to stand up in court and achieve a conviction. Thurloe being a lawyer himself did not wish to waste the court's time when there was so little evidence and so merely detained the suspects without trial. Although this is a reasonable expedient that has been used in our own times against terrorists in Ulster, it could be represented as being unjust. A way more in accordance with the traditions of English liberty and jurisprudence was found and on 18 May Cromwell signed a warrant for the detainees to be transported to Barbados as slaves.

While dealing with these preparations for Royalist rearming Thurloe had heard of a mutiny being planned by republican elements in the army. Robert Overton had already been arrested by Monck on suspicion of disloyalty and sent to the Tower. Soon others were rounded up. Allen the Adjutant General was arrested at his father-in-law's house in Devon. Allen was an Anabaptist and a republican as well as being a senior officer responsible for the army's discipline. He and like-minded officers had encouraged the printing of seditious pamphlets against the Protector and arranged to have them circulated between regiments. A general rising was being planned which included the seizure of key military locations, such as Hull, Portsmouth and Edinburgh Castle, and Cromwell's assassination. By publishing the seditious pamphlets the conspirators had made it relatively easy for Thurloe to identify those who were responsible and arrest all concerned.

Major John Wildman the Leveller was captured by a troop of horse on 12 February in lodgings at Exton, near Marlborough. He was surprised in the act of dictating a letter unwisely entitled 'A Declaration of the free and well-affected people of England, now in arms against the tyrant Oliver Cromwell'. On being imprisoned in Chepstow Castle, Wildman continued writing letters in the same vein. As these letters were of course intercepted they provided an intelligence bonus because they revealed other conspirators. These correspondents, including Lord Grey of Groby, were later arrested and placed in the Tower. Wildman was then examined personally by Thurloe, during which a deal was struck that the prisoner would be given his freedom in a year's time on condition that he worked as a double agent. It was typical of Thurloe that he should decide that it was better that Wildman should be turned into a potentially very valuable double agent rather than exact punishment. With Wildman neutralized and many leading Levellers and republicans behind bars, Thurloe was now on top of this particular threat, at least for the time being.

In Scotland Monck had already shown he was taking action against the dissident threat by his prompt arrest of Overton. He now warmed to the task and made every effort to gain intelligence to identify those whose adherence to the 'Good Old Cause' of republicanism outweighed their loyalty to the Protector. Some made this task easy by openly expressing their dissatisfaction with the regime. Those foolish enough to commit their anti-Cromwell thoughts to print in pamphlets such as *Some mementoes of the Officers and soldiers of the army*, written by 'some sober Christians', were soon identified. At least six officers were cashiered and sent to London under guard. A little later a more senior officer, Colonel George Fishwick, the Governor of Edinburgh and MP for Berwickshire, was also removed for suspected disloyalty to the Protector.

Monck was equally thorough about rooting out even the most junior who he thought might be engaged in subversive activity. Typical was a letter from Monck to Cromwell of 25 January 1655 about a trooper Miles Sindercombe whom he had discharged from Colonel Tomlinson's regiment in Scotland for 'being a busie and suspicies person ... who was forward to promote ... ill desigens' and advised his arrest in England. Thurloe was able to write later in that year that none 'in all the three nations was more loyal and dutiful to his Highness than he (Monck) nor one in whom His Highness is more indebted to weeding out the army troublesome and discontented spirits'.

Monck was using his network of spies to be equally vigilant about Royalist activists. Any Royalists captured had to surrender all arms except their sword and it was made clear that they would be automatically sentenced to death if they again took up arms against the Protectorate. Monck had a very hands-on approach to covert intelligence collection. Earlier he had personally suborned Major James Bothwick whose brother was a Royalist sent by Charles from Cologne to build Royalist support in Scotland. Through him Monck intercepted Royalist letters to and from the exiled court, including correspondence with the main Royalist players such as Middleton. Highly valuable information was obtained including details of Glencairn's whereabouts which was to lead to his arrest and imprisonment. Monck was able to reassure Cromwell that 'There are no letters of Charles Stuart or others which come into the hands of his friends but I shall know them.' Copies of all these letters were of course sent to Thurloe, together with accounts for the money spent to pay the spies and informants involved.

Back in England there was still the problem of Major General Thomas Harrison who, despite spells of imprisonment, was still carrying out active opposition. This was a man who had been Cromwell's right-hand man after the death of Ireton. The trouble was that the religious and republican verve that had made him so devoted to Cromwell the general had made him implacably opposed to Cromwell the Lord Protector. In February Cromwell had him arrested and brought before the Council of State, which was mainly composed of his brother officers.

As Harrison refused to give an undertaking to stop disturbing the peace there was now no real option but for his long-term imprisonment. He was sent to Carisbrooke Castle where he was to remain for three years before being released to live under close surveillance in his father-in-law's house in Highgate. The most prominent member of the Fifth Monarchists was therefore neutralized and the army shown that voicing opposition to the Protector could not be tolerated in anyone, however senior. Despite this, there would remain murmurings in many parts of the army that Cromwell had betrayed the 'Good Old Cause'.

In April the Council decided that all foreign and inland postage of letters and packets should be put under the Secretary of State after Manley's two-year monopoly contract expired in July. Thurloe had of course been working closely with Manley in running the intercept operation but now he would have direct control of the Post Office. Manley had made a sizeable fortune out of his monopoly but had created the effective postal system that he had been contracted to deliver. A weekly service had been set up using packet boats for the Milford–Waterford and Chester–Dublin crossings and a number of packet boats for foreign post. Stages were established throughout the country and four horses were to be available at each stage and these were only to be ridden over one stage. There were other refinements such as the enhancement of naval communications by the provision of weekly postal runs between Dover and Portsmouth, Plymouth and Salisbury and London and Yarmouth. Having an efficient postal service was an important factor in having an equally efficient service for the intercept of mail.

Now this whole activity was put under Thurloe's direct control. Good though the system was, Thurloe began making improvements, down to details like instructing that all mail be carried in leather bags. His more fundamental reforms were that mail to and from London was to operate three times a week and standard postage charges introduced of 2d a letter for up to 80 miles; 3d for anywhere further in England; 4d for Scotland and 6d for Ireland. His reforms included some to assist the intercept operation, such as that postmasters were to keep ledgers showing the day and time mail was received.

Under Thurloe's close supervision, the already effective intercept operation would gradually develop to achieve unprecedented sophistication. Thurloe's main contribution, other than overall professional coordination of the operation, was to introduce the concept of covert intercept. Previously correspondence that had been intercepted never arrived at its destination or occasionally arrived belatedly with broken seals having obviously been read by the authorities. The following are three reports that illustrate this somewhat unsubtle approach to intercept. First, an example of the robust measures sometimes employed as described in this translation of an intercepted letter from the Dutch Ambassador:

> We certainly know, that the mail was set upon a mile from this city on the way to Dover, and the mail cut open, the letters taken out, and flung down the highways. Some were taken up again; but without doubt many will be lost.

Another example is a letter from M. Chanut the French Ambassador at The Hague to the French Resident in London in December 1653. When an expected letter failed to arrive he wrote:

> But I find none for me. Now it may be, that their packet hath been opened, and that finding therein your's to me, they have taken it out to translate at leisure … I shall desire you, that you will send your letters to me under a merchant's cover, and I shall do the like from hence for the future. I have given my directions to a merchant, who will bring it to you.

And lastly the following translation of the intercepted letter of M. Bevering writing on 27 February 1654 to the Dutch States General soon after being appointed their ambassador in London:

> Whereunto I say only, that the same ought to have been in cipher since I very much suspect, that it has been seen and read, together with all the others in the packet, which I could see plainly to have been opened. And besides, I must renew by this opportunity what I have told you already, even from the beginning of our negotiations, that by the opening of our letters, and by comparing the same, the cipher of their high mightinesses, which is at best but indifferent and very common, has been discover'd without doubt long ago; and therefore that they would be pleased to provide new orders against the same.

Whether they were diplomats, Royalists, republicans or Anabaptists, anyone who wished to send confidential correspondence knew that it was likely to be intercepted and therefore took measures to reduce the chance of their information becoming known by using secret couriers instead of the postal system. They also made use of ciphers, veiled speech and white ink. White ink was invisible ink usually made from lemon juice. Also correspondents who realized that their mail had been intercepted normally took counter-compromise action by making major changes to the plans described in the intercepted letter, thus greatly reducing the damage incurred. By Thurloe introducing covert intercept it meant that each particular intercept operation could continue without the likelihood of discovery and the resultant counter-compromise action.

Two people in particular were responsible for aiding Thurloe in this initiative. Issac Dorislaus was all the time becoming more experienced in the different overt and covert courier systems, in recognizing handwriting and interpreting the plain language substitution codes of veiled speech. Reference to Charles II as 'R. Carolus' or 'Ch. Stew' had showed little imagination on behalf of their originators but it became more difficult when Charles was referred to as 'Mr Cross', 'Tom Giles' or 'Your Mistress' or when 'Normandy' was substituted for 'Scotland, 'Swedish' for 'Scottish or 'Essex' for 'France'. Dorislaus routinely 'developed' letters by holding them up to a candle to reveal white ink. Naturally having been developed it was clear that the documents had been intercepted, just as it was obvious that the seals had been broken, and in either case they could not be sent on to the addressee. This is where another person made a significant contribution. Samuel Morland, a former fellow of Magdalene College Cambridge, had joined Thurloe's staff in about May 1655. Instead of taking the normal career route of a don and becoming ordained, Morland had decided to try government service. He was selected to be part of the hundred-strong retinue of Bulstrode Whitelocke when he went as ambassador to Sweden at the end of 1653. There his linguistic capability and diplomatic skills won him Whitelocke's praise and when he returned to England a year later Thurloe took him on as one of his clerks and then entrusted him with being envoy to the Duke of Savoy and the distribution of aide to the Vaudois. When he came back he was rewarded by being made Clerk of the Pell (i.e. parchment) of the Exchequer on an annual salary of £150. As a secondary duty he worked at the Post Office on intercept. Being an inventive person he soon taught himself to forge letters and to copy out those which had been developed with such accuracy that the recipient would not know the difference. To assist in this process he obtained a wide inventory of different types of paper and inks so that a perfect match could be made. He also acquired the necessary equipment to create seals so that opened or forged copies of letters could be sent on with a seal that was a sufficiently good counterfeit to fool the addressee. Finally he invented in his own words a way of 'copying out any writing, though it be a whole sheet of paper close written on both sides, for which there is little more than one minute's time required'. How this was done is not known but it may have involved putting a letter into a press with damp tissue paper. These refinements, coupled with agents being tasked to identify and if possible suborn covert couriers, helped the intercept operation grow into an even more sophisticated and wide-reaching enterprise.

Of course becoming Postmaster General was another commitment of Thurloe's time. His astonishing capacity for hard work comes through again and again in his correspondence, such as in a letter to Whitelocke ending 'It is now midnight and I am extremely weary.' But all this working long into the night by candlelight and then having to have everything prepared for Council meetings at eight the next morning was beginning to take its toll. In February he had been ill for several days and he was also to be unwell seven months later; both illnesses were likely to have been stress related. On the credit side, to augment his £800 a year pay, having become Postmaster General he probably made an annual profit of £6,000 from the £10,000 a year rent that he paid the Council for running the monopoly.

Despite Charles having given instructions that Royalists in England should not take any action until the time was right, Hyde was being bombarded with plans for uprisings. This was partially because Royalists could see the Protectorate now getting resistance from the diehard republicans. The so-called 'Action Party' of Royalists in England were advocating insurrection, whereas the Sealed Knot was far more cautious having noted the failure of the Leveller rising. Thomas Ross of the Action Party was sent to Charles to make their case. Ross told Charles that part of the army was ready to declare against Cromwell and that there was enough Royalist support in Kent to take Dover Castle. With different reports coming from the Sealed Knot and the Action Party, in April it was finally decided that Wilmot, who had now become Earl of Rochester on his father's death, and Sir Joseph Wagstaffe should be sent to England to see if a rising was possible.

The pair landed in Margate in February and then took lodgings in Aldgate Street, London. The plan was for Rochester to go north and Wagstaffe to the west to rally support. Then Charles, under the assumed name of Mr Jackson, secretly positioned himself in Middleburg on the Dutch coast ready to sail to England if a general uprising got off the ground. Rochester travelled to Yorkshire where he joined a group under Lord Maulever and Sir Henry Kingsby. The Royalists had made a conscious decision not to involve Sir Marmaduke Langdale in the uprising because it might associate it too closely with his Catholicism. Given Langdale's quality of generalship and his popularity in much of the North, this was a fatal error. As it was this rising under an indifferent leadership was swiftly put down and Kingsby imprisoned in Hull. Rochester just managed to escape with his life. He travelled to London disguised as a grazier and managed to eventually escape to the Continent. Wagstaffe in the West had made contact with former Royalist officers Penruddock, Grove and Jones and with about 200 men planned to surprise Winchester during the March assizes.

At 5 am on 12 March they entered Salisbury, released prisoners from the gaol and arrested the sheriff and two judges in their beds. Disagreement soon broke out among the Royalists. Wagstaffe wanted to hang the judges but John Penruddock and the others would not agree. Wagstaffe then told the sheriff to proclaim Charles as King on threat of hanging. The sheriff refused. Having reached this impasse and paralysed by indecision, news reached them that a troop of government horses was on its way from Salisbury. Seeing that their rising was getting nowhere the Royalists left the town at about 3 pm. Some dispersed to their homes but the main body went off towards Devonshire.

The plan had been for other Royalists from Hampshire to link up with Wagstaffe in Salisbury. About 2,000 to 3,000 of them were on their way there when they received news that Wagstaffe and Penruddock had left Salisbury. All they could do now was to turn round and scurry back to their homes in disappointment. The government horse caught up with Penruddock's depleted group of about fifty at South Molton and captured the great majority. Wagstaffe managed to give him the slip and eventually escaped abroad. Of the captured, Penruddock and two minor leaders, Grove and Jones, were beheaded at Exeter and about fifteen others in Salisbury. The rest of the prisoners were sold as slaves to Barbados. There had been other much smaller attempted risings in Northamptonshire, Nottingham, Shropshire and Montgomery but all were even more feeble than Penruddock's. The Royalist uprising had proved a complete non-event. Charles quietly left Middleburg for Cologne.

This Royalist disaster caused them a double blow because it resulted in most of the disgruntled Republican element of the army rallying behind the government in opposing the Royalist insurrection. The whole embarrassing failure had been caused by exceptionally poor and unrealistic planning combined with inept leadership, but there was also another factor. As always there was excellent intelligence made available to the Protectorate from Thurloe. The spies of Thurloe were by then everywhere. When Prince Rupert had returned from his privateering and gone off to travel round the German States in January to collect his inheritance money he was closely monitored all the way by Thurloe's agents. Far greater intelligence effort was of course placed on the surveillance and penetration of Charles's little exiled court. In the words of Clarendon, Charles

> was the more troubled, because he was from several of his friends from thence advertised that all his councils were discovered, and that Cromwell had perfect intelligence of whatsoever he resolved to do, and all he said himself, so that it would not be safe for any bodies to correspond with him, or to meddle in his affairs and concernments.

With regard to the Rochester-led rising, Thurloe had known about it from the beginning and was able to monitor its progress. Charles's court in Cologne had been penetrated by Thurloe's agents. The two principal ones at this time were John Adams and Sir John Henderson. The latter sent not only his own information but that which he gleaned from Charles's Latin Secretary, Peter Massonet. Another useful Royalist source was Colonel Robert Werden in Cheshire who was in contact with the Action Party. The interesting point about Werden was that he was one of several useful sources who had been originally recruited by Thomas Scot, which confirms that Thurloe was able to make use of the good work done by his predecessor.

A feel for the intelligence and counter-intelligence operations of this time can be given by the tale of Henry Manning. This young man was a Roman Catholic who had been a page to the Earl of Pembroke. His father had been killed fighting for the late King and Manning himself had been wounded in action. How it came about we do not know, but Manning was recruited as an agent by Thurloe and tasked with penetrating the Royalist court. He arrived in Cologne with excellent credentials and the explanation that he had sold his estate to join the King. In time he got close to Rochester and then confided in him that he was in contact with the Earl of Pembroke who had the large sum of £3,000 at Wilton which would be passed to the King if he received a sealed paper delivered as a token of the King's authority. Rochester passed this information to Hyde who did not believe the story as he was himself in contact with Pembroke and knew that he had little spare money.

Meanwhile Rochester departed in secret to England and Charles in equal secrecy to Middleburg. Manning went to see Hyde and said that he wanted to be the first to draw his sword for the King but this attempt to get himself into the plot for the uprising received short shrift from Hyde. Manning then went to see Herbert Prince who was trusted by Rochester and knew the King was at Middleburg. Manning persuaded Prince that they should both go to Middleburg to offer their services to King. Prince located the King in Middleburg and had an audience with Charles in which he asked if he could bring Manning to meet him. Charles was none too pleased to have his secret whereabouts potentially compromised by two Cavaliers turning up uninvited and refused to see Manning and ordered them both to leave the town. While they had been away Hyde had been making enquiries about Manning. He had written to the Earl of Pembroke about him and learnt that Manning had been dismissed for dishonesty. He also discovered that Manning was receiving letters of credit from a merchant in Antwerp and also that correspondence to and from England was being carried out through this merchant.

Hyde arranged for this correspondence to be intercepted and obtained letters from Thurloe to Manning giving operational direction and instructions in tradecraft. One even said that Cromwell himself was pleased with his work. He also found a letter from Manning to Thurloe giving information which was untrue and obviously made up, including a plot to take Plymouth with a vessel and 500 men. One letter even boasted, as Clarendon later described: 'there was nothing so secret at Cullen (Cologne) of which he could not be informed if he had enough money and therefore desired a bill for a thousand crown to be dispatched'.

When Manning returned to Cologne he was arrested at his lodgings. His rooms were then searched and his cipher found for encrypting messages to Thurloe. Manning was brought before Hyde where he confessed that he had been recruited by Thurloe and that his motive had been simply that he needed the money. He went on to say that he despised himself and had never sent any reports that were true other than one that the King was in Middleburg. Manning was not being entirely candid, for Thurloe's records show that he had sent a report in May with true information which led to a search in Covent Garden resulting in the arrest of William Rumbold the secretary of the Sealed Knot. Hyde was not aware of this but he was in any case already fully convinced that Manning was a traitor. Traitors of course deserved death but that would not be acceptable to the Bishopric of Cologne. Manning therefore received no punishment from Hyde other than to be banished from the court in disgrace. Charles then ordered that an account of the whole event be published as propaganda to show Thurloe and the Protectorate being foolish enough to be fed with false information.

The whole affair demonstrates many things including the detailed personal involvement of Thurloe in the talent–spotting, recruitment and handling of agents. It is also a reminder that throughout history money is the prime motivator for the great majority of agents and that for these, unlike the ideological agent, there is a great temptation to invent or exaggerate intelligence to receive higher payments. This episode also shows the route an outsider such as Manning had to take to gain access to sensitive information. It was the slow process of contriving to meet and then cultivate a relationship with those who did have access, in this case Rochester and to a lesser extent Prince. By following this process Manning very nearly manoeuvred himself into a position of confidence with them which in time might have eventually gained him direct access to the innermost Royalist councils.

On the counter-intelligence side the story illustrates the importance of continual vigilance against hostile intelligence operations. Despite Manning's impeccable Royalist credentials, Hyde took the trouble to vet his loyalty with the Earl of Pembroke. When Hyde discovered Manning had lied, he conducted further investigations, which culminated with a successful intercept operation that provided the evidence against him and the grounds for his arrest. Finally, Hyde carried out the interrogation, which resulted in a full admission. Charles then turned the disadvantage of the treachery to advantage by publishing the case. It not only became useful propaganda but, more importantly, valuable security education for the Stuart court. It might seem unprofessional that Hyde let Manning leave in disgrace but like any other agent exposed as betraying both sides he could not expect a happy ending. To have executed Manning would have been regarded as murder by the authorities in Cologne. The following winter, two Royalists enticed Manning onto the lands of the Duke of Neuburg. With the consent of the Duke they took him to a wood where he was shot dead. In the words of Clarendon, 'the wretch soon after received the reward due to his treason'.

The Penruddock and other risings of the year had never put the Protectorate in any real danger but Cromwell decided to take no chances in the future. He therefore turned to those he could really trust, the army in general – now purged of Levellers, Fifth Monarchists and republicans – and his closest officers in particular. Urged on by Lambert, in August Cromwell divided the country into eleven (later twelve) military districts under officers given the rank of major general with the responsibility for civil government and law and order in their areas. This not only meant supervising security, such as the prevention of unlawful assemblies, but also acting as moral watch dogs for 'the suppression of vice and the encouragement of virtue, the very end of magistracy'. Part of this task was to review the clergy in their areas, eject those who did not meet strict Puritan standards and replace them with godly supporters of the Protectorate.

Given that the great majority of the population had strong religious faith and went to church every Sunday, the clergy were prominent members of their community who could strongly influence public opinion, particularly through the pulpit. Although the Protectorate allowed religious tolerance for the less extreme forms of Protestantism, the vetting of the clergy meant that those leaning towards sects such as the Fifth Monarchists could be removed from their positions of influence. In time the Protectorate would create a completely purged clergy who would not dare to openly oppose the Protectorate 'party line' if they valued their stipend. The major generals were given commissioners to help them in this task and the related work of moral improvement. The latter meant such things as ensuring that alehouses could not remain open, and no entertainment from plays to cock-fighting could take place, without the express permission of the local major general.

Every major general was given command of a militia unit of horse which had been set up in each district three months earlier to deal with any local insurrections. This was in some ways like the traditional role that Lords Lieutenant had held under the sovereign in the past. The big difference was that in this case the officers concerned were tough professionals backed by an effective military force in an active policing role, rather than local grandees holding a largely honorary post. Apart from being responsible for security and law and order in their areas, they provided oversight of civil government and so supervised the work of JPs, assizes and corporations. In short there were few aspects of life within their districts that a major general could not control or at the very least influence.

The South-West was given to Cromwell's brother-in-law Desborough who had been mopping up the remnants of the Penruddock uprising and this was followed in August by the appointment of his cousin Whalley and other reliable Protectorate men: his son-in-law Fleetwood (recently returned from Ireland to sit on the Council but remaining Lord Deputy), also Lambert, Berry, Kelsey, Goffe, Berry, Butler, Worsley and Barkstead. By the end of the year the country was in effect under martial law and was taking on the appearance of a military dictatorship.

The creation of the major generals had been just one of the reactions to the Penruddock rising but there were several others with which it was to be associated. In the rigorous government action after the rising about a thousand Royalist suspects had been rounded up and interned without trial. Most were held until August but others were not released until October. All those released were required to give substantial bonds that they would not take part in any future conspiracy. New laws had been introduced in August on censorship requiring all printers to be registered with the Secretary of State and no printing could be authorized without Thurloe's permission. Only two news letters were allowed, the government publications *Mercurius Politicus* and *The Publick Intelligencer*. The major generals were the obvious body to administer the bond system and enforce censorship. Thurloe was in constant contact with the major generals who kept him informed on all local matters and provided him with any covert information they managed to glean. He was also in correspondence with one or more contacts in every town in the three countries. These were usually sheriffs or justices but could be leading merchants or land owners. This type of information was not only useful in itself but enabled Thurloe to have a second opinion to help evaluate the veracity of the reports received from the major generals. Although the great majority of information received in this way was overt, it was nevertheless of considerable value in giving Thurloe, and therefore Cromwell, a really good feel for the situation in all parts of the Commonwealth. It also enabled Thurloe to act as a most effective public information officer for the Protectorate who could disseminate high-quality information to the general public through the two authorized news letters, provided of course the release of the information was in the interest of the Protectorate.

There was variance in the way major generals carried out their duties in the promotion of virtue. All of them took seriously the control of public gatherings such as race meetings which could be a cover for Royalists to conspire or even launch an uprising. As Whalley (major general for Lincolnshire, Nottinghamshire, Derbyshire and Leicestershire) said, it was not the intention 'to abridge gentlemen of that sport but to prevent the great confluence of irreconcilable enemies'. Most major generals banned all racing. John Barkstead, who as well as continuing to run the Tower was made major general for the City of London and Middlesex, completely suppressed racing, bear-baiting, cock-fighting and wrestling and went as far as having all fighting cocks and bears killed by his soldiers. He even confiscated the horses of anyone caught riding on a Sunday. William Boteler (major general for Bedfordshire, Northamptonshire, Rutlandshire and Huntingdonshire) fined a man £5 for saying 'damn'. He also went to great lengths to shut down all alehouses under his jurisdiction, as did two other major generals, Worsley and Berry, who together ran Worcestershire, Herefordshire, Shropshire and Monmouthshire. Few but the most Puritan in the land could take kindly to this constant interference in the everyday lives and traditional pleasures of the population.

December saw the introduction of the Decimation Tax, which was a 10 per cent levy on all known Royalists with annual incomes of more than £100 or property valued above £1,500. The practicable purpose of the tax was to pay for the upkeep of the horse militia in each major general's district but it also served to make Royalists permanently identified and disadvantaged second-class citizens. Both the collection of the tax and hearing of appeals against it were of course placed in the hands of the major generals who had an interest in raising as much as possible. They were very vigorous in collecting the money because even these high taxes were often insufficient to cover the cost of the militia. Indeed by April the next year, it was decided that militia troops would have to be reduced from 100 to 80 men as a money-saving measure. It became imperative that enough tax was raised to fund militias and the administrative apparatus needed to support the major generals in their duties.

These duties were being continually extended. For example, the Council decided that anyone who had supported Charles I in the previous seven years should be forced to give a financial pledge for them and their servants' loyal behaviour towards the Commonwealth. In addition their movement was to be restricted and any changes in residence reported. The major generals became the instruments for facilitating the monitoring of Royalist movement. A national registry office was established in London to record the location and movement of the whole Royalist community. Any Royalist wishing to visit London was required to first inform their local major general and then report to the registry office within twenty-four hours of arriving in London. In order that Royalists with residences in both London and the country did not slip through the net, a special measure was devised. In October such Royalists were given two weeks to leave London and report to the staff of the major general covering their county residence, then, of course, they were required to report back to the national registry on their return to London.

The new national registry was then given the additional remit of monitoring the movement of any person into England. To do this the registry had to establish deputy registrars at Dover, Deal, Gravesend, Rye, Plymouth, in fact at every major port. All new arrivals in England were required to report to the deputy registrars and give their name, destination and address of intended lodging. Those travellers going to London were then required to report to the registry office and those to the country to the staff of the appropriate major general. In short, a large and comprehensive organization was established to monitor and control all who might be enemies of the state and keep them under constant fear that they would lose the majority of their property if they were found to have been working against the Protectorate. The strength and extent of this state control was completely without precedent and had only been made possible by the creation of an effective bureaucracy and military efficiency. Its key elements were the major generals and their staff covering all areas of England and the central national registry office with its subregistrars at all the ports. In order to understand the huge scope of these measures the following figures speak for themselves. The major generals imposed bonds on over 14,000 suspect Royalists and from February 1655 to August 1657 over 1,000 arrivals in England were documented. Many of the records still exist and the value and detail of the information provided can be seen by taking just a few entries on some of the Sealed Knot members. These show Lord Belasyse and his servant leaving lodgings in Martin's Lane on 15 February for Dover to travel to France with a Council warrant; Sir Richard Willys lodging at the White Horse in Russell Street from 5 February to 14 March and then returning home to Fen Ditton and Sir William Compton lodging near Charing Cross at the beginning of April.

The man who provided the direction of both the major generals and the national registry, and therefore the coordination between the two, was of course Mr Secretary Thurloe. He was also able to ensure that information from his existing intelligence sources fed into the major general/national registry system and information from that system contributed to the overall intelligence assessment. The national registry had brought a new and comprehensive dimension to surveillance of Royalists in particular but specific targeted surveillance had been used for some time. For example, static surveillance of foreign diplomats was well established by 1653 when on 18 July the Dutch Ambassador to London, M. Bevering wrote back home:

> Sir, I dare not write much news. All our actions are spied. We have spies
> set to watch us in our houses. We can not be certain of anything we do,
> that it will not be know or miscarry. If you please to have anything sent to
> you from here, that this country afford, pray let me know it.

From the beginning, Thurloe had made extensive use of surveillance on intelligence targets but does not appear to have had his own government surveillance teams. Instead he seems to have outsourced the activity and paid groups of people to watch particular targets. These included static surveillance to watch the coming and goings of the principal foreign embassy residences and of course the Stuart court in exile. It is recorded that he had between fifty and sixty persons on this task in the first half of 1654 when Charles was still in Paris with the Queen his mother. Although most surveillance was static, some was mobile, such as that tasked to follow Prince Rupert round Germany or Queen Christina of Denmark after she had abdicated and was travelling the Continent and planning to take over the throne of Naples with French backing. Under these circumstances there was a fine line between a contracted surveillance operator and a casual contact or even agent. It matters little in what category they might be placed, the important point was that Thurloe presided over a surveillance operation of a magnitude that was unprecedented in British history and is only now being matched in the current war on terrorism.

At the same time that Cromwell was imposing these severe restrictions on freedom in the name of national security, he was engaged in a very different and humanitarian venture. The Protector had decided that Jews should be allowed back into England and be given freedom of worship. At first sight it is amazing that Cromwell, an arch-Protestant zealot, should wish to change laws that that had been in existence since the Jews were expelled from England in 1290. There were a variety of reasons why the Jews were beginning to be seen in a different light from a people who were thought to deserve persecution for the crucifixion of Christ. During the previous ten or so years a growing number of Protestants had begun to feel it was their duty to convert the Jews to Christianity. In fact the Fifth Monarchists went one step further and believed that the conversion of the Jews was an essential step in the overthrow of the Anti-Christ necessary for bringing about the Second Coming.

Naturally, if there was to be any hope of Protestants converting Jews they had to be able to live amongst them. As it happened Jews were already living covertly in England and had formed groups in London, York and Dover. These were known as Marranos and pretended to be Spanish and Portuguese Catholics who had settled in England for trade. The Marranos kept themselves to themselves and worshipped quietly in their secret synagogues. Few were aware of their existence as Jews and those who did turned a blind eye to these increasingly prosperous people who were making a welcome contribution to the country's commerce. For the Marranos themselves the situation was bearable but they naturally hoped that their presence might be given formal recognition. In fact in December 1648 their leaders approached Fairfax with such a suggestion which he passed to the Council of Officers for their consideration but it seems to have been put to one side. When Thurloe had visited Amsterdam as secretary to Oliver St John he had taken the opportunity to meet Menasseh ben Israel, a Maderian Jew, who had long been a principal religious leader in Amsterdam. Menasseh had been for some time campaigning for Jews to be able to openly return to England and take part in the increasing trade. On meeting Menasseh, Thurloe recommended that he applied to the Council. This he did and a committee was set up under Cromwell for its consideration. Other more urgent matters arose and the Jewish question was again put to one side.

Towards the end of 1655 Thurloe again raised the Jewish question with Cromwell and the subject was once more back on the table. It would seem that it was not out of a wish to convert them that Cromwell became an enthusiast for allowing the return of the Jews to England. It was because he was persuaded by Thurloe that the Jews were a major potential source of intelligence. The Jewish trading communities made use of their network of commercial contacts with other Jewish traders around the world to keep themselves informed on the economic situation and business opportunities. These many informal networks of contacts around the world enabled Jewish merchants to gather commercial and maritime intelligence as well as such political and military information which came their way that might have commercial implications.

If the Jews could be made to feel in the debt of Protectorate England, many would not only be prepared to provide valuable intelligence but do it for nothing. Thurloe did not put forward this proposal to Cromwell as a mere theory: he had already been using some Jews as informants with great success. These were men such as Antonio Carvajal who lived in Leaden Hall Street, and the Portugese Jew Manuel Martinez. The value of their information can be illustrated by a report to Thurloe in September from a Jew in Amsterdam that 11,000 men had left Spain under General Paulo de Contreros in eight warships accompanied by ten fire ships. A regular stream of such reports would provide the navy with a significant advantage in the forthcoming war against Spain. In fact it was the impending war that must have hastened the need to come to accommodation with the Jews who of course had a particular hatred of Spain, having been victims of the Inquisition.

Probably at Cromwell's invitation, Menasseh ben Israel arrived in London from Amsterdam, leading a small delegation of rabbis. When Cromwell met Menasseh he was quickly won over by his charm and learning. A petition requesting that Jews might be able to live in England 'under the shadow of your protection' was forwarded by Cromwell to the Council. The matter was discussed at length on

18 December and it was clear that there was plenty of opposition arising from traditional anti-Semitism and a fear that Jews would take profits from English merchants. Cromwell then assumed his role as Lord Protector and discreetly lifted the restrictions on Jews entering and working in England. This was not done by the enactment of new laws or repeal of the 1290 ruling, it just quietly happened because the Lord Protector wanted it so.

A first modest step towards formal recognition of the Jews came in March the next year when it was agreed that the Jews could have their own cemetery in London at Mile End. Three months later Don Antonio Bobles, a Marranos living in London, had his property seized because he was thought to be Spanish and so from a country with which Britain was then at war. He appealed to Cromwell and the Council ruled that he was a 'Jew born in Portugal' and his property returned. Following the creation of this precedent, Jewish merchants began openly settling in London and other parts of the country, so laying the foundation for the major economic and cultural contribution which their race has made to their adopted country. Their early position in England rested upon the personal guarantee of the Lord Protector which could have ended with the restoration of the monarchy. As it was, Charles II acknowledged the financial help he had received from Amsterdam Jews and in 1664 they were given formal legal authority to live and trade in England with freedom of worship. Since that time the relatively small number of Jews has made an entirely disproportionate contribution to all walks of British life. The intelligence requirements of the Protectorate were a catalyst in bringing this about.

Chapter 10

Rule of the Major Generals, 1656

By January 1656 the restrictions imposed by the major generals had become so tight that few would dare outright resistance to the Lord Protector. Although insurrection was becoming increasingly unlikely, there always remained the possibility that the Protectorate might be terminated by an assassin's knife or bullet. Towards the end of 1655 Thurloe had received a flurry of reports of assassination plots. One report in November was that the Spanish were plotting 'the means to help His Highness and some of the councillors out of this world'. Then there was a report that Sir Joseph Wagstaffe had obtained a secret weapon that would fire seven shots at once, almost silently and without smoke. This followed an assassination plot by James Halsall and Richard Talbot. The value of intelligence as a commodity was now generally known and Halsall's servant betrayed his master for money. Both were arrested and examined by Thurloe. By the end of the year a further three suspects had been arrested and placed in the Tower. None of these plots was likely to have succeeded but they all had to be dealt with seriously by Thurloe as he was well aware that Royalist assassins only needed to be lucky once. The speed with which they were discovered sent a message to all Royalists that any plot was very likely to be compromised and result in the loss of their estates, liberty and quite possibly life.

Intentionally or not Thurloe had created a climate of fear. Ironically this fear also extended to the Lord Protector himself, who was receiving Thurloe's continual reports of subversive activity that his agents had unearthed. Cromwell was of course an exceptionally brave man but while he was prepared to risk his own life when necessary he was not prepared to risk his work being left uncompleted through the loss of his life. Early in the year the Life Guard of Horse was purged and any whose loyalty was in the slightest doubt were dismissed. It was also increased in size to 160 and the pay was raised to 5 shillings a day. Significantly they were now placed under command of Major Richard Beke who had recently married Cromwell's niece Lavinia Whetstone, daughter of his favourite sister Catherine. Cromwell was ensuring that his security lay with those whom he could really trust through both obligation and family.

Such secret Royalists in opposition as remained in Britain must have felt that, what with the constant surveillance of the major generals and Thurloe's intelligence network, things could hardly get worse. They would have been wrong. Among the Royalists who had been arrested in the first part of 1654 was Sir Richard Willys. In August he sent a petition to the Protector for bail from the Tower in which he said that he 'would express his gratitude with obedience' if he was given freedom to raise a force to fight the Turks. The Council decided that he should be banished on condition that he did not act against the Protectorate. As it turned out Willys showed little sign of obedience and not only returned to live with his relations in Cambridgeshire but resumed work with the Sealed Knot. But even the most ardent opponents of a government can sometimes reposition their loyalty when beckoned along the alluring path of self-interest. Such was the case of Sir Richard, who like many Royalists had seen what wealth they had drain away in thankless service to a young man whose chances of regaining the throne were becoming remoter by the day. Willys was the second son of a Cambridgeshire lawyer and himself studied at Gray's Inn before deciding upon on a military career. As a professional soldier he had served under Monck in the Netherlands, followed by both the Scots wars, then joined the King's Life Guard at the start of the Civil War and was soon knighted for bravery in a cavalry action near Shrewsbury. He was captured twice in the war but got back to the army by first breaking his parole and then through a prisoner exchange. He later rose to the rank of major general and became Governor of Newark until removed by the King for taking Rupert's side. As a soldier he had been out of work since the end of the Civil War and had no family estates to fall back on. With his background there was absolutely no chance of being accepted into the New Model Army and now that his suggestion of fighting against the Turks had been turned down, he had no future.

Willys decided to write a letter to Thurloe signed 'John Foster' giving his terms for recruitment as an agent. These included that his real name once revealed should be known only to Thurloe and Cromwell and that he should receive £500 on appointment, as well as £50 enclosed with a reply to his letter and a further £500 for revealing conspiracies against the Protector. Willys also stipulated that Thurloe should send a reply to an apothecary in Charing Cross to be collected by Mr Foster or his servant. The use of a cut-out indicated at once that the author had a natural feel for espionage tradecraft and the sums requested showed that he could be expected to deliver vital intelligence. Thurloe duly replied, enclosing the £50, and so began running what was to be his most valuable Royalist intelligence asset. The timing was perfect. The Sealed Knot had been in complete disarray following the arrests after the Penruddock rising and bitter disputes between Belasyse and Willys, but had begun to reform in early 1656 under Edward Villiers, with Willys as a prominent member. They had got themselves sufficiently recognized as to resume secret communication with Hyde using a courier called Thomas Barret. With Willys now an accredited agent, Thurloe was in a position to know all the plans of the only active Royalist resistance movement and also the information communicated to them from the Stuart court.

The year 1656 saw the zenith of Protectorate intelligence. The major generals had England under tight control, as indeed Monck had Scotland. In Ireland Fleetwood was still nominally Lord Deputy but had been ordered back to England in September the previous year to take on one of the large major general districts of East Anglia. Some time before this Cromwell had sent out his younger son Henry to Ireland to keep an eye on Fleetwood, who seemed to be tolerating those like Ludlow who voiced opposition to the Protectorate. With Fleetwood back in England, Henry Cromwell, the Major General of the Army of Ireland, took over most of the powers of the Lord Deputy and began purging his army of potential dissidents, particularly Baptists and Quakers. So it was that by 1656 Cromwell's generals were in effective control throughout the three nations of the Commonwealth and were closely monitoring both their own forces and the public at large for any signs of disaffection to the Lord Protector. Thurloe was also at the height of his power at this time. Knowledge is often said to be power and Thurloe certainly had access to unprecedented amounts of knowledge and the mental capacity to use it to further the interests and security of the Protectorate. The great majority of the information he received was in his capacity as Secretary. This was the overt information on the current situation reported by major generals, justices, sheriffs and the like at home and the dispatches from the Protectorate's wide network of colonial governors, ambassadors and representatives overseas, to which should be added the naval commanders at sea. The Protectorate's diplomatic stations alone included residents in Spain, Portugal, France, Denmark, Sweden, United Provinces, Spanish Netherlands, Switzerland, Poland, Russia, Turkey and many of the Italian and German states such Leghorn and Hamburg. Given the fact that the coverage of these overt sources was so extensive and comprehensive, there was ample opportunity for comparing reports to obtain collateral and form judgements that established a realistic picture. These sources provided the basic information necessary to understand the situation at home and overseas and to inform government decision-making. Important though this overt information was, it was considerably enriched by secret intelligence. Thurloe was at the hub of an intelligence organization that coordinated the sources from intercept, interrogation, surveillance and agent handling. This is therefore a good period to pause for a few moments to examine how the intelligence apparatus functioned.

Captured or intercepted documents made a major contribution to the success of Protectorate intelligence. These could range from simple orders or messages to lengthy correspondence giving details of plots, military plans and diplomatic negotiation. This material could fall into government hands by chance, such as being found when a suspect was arrested or a ship searched after boarding. But even these chance finds needed the finder to be aware of the need to search, an ability to identify potentially useful documents and the means to convey them safely as soon as possible to Whitehall and the staff of John Thurloe. There had been a growing general awareness of the importance of enemy correspondence during the Civil Wars. Officers and most men of the Commonwealth army and navy were generally aware of the need to search for correspondence and incriminating documents and pass them back to higher authorities. This was a matter of discipline and loyalty. For the general public there was also awareness that such documents had a value and that to make them available to the appropriate authorities was likely to result in financial reward. All this was helpful to Thurloe and his intelligence department but was not enough to bring success. What was required and indeed what was provided was an intercept system based on hard work, painstaking attention to detail and sheer professionalism.

As we have seen, the intercept operation was run by Isaac Dorislaus. This was largely a night-time activity, with all letters received by the London General Letter Office that day being brought to Dorislaus' room where he would examine them from about 11 pm to 4 am. He would then use his skill to identify letters of potential intelligence interest from handwriting and seals. On average there would be about two or three such letters a night. Samuel Morland would arrive a little later then covertly open the letters and check them against a candle for secret ink. If secret ink was found Morland would forge a copy and reseal. In all cases Morland would make a working copy of the letter. Dorislaus would then read the working copy, not in itself easy, given the almost indecipherable handwriting of the time and lack of Standard English which could result in the same word being spelt in three different ways in a single document. The difficulty was further increased if the document was in a foreign language which Dorislaus would have to translate. If there was any cipher we may assume that Dorislaus would convert it to plain text if John Wallis had already identified the cipher key used by the correspondents. Any document with a new cipher would be sent to Wallis for cryptanalysis. The end product of Dorislaus's work would then be taken by Morland to Thurloe and seen by him the next morning. The intercepted mail would be returned to the General Letter Office before dawn to proceed without any delay in its transmission.

In order to carry out intercept it was first necessary to understand the means of communication, whether it was the formal system through postmaster or private systems, such as company couriers or diplomatic and military reporting. Then there were the covert channels for secret correspondence which were as various as ingenuity could devise. Agents and informants were essential in providing the information to at least understand the various mechanisms of communication, particularly clandestine communications. Once that method of communication was known, it was then necessary to decide how the intercept could be carried out. This again required agents and informants to help identify the couriers, servants, clerks and postmasters who might be prepared to pass the correspondence. Following this talent-spotting there was then the hardest task of all of approaching the targets to see if they could be bribed or suborned into handing over the documents in their charge. As Morland worked closely with Meadowe on agent handling in Thurloe's office, he was able to bring this essential element to the intercept operation.

Although intercept was usually carried out in a covert fashion there were sometimes occasions when this was not possible. In such cases Thurloe had to revert to either getting the Sergeant-at-Arms, Colonel Dendy, to send his sergeants to impound mail or hire thugs to mug couriers. Whether it was highway robbery that had to be organized or the more usual use of agents and bribery, the whole collection operation required a great deal of planning. Once received, the documents had to be processed in the normal way. A feel for the amount of effort involved in a fairly simple intercept is given on a note written by Thurloe attached to a copy of a letter from Charles to Sir Henry Slingsby. It reads as follows:

> Indors'd thus by secretary Thurloe, Charles Stewart's letter of 16 April 1656, to sir Henry Slingsby, brought by J. Cooper, and delivered to John Waters to be carried to Slingsby. It was delivered to me the 16 th of April old style: [The Continent had moved to the Gregorian Calendar but England retained the 'Old Style' or Julian Calendar which was 10 days behind] haveinge taken a coppy thereof, I gave it to Walters to be carried as he had directions.

Two points arise from this example. The first is that, although the document itself was merely a letter of condolence and contained nothing of intelligence value, it was processed with as much care as a letter of high intelligence importance and this included making a copy. The decision to make a copy and then send the original to its destination was obviously because Thurloe did not want the correspondents to be aware that their covert means of communication was being intercepted. Had either party realized that letters were not arriving, they would have changed the means of communication and Thurloe would have had to start the whole operation again from scratch. The second point is that, despite the professionalism that obviously went into keeping accurate records of covert collection, Thurloe may have made what today we would regard as a mistake. He has named both J Cooper and John Waters, which if those were their real names might be a breach of security because it disclosed his sources. It could well be that J Cooper was an overt member of Isaac Dorislaus's staff who was merely delivering the letter after it had been intercepted, but Waters seems to have been a Royalist courier working for Thurloe and therefore his identity, if real, warranted protection. Today the true names of agents and contacts are never included in documents showing the intelligence they provided. A two-word nickname would be used for the agent and a number allocated to the contact. A record of which nickname or number referred to which person would be held separately under secure arrangements to reduce the risk of source compromise. We know that Thurloe was very security-minded and would be unlikely to allow source identity information to be seen even by his small and trusted staff in their secure offices. It is therefore probable that this document was kept securely by Thurloe himself, for his eyes only. Perhaps we should give him the benefit of the doubt.

Intercept was not just carried out at the national level. In Scotland Monck and Lord Broghill, who had become Lord President of the Council of Scotland, were both running successful intercept operations against Royalists. Then there were agents like Joseph Bampfylde in Paris who managed to intercept correspondence between Charles and his court in Bruges about negotiations with Spain. This was probably achieved through a subsource Bampfylde was running in Madrid.

Whatever the form of intercept, the product always eventually arrived on Thurloe's desk for his formal assessment. This was of course true of all types of intelligence product. Reports from interrogation, or examination as it was called, were also received by Thurloe. As we have seen, examination was a matter in which Thurloe took a particular interest. He was a qualified barrister and had been made a bencher at Lincoln's Inn in 1654. He personally examined people of all types, including among others a tailor, butcher, schoolmaster and musician. The process followed legal procedures and consisted of taking evidence under oath. Surprisingly for the times it was conducted in a humane manner that was not to be guaranteed again in England until the Police and Criminal Justice Act of 1984.

As Lord Protector Cromwell must have taken over the royal prerogative of torture but certainly did not exercise it. Examinations during the Protectorate used no violence and depended upon the prisoner not putting their immortal soul at risk by committing perjury. There was one other incentive and that was for the interrogator to exploit the prisoner's self-interest. Deals could be done in which a prisoner would provide evidence against others in return for punishment being reduced or waived. Thurloe was a past master at creating these deals which would secure the conviction of others or in many cases turn them to become government agents. Thurloe was not alone in conducting interrogation/examination for it was also carried out by justices of the peace and military commanders, most notably Monck, and the Lieutenant Governor of the Tower, Colonel John Barkstead, who had also been made major general for the City of London. There were occasions when the Council of State itself or even the Lord Protector would wish to carry out examinations but these would be managed by Thurloe in his capacity as Secretary of the Council. These open sessions were not conducive to making deals. The best circumstances for examination were the Tower and it was there that most took place, not least because the great majority of prisoners of any status or intelligence value were imprisoned there. At the Tower Barkstead established a regime of tight security and harsh discipline, including regular searches of prisoners. His ability to make a prisoner's life distinctly uncongenial, by removing such comforts as outside food or visitors, created an atmosphere in which prisoners were more likely to cooperate to alleviate their conditions or secure their release. The examination of prisoners was normally conducted by the stern Barkstead but Thurloe usually took a hand when there was an opportunity for a deal to be done, indeed it was only really he who had authority to offer terms.

Thurloe was prepared to consider making deals in even the most extreme circumstances if he felt it would assist the intelligence effort. Towards the end of the year information was received from an agent named Corker that a certain Gregory Palden was a Royalist courier and also that he was plotting to assassinate Thurloe. Palden was seized and placed in the Tower, facing potential charges of attempted murder and treason. Even if there was insufficient evidence, Palden would have been aware that he could face long imprisonment without trial followed by the prospect of transportation to Barbados. He decided that discretion was the better part of valour and agreed to become a double agent in exchange for his freedom. Three months later he was released and returned to being a courier between Charles and his London contact for secret communications, John Barwick (Charles I's former London agent). who lived in St Paul's Churchyard. Thurloe had concluded the value of being able to intercept one of Charles's covert courier routes was preferable to any personal revenge. The Palden case provides an excellent example of how three different disciplines of intelligence, agent handling, interrogation and intercept, could be drawn together for maximum effect. It also exemplifies the value of centralized intelligence direction.

Thurloe's unique position of combining the appointments of Secretary of State, Secretary to the Council, director of foreign intelligence and Postmaster General meant that all aspects of intelligence could be centrally managed. Apart from Thurloe himself, the glue that often brought the differing sources of intelligence together was agent handling. As shown in the Palden case, agent information could result in arrests and subsequent interrogation which might in turn result in the creation of an agent who could be used to facilitate intercept. In addition most routine static surveillance was carried out by contacts, and more sensitive static and all mobile surveillance done by agents. Thurloe could not run all the agents and contacts himself. Philip Meadowe became Thurloe's right-hand man but did have had some help from Morland who seems to have been acting as Thurloe's private secretary. Thurloe had about twenty-eight agents, or what today we would term accredited sources, and these valuable assets such as Sir Richard Willys he largely ran himself. He also had about a hundred good-quality informers: what in today's terms would be called numbered contacts. Meadowe tended to supervise the handling of informants but Morland was responsible for the support side of agent handling. This is the less glamorous but important work of arranging such things as safe houses for debriefing agents and informants.

Before long Meadowe himself began to develop his own sources, as indeed all senior servants of the Protectorate were expected to do. Mention has already been made of Monck recruiting agents to conduct intercept but Lockhart the ambassador in France reported in July 1655 that he had recruited two agents for intercept. One was a messenger between Henrietta Maria and Cardinal Mazarin at the cost of £50. This in fact turned out to be not particularly productive because, although Mazarin was the power behind the throne in France, he had little time for Henrietta Maria. He was more concerned with an alliance with Cromwell and so wrote to her with the deference that was due to a daughter of France but with the circumspection of the great politician he was. More productive was the other agent recruited because he was one of Mazarin's own secretaries. Being an Italian like his master had helped him to gain the complete trust of the Cardinal and so French planning and policy at the highest level found its way through Lockhart to Thurloe. The value of this information may be judged by the fact that the agent was paid £2,000.

Thurloe would not only encourage Protectorate officials to recruit sources, he would actively direct them to talent spot. For example, Lord Broghill, the President of the Council of State for Scotland, was soon working as avidly as Monck in intelligence collection. He rapidly proved himself to be a good source handler and among his more successful agents was a one-eyed Cavalier called Colonel Blackadder (probably Montrose's former Scoutmaster) whom he recruited to infiltrate the Stuart court in Cologne. Thurloe knew he could rely on Broghill as an experienced handler and wrote to him in April asking him to recruit a Catholic priest to go to Spain and try to obtain intelligence about the impending Spanish/ Royalist alliance. This was rather a tall order as Catholic priests had become rather thin on the ground in Scotland following a recent proclamation that any caught would face execution. Despite this, Broghill was fortunate enough to find a Jesuit who agreed to go and live in Madrid and report back by sending correspondence to the Venetian resident living in Covent Garden who would act as a cut-out.

Thurloe's recruitment by proxy was often more complex. In the summer of 1654 Thurloe had used his influence to get Richard Bradshaw reappointed to the post of Deputy Governor of the English Merchant Adventurer Company in Hamburg. With Bradshaw now in Thurloe's debt he then asked him to identify someone 'to penetrate their [i.e. the exiled Stuart court] counsills and designs'. Bradshaw recommended Sir John Henderson who had been the Royalist Governor of Newark and had only recently been released from imprisonment. Henderson was a Scot with considerable knowledge and contacts on the Continent, having spent many years living in Germany and Scandinavia. An approach was made to Henderson, hinting that it might be time to consider which side his bread was buttered. This resulted in Henderson writing a letter to Cromwell himself offering his services. Soon after he was formally taken on by Thurloe as an agent and given his own cipher. The arrangement was that he should be based in Hamburg and be given a monthly wage and travel expenses. Henderson made contact with Charles who had by then moved to Spa and was received as someone who had proved his loyalty in the Civil War and been imprisoned for his devotion to the monarchy. Before long he had completely won Charles's confidence and was made privy to the plans for Middleton's expedition to Scotland to the extent that he was even offered the command of the infantry!

The recruitment of casual contacts and low-grade sources to act as static surveillance or occasional informants was never a problem for the Protectorate. There were always those such as discharged soldiers who were only too willing to make a bit of money on the side – and the Protectorate ensured that it had plenty of money for the purpose. However, the recruitment of sources who are likely to gain access to high-grade enemy information is always a major challenge and was so for the Protectorate. Thurloe was the first to try systematically to recruit agents by turning them, a practice which was then called 'gaining over'. There are three traditional reasons why someone can decide to work against their own side and start providing information to the enemy. These are blackmail, ideology or money. Blackmail, which was regularly used by both sides in the Cold War, tends to need quite a long period of cultivation and generally requires a greater expertise in tradecraft than was available at that time. Only one case comes to mind and it is no surprise that it was carried out by that devious and experienced intelligencer George Downing. Having served Cromwell effectively as Scoutmaster General of Scotland he was sent as the Protectorate Ambassador to The Hague where he soon began cultivating his own sources. As part of his recruitment effort he tried to get his hands on evidence of indiscretions that he might use to apply pressure on targets. He managed to buy some papers that had been originally acquired from a 'whoor' who had had a relationship with Thomas Howard. As Howard was the brother of the Earl of Suffolk, who was a member of Charles's inner circle, this was potentially useful. Downing decided to make an approach to Howard in the hopes that this would be a strong enough lever to win him over. What the papers contained we do not know but Howard felt that they were sufficiently embarrassing for him to be recruited as informant in exchange for Downing's silence.

Like blackmail, ideology played an important part as a motivator for agent recruitment in the Cold War. Burgess, Maclean, Blunt, Blake and Faux are just some of the successes achieved this way by the Soviet Union, while the West received intelligence from brave men of principle such as Oleg Godievsky. Ideological differences were just as strong if not even stronger in the mid-seventeenth century compared with the twentieth century because they combined ardent religious belief with political philosophy. The Roman Catholic or Anglican faith was irreconcilable with that of the Presbyterians or Puritan Sects, just as Monarchists were irreconcilable with Republicans. Despite this, there were few real cases of significant ideological spies. During the Civil Wars there had been supporters of one side or the other who found themselves in enemy-controlled territory and so would be prepared to assist their own side. Oxford was a good case in point. The city was the Royalist capital and dominated by Royalists but while the university overwhelmingly supported the King many of the townfolk were Puritan. These Puritans became potential informants for Sir Samuel Luke's Parliamentary scouts and could provide them with information of troop movements they had seen and careless talk they had overheard in the taverns.

By the time of the Protectorate all three countries were firmly under Cromwell's rule. Royalists were all identified, having revealed their sympathies during the Civil War, and were barred from office. Some such as Sealed Knot members would pass information back to the Stuart court in Cologne but as they were branded as delinquents, their opportunity of obtaining access to government information was virtually negligible. Certainly at this stage there was no reason why a Royalist should have an ideological reason for being prepared to become an agent for the Protectorate. Things were rather different on the Roundhead side. There were some like Fairfax who had supported Parliament throughout the Civil War but felt that things had gone too far with the execution of the King. Others like Monck were Royalist by inclination but had found themselves as professional soldiers serving the Protectorate. At this stage such people would not be interested in covertly supporting Charles for ideological reasons but this would change once the Protectorate was over and the return of the monarchy seemed the only way to restore order. Yet there was one group for whom ideology could make them change their allegiance.

These were the staunch republicans who could not forgive the betrayal of their cause by the creation of the Protectorate. One such person was Edward Sexby, who had gone from being a prominent Agitator, enthusiastic activist for the Commonwealth and agent of Thomas Scot, to reverting to his Leveller principles and defecting to the Royalists as a means of opposing the Protectorate. Like other prominent disaffected republicans, Thurloe tried to keep tabs on him. Reports came in of Sexby visiting Spain and then going to Cologne at the end of 1655. For Thurloe this could only mean that he had been representing the exiled Stuart court in discussions with Spain. Thurloe sent a letter to Gilbert Talbot, one of his agents in Cologne, tasking him with intercepting Sexby's correspondence. Unfortunately for Thurloe, this letter was intercepted by an agent of Ormonde. The fact that the letter was in cipher was enough to incriminate Talbot, who was seized by the Royalists – and he not only confessed but passed over his cipher. Although that source was blown, Thurloe was soon to learn by other means what Sexby had been up to, when he heard of a treaty that had been signed in early April 1656.

As we shall see, Sexby was not in fact responsible for making the alliance between Charles and Spain but he certainly helped to prepare the ground. The alliance at this stage had not become a formal treaty but more a draft understanding. The nub of it was that the Spanish would provide an invasion force of 4,000 foot and 2,000 horse to help Charles win the throne. In return, once Charles had become king, he would return Jamaica to Spain, provide twelve warships to fight the Portuguese and suspend penal laws against Catholics. In order to coordinate Spanish/Royalist military activity it was further agreed that Charles would move his small court to Bruges. Thurloe wrote to Henry Cromwell the next month to tell him about this development saying; 'the Spaniards, cavaliers, papists and Levellers are all come into a confederacy. What monstrous birth this womb will bring forth I can not tell.' Sexby's ideology had turned him into a freelance agent happy to work for the Royalist interest as a means of hitting back at his erstwhile comrades in arms. He could now draw satisfaction that his covert activity had helped to damage the Protectorate. Unfortunately for the Protectorate, Sexby's capacity to cause mischief was only beginning.

Although the Royalists might recruit the odd agent on ideological grounds, this was just not the case for the Protectorate. There was just one motive on which Thurloe could rely for recruitment and that was self-interest. This manifested itself in two forms. The first was recruitment in exchange for the state waiving its power to cause injury to an individual or their family. This was a form of blackmail. These were the deals done during the interrogation process. When faced with the prospect of a crippling fine, indefinite imprisonment or worse, the prospect of working for the government of the day became an attractive alternative. The other aspect of self-interest was simply money. In some case agents were recruited by outright bribery but for the most part they were walk-ins, offering their services for cash in the manner of Willys.

To this day, rescue from debt or just plain avarice has always accounted for the great majority of agents. Almost always those who were recruited as part of a deal struck during examination became paid agents. This was natural tradecraft and the reasons must have been the same then as they are now. These are that a paid agent is far more under control than one who has been recruited simply through fear. Payment creates a structure and professional relationship between the agent handler and the source. It makes the source more dependent upon the handler and is a constant reminder to the source that they are now part of his team and it is too late to return to former allegiances – they are what the KGB (now SVR) and GRU term 'on the hook'. The average salary for a Protectorate agent was £10 a month, to which might be added legitimate expenses for travel and accommodation. Of course top agents could expect much more. One of the best paid agents went under the cover name of 'Captain Holland' and received a total of £125 because he had vital access to the United Provinces' Cabinet at the time of the Dutch war.

The man responsible for the payment of sources, agents and indeed all government intelligence activity was a member of Thurloe's office called George Firbank. This money was made available from the Council of State's Contingency Fund. Firbank was responsible for payment and accounting of an extremely wide range of intelligence activities, from the paying of casual contacts and agents to the hiring of safe houses for debriefing, to the bribing of postmasters, messengers and anyone else who could facilitate intelligence collection. Whatever the intelligence activity, it was disguised in the ledgers for security reasons and entries merely read 'for public services'. The actual amount of money available from the Contingency Fund is not known. Pepys records in his dairy that Secretary of State Morris told the House of Commons in February 1668 that he only received £700 a year for intelligence whereas Thurloe had received £70,000. This is almost certainly a huge exaggeration. A more likely figure would have been in the region of £2,000–3,000 – but whatever it may have been, it was a great deal. Large though the amount of money allocated by the Protectorate to intelligence was, the chronic state of government finance meant that sometimes there was not the ready cash to pay Thurloe's own staff on time, let alone agents. An example of this can be seen in a note from Thurloe to Firbank on 26 September 1656 in which he directs that payment should be made to a particularly important source 'out of the first money you receive'. Records show that, despite the urgency, this payment did not take place until 14 November. Although there were these occasional financial hiccups, those on the Protectorate intelligence payroll could expect to receive their financial dues and so remained loyal to their paymaster.

The running of agents was not confined to the activities of talent-spotting, recruitment, debriefing and payment. There was the whole management process of both the sources themselves and the intelligence they produced. With regard to the management of the sources there was the matter of receiving the information in a covert fashion. Where face-to-face debriefing was possible between the handler and the source, a suitable safe house had to be found. Once found, care had to be taken that it was not compromised by poor tradecraft on behalf of either handler or sources. In the cases of sources overseas or too far away, arrangements had to be made for correspondence to be encrypted and sent to a cover address. These agent reports were called 'letters of intelligence'. One small but important point here was the need to prevent an own goal resulting from the excellent intercept service disrupting the source's communications. In a good example of joined-up government, Meadowe made Dorislaus ensure that the intercept service actually facilitated correspondence from agents. Agents were given a false address to send their letters of intelligence and Meadowe gave Dorislaus a list of these addresses so that as soon as he saw a letter with one of the addresses, he would pass it to Thurloe. The identity of these agents was almost always kept secret, identified only by their handler if they debriefed in person or by the cover address they used for correspondence. Their letters of intelligence would be usually unsigned but some agents used initials such as 'J M' in Cologne or 'John xx' in Antwerp, or an assumed name. Bampfylde for example used many different names, such as 'Rawley', 'Jo Williams' and 'J Beauple'. Although some of Thurloe's staff would have known or guessed the identity of different agents and contacts, only Thurloe would have held the records of all their identities. The information produced by letters of intelligence would have been briefed verbally direct by Thurloe to Cromwell or the Council and there would be no reason for any information pointing to the identity of a source ever going outside the secure environment of the department's offices.

Naturally, there was a considerable range in the quality of the different sources and the intelligence they provided. Thurloe carefully examined the intelligence product and was constantly assessing the intelligence and the source. As has been noted, his main way of doing this was to use his extensive collection capability to see if one source of information was corroborated by another. He did this even when he had complete faith in the integrity and professionalism of the source of information. Back in 1653 when the very capable Bulstrode Whitelocke was Commonwealth Ambassador to Sweden, Thurloe was comparing the information he received with two other sources. One was an agent in Stockholm being run personally by Thurloe and the other was from the interception of letters to and from the Dutch Ambassador to Sweden. Thurloe was a hard taskmaster of his sources and subsources. He wanted value for money and expected to receive regular weekly letters of intelligence that contained information of real use. For many sources this was extremely hard to achieve and they found themselves either filling up reports with trivia, such as rumoured affairs between members of the Stuart court or simply fabricating information. In either case they were likely to get short shrift from Thurloe. If they did not come up with the goods they were discarded, as was the case of an agent in Danzig called John Benson. On being sacked the luckless Benson wrote to Thurloe as follows:

Sir, Yours I received by yesterday's post, whereby you doe actually discharge me from this employment, by reason you finde my letters to speak nothing unto the business, about which I was first sent hither. I grant the truth of what you say therein, there being a great change of affairs since that time.

Despite continuing to plead his case, Benson remained sacked.

Centralization of intelligence is an often quoted basic principle, which is usually easier said than done. In UK today the government intelligence apparatus consists of several agencies which themselves are often large and diverse. Centralization is achieved by being coordinated through the Chairman of the Joint Intelligence Committee operating through Cabinet Office Committees and generally works very well. Even so, because of the complexity, there are bound to be occasions when for example the police fail to inform the security services (MI5) about information that might be of use to them or vice versa. The bigger the intelligence apparatus, the bigger the problem and in the case of the gigantic US apparatus, with huge agencies which are sometimes in potential rivalry with each other, the challenge of achieving centralization of direction and purpose is considerable. For Protectorate Britain intelligence centralization was achieved as the whole direction, collection and assessment process came together with one man. Although Thurloe was very clearly head of intelligence it should also be said that the supreme head of intelligence was Cromwell himself. Thurloe passed all intelligence of consequence to Cromwell, who had an insatiable appetite for it and was a highly informed intelligence user. It was Cromwell, and through him the Council of State, who authorized the intercept operations and other collection processes and he who agreed the considerable amount of funding to pay for it. Thurloe achieved an amazing amount for intelligence but the whole activity might have been a mere backwater had it not been for the constant interest and support of His Highness the Lord Protector.

While Thurloe, with Cromwell's support, ensured that Protectorate intelligence had the great advantage of centralization, he also brought disadvantages. Thurloe worked incredibly hard but no man could keep permanently on top of so punishing a workload. He did delegate quite a lot to Meadowe but always wanted to remain in the centre of things himself. Meadowe for his part became hugely overstretched, with his responsibilities expanding to cover both foreign affairs and agent handling. As a result the centralization of work in these two figures created a bottle neck, delaying correspondence and decision-making. This was particularly apparent when Thurloe had one of his bouts of illness or when Meadowe was dispatched abroad on diplomatic missions, leaving Thurloe to pick up his intelligence work and poor blind Milton to cover for foreign affairs.

It must be remembered that Thurloe did not have the opportunity to devote his whole time to intelligence. He had all the problems of the state on his shoulders, not least managing a government heading for bankruptcy. By the summer of 1656 the cost of the war with Spain was getting seriously out of hand. The total government debt was now £1.5 million, which equated to a whole year's revenue. As monarchs had discovered before him, Cromwell found himself forced to call a parliament to vote funds. Cromwell knew from bitter experience that parliaments could be fickle and so it was essential that the membership should be supportive of the Protectorate. The experiment of selecting MPs purely on their godliness had proved less than satisfactory in the Barebones Parliament, so this time the criteria were changed to loyalty to the Protector. In August it was therefore decided to summon a Parliament for 17 September but to take a number of prudent measures to reduce the risk of it becoming a forum for opposition. Selection was the key. Naturally Roman Catholics and Royalists were denied the vote and major opposition leaders such as Sir Harry Vane found themselves placed in custody, but more was needed.

Major generals were instructed to supervise the election process and encourage the choice of MPs supportive to the Protector. This worked pretty well in Scotland and Ireland, which were after all recently subjugated countries. The major generals fared less well in England and Wales where there was a backlash to their rule. A general cry of opposition went up: 'no soldiers and no courtiers'. Many electors declined to support the government candidate and voted for change. As a result 230 of the MPs elected had formally been members of the previous uncooperative parliament and 180 were new men whose loyalty to the Protectorate was unproved. This was not a good start. Fortuitously under the provisions of the *Instrument of Government*, 'only persons of known integrity and fearing God and of good conversation' could be MPs. No one elected could take their seats until they had received a certificate to that effect from the Chancery Clerk on the authority of the Council. As Secretary of the Council, Thurloe was largely responsible for making the decision on the granting of certificates. This he did using his extensive database and by making enquiries with the relevant major generals to determine whether an elected MP was politically reliable. The major generals thus added to their duties that of being part of an ad hoc government vetting agency. A hundred MPs such as Haselrig were excluded in this manner and barred from the door of the House by soldiers. A further fifty MPs refused to take their seats in protest, so indicating their lack of support for the Protector. It had taken a bit of effort and the process had not always been in the highest traditions of democracy but it looked as though Great Britain would at last have a parliament worthy of the Protectorate.

One of Cromwell's first acts once formal war had begun with Spain was to dispatch a fleet to attack the enemy in their own waters. Blake and Montagu were ordered to destroy shipping in Cadiz harbour and then carry out reconnaissance of Gibraltar with the intention of seizing it on a future expedition. While the English fleet was preparing for this operation, information reached Thurloe that there were objections to the righteousness of war among some of the captains and officers. Disaffection of this sort could not be tolerated and Desborough was sent down to weed out malcontents, which he did with his customary efficiency in such matters. With loyal crews, Blake and Montagu had set sail but, finding Cadiz harbour too strongly defended, left sixteen frigates as a blockade and sailed to Lisbon. The reason they went to Lisbon was because King John IV of Portugal was refusing to ratify the treaty with the Protectorate against their common enemy Spain because it contained a clause saying that English merchants and seamen should have freedom of worship in Portugal. King John prevaricated and had told Philip Meadowe who had been sent there as ambassador that he would have to refer the matter to the Pope. This had infuriated Cromwell who had directed Blake and Montagu to take the greater part of the Fleet to Lisbon to overawe King John.

The arrival of the English fleet had the desired effect and Meadowe was soon able to report to Blake that the King of Portugal had agreed to ratify the contentious issues. Blake then sent five frigates off to Malaga, sinking nine Spanish ships and spiking the harbour guns. In September he took the majority of the fleet to Lisbon for replenishment, leaving Vice-Admiral Richard Stayner with eight ships on the Cadiz blockade. A few days later the Spanish silver fleet appeared off Cadiz and Stayner attacked. Three Spanish ships were sunk, three were damaged but managed to make it to Cadiz and two were captured. The two captured galleons were found to be transporting 600,000 pieces of eight, worth over £250,000 in the money of the day. After this engagement Blake ordered Montagu to sail back to Portsmouth with the booty which, when unloaded, required thirty-eight wagons to carry the silver to the Tower of London mint for turning into coinage. This was a huge windfall for the indebted Protectorate Treasury but arriving as it did in November 1656 was too late to avoid the need for summoning a parliament, for by then the Second Protectorate Parliament had already been sitting for three months. What it did mean was that if Parliament proved too demanding over voting funds, it might if necessary be dissolved, as enough money could be scraped together to continue the Spanish war without it.

By the end of the year the Protectorate's fortunes were looking mixed. On the one hand Thurloe and the major generals had a tight grip of the country, the war with Spain was going well and the new Parliament seemed prepared to grant £400,000 for its cost. On the other hand Cromwell's health was deteriorating. He had the serious discomfort of bad gout coupled with severe pain from a gallstone, neither of which helped his temper. In addition he had personal worries over the health of his wife Elizabeth and favourite daughter Bettie Claypole who had bouts of illness. He was feeling his age and had to consider how the Protectorate should be continued after his death. Cromwell had always hoped that his sons would live private lives away from politics but his position as Protector had made his offspring semi-royal. Even Bettie had become a lady when Cromwell had knighted her husband John Claypole and made him Master of the Bedchamber. Certainly foreign ambassadors in London regularly called Cromwell's two unmarried daughters, Francis and Mary, 'princesses' and his two sons were now generally referred to as 'Lord Richard' and 'Lord Henry'. Given their situation it was natural that the two young men should find themselves drawn into public life. In the case of his second son Henry, this was embraced with enthusiasm. He had been made General of the Army of Ireland and in effect replaced Fleetwood as ruler of the country. Henry had settled well into the job and showed remarkable promise for a 28-year-old with no military or administrative experience. Cromwell's eldest son Richard was made of different stuff. He was a country gentleman who enjoyed a high standard of living well beyond his means. Like many a country gentleman he had become an MP and had sat in the 1654 Parliament but had taken little or no part in events and always been pleased to return to his rural existence.

By November 1656 there were a few members of the new Parliament who thought that the power of Protector should be hereditary. On two different occasions Cromwell received deputations making the proposal, both of which he declined. He well knew that most senior army officers were completely against the idea. It was with these background stirrings that Cromwell decided Richard should take on some government responsibility and so appointed him a member of the Committee of Trade and Navigation. It remained to be seen if this would be the making of him.

On Christmas Day Desborough addressed an understandably poorly attended House and proposed that the Decimation Tax should be made permanent. As this tax was the financial basis for the major generals, to make it permanent would be tantamount to making the major generals permanent. By this time the major generals' rule had got the backs up of nearly all sections of the country. The motion was opposed. Matters were not helped by Thurloe being taken ill on Christmas Eve and not being able to return to work until 10 February. Even if Thurloe had been able to act in his parliamentary role of government spokesman, it is most unlikely he could have swayed those who were now so sick and tired of the major generals. The Bill was again put forward on 7 January 1657 and two days later was defeated by 124 votes to 88. With such substantial opposition to the major generals it looked as though 1657 would be the year that might force Cromwell to give up his principal mechanism for England's internal security.

Chapter 11

Uncertain and Giddy Times, 1657–1658

When the second parliament of his Protectorate had assembled on 17 September 1656 Cromwell encouraged it to vote taxation by describing the threats facing the country. He said: 'Truly your great enemy is the Spaniard. He is a natural enemy … through that enmity that is in him against all that is of God.' He explained that it was from this anti-Christ that all other threats flowed and that Spanish Flanders was now providing troops to support a Royalist invasion through an agreement arranged by a Leveller colonel. He was able to present some of Thurloe's intelligence as proof, using information on Sexby, which probably came from Thurloe's source Wildman who had been part of the Royalist/Leveller negotiations with the Spanish in Flanders. Cromwell also spoke of threat information derived from mail intercept and examination of suspects and stated that some Spanish money sent to the Levellers in England had been seized, but for this he gave credit to 'God, in his providence', rather than his intelligencers. He also covered some of the recent threats against him, such as a plot to blow up his house, but these he described as no more than 'a mouse nibbling at the heal'.

The new Parliament was soon to discover that this mouse nibbling had to be taken very seriously. Sexby had returned in secret to England and began planning to shoot Cromwell as he rode through Hyde Park. After a time he realized that this operation was too difficult and returned to Flanders, leaving £1,500 with a cashiered Roundhead quartermaster Miles Sindercombe to come up with another plan for assassination. Sindercombe had previously been involved in the Overton plot against Monck in Scotland and now he recruited two Royalists, one called Boyes and another, a former soldier, called John Cecil. The group hired a tailor's room in King Street Westminster to plan the assassination. They decided that their best opportunity of killing Cromwell was when he could be guaranteed to be at a particular place at a particular time. The State Opening of Parliament was just such an opportunity and they obtained the use of a house which was conveniently near the east door of Westminster Abbey. Sindercombe and his two accomplices arrived at the house on the day of the Opening carrying a blunderbuss and ammunition hidden in a viola case. They took up position at a window overlooking the Protector's procession and awaited the arrival of Cromwell. The plan was perfect and there was a rear door from the house to make a reasonably easy escape in the confusion which would follow the assassination. What had not been foreseen was that the spectacle of the opening attracted large crowds which masked the Protector when he arrived, making it impossible to take aim. The operation was aborted and it was back to the drawing board. As it happened, Sindercombe was fortunate not to have been arrested. Thurloe had received intelligence from an agent that an assassin was lodging in King Street. The agent in question was a Swiss national called Jean Baptiste Stouppe who had been recruited by Thurloe in 1654 and had been sending high-quality reports back from Paris and the United Provinces and had some very good contacts in Brussels, Switzerland and Savoy. Unwisely, Thurloe took no action other than tasking Stouppe to write to his subsources in Brussels to obtain more information. The moment had passed and Sindercombe was long gone before any reply was received from Brussels.

Soon after this Sindercombe decided to follow the same modus operandi and attack Cromwell at a time when he was likely to be at a particular place but when crowds would not be present. He hired a house in Hammersmith, which was on a narrow section of the road by which Cromwell regularly travelled to Hampton Court for the weekend. Having decided upon a place where he could be certain Cromwell would be, Sindercombe now needed to find out the time. As Cromwell took the basic security precaution of varying his times of travel, inside information on his diary was needed. This Sindercombe obtained from a Henry Toope, a former military colleague now serving in the Protector's Life Guard. As encouragement, Toope was promised the huge sum of £1,500 for the information but given a more modest advance of £10. It seems the earlier purge of the Life Guard might have overlooked the possibility that some apparently loyal members could be open to bribery. Having decided on the place and time for the assassination, the conspirators set about arranging the method. In an upstairs room of the coachman's house Cecil rigged up a battery of seven blunderbusses able to be fired simultaneously at Cromwell's coach as it passed. With all prepared on the appointed day they waited for the passage of the Protector's coach, and waited and waited. Cromwell had changed his plans at the last moment and decided to travel to Hampton Court by boat. This change of plan might have been sheer bad luck for the conspirators, arising from a whim of the Protector, or perhaps more likely resulted from a tip-off by one of Thurloe's sources. We will probably never know. As Sindercombe was working under the general direction of the Leveller Sexby there is a good chance that Wildman was aware of this Leveller plot and reported it to Thurloe.

Undeterred by setbacks, the resourceful Sindercombe now decided that, as Cromwell regularly rode in Hyde Park, that would be the best opportunity for assassination. Sindercombe realized that it would not be too difficult to join in the general crowd that followed the Protector on these occasions and get near enough to shoot him. The problem would be to escape afterwards, as the nearest park gate on the Protector's customary route was kept locked. To overcome this, he arranged for the hinges of the gate to be filed through and obtained a particularly fast horse to ensure his getaway. The horse became ill just before the intended day and the operation was abandoned. Sindercombe then came up with a more dramatic idea of setting fire to Whitehall Palace and killing Cromwell as he was evacuated from the building. The conspirators set about bribing servants with access to Whitehall and organizing enough swift horses for a getaway. This was an overambitious plan which necessitated a large number of people being involved and therefore a greater risk of discovery. As it transpired, it was Toope who reported the plot to Thurloe. On 8 January Sindercombe and Cecil were arrested in Whitehall Chapel. The two of them and Toope had been found to have placed highly inflammable materials under the seat of General Lambert together with a slow-burning match which would have ignited about midnight. They had also bored holes into the woodwork to provide a draught for the fire and help it spread. Had this operation not been disrupted it would have been likely to cause the major fire that was intended.

This potentially effective operation was of course the last for Sindercombe and Cecil. They were personally examined by Thurloe the day after their arrest. Sindercombe remained silent but Cecil was able to corroborate the information provided by Toope. Four days later Sindercombe and Cecil were condemned to death for high treason. This did not prevent Sindercombe from having one last little plot. He arranged for his sister to bring him arsenic in paper on her farewell visit to him the night before his execution and the next morning he was found dead. Sindercombe was to plot no more but Sexby was still loose in Flanders, scheming new means of sedition.

Thurloe bore no hard feelings against Toope for trying to assassinate Cromwell and he remained on the pay roll as an agent till the end of the Protectorate. Cromwell on the other hand certainly did bear hard feelings against Thurloe. He was less than impressed that his head of intelligence had received information from a high-grade source that an assassin was living in King Street and then had done nothing to try to arrest him. During a highly uncomfortable interview with His Highness, Thurloe accepted his failure but explained that he was receiving information on assassination plots on so regular a basis that he could not possibly follow each one up without further confirmatory information. Cromwell angrily replied that he was the best judge of intelligence affecting his own life and it had been a dereliction of duty that he had not been informed about it. After Thurloe had again abjectly apologized and reminded the Protector of his excellent record of diligence in the past, Cromwell's rage subsided and a few days later they were back to their close relationship.

That this argument occurred emphasizes two things. First that Cromwell rightly regarded himself to be the prime consumer for national intelligence and took the greatest interest in his intelligence apparatus working in the best possible way to meet his needs. It also demonstrates an age-old problem of briefing threat intelligence. If an intelligence officer immediately briefs all the semi-raw threat information received they are likely to lose credibility when much of it is later found to be incorrect. If they wait till there is some confirmation, they take a chance that the threat is real and may be carried out before any further information has been received to aid assessment. They know that if they make the wrong choice they will be condemned by those who can enjoy the superior knowledge of hindsight.

The new Parliament had been horrified to hear of the Sindercombe plot and had appointed a day of thanksgiving for the saving of the Protector's life. But their concern for his well-being did not match their concern for his policies and a few days later they voted against renewing the Decimation Tax and therefore the authority of the major generals. This was not an intentional blow to Cromwell's authority but an expression of the widespread unpopularity with which the major generals were held. Parliament would not now be satisfied until the major generals were removed. Far from reducing Cromwell's authority there was now a movement to extend it. This was a direct result of the recent plots which had demonstrated how fragile was the Protectorate, resting as it did on the life of one man. It was argued that if Cromwell became king, then the succession would be assured through his family. On 23 February Sir Christopher Pack, a former Lord Mayor of London, stood up in the Commons and asked Cromwell permission to read a paper to him. To Cromwell's genuine surprise the paper proposed re-establishing the House of Lords and making him king. This was greeted with uproar, with staunch republicans and the majority of the army members calling Pack a traitor. Both Fleetwood and Desborough made particularly strong attacks against the motion. Others took Pack's side and the matter dominated proceedings in the House for nearly three months, with Pack's paper being eventually transformed into *The Humble Petition and Advice of the Parliament of England, Scotland and Ireland.*

This petition was eventually passed and on 31 March the Speaker formally asked Cromwell to accept the proposed new constitution and with it the crown. Cromwell asked for time to consider and appointed a committee to advise him on the matter. The less controversial proposal to re-establish the House of Lords met favour with Cromwell but only on condition that he nominated the members and was therefore able to use it as a counter-balance to any dissent in the Commons. In Thurloe's words: 'that this House [the Lords] just constituted will be a great security and bulwark to the honest interest ... and will not be so uncertain as the House of Commons which depends upon the electing of people'. Thurloe and Cromwell had only just been reminded by the defeat of the Decimation Tax that, however carefully managed, the 'electing of people' could seriously hinder government policy.

The matter of the House of Lords was of course trivial compared with the *Humble Petition's* explosive offer of kingship. Many of Cromwell's closest advisers including Thurloe, Whitelocke and Lord Broghill strongly recommended accepting the crown. Although there was a parliamentary majority for the proposal, there was also very strong opposition to kingship from those who were proud to call themselves republicans, especially within the army. For them to accept kingship would be to completely betray 'the Good Old Cause' for which so many had risked their lives and fortunes in a bloody civil war. In the face of such fundamental opposition, Thurloe set about covertly gauging the feelings of those with influence. The question was whether Sindercombe and the Protector's failing health might convince influential republicans that a hereditary ruler was necessary to preserve the reforms of the Commonwealth. The answer that came back was that hardened republicans were not yet convinced. For example, Thurloe was able to read the intercepted letters from Sir Harry Vane in The Hague to republican colleagues in England. These were trying to form a group which would restore the Commonwealth after Cromwell's death. Thurloe also established that Fleetwood and Lambert were planning to resign their commissions if Cromwell accepted the crown, an act which would have been likely to incite the majority of the army against kingship. Cromwell was doing his own sounding out and seeking legal and religious advice through the parliamentary committee set up for the purpose.

While the parliamentary committee conferred, the Fifth Monarchists acted. For them there could be 'no other king but Christ' and the prospect of Cromwell becoming king was a final betrayal. Thomas Venner, a London cooper, had become the leader of a Fifth Monarchy group and planned an uprising to take place on 9 April that would have its assembly point at Mile End Green. A leaflet titled *A Standard Set Up* was distributed and banners made with the lion of Judah and the words 'Who shall raise him up'. Feverish excitement soon spread among their supporters that this would mark the start of Christ's millennium. The less devout were attracted to the promise that such a millennium would have no taxes. Needless to say, Thurloe soon heard of these preparations, including the details of a planning meeting to be held in Shoreditch. When Venner and about twenty others assembled for the meeting they were seized, along with their supply of weapons, banners and pamphlets. The rising had been extinguished before it had begun and Venner and his associates found themselves in the Tower on what was to have been their day of destiny, 9 April. But there were other prominent Fifth Monarchists who might make trouble. Thurloe exploited the plot to justify the arrest of every Fifth Monarchy leader, all of whom joined Venner in the Tower. In the space of a few days an uprising had been prevented and potential leaders neutralized.

By now the question of kingship had become the matter of supreme public importance and Cromwell had to make up his mind. After months of agonizing indecision, Cromwell at last concluded that providence did not guide him towards kingship. With new moral certainty on 8 May he summoned the Commons to the Banqueting House and formally turned down the crown with the words: 'I cannot undertake this government with that title of King. And that is my answer to this great weighty business.' What he did do a few days later was to agree the other provisions of the *Humble Petition*, the most important of which were that he would be able to nominate his successor as Lord Protector and appoint a second House of Parliament, which would not be called the House of Lords but the 'Other House'. This compromise reassured the republicans, while at the same time giving confidence in the continuation of the Protectorate.

The petition also contained a clause which removed a considerable public grievance against the Protectorate regime by abolishing the rule of the major generals. While this measure must have offered the Protectorate a new beginning freed from association with the perceived injustices of the major generals, it also removed the country-wide structure of loyal functionaries so important to Thurloe and the security of the state. Of course Scotland and Ireland remained under military rule and the army garrisons across England and Wales could still be relied upon to swiftly stamp out any attempt at insurrection against the Lord Protector, their commander-in-chief. Thurloe still ran an efficient government service and his highly effective intelligence network, but the high water mark of national security was past. Cromwell's rule remained a military dictatorship which thanks to Thurloe was also a quasi police state, but it had lost an important mechanism for the Protector's authority. Naturally, there was a general relief at this lifting of military-imposed restrictions and Cavaliers could at last feel as though they were beginning to be treated as equal citizens. The removal of powers from the major generals was of course a welcome blow for English freedom, but from the purely government intelligence point of view it was a setback. The great majority of Cavaliers might be disorganized, dispirited and now more likely to learn to live with the Protectorate regime since the hated major generals had gone but there would always be a few who would continue to plot insurrection. The lifting of important restrictions such as the registration of movement made the identification and tracking of subversives far more difficult and put an end to the source-handling activities that many of the major generals had been running in their districts.

The next month Cromwell, in a robe of purple lined with ermine, was inaugurated as Lord Protector in a grand ceremony at Westminster Hall that was little short of a coronation – lacking only a crown. The question was left open as to who should be the successor to the man now proclaimed by the herald 'His Highness Protector of England, Scotland and Ireland'. Some might have speculated that precedence in the ceremony gave some clues, for behind Cromwell under his canopy of state were the Privy Council but closest to him were the Earl of Warwick, then Cromwell's son Richard and his sons-in-law Claypole and Fleetwood, whereas Lord Lisle, Edward Montagu and Bulstrode Whitelocke stood in front of him on a lower platform with swords drawn. Whether Cromwell would name one of his own children as his successor or a trusted man younger than himself, such as one of his sons-in-law or close advisers, only time would tell.

Beside Cromwell on the big day were the Speaker and the Lord Mayor and on either side of them were the ambassadors of France and the United Provinces. This was to demonstrate that the peace made with the Dutch was a durable union between two Protestant powers and that the new alliance with France was a challenge to the great enemy Spain. In fact the alliance had developed into something more tangible two months previously when Cromwell had agreed to join France in an attack on the Spanish Netherlands. Meanwhile, unaware of the pageantry in Westminster Hall, a seriously ill Blake was continuing to blockade Cadiz. There he received intelligence from Captain Young of the *Catherine* that the Spanish silver fleet had taken refuge in Santa Cruz harbour, Tenerife. Despite suffering from scurvy and dropsy he immediately set sail and arrived to find that the intelligence was correct but that the eight merchantmen carrying silver were protected not only by sixteen galleons, which outnumbered his own force, but the guns of seventeen batteries in the harbour's seven forts and castle. The Spanish position was clearly impregnable and the Spanish admiral sent Blake a playful message that he could come and take his ships if he felt like it. As it happened Blake did feel like it and at 8 am sailed into the harbour under the terrible weight of fire from the Spanish ships and batteries. First he silenced the fort's guns and then attacked the galleons. After four hours Blake's fleet had set fire to every Spanish ship in the harbour and all their surviving crews had swum for safety to the shore. The wind changed and Blake was able to extricate his fleet from the harbour and head for the open sea. Good intelligence had provided an opportunity for a major success but it was the leadership of Blake and the courage of him and his crew which made this a victory that was to be the talk of Europe for some time. Sadly, Blake was not to savour the gratitude of the nation, for he died on 7 August just as his fleet was entering Plymouth.

A few days after Blake's death, he was succeeded as admiral by Edward Montagu. He was a 32-year-old former Commissioner of the Treasury whose only naval experience had been during the previous last six months when he had served as Blake's deputy. The obvious professional successor to Blake would have been the popular and respected John Lawson. He had joined the navy as a common sailor and risen to become a ship's captain even before the start of the Civil War, during which he had served with distinction on the Parliamentary side. He had gone on to take a prominent part in virtually all Commonwealth naval operations, including the Dutch war, and had been made a vice-admiral. The problem with Lawson was that he had supported John Wildman when he stood for MP of his home town of Scarborough and so was tainted with being a Leveller. Cromwell had had enough of Levellers and their fellow travellers so in January 1656 he passed over Lawson and made Montagu a general-at-sea and Blake's deputy. Lawson resigned the next month. With Blake dead, Montagu was given the top job.

Montagu's naval experience might have been slight but he was known and trusted by Cromwell. Montagu had fought at Marston Moor, Naseby and the capture of Bristol and then resigned his commission to become MP for Huntingdon. He had proved his loyalty to Cromwell by taking his part against his own uncle the Earl of Manchester and had reinforced his devotion by being one of the leading MPs campaigning for Cromwell to accept the crown. It was a sign of the uncertain times that Cromwell decided, rather than have the fleet under an experienced sailor, to have it under a man who could be relied upon to purge it of radicals. Cromwell well knew that the foundation of his authority rested primarily with the army and secondarily with the navy and he was continually alert to ensuring the loyalty of both elements of the armed forces. As it turned out, Montagu became a good naval commander and so a testament to Cromwell's judgement in staff selection, even when tempered with political expedience.

By this time the contest for the Spanish Netherlands had begun in earnest. The French troops were led by the great Marshal Turenne and the Spanish by Don John of Austria and the French rebel, the Prince of Condé. Cromwell had sent Sir John Reynolds, a reliable Cambridgeshire man, with Thomas Morgan taken from Scotland to be his second-in-command. Reynolds landed near Boulogne with 6,000 men wearing for the first time abroad the red coats that were to become the hallmark of the British army. They were supported by a strong fleet under Montagu who patrolled the coast. Needless to say, Thurloe was using his agents to obtain military intelligence for the Flanders campaign. For example, he was giving very specific tasking to his agent Blanck Marshall to get enemy strengths of Spanish-held towns.

> This you are to doe, with a little paynenes, but do it exactly, that I may certainly knowe how many effective men they are, and not as they are computed; and how many Irish, English and Scotts there are amongst them ... a slight doeinge of this business will be of no use to me, nor can it be expected to be of any profit to you.

The agreement with the French was that the first joint objective was to be Gravelines which would become French, followed by Mardyke and Dunkirk which would become British. For Cromwell it was essential to take Dunkirk in order to counter any possibility of a Royalist/Spanish invasion being mounted from Flanders. When the young Louis XIV arrived at the coast and saw the British forces he was impressed and ordered that they should besiege Cambrai and other towns further inland. This was completely unacceptable and it took all the diplomacy of the Protector's ambassador, Sir William Lockhart, to get back to the original plan. Lockhart was a Scot who had been knighted by Charles I and fought on the Royalist side in the Civil War but had fallen out with Argyll, which led him to join the Commonwealth cause. He had been appointed ambassador in early 1656 and it was no coincidence that he was married to Cromwell's niece Robina Sewster. Not only could he be expected to be loyal to the Protector by being tied to his family, he was also chosen for his intelligence and charm. Lockhart had soon proved that he was worthy of Cromwell's confidence and struck up a close friendship with Mazarin, even going so far as to christen his new-born son 'Jules' in honour of the Cardinal. Lockhart drew on his friendship with Mazarin to persuade the French King to give up his idea of attacking Cambrai and besiege Mardyke instead.

With Louis and Mazarin now reluctantly content, Mardyke was taken after a siege of three days and put in the hands of the British troops. The joint forces now turned their attention to Gravelines but the Spanish opened the sluices and put the surrounding area under water. Turenne decided to place his army in winter quarters and so passed a lull in hostilities. Naturally the winter break saw no let-up in Thurloe's intelligence effort and he was receiving information from his many sources, including one Jo Dunch who sent his own 'night spies' to provide surveillance on Cavalier meetings. During this time there was the strange situation of fraternization between British troops on both sides, for the Duke of York was leading a Royalist contingent under the Spanish flag. On several occasions Reynolds himself had paid his respects to the Duke when they met out riding. This was reported by one of his officers to Thurloe who recalled Reynolds to London. Reynolds never had the opportunity to counter aspersions on his loyalty for he was drowned when his ship back to England was wrecked. The Duke of York took the opportunity of Reynolds's departure to try to retake Mardyke but was repulsed and the period of fraternization was over, with both armies settling in for the winter. Sir William Lockhart was given Reynolds's vacant post of Commander of British Forces in Flanders.

Back at home the Fifth Monarchist threat might be neutralized but Sexby was still on the loose, trying to raise resistance among the Levellers. He had written a pamphlet attacking Cromwell with the self-evident title *Killing no Murder*, which he had printed in the Netherlands and shipped to London. Following a tip-off, seven bundles of this pamphlet were found at St Katherine's docks disguised as bales of silk. Arrests followed and Barkstead obtained some useful information from his subsequent interrogations in the Tower. Of particular use was that Sexby was about to visit London in secret. Thurloe realized that without specific intelligence it would be impossible to watch all the ports to arrest Sexby when he landed. Indeed, he had not long before received a report from a Dutch agent that a Royalist could go through a Kent port for as little as 20 shillings. Thurloe therefore decided that the best chance of intercepting Sexby was when he embarked back to the Continent. Sexby returned to England in June disguised as a farm worker and with a long beard. He soon realized that he was a wanted man and that Thurloe's informants were on the look out for him, so he decided to slip back to Flanders. He paid passage for a ship and it was at this point that informants were able to identify him. Just as the ship was about to set sail Sexby was arrested. When he was examined in the Tower he proudly admitted his role in Leveller resistance, including the tasking of Sindercombe's assassination attempts and authorship of *Killing no Murder*. He would not be induced to reveal his accomplices but that mattered little as the unlikely and uneasy alliance between Royalists and the few remaining Levellers was at an end.

He remained in the Tower for just over a year until he died of an illness, having first gone insane. With him died all significant Leveller opposition but the Levellers' novel concept of equality of man was to live on in the minds of future generations and eventually lead through the Reform Acts of 1832, 1867 and 1884 to 1918, when at last all men over 21 were allowed to vote, and 1928, when this was extended to women.

Having become Lord Protector with additional powers, Cromwell had been busy with reviewing appointments. Above all he wanted to ensure the complete loyalty of his power base, the army. He decided that Lambert's conduct during the time of the debate over kingship had been two-faced as he had sympathies with the Fifth Monarchists and had been secretly supporting the republicans. The crunch came when Lambert declined to take the obligatory oath of allegiance for the new-style Lord Protector. Despite him being Cromwell's best general who had led with such distinction at Marston Moor, Dunbar and Worcester, and being one of the instigators of Cromwell being made Protector in the first place, Cromwell made no attempt to persuade him to take the oath. On 13 July Lambert was ordered to resign his commissions and all offices. This he did three days later. Exceptional service to the cause and years of the closest working relationship with Cromwell could not stand in the way of the security of the regime. Surprisingly, Lambert left without fuss and retired to put his energy into gardening on his Wimbledon estate. There appeared to be no reaction from the army at the loss of the man who was their de facto second-in-command and judged by many to be the Protector's most likely heir. Thurloe must have breathed a sigh of relief that this potentially explosive situation had passed off so well and Lambert had been quietly turned into yesterday's man. Or so it seemed.

In the bitter cold winter of 1657/8, when Thurloe was having one of his bouts of illness, Richard Cromwell and his wife Dorothy were summoned to London from their rural life in Hampshire. Cromwell had decided that Richard as his eldest son should have more responsibility. The previous summer he had added to Richard's status by making him Chancellor of the University of Oxford. Now he made him a Privy Councillor. Henry Cromwell was also given recognition by being promoted from General to Lord Deputy of Ireland. Richard and Henry were also made members of the Other House, but further appointments did not go so smoothly. Cromwell's friends in the nobility were obvious candidates but several were not at all keen to accept. They felt that it was their hereditary right to sit in what they regarded as the House of Lords and could not accept that they would only be members because they had been selected by the Lord Protector. The Earl of Manchester and Lord Saye and Sele flatly refused to be members and Cromwell had to resort to appointing many of his best Commons supporters to make up numbers. St John, Claypole, Monck, Fleetwood, Desborough, Skippon, Whalley, Goffe, Berry, Montagu and Whitelocke all found themselves in the Upper House.

One of the provisions of the *Humble Petition* was that there should be no exclusion of any MP elected to the Commons. This meant the new Commons included republican opponents such as Sir Arthur Haselrig and Thomas Scot just at a time when the chamber had been denuded of many of the Protector's main supporters. Another difficulty was that some lords who had agreed to be appointed to the Other House refused to take their seats, having taken one look at their fellow members. The Earls of Warwick and Musgrove both stated that they would not sit in an assembly with the likes of General Hewson, a former shoemaker, or Colonel Pride, a former drayman.

Things deteriorated further after the new parliament was opened in January because the two Houses were immediately at each other's throat. The Other House regarded itself at the successor to the Lords and therefore the Upper House, while the Commons considered itself the senior chamber because it was elected. Cromwell summoned both Houses and tried to make them work together but the genie was out of the bottle and Haselrig and his vociferous republican friends continued to attack not just the Other House but the authority of the Protector. In despair

Cromwell had no option but to dissolve the Parliament after it had sat for no more than a fortnight. On top of every thing, Thurloe became ill during the early spring and Cromwell found himself temporarily without his chief administrator and head of intelligence at a time when the regional infrastructure of the major generals had been removed. To make matters worse, Thurloe's right-hand man, Meadowe, was also away. Having achieved the ratification of the Portuguese treaty it might have been hoped that Meadowe would be able to return to his work in London but that was not to be. Cromwell felt that only Meadowe had the necessary skill to sort out the latest crisis between the two important Protestant powers of Denmark and Sweden. In February he was dispatched as ambassador to Denmark.

The crisis was as convoluted as the foreign affairs of the time. In May the previous year Lutheran Denmark had been encouraged by the United Provinces to invade the Lutheran Swedish Duchy of Bremen. The Danes were allied to Catholic Poland and Calvinist Brandenberg, who in turn allied to Catholic Hungary under the 8-year-old Arch Duke William, who was about to be elected Holy Roman Emperor. It is a tribute to the multi-talented Meadowe that he managed to negotiate the peace treaty of Roskilde between Sweden and Denmark. This was a major feat of diplomacy, which resulted in Meadowe being knighted by Cromwell when he returned to England. As it happened, the treaty between the two Protestant adversaries was soon broken and Meadowe would have been better employed at home. Andrew Marvell had been standing in for him as Latin Secretary but no one was acting as an intelligence focus while he and Thurloe were away. The whole strength of having intelligence centralized at the highest level became a severe handicap when both head and deputy were away and no one was authorized to stand in for them. Fortunately for the Protectorate, this only lasted for a short time and Thurloe was again back at his desk. Luckily there had been no crisis and so, apart from the great backlog of work, the provision of intelligence could be resumed.

Charles and his exiled court had been watching with dismay as Cromwell assumed the position of king in all but name. In January 1658 Charles had appointed Edward Hyde Chancellor on the death of the loyal but rather ineffectual Sir Edward Herbert. Hyde was now recognized as Charles's principal minister, a position he had held unofficially for some time. It had been with Hyde's encouragement that Charles had sought the alliance with Spain in spring 1656, following France becoming allied to Protectorate Britain. With France and Spain at war it should be natural for Spain to want an alliance with Charles in order to help destabilize the Protectorate. For all the logic there had been difficulties, not just because Charles was a Protestant but because Spanish diplomacy was very cumbersome. It was a major problem for an impoverished deposed King of Scotland to even have an opportunity to put across the case for an alliance. Luckily for Charles such a potential opportunity had arisen with the departure of Arch Duke Leopold as Governor of the Spanish Netherlands in early 1656 and his replacement by a soldier, Don John of Austria.

It has to be said that Don John was a competent rather than a great soldier, who had served in Naples, Sicily and Catalonia but seen little action. His significance lay more in his birth than his military prowess, for he was the illegitimate son of King Philip IV of Spain. Unkind people sometimes suggested that his actress mother may have extended her favours beyond the royal bed and could not help noticing that Don John's long raven locks and regular features bore little resemblance to the fair hair and huge chin of the Habsburgs. Be that as it may, King Philip had not only recognized Don John as his son but had given him positions of increasing importance. After some negotiation by Hyde it had been agreed that in March Charles should go in secret to Don John's capital Brussels. A hesitant Charles, unsure of Spanish etiquette and with only a smattering of the language, was eventually received by Don John. To his relief, Charles found Don John to be a man of charm, who after a few meetings agreed to use his good offices in securing an alliance with his father. Charles had left Brussels well pleased. Not only had he obtained the vital agreement of Spanish military support to help restore him to his throne but an agreement that he would receive a monthly pension of 3,000 crowns. The money was to prove as elusive as Mazarin's pension but Charles's credit rating was much improved and he was able to move his court from Cologne to Bruges and a fresh group of potential creditors.

The immediate euphoria of obtaining agreement to a Spanish/Royalist alliance very soon gave way to a major family quarrel. Charles's mother Queen Henrietta Maria was less than pleased that her son should have sided with Spain against her own country France. His sister Mary was angry that Charles should have allied with the country that the United Provinces had fought in such a bitter war of independence. She knew that this would make her already precarious position as Princess of Orange almost untenable. His brother James was furious to find that he could no longer serve in the French army and accept the promotion he had just been offered of the command in Italy. His promising military career now seemed to have run into the sand, all because of a clause stating that Royalists could only serve in the Spanish army.

Balanced against this damaging family upset there had at first been little gain to show for nailing Stuart colours to the Spanish mast. The Spanish bureaucracy ground exceedingly slow, in fact it would take another two years before the Royalist/Spanish treaty was formally ratified. That said, with Don John behind it there was no serious doubt that it would eventually come about and after a few months some military planning began to take place. Slowly, slowly, the Royalist bid to restore the monarchy by force began to take shape. On moving to Flanders Charles had begun raising four regiments of his own and also ordered an Irish regiment in French service to join him. This all took time because of the difficulties of obtaining hard cash to pay the troops. Naturally these activities were under the close scrutiny of Thurloe's agents in Bruges who reported that Charles's army numbered no more than 700, were badly equipped and, as they were given little or no pay, their loyalty was highly suspect. In fact one of Thurloe's informants described them as 'better versed in the art of begging than fighting'. They were indeed a rag-tag outfit but they were an outward and visible sign of the rebirth of the Royalist cause and provided the grounds for hope which had previously been so forlorn.

Charles might have been trying to meet his side of the bargain with Spain within his very limited means but Spain was in no rush for an invasion of England. Don John could see that Cromwell appeared secure as Lord Protector and not only had a strong army at his disposal but also a formidable fleet, part of which was stationed off the Flemish coast. After much understandable dragging of feet, in December 1657 Don John suggested that Charles send a senior figure in secret to England to see if the Royalists would indeed rise up if there was a Spanish-backed invasion force. Ormonde was chosen for this important assignment. It was a sign of Charles's financial straits that he had to pawn his beloved Garter insignia to pay the cost of Ormonde's travelling expenses. On a more cheerful note, the timing for the visit seemed to be just right. Charles must have been encouraged at the start of the new year when he learnt that what had been expected to be a wholly acquiescent Parliament was now at loggerheads with the Protector. There was at last the possibility that the tide was turning against Cromwell in England. Cromwell was still receiving some opposition from many of his former allies, whether it was staunch republicans or the last remnants of those still harbouring something of Leveller or Fifth Monarchist beliefs. This was not especially new in itself but the change was that there was now strong criticism of him being voiced by many of the people's representatives in the Commons. Cheered by this turn of events, some English Cavaliers thought that at last it just might be that there was sufficient dissent in Britain for an uprising to be viable. Some had sent letters to Charles in Bruges saying that the time was right for a rising, accompanied by a Spanish-backed invasion. It was therefore of utmost importance for Ormonde to judge for himself whether the level of support really existed and, in his own words: 'if their coucels were discreetly laid'.

Ormonde duly arrived at a small harbour near Colchester disguised as a peddler and with his fair hair dyed black. Before leaving he had taken the precaution to have letters sent indicating that he was still in Bruges, which he was confident would be intercepted. By February he had reached London and was staying at a Catholic surgeon's house in Drury Lane with his dyed hair gradually turning a startling orange colour. He now began to make contact with a wide variety of representatives of groups in opposition to Cromwell. These included Presbyterians such as Manchester, and Waller and other leaders like Lord Saye and Sele, who were prepared to accept Charles if he signed the agreement made by his father in the Isle of Wight. Meetings even took place with a few last Levellers but whoever he spoke to it became increasingly clear that such opposition as existed was highly fragmented and divided amongst itself. Ormonde naturally contacted the Sealed Knot in the form of Willys and Russell, who made it clear that they would not support a rising until Charles had landed in England with Spanish support. As the Spanish had already made it a condition that they would only launch an invasion force if an English port had been already seized by English Royalists as a bridgehead, there was an obvious impasse. Needless to say, throughout these fruitless discussions, Ormonde's disguise and the deception of his letters intended for interception had not fooled Thurloe. He had known all about the Ormonde's visit through his Sealed Knot source Sir Richard Willys. With a belated form of loyalty to his friends, Willys reported all Ormonde's movements but only after a short delay to ensure it was too late for him to be arrested.

As it happened this was of little consequence, as Ormonde was under close surveillance and there was no purpose in arresting him when every contact he made was of great assistance to intelligence in confirming Stuart sympathizers. Thurloe had told Cromwell of Ormonde's activities but Cromwell decided not to act against him or those who he had contacted. As well as appreciating Ormonde's indirect intelligence value, Cromwell reasoned that arresting Ormonde would only open old wounds and he did not want the embarrassment of taking prisoner a person who was generally regarded as an honest man for a Royalist. He therefore decided to engineer a discreet end to the visit. He called in his close Irish companion Lord Broghill and said to him: 'An old friend of yours is in town, the Marquis of Ormonde, now lodged in Drury Lane with a papist surgeon there. You had better tell him to be gone.' Broghill passed word to Ormonde that his whereabouts was known and the latter slipped back to the Continent to report his assessment. Amazingly Ormonde took the part of the Action Party and reported that Royalists would rise up and even suggested Yarmouth as a suitable place for an invasion force to land. Fortunately for Charles this appallingly poor assessment of the situation was not put to the test, because all too soon events in England proved it to be no more than wishful thinking.

Cromwell had spared Ormonde but that did not mean he had gone soft on Royalists. Thurloe had provided intelligence that a Spanish-backed Royalist plan for an invasion was being prepared, financed by 150,000 crowns from the King of Spain. Ostend had been decided upon as the point of embarkation. This intelligence was all correct in theory but as we know had failed to become substance. Thurloe would have known this. Nevertheless intelligence has its political uses. It was sufficient to justify putting the fleet supporting the British army in Flanders on particular alert and blockading Ostend. At home Cromwell exploited the intelligence to rally support and raise loans for the war. With no parliament to address, on 12 March he called for the Lord Mayor and Alderman of London and told them about Ormonde's visit and the invasion fleet assembling in Flanders. A few weeks later a High Court of Justice was established to try cases of treason. This was a new version of the court which had tried Charles I and had been agreed by Parliament back in September 1656 but had not been implemented because of its draconian nature. It consisted of 140 commissioners appointed by the Protector who would act as both judge and jury. In May commissioners began being appointed and it was soon ready for business.

While the High Court of Justice was being established, Thurloe and his intelligence staff were busy gathering information on Royalist activists to place before the court. As a preliminary measure all prominent Royalists and Roman Catholics were ordered out of London and required to remain within five miles of their country homes. The next phase was to carry out arrests and a good starting point were those who had been in contact with Ormonde but not influential figures, who might see the error of their ways and come round to supporting the Protectorate. The type of person who ended up being arrested was John Mordaunt, younger son of the Earl of Peterborough. Mordaunt had seen Ormonde when he had been over and had asked that he and John Stapeley, nephew of the Earl of Norwich, together with various other Cavalier gentlemen, should be given commissions to raise regiments of horse at their own expense in the event of a future rebellion. One of Stapeley's servants passed this information to Thurloe and provided all the names of those put forward for commissions. Cromwell himself decided to examine Mordaunt, who denied meeting Ormonde but naturally that did not save him from being sent to the Tower.

Thurloe examined John Malory, a friend of Mordaunt, and during the interrogation got him to agree Mordaunt's guilt, having tricked him into believing that he already had proof. This must be one of the oldest interrogation ploys but continues to get excellent results down to the present day. Malory joined Mordaunt in the Tower. Philip Meadowe, who had returned from his diplomatic spell abroad, also did his bit for this Royalist round-up. One source he recruited was Reverend Francis Corker who had been vicar of Bradford and was in touch with Royalists, particularly in Yorkshire and Sussex. He was able to report that Reverend John Hewett was holding services in London which were being used as a cover for Cavalier plots. This fitted with information Thurloe had also received when he examined Stapeley. Hewett was arrested and taken to the Tower. Many others were also arrested, including poor Sir Henry Slingsby who been held prisoner at Hull since the Penruddock rising. While in prison he was tricked by an agent provocateur into offering someone a Royalist commission and so was transferred to the Tower for treason. Six other Royalist activists were arrested in the Mermaid Tavern in Cheapside and they, together with Mordaunt, Stapeley, Slingsby and Hewett, appeared before the High Court of Justice and were swiftly condemned to death. The executions began with Slingsby and Hewett being beheaded and three others were hanged, drawn and quartered. Normally such spectacles of extensive bloody mutilation were greeted with interest and awe, but times were changing. There was so much public revulsion at the hideous form of execution carried out on fairly decent men that Cromwell decided to pardon the other conspirators. Stapeley, Mallory and Mordaunt were released. About a month later in July Cromwell authorized the release of the many other Cavaliers who had been rounded up for imprisonment but not charged, including all members of the Sealed Knot (among whom was Sir Richard Willys for obvious source protection purposes). Thurloe had Sir William Compton, Colonel John Russell and Willys brought before him at their release and personally warned of the consequences of further engagement in subversive activity. Neither the Sealed Knot nor any of the other Cavaliers seized had posed any immediate threat to the Protectorate but their arrest had demonstrated that those with Royalist sympathies were known to the authorities and execution awaited anyone who plotted the overthrow of the Protectorate. Cromwell clearly felt that a point had been made and so he adjourned the High Court in the knowledge that anyone contemplating what might fall into the broad definition of treasonous behaviour would know that it could be swiftly reconvened.

Any brief optimism at Charles's court following Ormonde's positive report on his trip to England was completely dispelled by the crackdown on Royalist activists. The hope of eventually mounting a Spanish-backed invasion to restore the King had become no more than a faint glimmer. The prospect had further worsened now that the Protectorate navy had established a tight blockade on the Flanders coast in general and Ostend in particular. All now depended on the successful progress of the campaign in the Low Countries. The Spanish with Charles's small force, and more importantly their ally Condé, were squaring up against France and its ally Protectorate Britain. The year 1658 had opened with the French army under Marshal Turenne and the British contingent under Sir William Lockhart besieging Dunkirk in the Spanish Netherlands. This caught Don John the Spanish commander by surprise as he had expected the allies to attack Cambrai. He was then obliged to advance against the allies at Dunkirk to raise the siege. Turenne and Lockhart did not wait for the Spanish to arrive but went off to meet them and intercepted them before they had received their ammunition supplies. On seeing the allies, Don John hastily deployed on some sand dunes, with the Duke of York commanding the right wing, Condé the left and himself in the centre. Just before battle was joined on 4 June, Lockhart was taken ill and his place was taken by Colonel Morgan whose English force was drawn up opposite the Duke of York who was commanding his wing of Royalist English and Spanish cavalry. Morgan's musketeers rushed up the sand hill and beat back the Royalist infantry. The Duke counter-attacked at the head of the Spanish cavalry and fought on with extreme bravery until first Condé's wing fell back and then the Spanish centre, leaving him and his men exposed. As the whole Spanish line then collapsed and began to flee the field, the Duke had no option but to rally as many as he could and flee with them.

This had been a great success for France and Turenne was generous enough to give credit for the victory to Morgan's English who had fought with such ferocity that they had barely any officers surviving the battle. Battles are won and battles are lost. The allies had won by their bravery and professionalism in the field but also by their decision to besiege Dunkirk and their subsequent decision to advance against Don John's approaching army. Conversely the Spanish lost because they could not match the allies on the field and that was in no small part caused because they were taken by surprise. Good intelligence is the antidote to enemy surprise and had Don John been aware first of the ally's intention to attack Dunkirk, and more importantly that they would advance to meet him, he would not have had to make a hasty unprepared deployment for battle without his ammunition supply. No military engagements are won by intelligence alone but they can be lost by the lack of it.

As a result of the victory at what was called the Battle of the Dunes, Dunkirk surrendered to the English, Gravelines was then taken and also Ypres and soon all the towns on the banks of the Lys had fallen to the allies. The Royalist hopes of support from Spain were now completely dashed and Cromwell and his Protectorate had achieved an unassailable position of strength which could be expected to last for the foreseeable future. In 1558 Queen Mary had supported her Spanish husband against the French and ended up losing Calais, the last remnant of the crown's once extensive territory on the continent of Europe. Calais had been under English rule since 1346 and its loss was such a huge blow to national prestige that Mary had said that when she was dead Calais would be found written on her heart. Now exactly a hundred years later the British Republic, allied this time with France against Spain, had come into possession of a town on the Continent. This very tangible result of the Dunes victory was a matter of considerable national pride and in many ways the high point of the Commonwealth and Protectorate. But the very success brought its own problems. Dunkirk had a population of 5,100, the great majority of whom were Catholic, who would be unlikely to take kindly to military occupation and the language, laws and government of the puritanical English. Lockhart sensibly allowed freedom of worship and a generally conciliatory attitude towards Britain's new subjects. There were a number of unfortunate incidents, such as English soldiers lighting their pipes from candles on the high altars of Catholic churches, but before very long an uneasy relationship of tolerance was built up between the soldiery and the citizens. Although the town was under firm military control there was the likelihood that it might become a centre for subversion against the Commonwealth. In order to counter this threat Thurloe devised a master stroke. The Jesuits were allowed to return Dunkirk and openly go about their work. This concession was obtained at a price. This was that they should inform on any subversion that came to their attention. They kept their bargain.

After the victory at the Battle of the Dunes, Cromwell became greatly respected, if not liked, by his fellow European rulers. He was now at the height of his power at home and abroad. Cromwell never forgot that this power rested ultimately with the army and, even in his now almost invincible position, did not take the army's loyalty for granted. Purges continued of those whose loyalty was found to be suspect. During the year Cromwell himself removed six troop commanders from his own cavalry regiment and his senior commanders, especially Monck, were equally energetic in routing out the unreliable. The commanders themselves were naturally of particular interest to Cromwell. He would have informal social gatherings with them as well as formal meetings so that he could better judge their feelings when their guard was down. He also made it a rule that generals could not meet together without his authority. This ensured that there was no opportunity for them to be tempted to secretly plan against him. As it happened, Cromwell had no need to doubt the loyalty of his generals, having removed the likes of Harrison and Lambert and being left only with those who were either members of his extended family or otherwise owed their position to him. There was no one in the army to begin to rival him and no reason to undermine the man on whom their fortune depended. For all that, circumstances can change and Cromwell was prudent not to neglect monitoring the loyalty of those closest to him.

Despite Cromwell's apparently invincible position there was always the possibility that his power might still be brought to an abrupt end by a single bullet from a Cavalier or republican assassin. Although this remained a possibility, the chance of it occurring was much reduced because of a major stepping up of the Protector's personal security. The days of Cromwell casually trying his hand at being a coachman were long over. Clarendon later wrote that he had become much

> less easy of access, nor so much seen abroad; and he seemed to be in some disorder when his eyes found any stranger in the room, upon whom they still remained fixed. When he intended to go to Hampton Court, which was his principal delight and diversion, it was never known till he was in the coach which way he would go; and he was hemmed in by his guards before and behind; and the coach in which he went was always thronged as full as it could be with servants, who were armed, and he seldom returned the same way he went and rarely lodged two nights together in one chamber, but had many furnished and prepared, to which his own key conducted him.

Although it seemed that all options to remove Cromwell were exhausted, the seeds of his end were already growing at this time of his greatest public fortune. The threat came not from his enemies but his personal circumstances. Cromwell's son-in-law Lord Rich had died suddenly on 11 February, leaving his pretty daughter Frances a young widow. This happened on the same day as the death of Cromwell's niece Lavinia Beke, of whom he was particularly fond. Two months later Lord Rich's grandfather, Cromwell's old friend and ally the Earl of Warwick, also died. At the same time Cromwell's favourite daughter Bettie Claypole was taken ill and did not seem to be responding to treatment – it was cancer. On top of this her 1-year-old son Oliver died in June. These personal sorrows had to be borne by the 59-year-old Cromwell at a time when his own health was deteriorating, with a bout of European malaria added to the pain of his gout and gallstone. He spirit must have also been worn down by the effort of keeping his ideals alive while faced with massive government debts and bloody-minded parliaments who would vote no money unless allowed to impose their own agendas. He still retained the loyalty of the massive army that was the prime source of both his power and debts but there was always the worry that its support would evaporate if money could not be found to provide regular pay. As he often said, the burden of government 'was too heavy for man', and that burden seemed to be getting heavier by the day. Throughout the stiflingly hot summer Cromwell was at his daughter's bedside in Hampton Court nearly day and night until on 5 August, when she died in excruciating pain. She was only 29. A light went out in his life. He was so overcome he could not bring himself to accompany Bettie's body down the Thames and attend her funeral at Westminster Abbey.

About a fortnight later, using every strength that he could muster from his faith, Cromwell managed to pull himself together but by then his health had severely deteriorated and he took to his bed. He was now a dying man. So larger than life was Cromwell that no one could believe that he was nearing death and it was assumed that the many prayers being offered would restore his health. It was not till 30 August that there was the first indication of anyone considering a Commonwealth without him. On that day Fauconberg made the first move by writing to his brother-in-law Henry Cromwell in Ireland saying that he would support him as Lord Protector and that Lockhart would as well. Thurloe could see that the end was coming but was beside himself with grief. Only on 2 September did the Council begin to accept that death was likely and start to consider arrangements for a successor. No successor had been formally nominated but it was thought that Cromwell had written the name of his heir in a sealed document. It was not the custom in those days to write a will until on the death bed, so it could be one was never written. Anyway, no amount of hunting the rooms of Whitehall Palace could locate it. The Council therefore asked the dying Lord Protector to name his successor. Cromwell muttered something indistinct and it was thought that he probably said 'Richard'; so Richard it was. In the early afternoon of 3 September, the anniversary of his great victories Dunbar and Worcester, the great man died. The Privy Council met at 8 that evening and then went to where Richard was staying to tell him he was the new Lord Protector.

Cromwell had never sought personal advancement, let alone greatness, but had relentlessly pursued the tasks that he felt God had entrusted to him. In doing so he had pushed through a revolution in which the three former kingdoms were a united Commonwealth with freedom of religion within the Protestant faith and equality before the law. His Great Britain was a major power in Europe and had the beginnings of an overseas empire. Cromwell had achieved all he had though his God-fuelled determination and the military brilliance that had brought him the command of the army. His power rested on three pillars: military might, parliamentary authority and a machinery of government. The New Model Army gave him the military might, Parliament had voted him the powers of Protector and the new breed of civil servants under Thurloe gave him the means to run the country effectively. Although a great parliamentarian, he like his Stuart predecessors had found it impossible to work with the House of Commons. He had been obliged reluctantly to marginalize Parliament, knowing that he could run the country through his civil service and be assured that their intelligence would provide warning of any opposition, which could then be quickly neutralized by his army. It was ironic that a man as principled as Cromwell should have found himself presiding over a government that fell little short of a combination of police state and military dictatorship. He had just about managed to push through his own policies despite the differing demands of the army and Parliament but as he said the burden had been getting 'heavier by the day'. The question was whether his successor would have the strength of character to carry that burden and the acumen to deal with those who for different reasons wanted to undermine the authority of the Protectorate.

Naturally the news of the Lord Protector's death was a cause of much rejoicing at the Stuart court in exile. Surely Charles's time had at last come and he would soon return to claim his own. But these days of Royalist celebration soon gave way to apprehension and then despondency, as the government of the three nations passed smoothly to a new Lord Protector. The person chiefly responsible for ensuring this orderly transfer of power was John Thurloe. The process went so well that Thurloe remarked 'there was not a dog that wag this tongue, so great a calm are we in'. Almost immediately all the ambassadors were falling over themselves addressing condolences and congratulations to Richard. From the City of London and throughout the country messages of support were coming for His Highness the new Lord Protector. Cromwell the Moses of the Republic was dead but there was a Joshua to lead the Commonwealth into the Promised Land. The post of Lord Protector had not only survived but become enhanced by the smooth succession. Oliver Cromwell was granted a state funeral modelled on previous royal funerals but with perhaps rather more pomp. After lying in state with an imperial crown beside him, Oliver was buried with considerable pageantry in Westminster Abbey. Richard called a Parliament and the business of government went on as normal. There was every indication that the Cromwell dynasty was now firmly established as Lord Protectors and for all anyone knew they might become a dynasty to rival the Plantagenets.

The *Petition and Advice* had given Oliver Cromwell the difficult decision of who was to be his successor. In some ways the obvious choice would have been his son Henry, who was not only a soldier and so potentially popular in the army but also Lord Deputy of Ireland and so highly experienced in government. Instead Cromwell seems to have chosen his eldest son Richard who was simply a rather impoverished country gentleman with very little political and no military experience. One can only speculate why Oliver made the choice of the son who was regularly referred to as 'indolent Dick'. First, perhaps because he was following primogeniture and so it was natural to him that his first son should succeed him. Second, perhaps because he felt it was time that the country ceased to be ruled by a soldier and a civilian might be able to enter into a more successful partnership with Parliament. Richard's lack of experience and leadership qualities would have been all too apparent to his father but he may have felt that he would get by with the support of his family. Oliver was fond of Richard's wife Dorothy and may have believed that she possessed a degree of resolution which her husband lacked. More important was the support of the extended Cromwell family who held so many positions of power. There was Richard's brother Henry in Ireland, his brother-in-law General Fleetwood, his uncle General Desborough and others of military influence such as cousin Whalley. Lastly there was the unfailing support that Richard could expect from Thurloe and through him the government service. Thurloe would probably have preferred his friend Henry Cromwell as successor but, ever the honest servant, he loyally followed his master's wishes and ensured Richard became the undisputed Lord Protector. It was a personal triumph for Thurloe that the transfer of power was so smooth. Whether the new Protector could retain that power would rest on Richard's ability to rise to the occasion and the strength of family loyalty of his military relations.

Almost at once Richard's family began to let him down. The Army Council began to question whether Richard should be commander-in-chief, which was his right under the *Petition and Advice*. In their view the commander-in-chief should be the most prominent general, as had been the case with Oliver Cromwell. As most of the Army Council were equally prominent generals, many of them were in effect throwing their own hats into the ring for the top job. Thurloe tried to defuse the situation by advising Richard to appoint his brother-in-law Fleetwood to the post of Lieutenant General of the Forces, at the same time making it clear that the post of commander–in–chief rested with the Lord Protector. The Army Council responded by demanding that Thurloe and Richard's other ablest councillors such as St John should be dismissed.

With the army getting difficult, Richard's hope lay with calling Parliament to use as a counterweight to them. The other imperative for a Parliament was that Richard had inherited a government deficit of £500,000, largely arising from his father's ambitious foreign policy. As well as the armies of occupation in Scotland and Ireland there were the garrisons in England and of course the army in the Low Countries. The navy was also sustaining two fleets at sea. One was blockading the Flemish Coast and the other was in the Baltic, defending the Commonwealth's ally Sweden against the Danes and Dutch. Both the army and navy had arrears of pay amounting to some £890,000. Certainly there was no money for pay to be had from the Treasury, as the total national debt stood at £32.5 million, at a time when government annual income was £12.4 million. In short the government was bankrupt and only a Parliament could make it solvent and stable.

The problem was that it would take five months before a Parliament could be assembled. It would be a matter of playing for time. For the remaining months of the year Thurloe set about doing all he could to ensure that when the Parliament did assemble it contained those who were favourable to the Lord Protector. One expedient was not only to call for MPs from the counties and larger boroughs but to extend the franchise to lesser and decayed boroughs who were easier to influence. Thurloe had previously used all the means at his disposal to try to get favourable MPs elected to the Parliaments called by Oliver Cromwell, but had only achieved limited success. Now it was imperative that he should succeed for his late master's son. Just at this critical time Thurloe had one of his bouts of illness that lasted from 13 September to mid-November. While an invalid Thurloe was attempting every available ploy to achieve the desired election results and the restless army commanders were considering their next move, Richard was quietly carrying out the functions of Protector. This he was doing in a dignified, steady manner that was unlikely to rouse any public hostility and calculated to build confidence in the new regime. January 1659 would show whether the combination of Thurloe's machinations and Richard's sensible low-profile performance would do the trick.

Chapter 12

Scramble for Power, 1659

Richard opened the third Protectorate Parliament in January 1659 with regal pomp. Even on this ceremonial occasion it was clear that the Commons would be as unmanageable as ever. When Richard made the traditional summons of the Commons to the Lords, only half the members obeyed because they did not want to recognize the other chamber. Richard still went ahead with his address to the two Houses which he ended by urging them to make this 'a happy parliament'. As it happened, it would turn out to be possibly the most fractious and unhappy of all British Parliaments.

The Commons was dominated by a group in fundamental opposition to the Protector. These were republicans who rejected the powers of both the Protector and the Other House, wanting the Commons to be the Commonwealth's supreme authority. The leaders of this opposition were those who had made life so difficult for Cromwell in the previous Parliament: Haselrig, Scot and Bradshaw. They were now joined by two major political figures with very differing reasons for opposition: Vane and Fairfax. Vane had returned from his French exile to further the republican cause and Fairfax had decided to come back to public life with the secret intention of helping a return to monarchy.

For all his efforts to create a benign parliament, Thurloe had failed to produce the goods. It was no surprise that this bitter Commons was uninterested in his attempts to raise urgently needed taxation. Violent argument took place for the first fortnight, culminating in a compromise resolution that the post of Protector should be retained with reduced powers. It then became a short step to decide that the Upper House should be the junior partner in government. At the end of March the Commons turned its attention to grievances against the heart of government, making accusations of embezzlement, oppression and illegal taxation. There was talk of the impeachment of the Protector's main advisers, with Thurloe the principal target.

The Commons knew that their power to authorize taxation had both the Protector and the army over a barrel and so made their increasingly extravagant demands a prerequisite to taxation. The army, which had little time for Parliament at best of times, became incensed by the Commons' behaviour. Although all generals were agreed in their opposition to Parliament they were otherwise divided into two groups. One group led by Whalley, Goffe and Ingoldsby met at Whitehall and maintained support for the Protector. An opposition group established their headquarters at Fleetwood's residence, Wallingford House, under the pretence of prayer meetings. This was led by Fleetwood and Desborough who, although related to Richard, wanted army ascendancy and through it greater power for themselves. Their immediate goal was for Fleetwood to be commander-in-chief, with Richard as his puppet Protector. Smelling an opportunity to fulfil his destiny, Lambert hastened to London from his Wimbledon retirement to join this group. Neither he nor anyone else seemed to bother that he no longer held a commission. He was after all a man of some charisma who had been Cromwell's best general and was still immensely popular in the army. To some, particularly himself, he was Cromwell's natural heir.

Desborough also led a subgroup which met at St James and consisted of middle-ranking officers who wanted the army to have the power and pay they felt it deserved. With the agreement of Fleetwood, the St James group formed a Council of Officers which drafted an address to Richard listing the army grievances, not least the arrears of pay. Fleetwood presented the address to Richard on 14 April. Richard quite rightly referred the address to Parliament. As soon as the Commons read the address they immediately suspected that the army was trying to outmanoeuvre them. Their response was to pass two votes. The first was that no senior officers should be allowed to meet without the express agreement of the Protector and the second that no officer could hold command at land or sea unless they signed an agreement that they would not prevent the free meeting of Parliament. They had thrown down the gauntlet to the army and the generals were swift to pick it up. Urged on by Lambert, Fleetwood and Desborough went to see Richard and advised him to dissolve Parliament. This was more than just advice, for Desborough made it clear, in his bluff manner, that if Richard did not consent he would be forcibly removed by the army.

Richard had to make a decision. Whalley and the Whitehall group of officers advised him to retain Parliament to block the ambitions of Lambert. They even offered to have Lambert killed but this was rejected by Richard. Thurloe advised dismissing Parliament – not surprisingly as the Commons were about to impeach him. With great reluctance Richard agreed to take note of the person whose advice had always stood him in good stead and came down on the side of Thurloe. On 22 April Richard signed the order dissolving Parliament.

Richard was now entirely dependent upon the army. He knew he could rely on a small group of generals such as Whalley and that most of the army rank and file were predisposed to support the son of Oliver Cromwell. The question was whether Lambert and Fleetwood would be satisfied with their rout of Parliament and rally round the Protector. The answer came quickly. The Council of Officers on their own authority dismissed Whalley, Goffe and all the senior officers supporting Richard. Radical officers removed by Cromwell, such as Harrison, were now welcomed back. Despite this successful military coup, Lambert and Fleetwood still had the problem of needing a compliant Commons to vote money to pay service arrears. They decided that the Rump Parliament which had been dismissed by Cromwell six years before would be sufficiently republican to support the army's wishes.

Without reference to Richard, Lenthall the old Speaker was quickly summoned, along with about fifty former members.

This Parliament met on 7 May but the proceedings descended into chaos when their right to sit was disputed by the members who had been excluded by Pride's purge eleven years earlier. Some eighty of these ageing gentlemen assembled at Westminster Hall to demand their seats. Lambert knew that those purged were largely Presbyterian and no friends of the army so ordered the Westminster guards to forcibly prevent any of them entering the Chamber. Despite the upheavals the Commons appointed a Council of State dominated by Lambert, Fleetwood, Desborough, Bradshaw, Haselrig and Vane. These names were no surprise but the Council also included Fairfax, Ashley Cooper, St John and Whitelocke. The latter three, who had always been cool towards the Protectorate, had decide to desert Richard and join the winning team. Monck in Scotland sent word that he was pleased to see the return of the Rump and Henry Cromwell in Ireland, realizing that the Cromwell dynasty had collapsed, resigned his office.

With no obvious opposition, the usurping officers now sent a list of demands to Parliament which were immediately passed. Foremost of these was that the Commonwealth should be governed by the Commons and the Upper House and the post of Lord Protector should be abolished. Knowing the esteem with which the name of Cromwell was still held, it was decided to sweeten the pill by granting both Richard and his mother a pension of £10,000 a year. During all this Richard had continued to live in Whitehall Palace with all the panoply of Lord Protector while being completely ignored. He had made one bold effort to re-establish his authority by ordering the officers of his personal bodyguard to arrest Fleetwood. When they refused the game was up. There was no way Richard could now come to some accommodation with the brother-in-law he had attempted to arrest. He had no choice but to resign the position of Protector, which he had never sought in the first place, and take the money. This he did on 25 June, although the pension was never paid. On the orders of the Council the replica crown, sceptre and other royal accoutrements that had been placed on Oliver Cromwell's monument in the chancel of Westminster Abbey were ordered to be publicly sold – they fetched £88 11s 6d. The country had lost enthusiasm for Lord Protectors.

To replace Henry Cromwell in Ireland, the Army Council appointed the staunch republican Lieutenant General Edmund Ludlow, whom Cromwell had sacked four years earlier for refusing to acknowledge the Protectorate. In Scotland Monck appeared to accept the new status quo. The Commonwealth of England, Scotland and Ireland was now effectively under a military junta working through a puppet Parliament. This new order had power but little respect at home or abroad and needed to quickly establish a government service loyal to the new regime. Barkstead was dismissed from the Tower and naturally Thurloe had been removed from all offices by the Council of State and was no longer even an MP. He retired to his mansion at Wisbech. The role of intelligence coordinator passed back to Thomas

Scot. The post of Secretary of State was left vacant until Scot was confirmed in the position in mid-January the next year.

Charles had been hearing of the events in England with mounting excitement. With the Protectorship ended and replaced with a makeshift military junta consisting of generals with conflicting personal ambitions, it was surely time to appeal to the majority of the population to rise up and restore legitimate government. For so many years Hyde had counselled waiting until the Commonwealth government was in sufficient disarray and sufficiently unpopular to provide the ingredients of a successful rising. The intelligence from all Hyde's sources pointed clearly to the unpopularity of the new regime and its inherent instability. This intelligence assessment was quite correct and Charles decided to authorize a Royalist uprising in support of which he would returning to England at the head of an army.

Although the ever cautious Sealed Knot had expressed concerns about the whole operation, other Cavaliers were more sanguine. Charles had agreed to John Mordaunt setting up a Royalist group called the 'Great Trust' in order to organize an uprising and made him a viscount as a mark of his support for the project. After some wrangling, most of the Sealed Knot agreed to plan for a rising on 1 August. In preparation for this Charles moved to Boulogne ready to take ship to the traditional Royalist strongholds of either Wales or Cornwall. It was planned that the Duke of York would also embark at Boulogne with some 600 veterans provided by Condé but would land on the Kent coast. Charles's younger brother the Duke of Gloucester was to assemble in Ostend with 4,000 troops. With Cavalier risings taking place across the country and armies led by the royal family advancing from different directions, the junta would not know which way to turn and would probably cave in. This was a plan based on a correct intelligence assessment that had a real chance of success.

The only problem was that the whole operation was blown by Sir Richard Willys. In late July Willys was arrested and brought before the Council for questioning and described the Royalist plans in detail. Then out of the blue in July a notice was posted on the Old Exchange in London branding Willys as a government agent. It appeared on the very day that Mordaunt returned to London to carry out final coordination meetings before the rising. Mordaunt and most Royalist activists refused to accept it and assumed that it must be black propaganda. Charles and Hyde however had reason to believe that Willys was indeed an agent. They rightly judged that the whole operation was compromised and sent urgent messages to abort both the invasion and the uprising.

In many cases the messages did not get through and Royalists appeared in arms at the rendezvous on 1 August only to discover that their expected comrades had not turned up. Commonwealth troops dealt quickly with these penny packets who had revealed their disloyalty to the regime. In Surrey Mordaunt only managed to raise thirty followers and fled to the Continent in dismay. The largest Royalist grouping that formed was in Cheshire where Sir George Booth, a Presbyterian, recruited 3,000–4,000 supporters and occupied Chester in the name of a free parliament. No sooner had he done this than he heard that the rising had been cancelled and that Lambert was marching towards him. Sir George and his followers fled to Nantwich but were overtaken by Lambert and routed. Those who escaped, like Sir George and the new Earl of Derby, were soon found, arrested and charged with high treason, as were several notables associated with the other half-cock risings. One conspirator managed to get away with it. That was Admiral Montagu who had been in secret correspondence with the King and sailed his fleet to the mouth of the Thames on the pretence of collecting provisions, when it was in fact to protect the intended Royalist landings. Although this manoeuvre made Montagu highly suspect in the eyes of Lambert, it was decided not to pick a quarrel with him at this stage and he was allowed to sail back to his station.

The unmasking of Willys and the failed rising all came about as a result of a complex series of intelligence activities, some of which are still not fully clear today. A certain George Paul had been an English merchant working in the Mediterranean for many years and then returned to live in England. While abroad he had somehow become a Royalist agent and back in London decided to use his own initiative to carry out some freelance subsource cultivation. He set his sights high and decided to try to penetrate Thurloe's department. To achieve this it seems that he got to know first one of Morland's servants and then Morland's wife. Morland had married Danielle de Milleville, an attractive French Protestant, who was the daughter of a landed gentleman from Normandy. Danielle seems to have been keenly aware of her genteel status and had expensive tastes which could not always be satisfied by her husband's salary as a government servant, especially as it was now often in arrears. In fact to be precise he was owed about £1,000 in arrears of pay and £20 in expenses. Morland had hoped to increase his income by taking on some government sinecure and had been pressing Thurloe for this throughout February but without result. He then decided to mortgage his London house and half his furniture to raise money for the country house his wife had set her heart on.

Just when the Morlands were in difficult financial straits, Paul made Danielle a gift of an Antwerp cabinet worth £50. Danielle was not only grateful to Paul but became open to the suggestion that more gifts or financial help would be forthcoming if her husband was occasionally prepared to share with him confidential government information. Danielle seems to have persuaded Morland to become a Royalist agent. Morland must have been brought up a Royalist, as his father was an Anglican parson and he had attended Winchester, which required an oath of loyalty to the King but his time in Puritan Cambridge turned him into a Roundhead. In later years he would attempt a moral self-justification for going over to the Royalists but the motivation for his treachery was clearly money. As Morland was a senior member of the intelligence department he was not prepared to contemplate being a mere source for Paul and so decided to become a loyal (but of course paid) servant of Charles and began communicating directly with him using a Thomas Henshaw as the covert courier. Then just when Morland had found a neat way to enhance his income, Richard Cromwell fell and with him Thurloe and all his clerks. Morland was out of a job.

The military junta soon realized that they needed experienced government servants and, although Cromwell supporters like Thurloe could not be trusted, many of the other secretaries could serve the new regime. Morland was given a job at Wallingford House working for John Bradshaw, who had been made Lord President. In other words Morland was in the heart of the ruling junta of Lambert, Fleetwood and Desborough. Charles and Hyde could not have wished for a better placed insider. One of Morland's earliest source reports to Charles was sent mid-June via Henshaw and contained a pile of Willys's letters to Thurloe. Naturally Willys had signed them 'Barret' or one of his other assumed names but they were written in his distinctive handwriting. Charles and Hyde had received a great deal of correspondence from Willys over the years and at once recognized the writing. Surely this was proof positive that Willys was a traitor. And yet, could it really be that the trusted Willys had abandoned his family, friends and honour by becoming a Roundhead agent? The information had come from Morland who was a new, untried source, whose whole career had been spent in opposing the Stuart cause. Morland was after all an experienced intelligencer and might be operating as a double agent. It could be that Hyde was aware that Morland was an accomplished forger who would have had little difficulty in producing documents in Willys's spidery hand with the intention of throwing the English Royalist resistance groups into disarray. Thoughts such as these must have been going through the minds of Charles and Hyde and made them feel the need to proceed with care. On the other hand, time was running out as there was by now barely a month before the 1 August date planned for the uprising. The situation needed to be clarified, and quickly.

Charles wrote two letters. One was to Morland asking for more information and even promising him the Garter if he came up with high-quality political intelligence. The other was to Willys summoning him to Charles in Bruges. Willys did not respond to his monarch's command but instead wrote that he had hired a property in Hythe which could be used as a safe house by Charles and his brother James if they landed there in secret at the time of the rising. At virtually the same time Henshaw the courier arrived with a letter from Morland saying that Willys was part of a plot to lure the royal pair to a place where they would be assassinated. If there had been any doubt about Willys's being a traitor, this was now completely dispelled. The rising was clearly compromised and the whole operation must be aborted. Messages were sent to Royalist activists in England but as we have seen some did not arrive in time. It is not known who placed the notice denouncing Willys as a traitor at the Old Exchange but it would be no surprise if it had been instigated by Hyde as a means of rapidly disseminating the threat he posed.

Meanwhile Morland clearly warmed to the idea of making his wife a lady and himself a Knight of the Garter, as he was inundating Hyde with intelligence material. Much of it was taken from Thurloe's records and included copies of ciphers and the identity of Commonwealth agents in Bruges such as Malcolm

Smith who had been reporting to Thurloe using the name Blanck Marshall. Poor Scot had no idea that an insider was sabotaging the junta's intelligence apparatus. He was probably quietly congratulating himself that the Willys debacle was not as damaging as it appeared. The reason was that Willys was still reporting in as an agent. This was because Willys had been so respected that many English Cavaliers thought that the accusations against him were simply a propaganda smear and continued to keep him in their confidence. Even Mordaunt, the leading Royalist activist, who had returned to Calais after the failed uprising, continued to believe in Willys and kept him abreast of Royalist activities for another two months. This short-term reprise in the flow of Royalist information to Scot did not of course make up for the damage he was being caused by Morland. It was perhaps as well for Scot's blood pressure that he was unaware that there was not only a Royalist insider in the office of the Lord President but also in his own. This was Henry Darella, a senior official in Scot's intelligence department, who had begun passing information via his wife to his brother-in-law Roger Palmer. Palmer was the husband of Charles's mistress Barbara Villiers who was later made Duchess of Cleveland in recognition of her services to the crown. Palmer passed on the information to Alan Broderick, a member of the Sealed Knot in London, who then passed it to Hyde. With information from Morland and Darella, Charles could be informed of both the junta government's plans and actions and current intelligence activity directed against the Stuart cause.

For the first time the Royalist court was almost winning the intelligence war but, with the uprising and invasion aborted, Charles was further away than ever from his objective. In a matter of days all Charles's careful plans for winning back the crown had turned to nothing. He decided to seize a long-shot chance of trying to get combined French and Spanish backing for another invasion. The opportunity that had presented itself was the peace negotiations between Mazarin and his Spanish opposite number Don Louis de Haro in Fuentarabia. So off Charles hurried to Fuentarabia. The visit was a total embarrassment. Although Charles was an ally of Spain, de Haro received him coldly and made it clear he had little interest in a pretender whose fortunes had sunk so low. Mazarin was well aware that it was the Battle of the Dunes victory, achieved with Commonwealth help, that was enabling him to make an advantageous peace with Spain. He had literally no time for Charles, France's one time pensioner now turned Spanish ally and refused even to see him. Charles quietly returned to Brussels, to his unsupportable personal debts and complete lack of future prospects. There the King and his impoverished followers spent the long cold winter. Try as he might Hyde was only able to raise enough money through loans for Charles to eat one meal a day. This was eaten off a few bits of pewter, as all the plate had gone to Cologne pawnbrokers three years before.

Although not realized at the time, there was one positive outcome from the preparations for the August rising. Hyde had attempted to contact as many potential supporters as possible to win them to the King's cause. These had ranged from stalwart Cavaliers to potential sympathizers like Admiral Montagu. George Monck was among those Hyde had wanted to sound out, as he was a former Royalist and came from a strong Royalist family. Sir John Grenville was Monck's cousin and a leading Devonshire Royalist. He was the patron of Monck's younger brother Nicholas as rector of the Devonshire village of Kilhampton on the unusually high stipend of £300 a year. Charles wrote to Grenville telling him to offer Monck £10,000 a year and enclosed a personal letter to Monck asking for his support. The problem of how to get this message to Monck was resolved by Grenville deciding to use Nicholas as the messenger. Grenville requested Nicholas to attend him in London without delay, and on his arrival asked for his help. Nicholas had Royalist sympathies which he had kept to himself and was prepared to undertake this errand for the patron he and his large family owed so much.

As Nicholas's daughter Mary happened to be visiting her Uncle George in Dalkeith, it was decided that the cover story for the visit would be that Nicholas was going to consult his elder brother as head of the family about Mary's marriage. It was also decided that for security Nicholas would not carry the King's letter or incriminating correspondence but learn it all by heart. As the roads north from London were full of soldiers marching to counter the Royalist rising, it was arranged that Nicholas should travel to Scotland by frigate. This he did and, having landed in Leith, reached Dalkeith on 8 August. On hearing the message, George Monck gave no indication of his feelings on the matter. Even though Nicholas remained in Dalkeith for a couple of months he never became any the wiser over his brother's intentions. Two weeks after George Monck had received the message, he did however sound out a few of those closest to him who he believed might harbour Royalist sympathies. These included his two chaplains, Thomas Gumble and John Price, and Colonel Ralph Knight, the commander of his cavalry regiment. They all said that they would support him if he decided to declare for the King. They then began making a few discreet arrangements, such as checking how much money was available in the treasury and drawing up lists of those in the army who might support the King and those who might not. They also drafted a declaration from the Army of Scotland to the Rump to urge it to fill up its vacant seats and then call free elections.

Everything was then put on hold when news arrived that Booth's uprising had been defeated by Lambert. As the Army of Scotland was not strong enough to take on Lambert and Fleetwood, Monck had little option but remain a loyal servant of the Commonwealth. Only his closest confidants had any inkling that his loyalty to the Republic had been wavering. In all his outward actions he had cracked down on Royalists in Scotland. From the moment that Monck had heard that there might be a Royalist uprising, he had banned all public gatherings and seized all unauthorized arms and horses belonging to known Royalists. He had also given his officers orders to 'get intelligence of intended meetings of Royalist planning risings and to keep in touch with adjacent garrisons and justices of the peace'. For good measure, he had made all his officers take an oath not to support the King. It was no surprise that Fleetwood and the Council of Ministers had complete confidence in Monck's loyalty. They even sent him £20,000 to ensure that his army remained well paid and therefore loyal. As it turned out, this large amount of money would become Monck's war chest for his move against them.

Parliament was naturally pleased with Lambert for so swiftly stamping out Royalist revolt in Cheshire and voted him £1,000 to purchase a jewel as a token of gratitude. Lambert with his usual flair for popularity, decided to distribute the money to the troops. Some would see this as a selfless act but others were more cynical. These included the majority of Parliament and military officers who did not want to see Lambert bribing his way into the army's favour. While marching back through Derby, a number of Lambert's officers signed a petition demanding that Fleetwood should be made permanent commander-in-chief and Lambert his Lieutenant General. Parliament immediately saw this as the army bypassing Parliament and once again making a bid for supreme power. Haselrig and Scot were incensed and called for Lambert and the authors of the petition to be sent to the Tower. Fleetwood intervened on Lambert's behalf and succeeded in at least partially reassuring them by agreeing that all copies of the petition should be seized and destroyed. Parliament then turned its attention to countering the army unrest that had given rise to the petition. On 4 October they voted a monthly amount of £100,000 to cover pay and arrears to be raised from the sale of rebel Royalist estates. It had taken a very long time to provide the army with the money it was owed but at last this was in hand. Surely this would herald a new beginning in army/parliamentary relations that could be the basis for a stable Commonwealth?

The honeymoon was short-lived. The Council of Officers produced a new petition saying that anyone who criticized the army should be punished. Haselrig had been making soundings within the army to see if there were any commanders who would support Parliament against the ambitions of Lambert and the Wallingford House group. He believed that he could probably rely on three regiments in London and also the armies of Monck in Scotland and Ludlow in Ireland. Encouraged by this, the Commons passed a vote declaring it high treason for anyone to raise taxation without the consent of Parliament. As the existing vote for taxation would expire on 1 January, Haselrig thought that this would force the army to be brought to parliamentary heel. The next day Haselrig went further and carried a motion that Lambert, Desborough, six colonels and a major should be cashiered for signing the last petition. Warming to the task, another vote was carried that Fleetwood should be removed from the post of commander-in-chief and merely made the president of a board of seven officers to manage the army. Haselrig had clearly forgotten the lessons learnt about who came off worst when Parliament opposed the army. He was soon to be reminded. The next day Lambert marched on Westminster at the head of 3,000 men. En route to Westminster Lambert came across Lenthall the Speaker who was pulled from his horse and put under house arrest. Westminster was guarded by two regiments of foot and three troops of horse drawn from the regiments Haselrig believed were loyal to Parliament. When they saw Lambert approach they at once went over to him and it was not many minutes later that the

Rump Parliament was again forcibly dismissed. It need hardly be said that Scot was immediately removed from being head of intelligence and the government service was again in chaos. Haselrig's assessment of parliamentary support within the army in London was so incorrect that it had led to complete disaster for the republican parliamentary cause.

Back in Scotland, Monck had been keeping himself informed of the growing rift between Parliament and the Council of Officers and decided to exploit the situation. He sent his brother Nicholas to London to deliver a message to his brother-in-law Dr Thomas Clarges, an MP. The message was to inform the Speaker that Monck was prepared to march his army south to support the Rump. Monck's message arrived on 12 October and it was that more than anything else that so emboldened the Rump that they decided to vote to cashier the leading members of the Council of Officers – the act that was to provoke Lambert's coup.

The citizens of London witnessing these events must have wondered who was now running the nation, since there was no Protector or Parliament. The rather unsatisfactory answer proved to be the Wallingford House Council of Officers. This body annulled the Commons votes of the previous few days and established a Committee of Safety of twenty-one members to replace the Council of State. But who was in charge? There were civilian members such as Sir Harry Vane and Bulstrode Whitelocke but the army was of course dominant. The question was who led the Army. There was Lambert who, as Cromwell's right-hand man at Naseby, Dunbar and Worcester, had been the obvious military heir until he had been dismissed by the Protector. Then there was Fleetwood, Cromwell's son-in-law, who was officially commander-in-chief but now rather overshadowed by the popular Lambert. Henry Cromwell, as the son of the great man, could have trumped both of them but he had now put himself out of the picture. On the subject of relations, there was also Desborough, the husband of Cromwell's sister Jane. It was he who was largely responsible for the Wallingford House officers who had set themselves up as managers of the army. The problem was that there was no outstanding leader but rather an uneasy triumvirate of Lambert, Fleetwood and Desborough whose authority was confused by the existence of the faceless Wallingford House officers and the Committee of Safety. To cap it all, with Scot now dismissed, the military junta found itself with virtually no government service and no coordinator of intelligence.

One prominent general who had not been party to the dismissal of Parliament was George Monck. The Committee of Safety wanted to ensure they received his belated support and sent a Colonel Ralph Cobbett to Edinburgh to explain their actions. They were right to be concerned over Monck's reaction, as he was by nature a conservative who firmly believed in the authority of Parliament. When Monck heard the news of the coup he was furious. Cobbett never did deliver his message but was arrested on Monck's orders as soon as he reached Berwick-on-Tweed. Monck immediately sent a letter to the Committee in London, copied to William Lenthall, the ousted Speaker, condemning the military action and saying that he would assert the liberty of Parliament. He then turned his attention to the loyalty of his army and whether it would support him or Fleetwood the commander-in-chief. On 19 October he issued an instruction to all officers 'to be faithful to the parliament of England' or be cashiered. Regiments were reorganized to ensure that commanders at all levels were likely to be loyal to Monck personally. Between 130 and 140 officers were removed or replaced. Most were arrested and taken under guard to the English border where they were released on the understanding that they would be hanged if they returned to Scotland.

When the Committee of Safety heard of Monck's declaration to restore Parliament, they authorized Lambert to take an army of 8,000 men to intercept Monck on his march south. It was their hope that Monck might be won over when met by his former military colleagues and Lambert would only have to fight as a last resort. After all, Monck had been a comrade-in-arms and like them a loyal supporter of Cromwell who had also dismissed the self-serving Rump by military coup when it proved obstructive. Surely Monck would not want to split the army or even risk civil war and the return of Charles Stuart. Lambert was confident of a happy outcome but wanted to negotiate from strength so sent word to Colonel Robert Lilburne the Governor of York to raise the local militia and occupy Newcastle. Monck then made it clear that he had no wish to divide the army and agreed to send three representatives to the Committee to conduct negotiations. It looked as though some solution would soon be found.

Meanwhile a distinguished retired officer had been watching events. Fairfax, like many who had supported Parliament in the Civil War, had been against the actions of Charles I but fully adhered to the constitutional concept of rule by a monarch and two Houses of Parliament. Fairfax had been keeping discreet contact with the Royalists and saw the opportunity to restore the monarchy. It happened that Colonel Thomas Morgan was passing through York on returning to the army of Scotland from serving in the Spanish Netherlands. While there, he visited Fairfax at Nun Appleton and agreed to take a letter saying that Fairfax would support Monck against Fleetwood and Lambert but indicating that he wanted the Rump replaced by a new parliament and the return of the King. After receiving the message on 8 November, Monck sent Clarges with an encouraging but rather ambiguous reply to Fairfax. Despite being unsure whether Monck would support the King, Fairfax began using his influence to discreetly rally the Yorkshire gentry for the King's return.

Monck continued to negotiate with both Lambert and the Committee of Safety but was just playing for time. He knew that Lambert did not have the money to pay his men and so his popularity might be tested to breaking point. When he received the draft agreement negotiated on his behalf by his three commissioners he found an excuse to repudiate it and demanded new talks to take place in York, roughly halfway between his headquarters in Edinburgh and Lambert's headquarters in Newcastle. Fleetwood and the Council of Officers tried their hardest to get Monck back on side and a whole series of his former friends including General Whalley trailed up to

Scotland to beg him not to split the army. Meanwhile Monck's commissioners had made clandestine contact with members of the Rump's former Council of State and relayed a message from them that they would make him commander-in-chief.

Haselrig had decided to drum up some support for Parliament on his own and went to Portsmouth where he was welcomed by the governor who was a friend of Monck. On hearing this Fleetwood ordered troops to restore order in Portsmouth but on arrival they went over to Haselrig. A backlash against the army and for Parliament now gathered momentum. London apprentices began taking to the streets and inciting others to demand the return of Parliament and even the King. The Committee reacted by dispersing them in skirmishes that resulted in some civilian deaths. This provoked greater anger and increased the scale of anti-army protest. Suddenly the Committee's fragile authority was being challenged from all directions.

Monck decided he was now sufficiently prepared to make to a move and occupied Berwick. Despite this act of aggression, Monck sent a message to Lambert that he would not advance further south if Lambert remained in Newcastle. On 8 December he set up his headquarters at the little village of Coldstream beside one of the fords across the Tweed. He then demanded that Lambert withdraw all troops from the North and begin a fresh peace conference, this time at Alnwick. While a frustrated Lambert saw his unpaid troops gradually drifting away, Monck had been in contact with the army in Ireland and persuaded them not only to support the Rump but to send a regiment to help secure Scotland in his absence.

Former members of the Council of State led by Thomas Scot then attempted a counter-coup against the military junta. They had persuaded Colonel Fitch, the new Lieutenant Governor, to hand over the Tower but the plan was compromised and Fitch and several of the conspirators arrested. Scot just managed to escape and took refuge with the Channel fleet at the Downs. The fleet was commanded by John Lawson who had been reappointed vice-admiral. Scot had made a wise choice, for the next day Lawson declared for Parliament and sailed his fleet into the Thames to establish a blockade. Meanwhile Haselrig took the troops that had gone over to him in Portsmouth and advanced on Westminster. When he arrived the soldiers guarding Westminster abandoned the military junta and joined Haselrig. On Christmas Eve this combined force marched to Lenthall's house in Chancery Lane. The surprised Speaker looked through his window to see this unexpected band of soldiery who proceeded to fire three volleys of musketry. This discharge was to announce that they declared Lenthall not only Speaker of the House of Commons but Lord General of the Army. When word had reached Lambert of the perilous situation in London he dispatched Desborough's regiment to the capital. They reached St Albans on 24 December and when they heard the news of Lenthall, they decided to also declare for Parliament.

While all this was happening Fleetwood and the Committee of Public Safety had been in Whitehall paralysed by inaction. They had received the dreadful news from Ireland. Ludlow had unwisely returned to London for discussions with the Committee after the dismissal of the Rump and in his absence his deputies had declared their forces for Parliament. From mid-December, the Committee had been witnessing the haemorrhaging of its army and a breakdown of law and order in London, with shops shut, the lawcourts closed and rioters on the streets. Fleetwood was urged to personally rally the London soldiers to prevent further desertions. A natural leader like Lambert would have had a go but not Fleetwood. He had proved himself a brave man in battle but there was a lack of character that had led to Cromwell referring to him on more than one occasion as 'a milksop'. Being an ardent Puritan, his response to the crisis was to fall on his knees in prayer. After a significant time in this posture he concluded that there was no prospect of divine intervention. To some like Whitelocke, the writing had been on the wall for a bit and they had already decided to quit Whitehall and try to make peace with the King. Vane and Desborough realized that the game was up but persuaded Fleetwood to try to save the Republic by making peace with Parliament. It was too late even for this. Late on that eventful Christmas Eve Fleetwood went to Speaker Lenthall and handed him the keys of Parliament. He then resigned his own post as commander-in-chief and on behalf of the whole Committee of Public Safety with the words that 'God hath spit in his face and would not hear him.'

Lenthall was making full use of this happy turn of events. Accompanied by his supporting soldiery, he went to the Lord Mayor to inform him that he was reassembling Parliament. The garrison in the Tower opened their gates to him and he sacked the officers appointed by the Committee of Public Safety. On Boxing Day the Rump met in the House of Commons and quickly passed a vote dismissing Lambert, Desborough and other leaders and ordering their banishment from London and Vane confined to his house at Raby. They then sent orders to Lambert's troops to desert their commander and return to their garrisons. This message reached Lambert's army at Northallerton, together with the news that the remainder of the army in the South had gone over to Parliament. But worse news was also coming in. Although suffering with gout, Fairfax had gone by coach to Marston Moor to the south of York and called the militia to join him. Being mainly Royalist, this they did but such was the magnetism of the former commander-in-chief that so too did the whole Irish contingent of Lambert's army who had been sent over as reinforcements against the Royalist rising in Cheshire. By the end of December, with almost one accord, Lambert's men decided to join their comrades and the general was left with no more than a hundred men. His career and ambitions in ruins, Lambert dismissed his tiny remnant of an army and went on the run, only to later give himself up. The road was now open for Monck to march to London unopposed.

Fairfax and his supporters advanced on York and demanded the surrender of the garrison. Lilburne put up no resistance and on 1 January 1660 York opened its gates. On the same day Monck began to march south through the deep snow from Coldstream. An impoverished Charles and his followers in Brussels, still unaware of these events, could hardly dare to hope that 1660 would bring a very happy new year.

Chapter 13

Honest George Monck, 1660

Monck was marching south but why? He had wanted to restore the Rump but the Rump was already restored. By 6 January Monck was in Newcastle and his advance guard had occupied Durham. Soon the whole North-East was in his hands. As he advanced southwards he sent messages to the Speaker of the Rump and others in authority assuring them of his good will. Typical was a letter to Oliver St John, the Chief Justice, confirming that it was his intention to avoid 'those two rocks of malignant and fanatical interest'. No one knew for sure what Monck's intention was. Even Fairfax who had seen him as he passed through York could not decide whether Monck was a Royalist or simply after his own ends. The Rump's re-established Council of State were certainly concerned and on 10 January formally appointed Thomas Scot as head of intelligence. The Council decided that Scot himself should travel up to meet Monck on his march south. Scot's official remit from the Council was formally to request Monck to swear an oath against Charles. His covert task was to keep close to Monck and gather intelligence that would indicate his intentions. Scot stuck to Monck like a limpet and even travelled in his coach all the way to the outskirts of London. For all his efforts, Scot was still no wiser about Monck's intentions. One thing of which Scot had become painfully aware was that wherever Monck went he was receiving petitions for the Rump to be replaced by a new free parliament.

Even at this stage Monck had confided in no one other than his two chaplains and Colonel Knight. Everyone else was speculating and there was even a street ditty:

> Monck's under a hood and not understood,
> The City pulls in their horns;
> The Speaker is out and sick of the goute
> And the Parliament sitts upon thornes.

When Monck arrived at Barnet on 2 February, he heard that the infantry regiment outside Somerset House, the Speaker's residence, had mutinied and declared for a free parliament and the return of Charles. Apprentices were also rioting and shouting the same demands. With the City in turmoil, the Council of State called upon Monck to restore order. The next day he led his army from Highgate, down Gray's Inn Road towards Somerset House where he was welcomed by Lenthall. The day after he attended the House of Commons and told the members that he had received many petitions for a full and free parliament and that he supported this so long as the new parliament did not become controlled by extremist sectarians or Royalists. This stance displeased both Royalist sympathizers and Republicans such as Haselrig and Scot, who had been appointed Secretary of State a few weeks before. The Lord Mayor and City Common Council were also annoyed because they wanted the Rump replaced as soon as possible by a free parliament. It was a dangerous game but Monck was again playing for time.

The Mayor now announced that he did not regard the Rump as a lawful parliament and the Rump responded by ordering Monck to enter the City, pull down barricades, arrest some of the leaders and dissolve the Common Council. Much to the dismay of some of his officers, Monck did enter the City on 9 February and began pulling down the barricades and making arrests. He realized that this would turn the City even more against the Rump. A couple of days later he wrote a letter to the Rump saying how much he regretted having been ordered to take such action against the City and asking them to issue writs for new elections by 17 February. The Council of State was astounded and sent Scot as Secretary of State to negotiate with him. They also showed their displeasure by instead of confirming Monck as commander-in-chief, directing that he was to be just one of five commissioners controlling the army, with the leading commissioner being Haselrig. Monck then told the Mayor that he was demanding a free parliament and soon the whole city was rejoicing with bonfires in the streets. Negotiations continued between Monck and the Council of State in which Monck assured them that he merely wanted to keep the three nations 'in a free state without King, Single Person or House of Peers'.

On 15 February Monck felt strong enough to demand Haselrig and Scot come to his headquarters near Drapers Hall to discuss a settlement. At the meeting Monck insisted on being appointed commander-in-chief, for army arrears of pay to be settled and for writs to be issued for a new parliament to meet on 20 April, after which the House should then dissolve itself. Haselrig and Scot were also obliged to agree that excluded members could take their seats and so on the morning of 21 February seventy-three were gathered together and taken to the House in a reversal of Pride's Purge of 1648. This influx of Presbyterians could only mean that the King would be recalled. The die was cast. The same day Monck summoned all London officers to St James' Palace, assuring them that the only reason for the return of these members was so that the House could be dissolved and writs quickly issued for a replacement. A similar written statement was then distributed by fastest messenger to commanders in the rest of England and in Scotland and Ireland. The restored Long Parliament confirmed Monck as commander-in-chief for all three nations and general-at-sea, along with Montagu. They appointed a fresh Council of State with the specific task of calling a new parliament to meet in April. Scot was dismissed as Secretary of State and, having been warned that his life was in danger, fled in disguise to Ostend and then laid low in Brussels. His post of Secretary of State was divided in two, both appointed on Monck's recommendation. One was

Colonel John Thompson, a loyal member of Monck's personal staff and the other was John Thurloe.

The choice of the latter may have been surprising, considering Thurloe's known loyalty to the House of Cromwell, but he was also an old and respected colleague of Monck, who now needed his expertise as intelligence coordinator. Thurloe no longer had all the powers he had previously built up as Secretary of State but he set to work on intelligence with his customary energy. There was of course a change of direction and Thurloe was well aware of how precarious was his own position. He thought it prudent to make contact with Hyde to put feelers out to the Stuart court but got little encouragement. George Downing who had been moved briefly back to a job at the Exchequer in London had been sent out once more as resident to the United Provinces. Thurloe wrote to Downing asking him to urgently find a high-level source at the Stuart court who he was prepared to pay up to £200. Naturally as well as trying to find out how the wind blew for him, there was the continuing routine of intelligence gathering. It was back to normal with reports coming from Admiral Lawson in the Downs about French naval movements in the Channel and Lockhart in France reporting on the negotiations at Bayonne. But as always the greatest intelligence effort was needed for internal security. What was the opposition to Monck's new regime and how could it be neutralized?

By no means all the army was happy with the readmittance of the excluded members of the Long Parliament. For example, Colonel Nathaniel Rich, a Fifth Monarchist sympathizer commanding a regiment in East Anglia, began to rally opposition to Monck but was promptly replaced. Similar resistance was encountered in Bristol and Hull but the commanders concerned were speedily removed. Anyone who might cause trouble was arrested, including Lambert who was sent to the Tower. All colonels were directed to keep tight discipline and a reward of £10 was offered for the arrest of anyone attempting to 'debauch the soldiers'. The army maintained its trust in Monck but no one was sure whether he intended the return of the King or to make himself Protector or even restore Richard Cromwell. Several of Monck's officers led by the Anabaptist Colonel John Okey asked Monck to sign a declaration against government by a single person. Monck merely asked them to await the new parliament, from which Royalists would be excluded, and leave Parliament to decide.

As it happened the Royalists, although not officially allowed to stand, had a landslide victory in the elections, as about a hundred took their seats under false colours. Only sixteen members of the Long Parliament were re-elected and the rest were Presbyterians. In total about 90 per cent of the MPs supported the restoration of the monarchy. What was more, the House of Lords began to reassemble even though it had not been constitutionally summoned. Too much was going on for anyone to raise objections. At the end of March, Monck had a secret meeting with his cousin Sir John Grenville who handed over the letter the King had sent in July 1659 with the offer of £10,000. A few days later Monck told Grenville to advise the King to issue a general pardon and guarantee liberty of conscience. He also advised the King to leave Brussels in the Catholic Spanish Netherlands and move to Breda in the Protestant Dutch Republic. No letter was written and Grenville had to learn the massage by heart. Some might have suspected but still very few knew for certain that Monck had resolved to restore the monarchy.

It was decision time and the more astute took the gamble of trying to jump into the Royalist fold before it was too late. Downing was typical and while writing letters of intelligence to Thurloe was using his principal Royalist source, Thomas Howard, as a go-between to Charles and providing Thurloe's correspondence and ciphers as a token of good faith.

Just as things appeared to be falling in place, the news arrived that Lambert had escaped from the Tower and was trying to raise a force in Warwickshire. Monck immediately sent Colonel Richard Ingoldsby with a force which managed to intercept Lambert at Edgehill. This, the site of the first battle of the Civil War, was also to witness the last military act of the drama. When Lambert saw he was hopelessly outnumbered, he tried to disengage but was pursued to Daventry, where he surrendered. With Lambert safely back in the Tower, this potentially dangerous distraction was over and plans for the King's return could proceed.

As soon as Charles received the message from Grenville, he moved to Breda. Grenville returned in late April with letters from the King to Monck, Montagu, the Lord Mayor and the speakers of the two Houses. In the letters Charles confirmed that there would be a general pardon and religious tolerance. Grenville briefed the Council of State the next day and on 1 May Charles's declaration, known as the 'Declaration of Breda', was read to both Houses at a joint meeting. That evening Monck read the King's letter to his officers in London and sent copies to army commanders in the three nations. Some officers tried to persuade Monck to become King himself, but he declined. On 5 May he was in a position to write to the King, with the approval of Parliament, that the army was loyal to the monarchy. It had been a close-run thing. Even so there were a few who resisted in the army. In Hull a Lieutenant Merry denounced the King but was swiftly arrested by the governor, Fairfax's son Charles. Naturally there were going to be other more prominent casualties of the Royalist upsurge. Thurloe was now an embarrassment and on 14 May Parliament gave orders for him to be arrested for high treason. He was committed to the Tower, his government career now ended for good.

About the same time as Thurloe's arrest, Montagu arrived with his squadron at The Hague's port Scheveningen to collect the King. As the flagship on which Charles was to travel was called the *Naseby*, the ship's carpenter had to do a quick job changing the name to *The Royal Charles*. When all was ready, His Majesty came on board and set sail for Dover, arriving on 25 May, where having knelt down and thanked God for his safe arrival, he was welcomed by Monck and the Corporation. The King and Monck then travelled with a large entourage to Canterbury where they stayed for the weekend and on 29 May went to Blackheath where Colonel Knight had drawn up the troops for His Majesty's inspection. That Charles was received by the troops in a disciplined manner but with no obvious enthusiasm, demonstrated just how great had been Monck's task to win them over to the Restoration. The King and his entourage then moved on through far more welcoming crowds to be officially received by the Lord Mayor and alderman at St George's Fields, then on to Whitehall. The procession then became even more spectacular as it made its way to the City of London. It was led by 300 cavalrymen from the City of London, all in silver doublets and had five cavalry regiments under Knight bringing up the rear. In the City His Majesty was given a truly rapturous welcome and Monck riding just in front of him was greeted with joyful cries of 'Hurray for honest George Monck!'

The day was Charles thirtieth birthday. Of the many thoughts that could have been rushing through the young sovereign's mind would have been the memory of another day back in 1642 when he had last seen London as a 17-year-old escaping the mob with his father and mother. So much had happened in the mean time. His father's three kingdoms had been united into a single Commonwealth whose powerful army, navy and foreign intelligence service made it respected throughout Europe. The new Republic had turned into a Protectorate, under a general with a powerful army and security service that made it a cross between a military dictatorship and a police state. Then when there was no adequate heir to continue the Protectorate the government destabilized and with bewildering speed a penniless prince in Brussels was now back in London as King, hearing the cheers of an ecstatic crowd. It could so easily have been otherwise.

It was Monck who had pulled it off – and against considerable odds. The stolid, thick-set, reliable, tobacco-chewing general had played an amazing game. It was probably in late summer of 1659 that he made up his mind to try to restore the monarchy. In the nine or so months that followed, he metamorphosed from being a predictably dependable general in far away Scotland, to become the most powerful man in Britain. By the end of that time he had managed to convince a sceptical Parliament to replace themselves with another which they were to discover too late was actively Royalist. He also succeeded in creating an aura of confidence in his judgement in the City of London and elsewhere that led the population to support his conclusion that monarchy was the only option. Greatest of all, he had managed to retain the army's support while he gradually coaxed it from being an implacable supporter of the Commonwealth and the 'Good Old Cause' of the Republic, to reluctantly acquiescing to the return of the monarchy.

He had achieved all this through guile and determination. In carrying out this undertaking he used all the intelligence skills he had learnt and perfected while commanding Scotland. He employed his own private intelligence network to establish who might or might not support him at each phase of his plan. He made best use of his full war chest to pay for information and use bribery when necessary. His officers and soldiers soon learnt that they should toe his line if they wanted to keep their jobs. Those who resisted were swiftly identified and purged. First, those opposing the Rump were removed and then those who did not support a free parliament and finally those who did not support the return of the King. And all this was done with the strictest of secrecy, with no more than three of his closest staff privy to his ultimate objectives. Parallel with this were his deception plans which obscured his true intentions, such as when he disciplined a soldier for saying that he intended to restore the King. It was a masterful display of intelligence professionalism, equal to that of Thurloe.

The intelligence produced under Thurloe's direction made a major contribution to the security and successes of the Protectorate. Sadly for him those successes were largely lost when the Protectorate period became a cul-de-sac of history. Thurloe's real legacy was secured by his last couple of months as Secretary of State. In this short time he was able to resurrect his battered intelligence organization and reorientate it to the Stuart cause. It was upon this foundation that Charles II's intelligencers could build and so help to perpetuate Thurloe's professional dedication and concept of coordination of all available sources that have been central themes in the development of British intelligence to this day.

The value of intelligence is best measured by identifying the successful outcomes that have occurred as a result of good decisions based upon correct intelligence assessments. Conversely, it may be measured by identifying unsuccessful outcomes that have occurred as a result of bad decisions based upon incorrect or inadequate intelligence. During the 1642–53 period there were many cases of the latter, such as Montrose's defeat at Philiphaugh or Hamilton's at Dunbar. During the Protectorate there were far more cases of the former, largely thanks to Thurloe's numerous successes in countering attempts at insurrection and assassination. However, the achievements of the Protectorate did not last and so the accolade for the greatest and most lasting success of the whole period must go to George Monck, and also Edward Hyde, the man who helped turn him to the Royalist cause. It was the intelligence skills of these two men which brought about the Restoration and enabled Great Britain to become a constitutional monarchy.

Epilogue

The Victors

Henrietta Maria lived to see her son Charles restored to his throne and returned to England as Queen Mother living in state at Somerset House. She also spent time in France with her youngest daughter Henrietta Anna, the wife of the Duke of Orleans, brother to the Queen's nephew Louis XIV. She died in France in 1669 aged 60 and received a state funeral befitting a daughter of France. Charles was sad but relieved that he would not be expected to pay for the event. He was to reign for twenty-five years with charm and cunning but with very little money. Britain's position in the world declined. Dunkirk was sold to the French, the army reduced from 50,000 to a strength of 3,000 and the great ships were laid up for lack of funds, as a result of which England was humiliated in a second war with the Dutch. So great were Charles's financial straits that he decided to make a secret treaty with his cousin Louis XIV which gave him money in exchange for promoting Catholicism and supporting France in war against the United Provinces. One positive aspect of Charles's rule was that he took a great personal interest in intelligence and knew its value even if that was sometimes stretched by paying Nell Gwyn and other mistresses from the secret Contingency Fund. He made the gifted Sir Henry Bennett (later Lord Arlington) his Secretary for the South and head of intelligence. Bennett's under-secretary, Sir Joseph Williamson, who coordinated all aspects of intelligence, was a colourful character who could dance six hours at a stretch, play musical instruments and do juggling acts. Whether or not these skills were advantageous to his work, he became one of the great intelligencers building on the work of Scot and Thurloe to found post-Restoration British intelligence.

Charles was succeeded by his brother James Duke of York, who reigned for just four years before opposition to his Roman Catholicism led to him fleeing the country and the crown being offered by Parliament to his Protestant daughter Mary and her husband and James's nephew, William of Orange.

Prince Rupert became a prominent member of Charles II's court, Lord High Admiral and a founder member of the Royal Society, spending much of his time in scientific experiments. He never married but entered into a long and happy relationship with his mistress the actress Peg Hughes, by whom he had a daughter Ruperta, whom he left as his heir. Had he married and had children, then the issue would have been offered the crown at the death of Queen Anne. As it was, it was to go to George I, the son of Rupert's younger sister, Princess Sophia, the Electoress of Hanover.

Edward Hyde remained Lord Chancellor under Charles II, running the government with his customary diligence and efficiency for the first years of the reign. He was rather unfairly blamed by Parliament for the failures of the second Dutch war and so dismissed in 1667. Fearing impeachment, he fled to France to live the rest of his life in exile. He spent his time completing his major work *The True Historical Narrative of the Rebellion and Civil Wars in England,* which was not to be published until some years after his death. This was a sad end to a major statesman and resourceful intelligencer who had been the principal architect of the Restoration. He had however been made Earl of Clarendon and his daughter Anne married the Duke of York. His grandchildren were to rule Great Britain as Queen Mary II and Queen Anne – overall not a bad achievement for a younger son of a Wiltshire squire.

George Monck did alright at the Restoration. As well as being made a Knight of the Garter he was created Baron Monck, Earl of Torrington, Duke of Albemarle, Master of Horse, Gentleman of the Bedchamber, Lord Lieutenant of Devonshire and Middlesex, Privy Councillor, Captain General, General-at-Sea and Lord Lieutenant of Ireland. He was awarded £7,000 a year out of royal revenues and retained lands in Scotland and Ireland worth £4,500 a year to add to the fortune he made from his offices such as Master of Horse. Despite his fortune he lived and dressed plainly and was never happier than when sitting quietly after a simple meal chewing tobacco in the company of his lady wife, Anne, the farrier's daughter, whom he was said to fear more than any battle. His brother Nicholas was made Bishop of Hereford and his cousin Grenville was created Earl of Bath.

The Vanquished

Oliver Cromwell was disinterred from Westminster Abbey on 30 January 1661, the twelfth anniversary of Charles I's execution. His body and those of John Bradshaw and his son–in–law Henry Ireton were dragged to Tyburn (now Marble Arch) where they were mutilated by the public executioner, after which their severed heads were placed on poles outside Westminster Hall. Sir Harry Vane was also executed, as was General Thomas Harrison, but Haselrig was merely imprisoned for life. The Marquis of Argyll, the arch-Covenanter and man who had actually crowned Charles II at Scone, found himself without friends at the Restoration. He was arrested in London and accepted his execution with courage in Edinburgh in May 1661. His head was stuck on the Tollbooth spike where Montrose's head had sat eleven years previously.

The Survivors

Elizabeth Cromwell, the Lady Protectoress, moved to France at the Restoration but later returned to England where she lived quietly with her son–in–law John Claypole at Northborough Manor in Nottinghamshire where she died in 1665. Henry Cromwell was allowed to keep his Irish estates after the Restoration and returned to his family's roots to live at Spinney Abbey in Cambridgeshire until his death in 1674. Richard Cromwell took on the name of Clarke and leaving his family behind fled to the Continent at the Restoration. There he lived a lonely, wandering and debt-ridden existence for twenty years before returning to England after the death of his wife Dorothy. He then lived discreetly as Richard Clarke at Cheshunt in Buckinghamshire and died in 1712. Mary Cromwell, Lady Fauconberg, was the one member of the family really to prosper after the Restoration where she became a familiar face at court. Her husband was made ambassador to Venice in 1669 then a Privy Councillor ten years later and ended up being created an earl by William III.

Lambert was given life imprisonment, which he spent pursuing his interest in botany, living in reasonable conditions with his wife, first in Guernsey and then St Nicholas Island in Plymouth Sound. Fleetwood was spared but excluded from public office and lived quietly at his manor in Stoke Newington until his death in 1694. Whalley and his son-in-law Goffe fled to America and lived under assumed names in Boston. Desborough was arrested and released several times before settling in Hackney. Anthony Ashley Cooper was made Charles II's Chancellor of the Exchequer in 1661, then created Earl of Shaftesbury and became Lord Chancellor in 1672.

Sir Richard Willys lived happily after the restoration. Fortunately he had married a rich widow the year before and so his financial troubles were over and he enjoyed a comfortable retirement on his estate at Fen Ditton until his death in 1690.

The Intelligencers

Sir Samuel Luke passed a contented rural existence in Bedfordshire and died in 1670. George Bishop spent the rest of his life in Bristol and became one of the leading members of the Society of Friends, writing over thirty Quaker tracts. Thomas Scot gave himself up to the King's resident in Brussels in the belief that he would be pardoned for his part in Charles I's execution. He had been tricked and was arrested on arrival in England. It seems that he might have been granted his life if he had revealed the identity of his sources but this he was not prepared to do. He was tried as a regicide and hanged, drawn and quartered at Charing Cross on 17 October 1660.

John Barwick, the long-serving Royalist agent, was rewarded by being made Dean of St Paul's at the Restoration. Sir Samuel Morland was given a baronetcy but was disappointed when he was not appointed second Secretary of State. He complained and threatened to denounce sixteen Royalist traitors. To keep him quiet he was given a gold medal for 'the great and important service Sir Samuel Morland did his Majesty from time to time, during the late usurpers power, by the faithful intelligence he so constantly gave him'. He did receive an intermittent pension and, although no longer employed in intelligence, joined other former intelligencers in the Royal Society, wrote *New Methods of Cryptography* and passed on his techniques for the covert examination of letters which were adopted by the Post Office.

The Post Office was farmed out at a rent of £21,000 a year but the management was given to Thurloe's Leveller source John Wildman, who ended up being knighted and made Postmaster General by William III. Isaac Dorislaus was retained in the Post Office and prospered under Charles II, eventually being elected a Fellow of the Royal Society. John Wallis, the great mathematician who had carried out cryptanalysis for Parliament, was soon in royal favour after the Restoration and again became the principal government cryptologist. In 1661 he was appointed a royal chaplain and was a founder member of the Royal Society, contributing to the origins of calculus. This cryptanalyst cleric died in 1705 at the ripe old age of 87, having thoroughly enjoyed bitter quarrels with most of the leading thinkers of the time including Hobbes, Descartes and Boyle.

At the Restoration word got out that Colonel Joseph Bampfylde had been an agent for the previous regime and he was imprisoned. He was released the next year through the intervention of Clarendon, who knew his value as an agent and decided to re-employ him. Needless to say Bampfylde changed his allegiance with alacrity and was soon working abroad pretending to be a republican and passing intelligence about the various English exiles. He then diversified by becoming a double agent against England for the Dutch and selling the odd bit of information to the French, but died back as an English agent in 1685.

Sir Philip Meadowe, who had been Thurloe's deputy, had his diplomatic skill recognized by Charles II and received a royal knighthood to replace the one given by Cromwell. He did not return to intelligence work but served on most of the main committees of Charles II and William III and died at the amazing age of 94.

George Downing, the former Scoutmaster General of Scotland and Protectorate Minister in the United Provinces, was knighted for his last-minute defection and retained in post. Nevertheless, Downing felt the need to further ingratiate himself with Charles II. Colonel John Barkstead, the former Lieutenant of the Tower, had fled with Colonel Okey to Germany and both had been granted asylum in Hanau. It should be remembered that Downing had been chaplain in Okey's regiment. In spring 1662 Barkstead came secretly to Delft with Okey to fetch his wife but Downing's informants tipped him off and arranged with the Dutch authorities for them to be arrested while they were relaxing in a tavern. They were then shipped back to England where Barkstead was executed. Downing returned to London and became a property developer, buying up leases in the Westminster area. On one rather boggy site he demolished the old buildings and put up fifteen rather jerry-built terraced houses to form a street that was to be named after him, which was later to become the home of Prime Ministers. So the name of this man, whom Pepys was to describe as 'a perfidious rogue', lives on far more than that of any other intelligencer in British history.

Thurloe was released from the Tower by Parliament on 27 June 1660 and authorized by Charles II to give assistance to Sir Henry Bennett when he replaced Sir Edward Nicholas as Secretary of State for the South and head of intelligence. In fact Bennett had no wish to associate with a former opponent like Thurloe, so his expertise was never again put to use. When his mansion and property in Wisbech were transferred to the Bishop of Ely, Thurloe went to live at Great Milton in Oxfordshire. There he passed a quiet life with at last time for his wife Ann, interspersed with business trips to his lodgings in Lincoln's Inn. It was while there in 1668 that he died of a sudden heart attack at the age of 51. The man who had held so much power and influence under Oliver Cromwell, who had been a role model for the government servant and one of the greatest English intelligencers, had died in almost obscurity. Thurloe like so many mandarins after him was soon forgotten and would have remained so if it had not been for a chance discovery in William and Mary's reign at his old chambers at XIII Lincoln's Inn. A false ceiling was found in the garret and concealed there was a very large bundle of Thurloe's papers. These were later edited by Thomas Birch and published in 1742. Great politicians and military leaders are commemorated with statues but the only memorials to intelligencers are the secret archives of their work. The seven volumes of Thurloe's State Papers not only provide clear evidence of his major contribution to the great events of the time but are one of the principal historical sources for the period and so make a fitting monument to this master intelligencer.

Appendix 1

Notes on Cryptography

Cryptology, the art of covert writing, was well established, if little used, in England in 1642. Then, as now, covert writing took two forms. The first is called steganography, coming from the Greek *steganos* meaning 'hidden' and *graphein* meaning 'to write'. The usual way to produce this hidden writing was with secret ink, often called 'white ink' in the mid-seventeenth century. The most common secret inks were concoctions based either on lemon juice or urine which left no mark on the paper but appeared when heated by a fire or candle. Many years later steganography would become more sophisticated, particularly when the microdot was invented by the Germans in 1941. Microdots are photographs of text or images that have been compressed to the size of a full stop but can later be expanded to reveal the full information. They were used with great success by the KGB and GRU throughout the Cold War for covert communication with agents. However, in the mid-seventeenth century steganography almost always meant dipping a quill into urine or lemon juice.

The other form of covert writing is cryptography, coming from the Greek for 'secret' and 'writing'. This is a matter of making the writing unintelligible to the reader and has two forms: codes and ciphers. Codes replace whole words or phrases with another word or symbol. As the Civil War developed so did the use of codes. They have always been useful for referring to military operations/activities such as 'Overlord' for the Allied invasion of Europe in 1945 or Operation 'Nimrod', the SAS attack on the Iranian embassy in London in 1980. During the Civil War they were used by both sides, such Royalist letters using 'Mr Cross' or 'my mistress' as substitutions for the King. The New Model Army went so far as to have a standardized code book. After the Civil War codes remained much in use to protect correspondence between either the government and its agent or the Royalists and their adherents. For example Thurloe's agent, Joseph Bampfylde, often used codes, such as 'Mr Phoenix' for the King of France and 'Mr Spencer' for the King of Spain. With the realization of government's growing capability to intercept mail so the use of code words grew as a basic method of retaining secrecy.

A more sophisticated method of keeping meanings secret was the other form of cryptology, cryptography. This is secret writing using a cipher which is a system of concealing the meaning of a message by replacing each letter in the original wording with another letter or symbol. When a document is enciphered the original wording (called 'plaintext') is replaced by a scrambled version that is unintelligible to the reader and is termed 'ciphertext'. The types of cipher used are termed encryption algorithms and each algorithm is defined by a key which provides the specific method of enciphering by the sender and deciphering by the recipient.

Cryptography in the seventeenth century, as indeed today, was divided into two methods, transposition and substitution. Transposition is the oldest method, which was first recorded in Sparta in the fifth century BC. In transposition the letters of the message are rearranged, thus generating an algorithm. For example, the word 'king' could be represented in transposition as 'ingk', 'gnik', 'nikg', 'ikgn'. However, to be a workable system for sender and recipient it needs to have a reasonably simple key. One way of doing this is for the key to be that every other letter is put on a second line then all the letters are put together, for example:

Plaintext: the king has arrived
Cipher: t e i g a a r v d
       h k n h s r i e
Ciphertext: TEIGAARVDHKNHSRIE (Conventionally always in capitals.)

Another example of transposition would be to switch letters, for example the first with the second, the third with the fourth, the fourth with the fifth, etc. For example:

Plaintext: the king has arrived
Ciphertext: HTKENIHGSARAIREVD

Needless to say there are numerous ways of doing transposition but it will be seen that in all cases the letters keep the identity they had in the plaintext but their order is changed. In substitution, the other main method of cryptography, each letter changes its identity but retains its position in the plaintext. Transposition was invented in India in the fourth century BC. It was most famously used by Julius Caesar for military correspondence during the conquest of Gaul. On some occasions he merely substituted Roman letters for Greek letters which would mean nothing to the Gallic tribes. More often he used what has become known as the Caesar shift cipher. This was a matter of replacing each letter in a message with a letter a certain number along in the alphabet. If the key was 'two' in a Caesar shift cipher algorithm for example, it would mean that the letter was replaced by a letter two along from it in the alphabet as shown below:

a b c d e f g h i j k l m n o p q r s t u v w x y z
C D E F G H I J K L M N O P Q R S T U V W X Y Z A B

Plaintext: the king has arrived
Ciphertext: VJCMKPIJCUCTTKXGF

Although transposition method was well known, it was the substitution cipher which was almost always used. In most cases the cipher was simply a matter of replacing each letter of the alphabet with another letter or symbol without any logical sequence, as is the case in the Caesar shift. An example would be:

```
a  b  c  d  e  f  g h i  j  k  l  m n  o  p  q  r  s  t  u  v  w  x  y  z
D  P  E  H  Q  Z  T MB A  W  S  N J  F  V  Y  K  C  X  R  L  O G  I  U
```

In this case the cipher alphabet becomes the key.

A more convenient variation of transposition was also quite common and that was using a word or phrase as a key that could be easily be remembered by sender and receiver and placing that at the front of the alphabet to create the ciphertext. For example if the key phrase was "God bless the King" then the cipher alphabet would be as follows:

```
a  b  c  d  e  f  g h i  j  k  l  m n  o  p  q  r  s  t  u  v  w  x  y  z
G  O  D  B  L  E  S TH E K  I  N P Q  R  U  V  W  X  Y  Z  A  C  F  J
```

Naturally as no letter can be used twice it means that the second recurring letter in a key word/phrase must be left out and the letters used in the key word must be omitted from the remainder of the alphabet following on from the last letter of the key word/phrase.

It is worth turning at this stage to cryptanalysis, the art of working out plaintext from ciphertext without knowledge of the key. Although the art of cryptography is old it did not start being used in medieval Europe until about the thirteenth century when the English Franciscan monk and scientist Roger Bacon wrote a book on the subject. From then on it became gradually more and more widely used by the Church and then by states for diplomatic correspondence. Naturally when an enemy intercepted a communication and found that it was unintelligible, they realized that it was enciphered and tried to determine what type of cipher algorithm was used and then to work out the key. It was not until the early sixteenth century that there was the first breakthrough in cryptanalysis. This achievement is credited to the Venetian Giovanni Soro and his technique, which is referred to today as 'frequency analysis', soon spread to most of the courts of Europe.

The concept of frequency analysis is to examine the number of times each letter or symbol occurs in the ciphertext and the relationship between the letters. This came about when it was discovered that certain letters are on average more frequently used in each language. For example, in English 'e' is the most frequent letter, followed by 'a' and then 'o. One looks at a ciphertext to see which is the most common letter/symbol occurring as it is likely that that letter/symbol is 'e'. Then the same process is followed to determine the likely symbol for 'a' and 'o'. Other factors relating to the structure of the English language can then be used to try to determine certain letters. For example in English 'h' never occurs after 'e' but often before it. As the word 'the' will be common in most messages it may be possible to identify the cipher letter/symbol frequently coming before what has been decided is 'e' to establish 'h' and then work out the cipher letter/symbol for 't'. As the word 'and' is also probably going to be used in a message and the cipher letter/symbol for 'a' has become known it may be possible to identify 'n' and 'd'. By progressing in this way, with much trial and error, the cryptanalyst using frequency analysis would hope to build up sufficient of the cipher alphabet to put enough plain alphabet letters into the encrypted message to try to make sense of parts of it and in doing so identify new letters and hopefully end up decrypting the whole message. Thus frequency analysis provided the potential to counter all the forms of transposition described above.

As the frequency analysis cryptanalyst technique was well known to those responsible for creating ciphers, various improvements to transposition encryption were invented. The earliest and most significant at the time was the use of what are termed 'nulls'. These are letters/symbols which are not substitutions for letters in the plain alphabet but blanks meaning nothing. These nulls can be scattered among the ciphertext in a way which could totally confuse a cryptanalyst carrying out frequency analysis. They are particularly useful if symbols are being used for a cipher alphabet because additional symbols can be added at the end which can be included in the ciphertext key by the message sender and will be disregarded by the recipient. Even using an ordinary cipher alphabet the cipher letters for the infrequently occurring plain alphabet letters 'z' and 'x'' could be used as nulls and distributed in such quantity among the ciphertext to make them appear an 'e' and an 'o'.

Another way to confuse frequency analysis was simply by having several different numbers or symbols to represent a particular letter, so for example 'e' could be 7, 13, or 45 in the cipher alphabet. When there are alternatives in a cipher alphabet, these are called homophones. This could be further complicated by combining a cipher alphabet with a small number of code words, a system that is called 'nomenclatures'. In this case symbols (or numbers) would have to be used for the cipher alphabet and so the key would show the plain alphabet above the cipher alphabet (in symbols) and then a list of symbols with their meaning (such as '*' for 'king', '↑' for 'attack' and '⊥' for 'London') and then possibly the list of any symbols for nulls.

In the mid-fourteenth century the great Renaissance man Leon Alberti came up with the idea of having more than one cipher alphabet. This is called 'polyalphabetic' (as opposed to 'monoalphabetic' for a single cipher alphabet). He invented the cipher disk: two copper disks, the outer one larger than the inner and both with the letters of the alphabet marked on them. The inner disk which was the plaintext alphabet in jumbled sequence would be able to rotate and each letter opposite on the static outer disk would be the cipher letter. Both the originator and recipient of the cryptograms would have the same disk and would have a key, such as starting with 'a' plaintext opposite 'k' ciphertext and after four words moving the inner disk so that 'a' moved say three spaces to be opposite 's' and after a further four words moved again three spaces and so on. Alberti also added more complex nomenclature versions of the cipher disk system.

Another form of polyalphabetic cipher was published by the Frenchman Blaise de Vigenère in his *Traicté des Chiffres* in 1586. The 'Vigenère cipher' as it became known made frequency analysis very difficult because it used twenty-six cipher alphabets, each based upon an additional Caesar shift. In other words:

	a	b	c	d	e	f	g	h	i	j	k	l	m	n	o	p	q	r	s	t	u	v	w	x	y	z
Shift 1:	B	C	D	E	F	G	H	I	J	K	L	M	N	O	P	Q	R	S	T	U	V	W	X	Y	Z	A
Shift 2:	C	D	E	F	G	H	I	J	K	L	N	M	O	P	Q	R	S	T	U	V	W	X	Y	Z	A	B

and so on for twenty-six shifts.

In this system the key would state which number of shifts would be used. If, for example, it was 2, 16 and 24, the first letter of the ciphertext would use the cipher alphabet letter corresponding to shift 2, the second letter of the ciphertext would use the cipher alphabet letter corresponding to shift 16 and the third would use the cipher alphabet letter corresponding to shift 24, and then the next would go back to the cipher alphabet letter corresponding to shift 2. This was further refined by expressing the key not as the numbers of the shift lines but as an easily remembered key word. The key word is placed above the message plaintext and repeated again and again. Each letter of the key word shows which shift number cipher alphabet should be used for example if the key letter was B it would mean that Shift 1 should be used and if it was C it would mean shift 2 would be used.

Although both the cipher disk and the Vigenère cipher were known to be highly effective, they were also regarded as being too complicated for practical purposes and so were just not used in the mid-seventeenth century. In 1641 a young English chaplain called John Wilkins published a book called *Mercury, or the Secret and Swift Messinger*. This described most of the types of cryptology by then invented but neither he nor anyone else seems to have put this knowledge into practice in the Civil War. During the period covered by this book encryption was carried out simply using monoalphabetic substitution, often with homophones, nomenclature and nulls. Cryptanalysis relied up frequency analysis and letter characteristics. If it was intended to use homophones, nomenclature or nulls, numbers were used as substitutes for letters. Because the use of cipher was time consuming it was normally reserved only for sensitive sections of the text. A typical example of encryption found in letters intercepted by Thurloe is the following extract from an intercepted letter from the Dutch Ambassador in July 1653:

> We think ourselves bound to tell you plainly, that we think the constitution of the government and the interest of the governors 25. 64. 15. 48. to have learnt to know them so well. That we make certain 13. 16. 50. 44. 17. 48. 5. 18. 52. and not only to 24. 8. 37 ...

The same principle was used in Thurloe's ciphers for communication to agents, for example, this short extract from agent S's letter of intelligence to Thurloe dated 20 March 1655:

159. 6. 36. 9. 36. 9. 36. 3. 28. 5. 12. 3. 31. 30. 39. 3. 19. 17. 25. 30. 36. 19. 41. 31. 11. 40. 37. 1. 35. 40. 3. 19. 41. 16. 30. 35. I am sure it is 35. 40. 18. 28. 12. 28. 41. 31. 40. 37. 5. 25. 36. 7. 6. 37. 12.

Pray sir be pleased to decipher this letter yourself.

This cipher is monoalphabetic substitution, with homophones as follows:

Plain alphabet: a b c d e f g h i/j k l m n o p q r s t u/v w y
Cipher alphabet: 9 18 17 16 12 11 10 7 6 5 3 2 1 27 19 29 25 26 22 23 25 21 43 42 40 39 38 37 36 35 34 33 31 30 28 41

It also contains nomenclature in so far as a symbol is used for 'Lord Protector', the code word 'Overton' means 'Cromwell' and there are other numerical code words such as 158 (designs), 159 (Hull), 82 (from), 81 (which), 67 (England), 62 (army), 1 (Charles Stuart as well as n).

Now knowing the basic cipher, the reader might like to 'decipher' the letter from S, bearing in mind seventeenth-century spelling.

Even today there is little fundamental change in the cryptology techniques that had been invented by the mid-seventeenth century, in that it is still based on ciphers that are substitution, transposition or, more usually, a polyalphabetic combination of the two. The great difference is the advances in technology. First a combination of mechanization and simple circuits enabled the Enigma encryption machine to be invented in 1919 to exploit the strength of the Vigenère algorithm. This had revolving disks with the letters of the alphabet that could be set to a particular order based on a code book used by the originator and recipient and was used by the Germans in the Second World War. Each time a letter was typed on the keyboard and encrypted, the disks would turn to change the algorithm. The Enigma cipher was broken by the Government Code and Cipher School at Bletchley Park in 1940, largely due to the work of mathematician Alan Turing who invented a machine called 'bombs'. Based upon his work in 1943 Bletchley were able to decode the similar but more complex German Lorenz SZ40 cipher machine used for communication between Hitler and his generals. This was done using 'Colossus', the first ever computer, running on 1,500 valves.

After the war GCHQ was formed and in 1952 the US established the National Security Agency (NSA), which soon became the largest employer of mathematicians in the world. Computers began to be used for encryption because they were able to mimic vast numbers of mechanical scramblers. In 1960 IBM began using computers for encryption and in 1977 the US government introduced the Data Encryption Standard (DES). About the same time the problem of key distribution and control was resolved by the creation of Public Key Infrastructure (PKI) and the RSA standard for PKI encryption was created. Since then cryptology has remained centred on computers and has developed with the same amazingly rapid advances of information technology. Data today can be encrypted to several standards with the difficulty of cryptanalysis depending upon the key length. An 8 bit key allows 2 power 8 (256) permutations, which modern computers could crack very quickly. Most encryption today uses 128 bit Advanced Encryption Standard (AES) which has 2 power 128, i.e. 340 followed by 36 zeros, of possible permutations. Higher level encryption uses 256 bit AES and other more complex standards which make cryptanalysis extremely challenging even with the aid of exceptionally powerful computers. For all that, cryptanalysis still depends upon men and women with the mathematical and analytical skills that were exemplified by John Wallis.

Cromwell's Family Connections

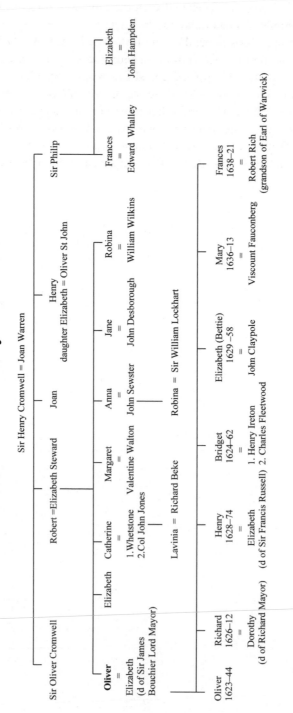

Notes: Not all family members are shown. The connections show five generals, three rulers of Ireland, two important envoys, two senior members of Household, the Lord High Admiral and the Chief Justice: all valuable personal sources of information.

Potentially Subversive Groups of Intelligence Interest to the Protectorate

Agitators

This was originally the name for the two soldiers from each regiment who were elected by their peers to be members of the army council in 1647. These representatives all had the same objective of refusing to allow any disbandment of the army unless Parliament agreed to give them the back pay which was in arrears, grant pensions to widows and the wounded and grant indemnity for actions during the Civil War. Once they achieved these objectives they continued general opposition to the Rump Parliament. The name 'Agitator' then began to be used for politically active members of the army who opposed government policy. They tended to be strong republicans and when the Protectorate was formed many opposed Cromwell who they considered had taken on the role of king in all but name. Some original Agitators began to join other religious or political groups: for example, John Wildman became a leading Leveller and so would be described by contemporaries as either an Agitator or Leveller.

Anabaptists/Baptists

This sect began in Zurich in 1524 and believed in adult rebaptism. Although not necessarily subversive in itself it came to be a byword for extreme Puritanism. Many members of the more extreme cults such as the Fifth Monarchists were labelled 'Anabaptists'. By 1654 these extreme Puritans of one sort or another were describing Cromwell as 'the Beast of the Apocalypse', a nomenclature which they would have previously reserved for the Pope. 'Baptists' on the other hand were a break away sect from the Church of England that sprang up in Lincolnshire in 1606 under Reverend John Smyth. By 1611 they had established their own church in Spittlefield in London. They believed in adult rather than infant baptism and the separation of church from state but were not religious extremists. The sect grew and there were many Baptists in the New Model Army but they were just another 'Independent' sect and did not as such pose a threat to the Protector, himself an Independent. The most prominent Baptist of the time was Lieutenant General Ludlow who was second-in-command in Ireland to first Ireton and then Fleetwood. He was dismissed from the post because he refused to recognize the legality of the Protector. His opposition to Cromwell was because of his own republican beliefs rather than his religious faith.

Cavaliers and Catholics

It goes without saying that all those who had supported the King in the Civil Wars were potential Royalist sympathizers, as were their families. All former Royalist officers and any Cavalier with sufficient land or money to be a person of influence needed to be monitored to see if they were involved in plots to help restore the monarchy. As Roman Catholics had been highly likely to have supported the monarchy rather than Parliament during the Civil Wars they too were regarded as Royalist sympathizers irrespective of whether they had actually ever taken up taken up arms for the Royalist cause.

Diggers

This was a small group who in 1649 wanted to establish a form of agrarian communism and took over common land at St George's Hill in Surrey. Their colony met considerable harassment from local land owners and they dispersed the following year. Diggers were gentle people who believed in passive resistance and posed absolutely no threat to the state but their concept of equality was one that challenged the social fabric and was a manifestation of the feelings that more militant groups such as the Levellers were expressing at the same time.

Fifth Monarchists

This movement began about 1651 when some London tradesmen decided to place great emphasis on Revelations and the Book of Daniel. Passages from these books of the Bible were interpreted as indicating that there would be four monarchies (Babylonian, Persian, Greek and Roman) which would be followed by a fifth under the Papacy which would rule for a thousand years and be replaced by the reign of Christ on Earth. Immediately before Christ's return the old order would be overthrown by violence (the Civil War and execution of Charles I proved that this had taken place) and there would be a period of Rule by the Saints. There was some disagreement over the precise timing of the Second Coming but most Fifth Monarchists agreed it would be either 1660 or 1666. There were many Fifth Monarchists in the Barebones Parliament who had seen parliament as a way of putting the Rule of the Saints into action. Cromwell's dissolution of that parliament and his acceptance of the position of Lord Protector made them regard him as someone trying to prevent the Second Coming. There were a significant number of Fifth Monarchists in the New Model Army, the most notable of whom was the much respected Major General Thomas Harrison. As Harrison and other Fifth Monarchists refused to accept Cromwell in the office of Lord Protector they had to be dismissed from the army. Despite this purge Fifth Monarchists still posed a threat to Cromwell's life, as was shown by the Venner Plot of 1657.

Levellers

This organization began among a group of MPs in 1645 but caught on with many of the lower ranks of the New Model Army. They stood for complete equality (naturally only for men) and the end of social distinction. The monarchy and nobility should be replaced by a sovereign parliament elected by manhood suffrage. In 1647 their radical manifesto was published in the Agreement of the People and included the dismantlement of the Church. Although the Levellers were largely suppressed in 1649, the ideology lived on and former Levellers or those influenced by their ideas were completely opposed to Cromwell becoming Lord Protector and therefore a king in all but name. After 1649 many of those who had been Levellers gravitated to other opposition groups, indeed John Lilburne the firebrand leader of the Levellers became a Quaker after his final imprisonment in 1653. Edward Sexby remained a Leveller but convinced himself that opposition to the Protectorate would be best served by joining the Royalists. Sexby was to be a thorn in the side of the Protectorate with his subversive writings and assassination plots, particularly the Sindercombe Plot, until his arrest in June 1657.

Presbyterians

Many of the Parliamentary leaders in the Civil War were Presbyterians but by 1651 some were beginning to support Charles. They had found themselves excluded from Parliament and, since Charles had taken the Covenant in Scotland, saw him as someone who could support their faith far more than Cromwell and the Independents. A Presbyterian minister called Love was arrested in London in May 1651 for conspiring for the Royalists and executed with another minister in early August.

Quakers

A movement founded about 1645 by George Fox which became officially called the Society of Friends. The Quakers challenged church authority because they believed that God spoke directly to individuals through the 'inner light' and for that reason priests were unnecessary. The Quakers attracted support in the North of England and also had followers in the New Model Army. Some Quakers would disrupt church services because they considered them an artificial activity that served to separate believers from direct communion with God. Although Quakers are today known for being non-violent and pacifists, those policies were only adopted by Fox in 1661. Apart from being an annoyance by sometimes disrupting services, Quakers were subversive in that they believed in equality among men and so were not unlike the Levellers in that respect.

Ranters

These were not an organized group or sect but the generic term at the time for the various self-proclaimed messiahs, prophets and preachers who emerged from 1647 until about 1658. They were sometimes associated in people's minds with Quakers.

Ranters believed in the individuality of the spirit which placed their personal relationship with God above everything else. Because of this they had no respect for authority, did not feel bound by the rules of society and were against organized religion and even the Bible. A Ranter would feel justified in walking around naked, engaging in free love or getting blind drunk if he felt the spirit moved him to do so. A number of these people who might today be termed 'religious nuts' were to be found in the New Model Army and shared the Levellers' concepts of equality. It need hardly be said that the Ranters' unpredictable and anti-social habits were not conducive to good conduct and military discipline.

Republicans

These were those who had supported the removal of the King and wanted a republican Commonwealth run by a council answerable to a parliament consisting only of the House of Commons. Most members of the army felt that parliament should reflect the needs of the army and the more militant felt that if parliament failed to do so the army's will should prevail. Republicans were completely opposed to the Protector because he had kinglike powers and had therefore betrayed the 'Good Old Cause' of republicanism.

Notes

My approach in writing this book has been to sift through the generally accepted history of the period and highlight and comment upon intelligence-related matters.

For the period as a whole I have relied heavily upon Clarendon's *The History of the Rebellion and Civil Wars in England* (Oxford, 1888) with his often caustic comments about Hyde's contemporaries and on the *Oxford Dictionary of National Biography* for all prominent characters. For a general overview of English history of the period, I have drawn on Maurice Ashley's *England in the Seventeenth Century (1603–1714)* (London, 1978) and Derek Hirst's *Authority and Conflict: England 1603–1658* (London, 1990). For an overview of the three kingdoms I have used John Kenyon and Jane Ohlmeyer's *The Civil War: A Military History of England Scotland and Ireland* (Oxford, 1998), Christine Kinealy's *A New History of Ireland* (Stroud, 2004), Norman Davies's *The Isles* (London, 1999), Michael Fry's *Wild Scots: Four Hundred Years of Highland History* (London, 2005) and Peter Gaunt's *The British Wars* (London, 1997). Below are the sources I have made most use of for particular chapters.

Chapter 1: 1642

For the lead-up to the Civil War I have relied upon Kevin Sharpe's *The Personal Rule of Charles I* (London, 1992), and C V Wedgewood's *King's Peace* (London, 1972). For the Civil War itself in this and subsequent chapters, I have been indebted to C V Wedgewood's excellent *King's War* (London, 1972), John Barratt's *Cavaliers: The Royalist Army at War* (Stroud, 2000), Martyn Bennett's *The Civil Wars 1637–1653* (Stroud, 1998), Mark Bence-Jones's The Cavaliers (London, 1976), Bob Carruthers's *The English Civil War* (London, 2000), Charles Carlton's *Going to the Wars: The Experience of the British Civil Wars 1638–1651* (London, 1995), Taylor Downing and Maggie Millman's *Civil War* (London, 1991) Christopher Hibbert's *Cavaliers and Roundheads: The English War 1642–1649* (London, 1993) and Roy Sherwood's *The Civil War in the Midlands 1642–1651* (Stroud, 1992).

Chapter 2: 1643

For detailed information on Charles I, I have used D R Watson's *The Life and Times of Charles* (London, 1993). For Prince Rupert I have relied upon Maurice Ashley's *Rupert of the Rhine* (London, 1976) and Frank Kitson's *Prince Rupert: Portrait of a Soldier* (London, 1994). For Fairfax, I have relied upon John Wilson's *Fairfax, General of Parliament's Forces in the English Civil War* (London, 1985). For Henrietta Maria I have used Rosalind K Marshall's *Henrietta Maria the Intrepid Queen* (London, 1990) and Alison Plowden's *Henrietta Maria Charles I's Indomitable Queen* (Stroud, 2001). For Wallis I have used C J Scriba's *The Autobiography of John Wallis FRS: Royal Society 25* (London, 1970) which gives a good account of his mathematical career. To get a feel for the major battles during the Civil Wars

I have used John Kinross's enjoyable book *Walking and Exploring the Battlefields of Britain* (London, 1993).

Chapter 3: 1644

The book I have found most useful on Cromwell and for the period 1643 to 1658 is Antonia Fraser's excellent *Cromwell our Chief of Men* (London, 2001). Other books I have found useful are Christopher Hill's Cromwell and the English Revolution (London, 2000), J C Davies's *Reputations: Oliver Cromwell* (London, 2001), Simon Robbins's *God's General, Cromwell the Soldier* (Stroud, 2003). My principal source on *General Monck* was Maurice Ashley's General Monk (London, 1997). The information on Luke and his scouts is drawn entirely from Luke's own diary to be found in *Journal of Sir Samuel Luke, Scoutmaster of the Earl of Essex 1643–44* (Oxford, 1950) and the Oxfordshire Record Society, *Journal of Sir Samuel Luke* (Oxford, 1953).

Chapter 4: 1645

For the New Model Army I have used Keith Robert's *Cromwell's War Machine* (Barnsley, 2005) and Maurice Ashley's *Cromwell's Generals* (London, 1954). My main source for Montrose has been Max Hastings's *Montrose the King's Champion* (London, 1977), which gives an adventurous account of a man who might not in fact quite live up to his legend.

Chapter 5: 1646-1648

No additional sources to those previously mentioned.

Chapter 6: 1649–1651

For general information on the Commonwealth I have used Tom Barnard's *The English Republic 1649–1660* (Harlow, 1997). My principal source for Charles II and the Stuart court in exile has been Antonia Fraser's *King Charles II* (London, 1979). More detailed information on Milton that I have not been able to include can be found in Barbara K Lewalski's *The Life of John Milton* (Oxford, 2002) and Christopher Hill's *The Experience of Defeat: Milton and Some Contemporaries* (London, 2000).

Chapter 7: 1652–1653

There is little material on Thomas Scot and I have drawn almost entirely on his own record which can be found as part of C H Firth's article in the *English Historical Review* of 1897, 'Thomas Scot's Account of his Actions as Intelligencer During the Commonwealth'. A useful book about the strange Queen Christina of Sweden and politics in Continental Europe is Veronica Buckley's *Christina Queen of Sweden* (London, 2005).

Chapter 8: 1654–1655

For the workings of the court of the Lord Protector I have used Roy Sherwood's *Oliver Cromwell, King in All But Name* (Stroud, 1997). For Thurloe I have relied on D L Hobman's *Cromwell's Master* Spy (London, 1961) and Philip Aubrey's *Mr Secretary Thurloe Cromwell's Secretary of State 1652–1660* (London, 1961) and of course on the Thurloe State Papers themselves, all seven volumes of which are available on the British History on Line website (www.british-history.ac.uk).

Chapter 9: 1655

For details of Thurloe's contribution to intercept I have used Firth's article 'Thurloe and the Post Office' in the *English Historical Review* (1898).

Chapters 10 and 11: 1656–1658

No sources other than those previously mentioned, particularly Thurloe's State Papers and also *The Diary of Thomas Burton Esq* (London, 1828) for extracts from Cromwell's speech opening the Second Protectorate Parliament and all other parliamentary business during the period 1653 to 1658. This useful resource is available on the British History on Line website.

Chapter 12: 1658–1659

Information on Samuel Morland comes from H W Dickinson's *Sir Samuel Morland Diplomat and Inventor, 1625–1695* (Cambridge, 1970), which also gives a good account of his work as an inventor after the Restoration. Also from the 'Autobiography of Samuel Morland, in a letter addressed to Dr Thomas Tenison, 3 May 1689', contained in MMS Lambeth 931 but I feel that he has embroidered the Weston Hanger plot to kill Charles in order to ingratiate himself with William III and consider it most unlikely that Willys would have been party to murdering the King.

Chapter 13: 1660

To complement previously mentioned sources, for the Restoration I have used Claire Tomalin's *Samuel Pepys, the Unequalled Self* (London, 2002).

Epilogue

For Charles II's intelligence service I have drawn from Alan Marshall's authoritative *Intelligence and Espionage in the Reign of Charles II, 1660–1685* (Cambridge, 2002) which also has valuable descriptions of intelligence activity during the Civil War and Commonwealth.

Notes on Cryptography

To supplement my own knowledge I have been indebted to Simon Singh, *Code Book* (London, 2000) which gives a very readable history of cryptography and also David Khan's comprehensive history *The Code Breakers: The Story of Secret Writing* (New York, 1996).

Index